Smart City Blueprint

The smart city movement, during the last decade and a half, advocated the built environment and digital technology convergence with the backing of institutional capital and government support. The commitment of a significant number of local governments across the globe, in terms of official smart city policies and initiatives, along with the constant push of global technology giants, has reinforced the popularity of this movement. This two-volume treatment on smart cities thoroughly explores and sheds light on the prominent elements of the smart city phenomenon and generates a smart city blueprint.

The first volume, with its 12 chapters, provides a sound understanding on the key foundations and growth directions of smart city frameworks, technologies, and platforms, with theoretical expansions, practical implications, and real-world case study lessons. The second companion volume offers sophisticated perspectives on the key foundations and directions of smart city policies, communities, and urban futures, with theoretical expansions, practical implications, and real-world case study lessons.

These volumes offer an invaluable reference source for urban policymakers, managers, planners, practitioners, and many others, particularly to benefit from it when tackling key urban and societal issues and planning for and delivering smart city solutions. Moreover, the book is also a rich and important repository for scholars and research and undergraduate students.

Tan Yigitcanlar is an eminent Australian researcher and author with international recognition and impact in the field of smart and sustainable city development. He is a Professor of Urban Studies and Planning at the School of Architecture and Built Environment, Queensland University of Technology, Brisbane, Australia.

Smart City Blueprint

Policy, Community, Futures

Tan Yigitcanlar

CRC Press
Taylor & Francis Group
CHAPMAN & HALL

Designed cover image: Shutterstock

First edition published 2024
by CRC Press
2385 NW Executive Center Drive, Suite 320, Boca Raton FL 33431

and by CRC Press
4 Park Square, Milton Park, Abingdon, Oxon, OX14 4RN

CRC Press is an imprint of Taylor & Francis Group, LLC

© 2024 Tan Yigitcanlar

Library of Congress Cataloging-in-Publication Data
Names: Yigitcanlar, Tan, author.
Title: Smart city blueprint. Policy, community, futures / Tan Yigitcanlar.
Other titles: Policy, community, futures
Description: First edition. | Boca Raton, FL : Routledge, 2024. |
Includes bibliographical references and index.
Identifiers: LCCN 2023018243 (print) | LCCN 2023018244 (ebook) |
ISBN 9781032517209 (hbk) | ISBN 9781032517193 (pbk) | ISBN 9781003403647 (ebk)
Subjects: LCSH: Smart cities–Political aspects. | Smart cities–Forecasting. | Public administration.
Classification: LCC TD159.4 .Y553 2024 (print) | LCC TD159.4 (ebook) |
DDC 307.1/416–dc23/eng/20230815
LC record available at https://lccn.loc.gov/2023018243
LC ebook record available at https://lccn.loc.gov/2023018244

ISBN: 978-1-032-51720-9 (hbk)
ISBN: 978-1-032-51719-3 (pbk)
ISBN: 978-1-003-40364-7 (ebk)

DOI: 10.1201/9781003403647

Typeset in Times New Roman
by Newgen Publishing UK

This book is dedicated to the following four beloved, beautiful, and brilliant women that have shaped my life: Cahide, Susan, Ela, Selin

Contents

Foreword

In 1989, when I first researched the term "urban technology", I was able to find only one use of the term—in an in-house edited book published in 1976 by what was then called Polytechnical University and edited by the university's president, George Bugliarello. In 1988, the U.S. National Academy of Engineering published a book edited by Jesse Ausubel with an ambitious title *Cities and Their Vital Systems: Infrastructure Past, Present, and Future*. That book had a chapter, "Combining Communications and Computing: Telematics Infrastructure", which only hinted at what was to come. But the book was an early work that started to move infrastructure toward the centre of the study of cities. Perhaps more influential was another volume edited by Joel Tarr and Gabriel Dupuy and also published in 1988, *Technology and the Rise of the Networked City in Europe and America*.

The integration of telecommunications and information technologies into urban infrastructures grew in the next decade and gave rise to Manuel Castells' magnum opus, *The Information Age: Economy, Society, and Culture*. Volume 1 of that work, *The Rise of the Network Society*, was published in 1996. The move of infrastructure to the centre of urban studies was completed by two works of Stephen Graham and Simon Marvin: *Telecommunications and the City: Electronic Spaces, Urban Places* (1996) and *Splintering Urbanism: Networked Infrastructures, Technological Mobilities, and the Urban Condition* (2001). Another publication significant to cities and their infrastructures was *The Report of the United Nation's Conference on Environment and Development* (Rio de Janeiro, June 1992).

And now, finding a place among these seminal works and explaining the way cities are and the way they should be, is Tan Yigitcanlar's two-volume *Smart City Blueprint*. This book explains how in the second decade of the twenty-first century information and communications technologies (ICTs) are ubiquitous and part of every urban network, every urban infrastructure. To a term—smart city—whose definition still is not settled, he offers a succinct, aspirational definition: "an environment that uses innovative technologies to make networks and services more flexible, effective, and sustainable with the use of information, digital, and telecommunication technologies, improving the city's operation for the benefit of its citizens".

Yigitcanlar, a widely published scholar, researcher, and teacher is well positioned to make that definition stick, as this book, with its sweeping use of methodologies and its wide-ranging use of geographical examples will become a key resource of what smart cities are and what they should become. His chapter on "Green Artificial Intelligence", for example, allows him to do this by explaining how smart cities should move away from the goal of purely technocentric efficiency and towards a consolidated AI approach that would support sustainable urban transformation.

Running throughout the book is Yigitcanlar's concern that too many smart city implementers have a too narrow focus on technological efficiency and do not appreciate or account for the human and social complexities of cities. This, he fears, can lead to new forms of social inequities and other deleterious consequences. He also does not believe that such approaches lead to the creation of sustainable cities absent community engagement and participatory governance.

Yigitcanlar ends this two-volume important book on *Smart City Blueprint* with two fundamental questions: The first asks whether policymakers and the public can be convinced of the need for "a post-anthropocentric urban turnaround". The second asks, *if the answer is yes*, then "how do the public, private, and academic sectors along with communities pave the way for post-anthropocentric cities and more-than-human futures?" He leaves unasked an even more difficult question: *What if the answer is no?* But Yigitcanlar is too hopeful to entertain that question in this magisterial, comprehensive, hopeful book.

Richard E. Hanley
The City University of New York, USA
Founding Editor, *Journal of Urban Technology*

Preface

No or inadequately regulated urbanisation and industrialisation practices since the beginning of the industrial revolution in the 1850s have resulted in climate change, environmental degradation, and unsustainable development worldwide with immense negative externalities on our cities, societies, and the planet. During the last couple of decades, the concept of the smart city has become a hot topic among urban policy circles, and today more and more cities are channelling their planning and development energy, strategies, and investments for becoming a smart locale—to somehow tackle the negative externalities.

Nevertheless, the smart city concept is neither new, nor always had the same emphasis. In the 1800s, this concept was used for the first time and referred to the efficiency and self-governance of cities in the western USA. In the 1960s, the modern smart city concept was referred to as smart urban growth management, and relevant strategies were introduced to avoid sprawling development and concentrating growth in compact walkable urban centres. Vancouver is one of the best practices for such smart growth management.

In the 1990s, the smart city concept emphasised technology-based innovation in the planning, development, operation, and management of cities. Nonetheless, some cities laid the foundations of this technocentric approach much earlier. For example, in the 1970s, Los Angeles created the first urban big data project, and in the early 1990s, Amsterdam built its virtual digital city. The conception of the last boom of the smart city dates to 2008, which was due to a strong push of major global technology, development, and consultancy firms—including CISCO, IBM, KPMG—as a business strategy to survive the global financial crisis (GFC).

This has led to the emergence of a corporate sector driven sociotechnical imaginary of the smart city movement. The best practice—e.g., Songdo, Masdar City, Gujarat International Finance Tec-City, Hudson Yards, Jurong Lake District, Amsterdam, City Verve, Barcelona, Tel Aviv—of this movement followed different pathways for their smart city transformation.

The first wave of the contemporary smart city emerged as a response of global technology, development, and consultancy firms to the GFC and perceived cities as enterprises that need the state-of-the-art digital technologies and infrastructures and an innovation culture to become internationally competitive. The meaning of "smart" in the smart city has shifted from a pre-GFC emphasis on sustainability and climate change to a post-GFC engagement with entrepreneurship and platformisation.

In that perspective, smart city is widely conceptualised as the convergence of digital technology and the built environment, institutional capital, and government support over long periods of time. An example of this would be public–private partnership in initiatives for convergence of blockchain and artificial intelligence (AI) in the Internet of Things (IoT) network for smart precinct development.

Despite some success examples and progress, this smart city perspective has proved insufficiently nimble to respond to shifting public attitudes about the ethics of urban technology and the governance of large-scale urban development. The most obvious example of the inadequacy of the existing algorithmic approach to smart cities is the termination of Sidewalk Labs' signature smart city development in Toronto waterfront.

The COVID-19 pandemic accelerated digital transformation efforts across the globe that have provided an invaluable opportunity for technology companies. Now, urban tech is on the rise, as venture investors move in with much more focused short-term plays. This is leading to the creation of the second wave of the smart city that is producing global supply chain of smart city solutions and an emerging urban innovation industry for delivery. On the one hand, it is also cultivating the emergence of the global urban innovation industry, moving from standalone solutions to standardised frameworks/systems/processes that produce novel/bespoke/tailored solutions. On the other hand, this poses risks of urban innovation industry following the business-as-usual of laissez faire ruthless capitalist practices for smart city (trans)formation, resulting in unsustainable outcomes.

During a debate at the Harvard Museum of Natural History, in the early days of the smart city movement in 2009, American sociobiologist Edward O. Wilson underlined the real problem of humanity as follows: "We have Palaeolithic emotions, medieval institutions, and god-like technology". Now, hence, we need to figure out how we are going to utilise existing and emerging powerful technologies, such as AI, wisely in our cities and societies.

The consolidated smart city concept advocates, developed by exclusively technocentric solution sceptic scholars, the emerging global urban innovation industry to adopt a responsible innovation practice for smart city (trans)formation, delivering accountable, ethical, frugal, sustainable, and trustworthy outcomes— and also forming a most needed responsible urban innovation industry and skilled and informed policymakers and planners to support the efforts in building sustainable and liveable futures for all.

Against this backdrop, this first volume of the Smart City Blueprint book (Smart City Blueprint: Framework, Technology, Platform) thoroughly explores and sheds light on the prominent elements of the smart city phenomenon and generates insights into a smart city blueprint. This first volume, with its dozen chapters, provides a sound understanding on the key foundations and growth directions of smart city frameworks, technologies, and platforms, with theoretical expansions, practical implications, and real-world case study lessons. This first volume is accompanied by the second volume titled Smart City Blueprint: Policy, Community, Futures.

This book is also part of the author's book trilogy on smart cities—i.e., *Technology and the City: Systems, Applications, and Implications* (2016), *Smart City Blueprint: Framework, Technology, Platform* (2023), and *Smart City Blueprint: Policy, Community, Futures* (2023). The books in the trilogy are invaluable reference source for urban policymakers, managers, planners, and practitioners, and many others, particularly to benefit from it when tackling key urban and societal issues and planning for and delivering smart city solutions. Moreover, these books also form a rich and important repository for scholars and higher degree research and undergraduate students as they communicate the complex smart city phenomenon in an easy to digest form, by providing both the big picture view and specifics of each component of that view, and hence offering a smart city blueprint.

The volume *Smart City Blueprint: Policy, Community, Futures* is structured under three main parts and elaborated briefly as below:

Part 1, Smart City Framework: This part of the book concentrates on providing a clear understanding on the policy dimension of smart city practice. The part offers lessons from the examples on policy in action, policy outcomes, policy acceptance, development pathways, and best practice.

Part 2, Smart City Community: This part of the book concentrates on providing a clear understanding on the community dimension of smart city practice. The part offers lessons from the examples on digital commons, participatory governance, good enough governance, augmenting community engagement, and alleviating community disadvantage.

Part 3, Smart City Futures: This part of the book concentrates on providing an understanding beyond the current smart city practice. The part offers insights into having a smart city focus beyond service efficiency, and rethinking smart cities considering the big picture view of the humanitarian and planetarian challenges that are upon and ahead of us.

Author

 **Tan Yigitcanlar** is an eminent Australian researcher with international recognition and impact in the field of urban studies and planning. He is a Professor of Urban Studies and Planning at the School of Architecture and Built Environment, Queensland University of Technology, Brisbane, Australia. Along with this post, he holds the following positions: Honorary Professor at the School of Technology, Federal University of Santa Catarina, Florianopolis, Brazil; Director of the Australia-Brazil Smart City Research and Practice Network; Lead of QUT Smart City Research Group; and Co-Director of QUT City 4.0 Lab. He is a member of the Australian Research Council College of Experts.

He has been responsible for research, teaching, training, and capacity building programs in the fields of urban studies and planning in esteemed Australian, Brazilian, Finnish, Japanese, and Turkish universities. His research aims to address contemporary urban planning and development challenges—that are economic, societal, spatial, governance or technology related in nature. The main foci of his research interests, within the broad field of urban studies and planning, are clustered around the following three interdisciplinary themes:

- *Smart Technologies, Communities, Cities, and Urbanism*—e.g., examining the disruptive externalities and beneficial impacts of urban technologies and digital transformation of urban services and infrastructures on our cities and societies.
- *Sustainable and Resilient Cities, Communities, and Urban Ecosystems*—e.g., exploring the urban and environmental dynamics and challenges to determine strategies for planning and designing sustainable, resilient, responsive, healthy, and liveable natural and built urban environments.
- *Knowledge-Based Development of Cities and Innovation Districts*—e.g., scrutinising the impacts of global knowledge and innovation economy on our cities and societies, and developing strategies for space and place making for knowledge-based activities in cities.

He has been providing research consultancy services to all tier governments (i.e., federal, state, local)—along with for international corporations, and non-governmental organisations—in Australia and overseas. These services have helped government and industry form their key strategies, become more resilient, and better prepared for the emerging disruptive conditions. He has received over $4 million funding from research consultancy projects and national competitive grant programs.

He is the lead Editor-in-Chief of Elsevier Smart Cities Book Series and carries out senior editorial positions in the following 11 high-impact journals: *Sustainable Cities and Society, Cities, Land Use Policy, Journal of Urban Technology, Sustainability, Journal of Open Innovation: Technology, Market, and Complexity, Journal of Knowledge Management, Knowledge Management Research and Practice, Global Journal of Environmental Science and Management, International Journal of Information Management,* and *Measuring Business Excellence.*

He undertook the Chairman role of the annual Knowledge Cities World Summit series between 2007 and 2019. Under this brand, he organised 12 international conferences in the following locations: Monterrey (Mexico); Shenzhen (China); Melbourne (Australia); Bento Gonçalves (Brazil); Matera (Italy); Istanbul (Turkey); Tallinn (Estonia); Daegu (Korea); Vienna (Austria); Arequipa (Peru); Tenerife (Spain); and Florianopolis (Brazil). He also contributed to the organisation of over two-dozen other international conferences in various capacities. He has also delivered over 70 keynote and invited talks at prestigious international academic conferences and national industry events.

He has disseminated his research findings extensively, including over 300 articles published in high-impact journals, and the following 24 key reference books published by the esteemed international publishing houses:

- *Innovation District Planning* (CRC Press, 2024)
- *Smart City Blueprint: Framework, Technology, Platform* (Routledge, 2023)
- *Smart City Blueprint: Policy, Community, Futures* (Routledge, 2023)
- *Companion of Creativity and the Built Environments* (Routledge, 2023)
- *Internet of Things for Smart Environments and Applications* (MDPI, 2023)
- *Urban Analytics with Social Media Data* (CRC Press, 2022)
- *Distributed Computing and Artificial Intelligence* (Springer, 2022)
- *State of the Art and Future Perspectives in Smart and Sustainable Urban Development* (MDPI, 2022)
- *Sustainable Mobility and Transport* (MDPI, 2022)
- *Reviews and Perspectives on Smart and Sustainable Metropolitan and Regional Cities* (MDPI, 2021)
- *Smart Cities and Innovative Urban Technologies* (Routledge, 2021)
- *Approaches, Advances and Applications in Sustainable Development of Smart Cities* (MDPI, 2020)
- *Geographies of Disruption* (Springer, 2019)
- *Planning, Development and Management of Sustainable Cities* (MDPI, 2019)
- *Urban Knowledge and Innovation Spaces* (Routledge, 2018)

- *Technology and the City* (Routledge, 2016)
- *Knowledge and the City* (Routledge, 2014)
- *Sustainable Urban Water Environment* (Edward Elgar, 2014)
- *Building Prosperous Knowledge Cites* (Edward Elgar, 2012)
- *Knowledge-Based Development for Cities and Societies* (IGI Global, 2010)
- *Sustainable Urban and Regional Infrastructure Development* (IGI Global, 2010)
- *Rethinking Sustainable Development* (IGI Global, 2010)
- *Knowledge-Based Urban Development* (IGI Global, 2008)
- *Creative Urban Regions* (IGI Global, 2008)

His research outputs have been widely cited and influenced urban policy, practice, and research internationally. His research was cited over 20,000 times, resulting in an h-index of over 80 (Google Scholars).According to the 2022 Science-wide Author Databases of Standardised Citation Indicators, amongst urban and regional planning scholars, he is ranked #1 in Australia and a top-10 ranked researcher worldwide. He was also recognised as an "Australian Research Superstar" in the Social Sciences Category at the Australian's 2020 Research Special Report.

Part 1

Smart City Policy

This part of the book concentrates on providing a clear understanding on the policy dimension of smart city practice. The part offers lessons from the examples on policy in action, policy outcomes, policy acceptance, development pathways, and best practice.

DOI: 10.1201/9781003403647-1

1 Policy in Action

1.1 Introduction

Smart urban technology adoption is a popular trend in cities as it is often portrayed as a solution to the many contemporary challenges that cities face [1]. In most cases, these technologies are promoted as part of a broader smart city agenda [2], but despite the increasing practice, there is no commonly agreed definition for smart cities [3–5]. The key perception difference comes from what smart means. For instance, for some, the smartness element in a smart city is the technology and data, and for some it is the people and policy, while for others it is a combination of both [6]. This difference in the conceptualisation and perception of what a smart city is reflects on how a city strategises its smart city planning [7].

This conceptualisation and perception difference has an impact on urban policy. [8] identify that each city has unique urban priorities that affect the conceptualisation of a smart city policy; however, aspects such as the application of information and communications technology (ICT) to the urban infrastructure, a collaboration of the stakeholders in all stages of planning and development, and investment in innovation are some of the basic building blocks of the smart city concept that apply pretty much to all smart city initiatives [9–11].

Given their broad scope and contextually varied applications in urban settings, smart city policies nevertheless have continued to attract funding from local governments to take advantage of the proposed benefits [12,13]. Most recently, the COVID-19 pandemic stimulated smart city technologies to develop rapidly in response to the urban crisis that it generated worldwide [14]. The contribution of smart technologies in dealing with the COVID-19 pandemic [15] prompted a drastic increase in the long-term and widespread use of technology in urban governance and permanently altered the dimensions of health, data, logistics, and crisis management [16–18]. These changes in planning trends have brought both benefits and challenges, while increased digitisation has created the benefit of accelerating innovation for how cities plan, manage, and govern their urban infrastructures. According to [19], the COVID-19 pandemic is turning into a "welcomed lubricant for the innovative stakeholders of many smart city development policies". This will likely boost smart city development during the post-COVID-19 era [20–22].

DOI: 10.1201/9781003403647-2

Nonetheless, it has also intensified the challenges of the digital divides between vulnerable community members, with technology progressing faster than device serviceability. This challenge highlights the recent trends in smart city discourse and its relationship to participatory and collaborative governance, for though communities are identified as key components of a smart city, top-down initiatives dominate policymaking [23,24]. The concept inspires suggestions that smart city strategies should focus on institutional changes to provide context-sensitive outcomes in local urban areas [25,26]. This may include changing the structure of smart policy creation from being conceived within institutions and industries outwards to instead begin from the bottom-up for a more community-based approach.

Research into the effectiveness of existing smart city policies is limited [27,28]. This may be attributed to the relative newness of smart cities as a concept and the variety in how policies are incorporated in worldwide contexts. Most of the literature in this domain focuses on a single city's or only a few cities' policy analyses [29,30]. For instance, Clement and Crutzen [31] investigated how local policy priorities set the smart city agenda in the cases of London and Melbourne; Angelidou [32] analysed four European cities' smart city strategies; and Mancebo [33] compared the smart city strategies of Amsterdam, Barcelona, and Paris. There are a relatively limited number of studies that compare, contrast, and analyse smart city policies in a large number of city cases. For example, Yigitcanlar [27] scrutinised the smart city development strategies of 15 cities; Angelidou [34] conducted research on 15 smart city policies and provided insights into the roles that ICTs play in urban systems; and Joss et al. [35] captured the smart city storylines and critical junctures of 27 cities.

Moreover, the global rise in urbanisation levels and associated economic, social, environmental, and governance challenges have been at the forefront of urban discourse in recent years. The concept of the smart city has been closely linked to these issues as a possible solution. Subsequently, the development of smart city strategy frameworks, in the form of smart city policy bundles, is gaining prominence globally. Today, many cities are interested in developing or adopting smart city policy frameworks; however, the complexity of the smart city concept combined with complicated urban issues makes it a highly challenging task. Moreover, as mentioned above, there are limited studies to consolidate our understanding of smart city policymaking.

Against this background, the study at hand discusses the existing knowledge gaps in smart city policy frameworks to offer understanding into how different cities are adapting smart urban technologies in response to their urban needs, with their own set of smart city characteristic measures. The chapter focuses on addressing the following research questions: (a) What do smart city policies target in terms of key planning issues, goals, and priorities? (b) How do smart city policies address these key planning issues, goals, and priorities? The study aims to aid in the understanding of a smart city policy that would lead to a consolidated view on how smart city policies can be utilised in tackling the urban challenges faced by cities worldwide more effectively.

For the empirical analysis, the study identified 52 smart city frameworks from the local governments of 17 countries—Australia ($n = 17$), Austria ($n = 1$), Canada ($n = 6$), China ($n = 1$), Croatia ($n = 1$), England ($n = 9$), Germany ($n = 1$), Ireland ($n = 2$), Malaysia ($n = 1$), New Zealand ($n = 1$), Northern Ireland ($n = 1$), Poland ($n = 2$), Scotland ($n = 2$), Sweden ($n = 1$), Switzerland ($n = 1$), the USA ($n = 4$), and Wales ($n = 1$).

The policy data then underwent a qualitative and quantitative content analysis with the guidance of six overarching smart city themes, namely, smart economy, smart environment, smart governance, smart living, smart mobility, and smart people [36]. The findings inform urban policymakers and planners on the common and distinctive policies being adopted in other cities and provide insights into smart city policy formulation.

Following this introduction, Section 1.2 of the chapter outlines the research design. Next, Section 1.3 presents the results of the analysis, and Section 1.4 offers a discussion on the findings. Finally, Section 1.5 presents the conclusions of the study.

1.2 Methodology

This study concentrates on addressing the following research questions: (a) What do smart city policies target in terms of key planning issues, goals, and priorities? (b) How do smart city policies address these key planning issues, goals, and priorities? Most academic and practical references outline that there is no singular or uniform policy perspective that exists for smart city transformation that is generic enough to be adopted directly [37]. By extension, this issue also carries over when analysing smart city policies that vary in scope and focus based on the local context and characteristics. Considering the contextual differences worldwide, smart city initiatives largely vary in focus depending on the planning issues of each locality. To simplify the scope of the research, the EU's smart city wheel was utilised under its six central characteristics: (a) smart economy; (b) smart environment; (c) smart governance; (d) smart living; (e) smart mobility; and (f) smart people [26]. A study by [38] identified these six characteristics "as a roof for the further elaboration of smart cities", and this smart city wheel approach is widely utilised in both academic and policy studies [39,40]. The use of this categorisation aids in the analysis of smart city policies, given that for a city to be considered truly smart it must perform well under all the smart wheel areas/categories [41].

The study adopts a qualitative and quantitative thematic analysis of keywords as the primary data collection method. The basis for selecting this method for smart city policies was that "thematic analyses move beyond counting explicit words or phrases and focus on identifying and describing both implicit and explicit ideas within the data, that is, themes" [42]. This study, hence, identified themes with guidance from the abovementioned six smart city characteristics for a holistic view of smart city policies.

The methodological approach for the thematic analysis was undertaken using the NVivo software (v.12) to analyse the smart city policies both qualitatively and quantitatively. The software is used widely in qualitative and mixed-methods research and in this study, it was used for analysing and organising the smart city policy documents. To develop a comprehensive analysis with NVivo, the research initially collected data through search queries executed on the Google search engine. This search was intended to provide the widest range of results for smart city policy documents globally. Given the variety of smart city policy document titles, different combinations for the search statements were selected to ensure accuracy in the query results.

The search Boolean string used was as follows: ("smart city" AND "digital" AND "smart communit *") OR ("government" OR ["policy" AND "strateg *" AND "plan" AND "blueprint" AND "framework" AND "roadmap" AND 'masterplan']). Additionally, the following Boolean string was also used to make sure of the capture of the policy documents of the renowned smart cities: ("smart city" AND "digital" AND "smart communit *") OR ["government" OR ("policy" AND "strateg *" AND "plan" AND "blueprint" AND "framework" AND "roadmap" AND 'masterplan')] AND ("smart city name")—such as ("San Francisco"). The list of smart cities used for this purpose was obtained from the IMD Smart City Index 2021 that provides the international ranking of smart cities [available at www.imd.org/smart-city-obse rvatory/home (accessed on 28 March 2022)]. Figure 1.1 shows the specifics of the policy document selection process.

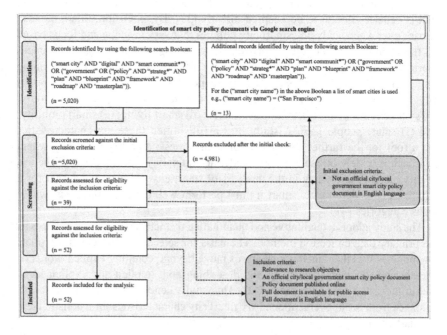

Figure 1.1 Policy document selection process.

The inclusion criteria for the search included the requirement that the policy documents must have been written in English and available online. Documents that did not meet these criteria were excluded from the analysis. The search results produced a total of 52 documents from local governments globally. Those cities varied demographically and geographically. Table 1.1 presents the salient characteristics of these 52 cities from 17 countries—Australia ($n = 17$), Austria ($n = 1$), Canada ($n = 6$), China ($n = 1$), Croatia ($n = 1$), England ($n = 9$), Germany ($n = 1$), Ireland ($n = 2$), Malaysia ($n = 1$), New Zealand ($n = 1$), Northern Ireland ($n = 1$), Poland ($n = 2$), Scotland ($n = 2$), Sweden ($n = 1$), Switzerland ($n = 1$), the USA ($n = 4$), and Wales ($n = 1$).

Table 1.1 Salient characteristics of the case cities

City	Country	Capital	State capital	Metropolitan	Population
Brisbane	Australia	No	Yes	Yes	2,560,720
Canterbury Bankstown	Australia	No	No	No	380,406
Casey	Australia	No	No	No	364,600
Charles Sturt	Australia	No	No	No	120,733
Marion	Australia	No	No	No	88,618
Darwin	Australia	No	Yes	Yes	147,231
Geelong	Australia	No	No	No	282,412
Hobart	Australia	No	Yes	Yes	238,834
Hobsons Bay	Australia	No	No	No	98,189
Newcastle	Australia	No	No	No	167,363
North Sydney	Australia	No	No	Yes	75,094
Norwood Payneham and St Peters	Australia	No	No	Yes	37,462
Parramatta	Australia	No	No	Yes	260,296
Sunshine Coast	Australia	No	No	No	348,343
Sydney	Australia	No	No	Yes	248,736
Townsville	Australia	No	No	No	183,32
Wyndham	Australia	No	No	No	283,294
Vienna	Austria	Yes	No	Yes	1,944,910
Winnipeg	Canada	No	Yes	Yes	632,063
St. Albert	Canada	No	No	No	65,589
Ottawa	Canada	Yes	Yes	Yes	812,129
Mississauga	Canada	No	No	Yes	668,549
Edmonton	Canada	No	Yes	Yes	712,391
Calgary	Canada	No	No	Yes	1,019,942
Hong Kong	China	Yes	No	Yes	7,598,189
Zagreb	Croatia	Yes	No	Yes	806,341
Birmingham	England	No	No	Yes	1,020,589
Bristol	England	No	No	Yes	399,633
Cambridge	England	No	No	Yes	116,701

(Continued)

Table 1.1 (Continued)

City	Country	Capital	State capital	Metropolitan	Population
Greenwich	England	No	No	Yes	286,186
Leeds City	England	No	No	Yes	726,939
Liverpool	England	No	No	Yes	467,995
London	England	Yes	No	Yes	7,074,265
Manchester	England	No	No	Yes	430,818
Sheffield	England	No	No	Yes	530,375
Munich	Germany	No	No	Yes	1,553,373
Cork	Ireland	No	No	Yes	208,669
Limerick	Ireland	No	No	Yes	94,192
Putrajaya	Malaysia	No	No	Yes	91,900
Wellington	New Zealand	Yes	No	Yes	212,700
Belfast	Northern Ireland	Yes	No	Yes	483,418
Krakow	Poland	No	No	Yes	755,050
Warsaw	Poland	Yes	No	Yes	1,702,139
Edinburgh	Scotland	Yes	No	Yes	448,850
Glasgow	Scotland	No	No	Yes	616,430
Stockholm	Sweden	Yes	No	Yes	975,551
Zurich	Switzerland	No	Yes	Yes	402,762
Chula Vista	USA	No	No	Yes	268,920
Las Vegas	USA	No	No	Yes	634,773
Philadelphia	USA	No	No	Yes	1,603,797
San Francisco	USA	No	No	Yes	874,961
Cardiff	Wales	No	Yes	Yes	315,040

All the smart city policy documents identified in the search were produced by or associated with the respective city's local government body and are presented in Table 1.2. The 52 policy documents related to a total of 16 countries, with Australia ($n = 17$), England ($n = 9$), and Canada ($n = 6$) as the countries with the most policy documents included in the research. The recency of the policy document publication dates was also prioritised in the search results. Consequently, the documents were all dated within about the last 10-year period, ranging between 2011 and 2021.

After the initial identification of the 52 relevant policy documents from online searches, the documents were read thoroughly to ensure suitability before commencing the analysis. Once the documents were identified as appropriate, the collected policies underwent a thematic analysis to identify the most significant nodes and sub-nodes related to the smart city content. To guide the identification of nodes in a subject as broad as smart cities, six smart city characteristics were used as the following six nodes: smart economy; smart environment; smart governance; smart living; smart mobility; and smart people [38]. From the six overarching nodes, nine sub-nodes corresponding to each characteristic were manually identified from reading the contents of each policy document. Table 1.3 lists the nodes and their associated sub-nodes.

Table 1.2 Salient characteristics of the policy frameworks

Local government	Policy framework	Year	References
Brisbane City Council	Smart, Connected Brisbane Framework	2019	[43]
City of Canterbury Bankstown	The SMART CBCity Roadmap	2018	[44]
City of Casey	Smart Casey Launchpad	2021	[45]
City of Charles Sturt	Smart City Plan	2018	[46]
City of Marion	Smart CoM Strategy Plan	2020	[47]
City of Darwin	Smart Darwin: Our Smart City Strategy	2019	[48]
City of Greater Geelong	Smart City Framework	2021	[49]
City of Hobart	Connected Hobart Smart Cities Framework	2019	[50]
Hobsons Bay City Council	Enterprise Digital Strategy	2018	[51]
Newcastle City Council	Smart City Strategy	2017	[52]
North Sydney Council	North Sydney Smart City Strategy	2019	[53]
City of Norwood Payneham and St Peters	Smart City Plan	2020	[54]
Parramatta City Council	Smart City Masterplan	2018	[55]
Sunshine Coast Council	Smart City Implementation Plan	2016	[56]
City of Sydney	Smart City Strategic Framework	2020	[57]
Townsville City Council	Townsville City Council Smart City Draft Strategy	2018	[58]
Wyndham City Council	Wyndham Smart City Strategy	2019	[59]
City of Vienna	Smart City Wien Framework Strategy	2019	[60]
Calgary City Council	Calgary's Smart City Approach	2018	[61]
Edmonton City Council	Edmonton Smart Cities	2019	[62]
Mississauga City Council	SMRTCTY Master Plan	2019	[63]
City of Ottawa	Ottawa Smart City 2.0	2019	[64]
City of St. Albert	City of St. Albert Smart City Master Plan	2016	[65]
City of Winnipeg	Winnipeg Smart Cities Proposal	2018	[66]
City of Zagreb	Integrated Action Plan: City of Zagreb	2018	[67]
Birmingham City Council	The Roadmap to Smarter Birmingham	2014	[68]
Bristol City Council	Connecting Bristol	2019	[69]
Cambridgeshire City Council	Connecting Cambridge	2018	[70]
Royal Borough of Greenwich	Greenwich Smart City Strategy	2014	[71]
West Yorkshire Combined Authority	Leeds City Region Digital Framework	2019	[72]
Liverpool City Region	LCR Digital Strategy	2021	[73]
London City Hall	Smart London Plan	2015	[74]
Manchester City Council	Manchester Digital Strategy	2020	[75]
Sheffield Executive Board	Smart Sheffield Report	2015	[76]
City of Munich	Project Smarter Together Munich	2016	[77]
Government of Hong Kong	Hong Kong Smart City Blueprint 2.0	2020	[78]
Belfast City Council	The Smart Belfast Framework	2018	[79]

(*Continued*)

Table 1.2 (Continued)

Local government	Policy framework	Year	References
Cork City Council	Cork City Digital Strategy	2018	[80]
Limerick City and County Council	Smart Limerick Roadmap	2018	[81]
Perbadanan Putrajaya	Smart City Blueprint	2019	[82]
Wellington City Council	Wellington Towards 2040: Smart Capital	2011	[83]
Krakow Metropolitan Authority	Smart_Kom Strategy	2015	[84]
City of Warsaw	Warsaw Towards a Smart City	2018	[85]
The City of Edinburgh Council	Edinburgh Digital and Smart City Strategy	2020	[86]
Glasgow City Council	Digital Glasgow Strategy	2018	[87]
City of Stockholm	Strategy for Stockholm as a Smart & Connected City	2017	[88]
Zurich City Council	Smart City Zurich	2018	[89]
City of Chula Vista	City of Chula Vista Smart City Plan	2017	[90]
Las Vegas City Council	Smart Vegas: A Forward Focused Plan	2019	[91]
City of Philadelphia	Smart City PHL Roadmap	2019	[92]
City and Council of San Francisco	Strategic Vision for Smart Cities and the Internet of Things	2018	[93]
Cardiff Council	Cardiff Smart City Road Map	2018	[94]

Table 1.3 Coding of the policy framework data

Node	Sub-node
Smart Economy	Business competitiveness, Business efficiency, Business intelligence, Business technology, Digital assets, Digital innovation, Economic business growth, Entrepreneurship, Market
Smart Environment	Carbon neutral, Climate change, Environmental conservation, Natural disaster, Reduce energy consumption, Renewable energy, Sustainable city, Sustainable Development, Waste and water management
Smart Governance	Citizen engagement, Collaborative leadership, Community engagement, Digital democracy, E-government, Multi-sector collaboration, Open data portal, Stakeholder engagement, Urban innovation
Smart Living	Attractive city, Cultural diversity, Data privacy, E-services, Entertainment, Liveability, Sense of place, Smart home, Urban infrastructure
Smart Mobility	Active transport, Electric vehicle, Mobility as a service, Noise and air pollution, Public transport, Smart parking, Sustainable mobility, Traffic management, Transportation management
Smart People	Collaboration networks, Community environment, Digital citizenship, Digital education, Digital inclusion, Diverse population, Equal opportunity, Resilient community, Skill development

1.3 Results

1.3.1 Quantitative Content Analysis

The smart city policy data were evaluated using quantitative content analysis tools within NVivo software (v.12). Initially, word clouds were created to present word frequencies within the policy documents where the largest words were the most repeatedly mentioned. Figure 1.2 presents the frequency of words throughout all 52 policy documents, while Figure 1.3 presents the frequency of words within the coded data. Following the initial analysis, the mentioned frequencies of the nodes and sub-nodes were analysed. Table 1.4 contains a list of all the analysed nodes, sub-nodes, number of sub-nodes mentioned within policies, frequency of sub-nodes, and total frequencies. From the six nodes, the three with the highest total sub-node frequencies were "smart mobility" (n = 307), "smart living" (n = 306), and "smart environment" (n = 302). The least referenced nodes were "smart people" (n = 193), and "smart governance" (n = 224). All the sub-nodes were mentioned throughout all 52 policy documents, where "economic business growth" (n = 37) was the most frequently mentioned individual sub-node, followed by "urban infrastructure" (n = 30).

Figure 1.2 Word cloud of the policy content.

Figure 1.3 Word cloud of the coding.

Table 1.4 Nodes, sub-nodes, and mentioned frequencies

Node and node frequency	Sub-node	Sub-nodes mentioned in policies	Frequency of sub-node	Total frequency of sub-nodes
Smart Economy = 29	Business competitiveness	1	2	=284
	Business efficiency	1	1	
	Business intelligence	9	18	
	Business technology	1	3	
	Digital assets	6	7	
	Digital innovation	14	35	
	Economic business growth	37	107	
	Entrepreneurship	24	43	
	Market	28	68	
Smart Environment = 18	Carbon neutral	10	17	=302
	Climate change	26	80	
	Environmental conservation	2	12	
	Natural disaster	1	1	

Table 1.4 (Continued)

Node and node frequency	Sub-node	Sub-nodes mentioned in policies	Frequency of sub-node	Total frequency of sub-nodes
	Reduce energy consumption	6	8	
	Renewable energy	25	75	
	Sustainable city	14	22	
	Sustainable development	15	48	
	Waste and water management	16	39	
Smart Governance = 8	Citizen engagement	13	21	=224
	Collaborative leadership	4	4	
	Community engagement	22	42	
	Digital democracy	2	7	
	E-government	6	13	
	Multi-sector collaboration	2	3	
	Open data portal	10	30	
	Stakeholder engagement	12	81	
	Urban innovation	7	20	
Smart Living = 16	Attractive city	4	4	=306
	Cultural diversity	5	11	
	Data privacy	7	18	
	Entertainment	23	45	
	Liveability	27	101	
	E-services	8	35	
	Sense of place	2	5	
	Smart home	6	8	
	Urban infrastructure	30	79	
Smart Mobility = 27	Active transport	2	3	=307
	Electric vehicle	15	26	
	Mobility as a service	8	14	
	Noise and air pollution	17	32	
	Public transport	18	80	
	Smart parking	20	41	
	Sustainable mobility	5	6	
	Traffic management	16	23	
	Transportation management	22	82	
Smart People = 21	Collaboration networks	1	1	=193
	Community environment	2	2	
	Digital citizenship	3	5	
	Digital education	18	54	
	Digital inclusion	29	94	
	Diverse population	5	12	
	Equal opportunity	2	3	
	Resilient community	3	5	
	Skill development	13	17	

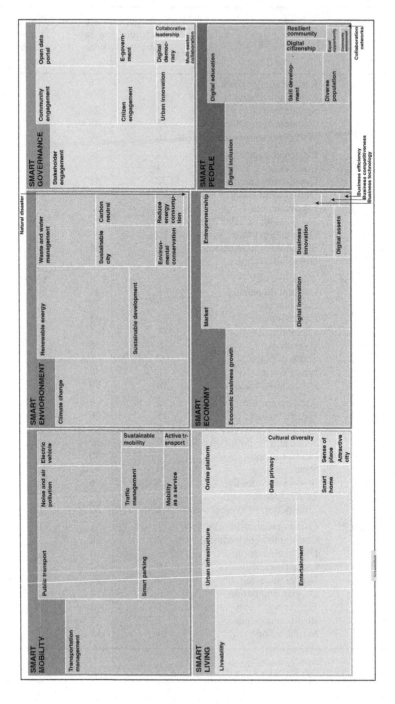

Figure 1.4 Hierarchy of nodes and sub-nodes.

Following the word frequency analysis, Figure 1.4 presents a hierarchy chart created in NVivo software of all the nodes and sub-nodes with the aggregated policy document data. The size of each rectangular section is relative to the node frequency and provides a holistic view of each of the six nodes and their nine corresponding sub-nodes. The chart demonstrates that the most prominent nodes in the policy analysis were those of 'smart mobility', 'smart living', and 'smart environment'. Additionally, the hierarchy chart displays the prominence of the nine sub-nodes within the overarching nodes. The frequency is reflected by the comparative rectangle size, with the largest being the most frequent and the smallest being the least frequent.

1.3.2 Qualitative Content Analysis

Following the quantitative analysis task, a qualitative content analysis task was undertaken. Figure 1.5 presents a concept map for each of the six nodes and corresponding sub-nodes that were analysed against the smart city policy frameworks. The map presents the aggregated text searches and their coding which were used to develop the total frequency figures for quantitative analysis. The results are presented under the six category areas described below.

1.3.2.1 Smart Economy with Economic Growth Focus

The findings from the 'smart economy' category offered insight into the economic priorities that the smart city policies were focusing on in the context of local governments. The most noticeable economically linked policy implementations fell under the following categories: (a) business competitiveness; (b) business efficiency; (c) business intelligence; (d) business technology; (e) digital assets; (f) digital innovation; (g) economic business growth; (h) entrepreneurship; and (i) market. The categories identified many conventional economic goals that the local governments pursued, with the most prominent being an overall business and economic growth. Smart city policies were seen to focus on traditional technological implementations to achieve growth, such as innovation, investment, and entrepreneurship; however, the local governments were also concentrating on new digital assets that their economies engaged with, such as data and artificial intelligence (AI). The Digital Glasgow Strategy [87] elaborated on this new economic and business growth focus as follows:

> The growth in digital technology is no longer about traditional software and hardware technologies. Increasingly digital innovation is being driven by the power of data, data analytics and artificial intelligence.

Due to the prominence of data in modern cities, the discussion of how to best utilise this asset to improve business and economic functions was encouraged in various smart city policies as outlined by the St. Albert Smart City Master Plan [65] as follows:

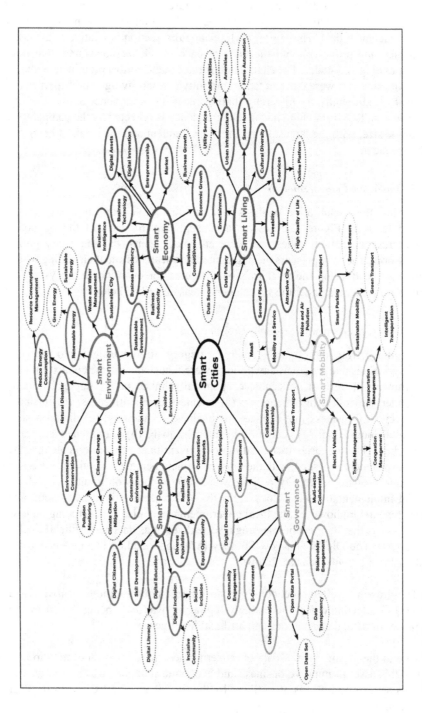

Figure 1.5 Smart city policy concept map.

A smart city promotes entrepreneurship and supports business requirements, particularly as the cost or ability to obtain valued data and education is a barrier to some businesses. A city can support the growth and success of its existing businesses, the attraction of new businesses, and the commercialization of its data through specific smart city services.

In another example from Ottawa's Smart City 2.0 [64], harnessing data for economic benefits also extended to the socioeconomic benefits that smart city policies encompass as described next:

The premise behind this is that shared data encourages community participation in smart city solutions. Equally important, it also facilitates knowledge-based business growth by providing third parties with data that enables the development of digital applications and smart city solutions. Essentially, it enables socioeconomic growth by providing access to data to those trying to analyze and solve problems.

Alongside the outlined benefits of data innovation, the smart policies were also considering the dilemmas that may arise with new technologies and their influences on economic growth. The Smart City Wien Framework Strategy [60] discussed this alternative perspective as follows:

End-to-end digitalization is penetrating all spheres of life. This phenomenon raises a host of new issues, for instance regarding the transparent handling and careful treatment of large quantities of data, the ethical and moral boundaries associated with the use of digital innovations such as artificial intelligence, and equitable distribution of the benefits and opportunities afforded by new technologies.

The benefits of applying new technologies to achieve economic and business growth in the identified policy frameworks were prominent. Nevertheless, the local governments were also increasingly aware of the negative consequences that may arise if these technologies are not handled appropriately to achieve not only economic growth but also to work in unison with other smart city objectives. For example, if local governments focus solely on advancing their economy through new technologies, they risk neglecting other characteristics that create a smart city. Recognising the need for this balance facilitates economic growth while also providing an enriching opportunity for their communities overall [95].

1.3.2.2 Smart Environment with Climate Change Focus

The findings from the 'smart environment' category assisted in finding the most prominent environmental foci within the identified policies. From the local government perspective, the main categories associated with environmental smart city policy included: (a) carbon neutral; (b) climate change; (c) environmental conservation; (d) natural disasters; (e) reduce energy consumption; (f) renewable energy; (g); sustainable city; (h) sustainable development; and (i) waste and water management. Of these categories, the most frequently recurring smart city initiatives focused on climate change and the importance of renewable energy. This prominence was related to the perception that renewable energy is a means of achieving overarching environmental objectives. As an example, Sydney's Smart City Strategic Framework [57] described the drive towards renewable energy as follows:

Technological advancements can support us to accelerate the transition to affordable, renewable energy and a carbon-neutral future. Data and digital technology can help to manage flows of materials and assets across the city, fostering an urban system that is regenerative and restorative.

After commenting on the perceived value of renewable energy as a method and a means to ensure a healthier environmental future, several frameworks outlined the renewable energy adoption methods currently operating in their councils. The Smart City Wien Framework Strategy [60] outlined their approach as follows:

The energy supply of Smart City Wien is based almost exclusively on renewable energy sources that are also used locally: solar installations on rooftops and facades generate power and heat. Efficient heat pumps allow waste and ambient heat to be used for heating and cooling of buildings. Deep drilling draws hot water from a depth of 3000 m underground and feeds it into the district heating network. Wind turbines, photovoltaic installations, hydroelectric and biomass plants both inside and outside the city use renewables to meet the city's daily energy requirements.

Likewise, the Digital Glasgow Strategy [87] stated the following as their renewable energy priorities:

Smart grid technologies, together with digitally-enabled renewable energy sources are allowing energy companies to improve the efficiency of energy supply, and technologies such as electric vehicles and autonomous vehicles provide opportunities to transform transport and to reduce pollution.

These approaches highlight the importance of renewable energy as a prominent policy method for tackling urban environmental challenges. Nonetheless, given the vast number of complex environmental externalities—e.g., carbon emissions, pollution, and climate change—renewable energy policies alone are not enough to overcome these issues. Smart city policies establish that renewable energy is most effective when implemented alongside technology that enhances its overall effectiveness. Ultimately, for a city to be smart, it must consider the environmental policies that it can implement to improve its chance of overall success. This brings the necessity for smart cities to also become sustainable cities, providing a triple-bottom-line sustainability [96,97].

1.3.2.3 Smart Governance with Stakeholder Engagement Focus

The findings from the 'smart governance' category offered insight into the structural changes that local governments present to achieve their smart city objectives. The central governance categories from the selected policies were: (a) citizen engagement; (b) collaborative leadership; (c) community engagement; (d) digital democracy; (e) e-government; (f) multi-sector collaboration; (g) open data portal; (h) stakeholder engagement; and (i) urban innovation. The categories generally displayed growing interest in increasing community interaction and transparency in the application of new technologies. Moreover, the local governments perceived that community and stakeholder participation policies are a viable method of adapting the existing top-down government practices to better target urban issues. The Greenwich Smart City Strategy [71] outlined how they are implementing this approach in the following words:

> In a consultative and collaborative approach, the council sees service delivery as a collaborative process in which citizens are active co-creators of public services. It will empower people to create their own solutions both to their own needs and to the needs of others in Greenwich. It will also use new, digitally enhanced forms of civic engagement to ensure direct, meaningful, and real-time participation of citizens in the planning, policy, budgeting, and management decisions of the Council.

Additionally, Wyndham's Smart City Strategy [59] displayed an example of their methods as outlined here:

> Emerging technology offers exciting opportunities to enhance both the transparency, accountability, and integrity of planning and decision-making and the physical safety aspects of the city. Real time reporting, smart sensors, open data, and digital democracy will be key elements of this change and Wyndham will embrace these advancements.

Smart governance is critical for smart cities as it is the enabler domain for the other five smart city domains; therefore, smart governance has a special importance as it aligns closely with the planning, development, execution/implementation, and management of all smart city policies. For this reason, local government agencies should pay special attention to this domain—particularly wider stakeholder engagement that will increase the legibility and acceptability of the policy.

1.3.2.4 Smart Living with Enhanced Liveability Focus

The findings from the 'smart living' category provided insight into the smart city priorities that the local governments implemented to enhance the overall quality of life. From this perspective, the categories most prominent under the smart living umbrella included: (a) attractive city; (b) cultural diversity; (c) data privacy; (d) e-services; (e) entertainment; (f) liveability; (g) sense of place; (h) smart home;

and (i) urban infrastructure. Given the significance of liveability as one of the primary objectives of smart cities, this theme also translated to smart city policy. Newcastle's Smart City Strategy [52] explained this priority as follows:

> Livability is crucial to the creation of a sustainable city community, as is the quality of amenity within its built urban fabric. The livability, amenity and attractiveness of a city refers to the quality of social space, its economic dynamism, and the overall ability of local authorities and other stakeholders to develop a progressive and inclusive economy.

Alongside establishing the importance of liveability for smart cities, the local governments were discovering how to integrate new technologies to achieve their community goals. Primarily, the smart city policies discussed the technologies being implemented in public infrastructure and in transforming existing communal areas.

The St. Albert City Smart City Master Plan [65] outlined how they were incorporating technology to realise the smart city objective of improved liveability as follows:

> In St. Albert, local amenities, street furniture, public art, and events are infused with technologies that seek to inspire and delight. Modern convenience features such as charging stations and Wi-Fi connectivity are widely available, digital information and wayfinding kiosks are integrated into the community's tourist sites, and the city offers a host of e-services for its residents to ensure maximum flexibility and convenience.

In another example, Ottawa's Smart City 2.0 [64] elaborated how they were introducing technologies into urban infrastructure and receiving feedback from multiple social levels to understand improvements to liveability in the following blurb:

> Smart Community Pilots: The pilot smart city technology and amenities in Ottawa communities will allow for the demonstration and development of smart city applications at the residential, business, and entrepreneurial level, while at the same time allowing the community the unique opportunity to evaluate technology and observe socioeconomic impacts.

These policies outlined the importance of liveability in the development of a smart city world-wide. Increasingly, a primary aspect that the local governments had adopted was the integration of technologies to improve the quality of life for their communities; however, feedback on the viability of these technologies is still required. This is where the governance and community engagement aspect of smart cities is necessary. If no communication or follow-up is provided, the investments into new technologies and infrastructure may not reflect the needs of communities. Effectively, to increase the liveability in smart cities, local governments must also adapt their governance strategies to ensure that their citizens are part of the process [98].

1.3.2.5 Smart Mobility with Transportation Management Focus

The findings from the 'smart mobility' category provided an understanding of the importance that smart city policymakers placed on the provision of efficient transportation methods. The predominant mobility-linked policy implementation fell under the following categories: (a) active transport; (b) electric vehicle; (c) mobility-as-a-service; (d) noise and air pollution; (e) public transport; (f) smart parking; (g) sustainable mobility; (h) traffic management; and (i) transportation management. The categories presented multiple transport-related foci that the smart city policies were targeting. A common theme throughout the policies was a push towards public and active forms of transport, but many local governments were still providing smart solutions for more efficient car use. This resulted in many frameworks having a combination of policies to increase public transport while, conflictingly, also improving the smart experience for car users. Specifically, the traffic management and smart parking categories identified smart technology that improves car use through smart sensors and parking apps. Wyndham's Smart City Strategy [59] mentioned examples of the benefits that this technology provides as follows:

> Information about parking bay availability makes it easier for citizens to find parking when and where they need it, assists with infrastructure planning and can also reduce air pollution by minimizing time spent looking for free spaces.

Additionally, the City of Norwood Payneham and St Peters Smart City Plan [54] elaborated on the technologies they were implementing for both car use and other modes of travel in the following blurb:

> Mobility outcomes such as parking, wayfinding and journey-planning were identified as areas of our city that can be enhanced through smart technology. The availability of real-time data, collected from smart sensors and devices, can be used to enhance a range of smart mobility outcomes in our city.

Traditionally, car use can be associated with various urban issues including traffic, noise, and air pollution; however, the smart mobility concept for many local governments raises the conflict between either investing more in improving car use or improving more efficient modes of transport. If a council prioritises smart technologies that make car use more efficient, it may impact the effectiveness of investment in smart technologies for public or active transport that reduce the negative impacts of car use. Various policy frameworks aimed to address this issue by facilitating electric vehicle use. The Hong Kong Smart City Blueprint 2.0 [78] presented one of the common approaches as follows:

Implement a pilot subsidy scheme to promote installation of electric vehicle charging-enabling facilities in car parks of existing private residential buildings.

The smart mobility category identified that the smart city policies were aiming to address complex and often contradicting transport issues. Overall, many local governments were prioritising smart technologies to increase public transport use while at the same time encouraging private motor vehicle use. There is a significant concentration in smart city policymaking on making transport autonomous, connected, and platform-based—such as mobility-as-a-service (MaaS). Nevertheless, there is a major gap in the smart city policy field in making transport affordable and accessible for all citizens, particularly for those socially excluded and disadvantaged [99].

1.3.2.6 Smart People with Digital inclusion Focus

The findings from the 'smart people' category offered insight into how local governments were putting efforts into including their communities in creating a smart city. The predominant policies under the smart people category included: (a) collaboration networks; (b) community environment; (c) digital citizenship; (d) digital education; (e) digital inclusion; (f) diverse population; (g) equal opportunity; (h) resilient community; and (i) skill development. These categories provided a wide range of people-based policies that were currently being implemented in local governments. In particular, the concept of a digital presence was prominent within the categories of digital citizenship, digital education, and digital inclusion. Mississauga's SMRTCTY Master Plan [63] highlighted these interconnected concepts in the lines of the following:

Success in the increasingly digitized social and economic realms requires a comprehensive approach to fostering inclusion. Digital inclusion brings together high-speed internet access, information technologies, and digital literacy in ways that promote success for communities and individuals trying to navigate and participate in the digital realm.

Significantly, the smart city policies were identifying a correlation between digital exclusion and other forms of exclusion including poverty, education, age, gender, and several other issues prevalent in urban centres. Further, the concept of digital inclusion identified that providing digital services was not enough. Many smart city policies were actively addressing the fact that citizens need to be educated on how to use the technologies available to them rather than simply assuming that people will immediately understand how to use those services. The Smart Casey Launchpad [45] was one such policy that identified and addressed this notion in the following way:

Digital inclusion is critical to maximizing and sharing the benefits of the digital revolution. Free public Wi-Fi, digital training sessions, and online-safety courses help to ensure everyone in the community can participate and benefit.

Similarly, the Smart Sheffield policy [76] presented an example of the same concept along the lines of the following:

> However, having access to the Internet and knowing generally how to use it is not enough—a truly digitally included person also knows how to apply these technologies to their own social and economic advantage.

Exclusion is a widespread and complex urban issue; however, using technology to improve this concern was one of the primary themes identified in the smart city policies. In addressing this, the smart city policies were increasingly concentrating on the integration of the feedback and participation of citizens in the entire governance process to ensure that infrastructure would effectively meet the needs of each community. For example, by ensuring that citizens have a digital identity and voice, local governments can implement enhanced smart city policies in the future. Citizens who previously were excluded from governance processes can voice their concerns digitally and local governments can approach urban issues with a greater perspective. Moreover, the presence of digital inclusion policies demonstrates that local governments understand the value of citizen input in the function of a successful smart city [100].

1.4 Discussion

1.4.1 Insights from International Smart City Policy Frameworks

The study at hand focused on capturing smart city themes that arose in policies from cities worldwide. For that purpose, 52 smart city frameworks from the local councils of 17 countries—Australia ($n = 17$), Austria ($n = 1$), Canada ($n = 6$), China ($n = 1$), Croatia ($n = 1$), England ($n = 9$), Germany ($n = 1$), Ireland ($n = 2$), Malaysia ($n = 1$), New Zealand ($n = 1$), Northern Ireland ($n = 1$), Poland ($n = 2$), Scotland ($n = 2$), Sweden ($n = 1$), Switzerland ($n = 1$), the USA ($n = 4$), and Wales ($n = 1$)—were placed under the microscope. The results provided an understanding of the key urban planning issues that these policies were often targeting. The study on smart city policies revealed that local governments implemented smart city strategies in response to a wide range of urban concerns or issues. These are discussed below under the six smart city domains.

Smart economy: As the node frequency analysis (see Table 1.4) has indicated, smart economy was the most popular policy domain amongst the investigated smart city policy documents. The main challenge for most of the investigated smart cities was to become economically competitive or to maintain their already established competitive edge. Economic business growth was, thus, reflected as the primary issue for smart city policies when discussing the relevance of "smart economy" foci—whether it is technology or creativity concentrated [101,102]. In response to this issue, the policies encouraged the investment in smart city technologies as crucial business infrastructures to attract innovative businesses that, in turn, would increase employment opportunities. In support of this, the policies mentioned how the adoption of data, data analytics, AI, and other new technologies can support the overall planning goals and priorities of business and economic growth by driving innovations in communities. The existing research has suggested that the emergence of data and AI can substantially aid urban economic growth [103–106], and that the priority smart city policies give this aspect is reflective of this knowledge.

The policies also identified the socioeconomic benefits from the incorporation of these new technologies. Specifically, shared data were outlined with their benefit of enabling community and business participation in the formation of smart city solutions. Given the dominance of economic efficiency goals for the use of data, the mention of data-related concerns is a new form of rhetoric that raises concerns around data use [107]. This rhetoric was also reflected in the smart city policies where the transparency of data, AI boundaries, and the overall equitable distribution and ethical use of new technologies were identified as possible areas of concern—in line with the literature [108].

Smart environment: For many of the investigated smart cities, one of the leading challenges was to tackle, through their policy frameworks, the unsustainable development problem. In this perspective, the central planning issue identified under the "smart environment" aspect of the smart city policies was climate change. Together with climate change, renewable energy was derived as both a goal and a priority for targeting multiple environmental urban challenges. The strategies mentioned various technologies—e.g., solar installations, wind turbines, heat pumps, photovoltaic installations, and smart grids—being utilised to contribute to renewable energy goals and objectives. The incorporation of these technologies in the smart city policies reflects renewable energy's wide regard as a key solution for climate change and energy security challenges in urban centres [109]. The findings from the smart city initiatives reflected the existing knowledge that technological innovations are highly interconnected with sustainability, as well as with the values and concerns that invariably shape the discourse and aims of new technologies [110].

Though many policies prioritised the importance of smart grids to increase the effectiveness of renewable energy [111], few policies fully mentioned how their renewable energy targets functioned beyond the local government level. The study findings of [112] indicate that local renewable energy strategies need to be coordinated with global, national, and neighbouring cities to meet the challenges of climate change effectively. Considering that the existing policies lacked this focus, future smart city policies are provided with an opportunity for extending renewable energy contributions beyond their localities. Overall, the local governments were optimistic about policies related to the outcomes of renewable energy sources in combination with technology that improves its effectiveness to contribute to a smarter environment; however, improvements can be made to extend the positive impacts beyond the local level.

Smart governance: Good governance practice is the enabler of smart city (trans) formation, and in that respect, governance to become smart(er) would help in the efficiency and effectiveness of smart city decisions [113]; however, the lack of or limited stakeholder and public participation in the decision-making process is an important issue for cities. This was also the case for smart cities. The investigated smart city cases showed that stakeholder engagement was the prevalent issue for "smart governance" in the identified smart city policies. Engagement at all levels was the major focus for many of the local councils, where community and citizen engagement were identified as goals and priorities for smarter governance. Technologies for civil engagement, real-time reporting, smart sensors, and open data were among the technologies being implemented by various policies. Where previous studies have raised concerns in relation to the ethical implementation of data in smart city economies, smart governance plays a central role in managing these concerns. A study by [114] similarly suggested that policy based on data analysis promotes technocratic decision-making and that the priorities of stakeholder, community, and citizen engagement in policy is reflective of this.

The concept of community engagement also significantly overlapped between the smart governance and smart people nodes within the policies. This is indicative of the growing importance for citizens to hold participative roles in the decision-making process [115]. This focus additionally supports the existing suggestions that there is a current transition from the dominance of traditional top-down planning initiatives to a model that incorporates citizens not only as users but as collaborators [116,117]. Nonetheless, though the policies suggested the importance of stakeholder engagement, many policies did not provide specific bottom-up planning approaches. The smart governance results reflected this, as it was one of the least mentioned characteristics in the smart city policies. These results mirror the study findings of [34], whereby many policies were addressing the issue of engagement but in a limited capacity. With evidence to suggest that smart cities need adjusted governance to support stakeholder engagement, future smart city policies need to increase this priority for smart governance.

Smart living: One of the main promises of the smart city movement is to increase the quality of life/living in cities through infrastructural and technological innovation offerings; however, a lack of significant quality of life improvements or improvements for only a small group of privileged locations/people remains an important problem for so-called smart cities. In most of the investigated smart city cases, hence, liveability was suggested to be the prominent issue under the "smart living" aspect of the smart city policies. The policies targeted and prioritised new technologies with the goal of effective integration into public infrastructure and amenities. This was often targeted in the form of Wi-Fi and e-services that provide digital information for public users. Primarily, the presence of liveability as a central priority in the smart city policies shows that local governments understand that smart cities can generate safe, healthy, and sustainable communities [118]. Smart city applications were also utilised to enable direct feedback and evaluations from the public on the impacts of these technologies and their effectiveness. The prioritisation of these technologies demonstrates that the local councils were endeavouring to integrate citizens into the decision-making process of local government, and it highlights the interrelation of the smart living, smart governance, and smart people aspects.

Smart mobility: As the node frequency analysis has indicated, smart mobility was the second most popular focus in smart city policy, after a smart economy. This was probably due to the rapid advancements in urban mobility domain—such as autonomous driving, electric vehicles, and mobility-as-a-service (MaaS) [119]— and the importance of addressing urban mobility problems as negative externalities of the environment and societies, causing transportation disadvantage and social exclusion [120,121]. In this perspective, this study outlined various policy implementations related to "smart mobility" with the most prominent issue being transportation management. It is widely accepted that governments worldwide identify public transport as a primary goal and priority over private vehicle use [122]. This factor was further reflected in the smart city policies with public transport being the second most mentioned characteristic; however, there was also a significant focus on investing in private vehicle use. These priorities may be reflective of the wide range of contexts that the policies originated from, with many being in areas that have a significant reliance on private vehicles. Additionally, COVID-19 exacerbated the dependence on individual vehicle use and local governments should adjust their future transport policies to improve public transport that is safe and efficient beyond the pandemic [123].

Many policies referenced parking sensors, parking applications, wayfinding applications, and electric vehicles as some of the most beneficial technologies for effective transportation management. These technologies indicate that smart city policies are aiming for overall improvements in transport by increasing the efficiency of car use and other modes of transportation at the same time; however, applying these technologies for use in the development of shared mobility transit enables a greater benefit to the overall social and environmental goals [115]. In future, these findings suggest that smart city policies should adjust their transport management values and priorities for public transport above private vehicles in their cities.

Smart people: As the node frequency analysis has indicated, smart people was the third most popular focus in smart city policy. This importance is warranted as smart cities should place people in the centre of the development—e.g., forming smart communities [124]. One of the main challenges in the progress towards a smart community formation is the lack of or limited initiatives or opportunities for inclusion/involvement [125,126]. In this regard, digital inclusion was suggested as the most prevalent "smart people" planning issue within the analysed smart city strategies. Many frameworks created goals and priorities related to digital inclusion and access to urban amenities. Additionally, these priorities were frequently identified as critical challenges related to responsible and ethical governance [127]. In response, the policies often referenced how the technologies they were implementing could be utilised to public advantage and how they could reduce exclusion by providing training that focuses on general digital education and safety.

Additionally, the digital inclusion focus further strengthens the intrinsic link between the smart governance and smart people aspects of policy to construct a form of urban digital governance. A study by [128] suggested that community-led smart initiatives increase inclusion and better address urban issues. By prioritising digital inclusion, smart city policies are signifying a shift in the approach to the community as both users and collaborators of a smart city [129–131]. The inclusion and engagement of communities ensure that smart city frameworks are account-able for planning outcomes and further indicate a paradigm shift in the governance and structure of planning processes to become more user-centred and co-designed [132–135].

The study findings presented in this chapter are insightful and should be considered in the discussion and formation of future smart city policies, specific-ally in the identification of urban issues that exist contextually in a local council area and of how smart city technologies can be directly implemented to achieve targets. Additionally, the research presents goals and priorities that existing policies are implementing alongside key planning issues to provide guidance in planning processes. The data provide an insight into the interpretation of the major urban challenges worldwide and how the current policies and technologies are being used to overcome them in the creation of a smart city. Though each policy document provided varying levels of focus and represented differing contexts, each smart city strategy incorporated some element from each of the six central categories that provided the foundation for the study. The results suggest that each element is crucial for overall smart city policy success, and a holistic approach is needed for smart city policy.

1.4.2 Limitations of the Study

The study explored primary urban planning issues, goals, and priorities that smart city policies worldwide are intending to target and tackle; however, four limitations should be noted when interpreting the study findings. Firstly, though the study included a significant number of smart city policies ($n = 52$) from multiple coun-tries ($n = 16$), a wider range of policies may provide a more accurate view of overall urban target issues. Secondly, the study was limited by its identification of policies written in English. If other languages were included in the study, the results may have afforded a richer discussion with the inclusion of wider country and city contexts. This limitation is particularly reflective with the prominence of smart city policies from Australia, England, and Canada in the study. Thirdly, although the smart city policies were thorough in nature, they do not fully consider broader—or other complementary—policies and government operations that could impact their implementation and, thus, their success levels. Lastly, the methodological choices give space for inadvertent researcher biases to form in the selection of the nodes and themes when examining the policy documents. Our prospective studies into this area will aim to consider these limitations to provide a more comprehensive and contextually accurate analysis of the smart city policies.

1.5 Conclusion

The study reported in this chapter focused on tackling the research questions of: (a) What do smart city policies target in terms of key planning issues, goals, and priorities? (b) How do smart city policies address these key planning issues, goals, and priorities? In total, 52 smart city policy frameworks were put under the

policy analysis microscope with the guidance of smart economy, smart environment, smart governance, smart living, smart mobility, and smart people domains
to generate insights into urban planning issues and their associated priorities and
goals. With respect to each of these six domains, the following most predominant
and challenging planning issues were identified: economic growth, climate change,
stakeholder engagement, liveability, transport management, and digital inclusion.

In terms of the first research question of "What do smart city policies target in
terms of key planning issues, goals, and priorities?", the key findings include the
following.

When discussing the goals and priorities of each smart city domain, the smart
city policies identified various foci that are highly dependent on context. When
addressing the economic growth issue, many policies identified innovation as a
goal and new technologies as the priority to achieve this outcome. For addressing
the climate change issue, the frameworks identified renewable energy as both a
goal and a priority. When addressing stakeholder engagement planning issues,
many frameworks centred their priorities and goals on increasing community and
citizen engagement. The liveability issue was identified to be primarily addressed
from the perspective that it is an overarching goal for smart cities, hence, the priorities and goals were aimed at successfully implementing technologies within the
infrastructure to the benefit of users. The transport management issue presented
conflicting goals and priorities depending on the context of each city. While many
frameworks specified a priority for public transport, many of the technologies
being implemented benefitted individual vehicle use. Regarding the digital inclusion issue, the smart city policies largely generated goals centred on ensuring that
communities were able to effectively benefit from new technologies and prioritised
a reduction in digital exclusion.

In terms of the second research question of "How do smart city policies address
these key planning issues, goals, and priorities?", the key findings include the
following.

Many policies accredited the deployment of new smart urban technologies and
their implementation into the daily functions of their cities to achieve their policy
targets. Overall, the policies supported the integration of smart urban technologies to advance each domain of the smart city policy, but the analysis also raised
an appreciation for the interconnected nature of each smart city domain. This was
particularly evident in the correlations between the smart governance, smart living,
and smart people domains, where the policies presented a holistic prioritisation
for incorporating citizens in the urban planning, development, and management
decision-making processes.

In sum, in the first decade of the smart city movement, there were not any/many
local governments with official and publicly available smart city policy documents.
During the last decade, particularly the last five years, local governments have
started to formalise their overall smart city perspectives through official policy
documents. An analysis of 52 of these documents from 17 countries disclosed that
while the existing smart city policies seemed to be headed in a somewhat more
focused direction—that is (at least at the policy-level) targeting desired urban

outcomes that ranged from sustainable development to good governance, and from digital inclusion to community formation—future policies should learn from their drawbacks and apply the concept of smart cities at a holistic level considering all smart city domains.

Additionally, the provided summative collection of the existing smart city policy frameworks from the investigated 52 cities of 17 countries, informs urban policymakers, planners, and practitioners in applying a gained understanding into their future smart city policy, planning, development, and management decisions, hence enhancing the existing governance processes to create smarter cities.

While this study generated insights into smart city policymaking, further research is needed to reinforce such understanding. Moreover, as stated by [126], "the presentation of smart city initiatives must be compared against the actions that are implicit or explicit in these policies". Prospective studies, hence, will also need to concentrate on identifying the impact of local government smart city policies, outlined in their policy documents. This will help in understanding the success and failure factors in translating smart city policies into desired smart city outcomes and will support local governments in forming a consolidated view on how smart city policies can be utilised for tackling urban challenges more effectively [136].

Acknowledgements

This chapter, with permission from the copyright holder, is a reproduced version of the following journal article: Micozzi, N., & Yigitcanlar, T. (2022). Understanding Smart City Policy: Insights from the Strategy Documents of 52 Local Governments. *Sustainability*, 14(16), 10164.

References

1. Komninos, N., Kakderi, C., Panori, A., Tsarchopoulos, P. (2019). Smart city planning from an evolutionary perspective. *Journal of Urban Technology* 26, 3–20.
2. Nili, A., Desouza, K., Yigitcanlar, T. (2022) What can the public sector teach us about deploying AI technologies. *IEEE Software* 39(6), 58–63.
3. Yigitcanlar, T., Kankanamge, N., Vella, K. (2021) How are smart city concepts and technologies perceived and utilized? A systematic geo-Twitter analysis of smart cities in Australia. *Journal of Urban Technology* 28, 135–154.
4. Allwinkle, S., Cruickshank, P. (2011) Creating smarter cities: An overview. *Journal of Urban Technology* 18, 1–16.
5. Hollands, R. (2008) Will the real smart city please stand up? *City* 12, 303–320.
6. Yigitcanlar, T., Degirmenci, K., Butler, L., Desouza, K. (2022) What are the key factors affecting smart city transformation readiness? Evidence from Australian cities. *Cities* 120, 103434.
7. Desouza, K., Hunter, M., Jacob, B., Yigitcanlar, T. (2020) Pathways to the making of prosperous smart cities: An exploratory study on the best practice. *Journal of Urban Technology* 27, 3–32.
8. Mosannenzadeh, F., Vettorato, D. (2014). Defining smart city. A conceptual framework based on keyword analysis. *Journal of Land Use, Mobility and Environment* 2523, 683–694.

9. Olivadese, R., Alpagut, B., Revilla, B., Brouwer, J., Georgiadou, V., Woestenburg, A., Van Wees, M. (2021). Towards energy citizenship for a just and inclusive transition: Lessons learned on collaborative approach of positive energy districts from the EU Horizon 2020 smart cities and communities projects. *Proceedings* 65, 20.

10. Bricout, J., Baker, P., Moon, N., Sharma, B. (2021). Exploring the smart future of participation. *International Journal of E-Planning Research* 10, 94–108.

11. Malek, J., Lim, S., Yigitcanlar, T. (2021). Social inclusion indicators for building citizen-centric smart cities: A systematic literature review. *Sustainability* 13, 376.

12. Caragliu, A., Del Bo, C. (2019). Smart innovative cities: The impact of smart city policies on urban innovation. *Technological Forecasting and Social Change* 142, 373–383.

13. Metaxiotis, K., Carrillo, F., Yigitcanlar, T. (2010). *Knowledge-Based Development for Cities and Societies: Integrated Multi-Level Approaches*. IGI Global: Hersey, PA, USA.

14. Lim, S., Malek, J., Yussoff, M., Yigitcanlar, T. (2021). Understanding and acceptance of smart city policies: practitioners' perspectives on the Malaysian smart city framework. *Sustainability* 13, 9559.

15. Sharifi, A., Khavarian-Garmsir, A., Kummitha, R. (2021). Contributions of smart city Solutions and technologies to resilience against the COVID-19 pandemic: A literature review. *Sustainability* 13, 8018.

16. Kharlamov, A., Raskhodchikov, A., Pilgun, M. (2021). Smart city data sensing during COVID-19: Public reaction to accelerating digital transformation. *Sensors* 21, 3965.

17. Toh, C., Webb, W. (2020). The smart city and Covid-19. *IET Smart Cities* 2, 56–57.

18. Kankanamge, N., Yigitcanlar, T., Goonetilleke, A., Kamruzzaman, M. (2019). Can volunteer crowdsourcing reduce disaster risk? A systematic review of the literature. *International Journal of Disaster Risk Reduction* 35, 101097.

19. Kunzmann, K. (2020). Smart cities after COVID-19: Ten narratives. *DISP Planning Review* 56, 20–31.

20. Hassankhani, M., Alidadi, M., Sharifi, A., Azhdari, A. (2021). Smart city and crisis management: Lessons for the COVID-19 pandemic. *International Journal of Environmental Research and Public Health* 18, 7736.

21. Kakderi, C., Oikonomaki, E., Papadaki, I. (2021). Smart and resilient urban futures for sustainability in the post COVID-19 era: A review of policy responses on urban mobility. *Sustainability* 13, 6486.

22. Das, D., Zhang, J. (2021). Pandemic in a smart city: Singapore's COVID-19 management through technology & society. *Urban Geography* 42, 408–416.

23. Capdevila, I., Zarlenga, M. (2015). Smart city or smart citizens? The Barcelona case. *Journal of Strategy and Management* 8, 266–282.

24. Lim, S., Yigitcanlar, T. (2022). Participatory governance of smart cities: Insights from e-participation of Putrajaya and Petaling Jaya, Malaysia. *Smart Cities* 5, 71–89.

25. Masik, G., Sagan, I., Scott, J. (2021). Smart city strategies and new urban development policies in the Polish context. *Cities* 108, 102970.

26. Lim, S., Mazhar, M., Malek, J., Yigitcanlar, T. (2021). The right or wrong to the city? Understanding citizen participation in the pre-and post-COVID-19 eras in Malaysia. *Journal of Open Innovation: Technology, Market and Complexity* 7, 238.

27. Yigitcanlar, T. (2018). Smart city policies revisited: Considerations for a truly smart and sustainable urbanism practice. *World Technopolis Review* 7, 97–112.

28. Lim, S., Malek, J., Yigitcanlar, T. (2021). Post-materialist values of smart city societies: International comparison of public values for good enough governance. *Future Internet* 13, 201.

29. Brandl, J., Zielinska, I. (2020). Reviewing the smart city Vienna framework strategy's potential as an eco-social policy in the context of quality of work and socio-ecological transformation. *Sustainability* 12, 859.

30. Alizadeh, T., Irajifar, L. (2018). Gold Coast smart city strategy: Informed by local planning priorities and international smart city best practices. *International Journal of Knowledge-Based Development* 9, 153–173.

31. Clement, J., Crutzen, N. (2021). How local policy priorities set the smart city agenda. *Technological Forecasting and Social Change* 171, 120985.

32. Angelidou, M. (2016). Four European smart city strategies. *International Journal of Social Science Studies* 4, 18.

33. Mancebo, F. (2020). Smart city strategies: Time to involve people—comparing Amsterdam, Barcelona and Paris. *Journal of Urbanism: International Research on Placemaking and Urban Sustainability* 13, 133–152.

34. Angelidou, M. (2017). The role of smart city characteristics in the plans of fifteen cities. *Journal of Urban Technology* 24, 3–28.

35. Joss, S., Sengers, F., Schraven, D., Caprotti, F., Dayot, Y. (2019). The smart city as global discourse: Storylines and critical junctures across 27 cities. *Journal of Urban Technology* 26, 3–34.

36. Manville, C., Cochrane, G., Cave, J., Millard, J., Pederson, J., Thaarup, R., Liebe, A., Wissner, M., Massink, R., Kotterink, B. *Mapping Smart Cities in the EU.* Available online: http://resolver.tudelft.nl/uuid:1fac0e18-8dd3-406d-86fe-ce1e6a22e 90c (accessed on 28 March 2022).

37. Korachi, Z., Bounabat, B. (2020). Towards a frame of reference for smart city strategy development and governance. *Journal of Computer Science* 16, 1451–1464.

38. Giffinger, R., Fertner, C., Kramar, H., Kalasek, R., Pichler-Milanovic, N., Meijers, E. *Smart Cities: Ranking of European Medium-Sized Cities.* Available online: www. smart-cities.eu/download/smart_cities_final_report.pdf (accessed on 28 July 2022).

39. Qonita, M., Giyarsih, S. (2022). Smart city assessment using the Boyd Cohen smart city wheel in Salatiga, Indonesia. *GeoJournal.*

40. Lu, H., Chen, C., Yu, H. (2019). Technology roadmap for building a smart city: An exploring study on methodology. *Future Generation Computer Systems* 97, 727–742.

41. De Filippi, F., Coscia, C., Guido, R. (2014). From smart-cities to smart-communities: How can we evaluate the impacts of innovation and inclusive processes in urban context? *International Journal of E-Planning Research* 8, 24–44.

42. Guest, G., MacQueen, K., Namey, E. (2012). *Applied Thematic Analysis.* SAGE Publications: London, UK.

43. Brisbane City Council. (2019). *Smart, Connected Brisbane Framework.* Available online: www.brisbane.qld.gov.au/sites/default/files/20190904-smart-connected-brisb ane-roadmap.pdf (accessed 28 March 2022).

44. City of Canterbury Bankstown. (2018). *Supporting Plan: The SMART CBCity Roadmap.* Available online: https://webdocs.bankstown.nsw.gov.au/api/publish?documentP ath=aHR0cDovL2lzaGFyZS9zaXRlcy9Db21tdW5pdY2F0aW9ucy9QdWJsaWNhd GlvbnMvV2Vic2l0ZSBEb2N1bWVudHMvU21hcnQgQ2l0aWVzIFJvYWRtYXAt Y29tcHJlc3NlZC5wZGY=&title=Smart%20Cities%20Roadmap-compressed.pdf (accessed 28 March 2022).

45. City of Casey. (2021). *Smart Casey Launchpad 2021–2025.* Available online: www.casey. vic.gov.au/sites/default/files/2021-02/City%20of%20Casey-Smart%20Casey%20La unchpad.pdf (accessed 28 March 2022).

46. City of Charles Sturt. (2018). S*mart City Plan 2018–2025: Charles Sturt A Leading, Livable City*. Available online: www.charlessturt.sa.gov.au/__data/assets/pdf_file/0037/159976/Smart-City-Plan-2018-2025.pdf (accessed 28 March 2022).

47. City of Marion. (2020). *Smart CoM Strategic Plan*. Available online: https://cdn.marion.sa.gov.au/sp/Smart-CoM-Strategic-Plan-2020_2020-10-15-003604.pdf (accessed 28 March 2022).

48. City of Darwin. (2019). *#SmartDarwin Our Smart City Strategy*. Available online: www.darwin.nt.gov.au/sites/default/files/page/file/Smart-Darwin-Strategy.pdf (accessed 28 March 2022).

49. City of Greater Geelong. (2021). *The City of Greater Geelong: Smart City Strategic Framework*. Available online: www.geelongaustralia.com.au/common/Public/Documents/8d8eea93d413524-attachment2-smartcitystrategicframeworkmarch2021.pdf (accessed 28 March 2022).

50. City of Hobart. (2019). *Connected Hobart Smart City Framework: Towards Australia's Most Economically, Socially, and Environmentally Connected Community by 2030*. Available online: www.hobartcity.com.au/files/assets/public/strategies-and-plans/hcc4578-smart-cities-framework_110919.pdf (accessed 28 March 2022).

51. Hobsons Bay City Council. (2018). *Enterprise Digital Strategy 2018–2022*. Available online: https://s3.ap-southeast-2.amazonaws.com/hdp.au.prod.app.hobs-participate.files/4715/7120/4112/Enterprise_Digital_Strategy_2018-2022.pdf (accessed 28 March 2022).

52. Newcastle City Council. (2017). *Newcastle City Council Smart City Strategy 2017–2021*. Available online: www.newcastle.nsw.gov.au/getmedia/392db4be-d418-48d8-a593-7a17a4b482bb/2752_Smart-City-Strategy-FINAL-WEB.aspx (accessed 28 March 2022).

53. North Sydney Council. (2019). *North Sydney Smart City Strategy 2019–2022*. Available online: www.northsydney.nsw.gov.au/files/assets/public/docs/8_business_amp_projects/business/201909_smart_city_strategy_final.pdf (accessed 28 March 2022).

54. City of Norwood Payneham and St Peters. (2020). *Smart City Plan*. Available online: www.npsp.sa.gov.au/about_council/strategic_planning/smart-city-plan (accessed 28 March 2022).

55. Parramatta City Council. (2018). *Smart City Masterplan*. Available online: www.cityofparramatta.nsw.gov.au/sites/council/files/2018-12/PCC_Smart_City_Masterplan-12.08.15S.pdf (accessed 28 March 2022).

56. Sunshine Coast Council. (2017). *Sunshine Coast Council Smart City Implementation Plan 2016–2019*. Available online: https://d1j8a4bqwzee3.cloudfront.net/~/media/Corporate/Documents/Smart%20Cities/Smart%20City%20Implementation%20Program.pdf?la=en (accessed 28 March 2022).

57. City of Sydney. (2020). *Smart City Strategic Framework*. Available online: www.cityofsydney.nsw.gov.au/-/media/corporate/files/2020-07-migrated/files_s-2/smart-city-strategic-framework.pdf?download=true (accessed 28 March 2022).

58. Townsville City Council. (2018). *Smart City Draft Strategy*. Available online: www.townsville.qld.gov.au/__data/assets/pdf_file/0018/49122/TCC-SmartCityDraftStrategy_A4.pdf (accessed 28 March 2022).

59. Wyndham City Council. (2019). *Smart City Strategy 2019–2024*. Available online: www.wyndham.vic.gov.au/sites/default/files/2019-06/Wyndham%20Smart%20City%20Strategy%202019_2024%20FINAL-web.pdf (accessed 28 March 2022).

60. City of Vienna. (2019). *Smart City Wien Framework Strategy 2019–2050: Vienna's Strategy for Sustainable Development*. Available online: www.wien.gv.at/stadtentwicklung/studien/pdf/b008552.pdf (accessed 28 March 2022).

61. Calgary City Council. (2018). *Calgary's Submission for The Smart Cities Challenge.* Available online: www.calgary.ca/content/dam/www/general/documents/smartcities/smartcitiessubmission2018.pdf (accessed 28 March 2022).

62. Edmonton City Council. (2019). *Smart Cities Challenge: Edmonton Final Proposal.* Available online: www.edmonton.ca/sites/default/files/public-files/assets/CityofEdmontonSmartCitiesProposal_21MB.pdf (accessed 28 March 2022).

63. Mississauga City Council. (2019). *SMRTCTY Master Plan: A Smart City for Everybody.* Available online: www7.mississauga.ca/websites/smartcity/SMRTCTY_Master_Plan_Final.pdf (accessed 28 March 2022).

64. City of Ottawa. (2017). *Ottawa Smart City 2.0.* Available online: https://documents.ottawa.ca/sites/documents/files/smart_city_strategy_en.pdf (accessed 28 March 2022).

65. City of St. Albert. (2016). *City of St. Albert Smart City Master Plan: Full Reference Version.* Available online: https://stalbert.ca/site/assets/files/1895/smart_city_master_plan-full.pdf (accessed 14 March 2022).

66. City of Winnipeg. (2018). *Smart Cities Challenge Proposal.* Available online: www.winnipeg.ca/interhom/SmartCitiesChallenge/CoW-Smart_Cities.pdf (accessed 28 March 2022).

67. City of Zagreb. (2018). *Integrated Action Plan City of Zagreb.* Available online: https://urbact.eu/sites/default/files/000_integrated_action_plan_city_of_zagreb_-_final.pdf (accessed 28 March 2022).

68. Birmingham City Council. (2014). *The Road to a Smarter Birmingham.* Available online: http://s3-eu-west-1.amazonaws.com/digitalbirmingham/resources/Birmingham_Smart_City_Roadmap_revised-Nov-2014.pdf (accessed 28 March 2022).

69. Bristol City Council. (2019). *Connecting Bristol: Laying the Foundations for a Smart, Well-Connected Future.* Available online: www.connectingbristol.org/wpcontent/uploads/2019/09/Connecting_Bristol_300819_WEB.pdf (accessed 28 March 2022).

70. Cambridgeshire County Council. (2019). *Smart Cambridge 2019–2020.* Available online: www.connectingcambridgeshire.co.uk/wp-content/uploads/2019/09/Smart-Cambridge-brochure-2019-2020.pdf (accessed 28 March 2022).

71. Royal Borough of Greenwich. (2014). *Greenwich Smart City Strategy.* Available online: www.digitalgreenwich.com/wp-content/uploads/2014/06/Greenwich-Smart-City-Strategy1.pdf (accessed 28 March 2022).

72. West Yorkshire Combined Authority. (2019). *Leeds City Region Digital Framework.* Available online: www.westyorks-ca.gov.uk/media/5390/digital-framework-final-april-2019-002.pdf (accessed 28 March 2022).

73. Liverpool City Region. (2021). *Liverpool City Region (LCR) Digital Strategy, 2021–2023.* Available online: www.liverpoolcityregion-ca.gov.uk/tockholm-city-region-lcr-digital-strategy-2021-2023-draft/ (accessed 28 March 2022).

74. London City Hall. (2015). *Smart London Plan.* Available online: www.london.gov.uk/sites/default/files/smart_london_plan.pdf (accessed on 28 March 2022).

75. Manchester City Council. (2020). *Manchester Digital Strategy: Creating an Inclusive, Sustainable & Resilient Smart City.* Available online: https://democracy.manchester.gov.uk/documents/s21579/Digital%20Strategy%20presentation.pdf (accessed 28 March 2022).

76. Sheffield Executive Board. (2015). *Smart Sheffield Report.* Available online: https://sheffield.digital/wp-content/uploads/2016/11/SmartSheffield-Report-Final-draft.pdf (accessed 28 March 2022).

77. City of Munich. (2017). *EU-Project Smarter Together Munich Documentation of Activities and Achievements.* Available online: www.wirtschaft-muenchen.de/publikationen/pdfs/Smarter-Together-Muenchen-Documentation19-en.pdf (accessed 28 March 2022).

78. Government of Hong Kong. (2020). *Smart City Blueprint for Hong Kong Blueprint 2.0.* Available online: www.smartcity.gov.hk/modules/custom/custom_global_js_css/assets/files/HKSmartCityBlueprint(ENG)v2.pdf (accessed 28 March 2022).
79. Belfast City Council. (2017). *Supporting Urban Innovation: The Smart Belfast Framework 2017 to 2021.* Available online: https://smartbelfast.city/wp-content/uploads/2018/04/Smart-Cities-Framework.pdf (accessed 28 March 2022).
80. Cork City Council. (2018). *Building a Connected City: A Digital Strategy for Cork City.* Available online: www.corkcity.ie/en/doing-business-in-cork/smart-cork/digital-strategy/cork%20city%20digital%20strategy.pdf (accessed 28 March 2022).
81. Limerick City and County Council. (2018). *Building Ireland's First Digital City Smart Limerick Roadmap.* Available online: www.limerick.ie/sites/default/files/media/documents/2018-08/Limerick%20Digital%20Strategy%20Roadmap.pdf (accessed 28 March 2022).
82. Perbadanan Putrajaya. (2019). *Putrajaya Smart City Blueprint.* Available online: www.ppj.gov.my/storage/putrajaya07/489/489.pdf (accessed 28 March 2022).
83. Wellington City Council. (2011). *Wellington towards 2040: Smart Capital.* Available online: https://wellington.govt.nz/-/media/your-council/plans-policies-and-bylaws/plans-and-policies/a-to-z/wellington2040/files/wgtn2040-brochure.pdf (accessed 28 March 2022).
84. Krakow Metropolitan Authority. (2015). *Smart_Kom Strategy: Roadmap for Smart Solutions in Krakow Metropolitan Area.* Available online: www.kpt.krakow.pl/wp-content/uploads/2015/03/smart_kom-strategy_ang.pdf (accessed 28 March 2022).
85. City of Warsaw. (2018). *Warsaw: Towards a Smart City. City of Warsaw.* Available online: https://pawilonzodiak.pl/wp-content/uploads/2018/10/warsaw-towards-smart-city-april-2018.pdf (accessed 28 March 2022).
86. City of Edinburgh Council. (2020). *Digital and Smart City Strategy: 2020–2023.* Available online: https://democracy.edinburgh.gov.uk/documents/s26745/7.10%20-%20Digital%20and%20Smart%20City%20Strategy.pdf (accessed 28 March 2022).
87. Glasgow City Council. (2018). *Digital Glasgow Strategy.* Available online: www.glasgow.gov.uk/ChttpHandler.ashx?id=43572&p=0 (accessed 28 March 2022).
88. City of Stockholm. (2017). *Smart & Connected.* Available online: https://international.stockholm.se/globalassets/ovriga-bilder-och-filer/smart-city/summary-of-the-strategy-for-stockholm-as-a-smart-and-connected-city.pdf (accessed 28 March 2022).
89. Zurich City Council. (2018). *Strategy Smart City Zurich.* Available onlinewww.stadt-zuerich.ch/content/dam/stzh/portal/Deutsch/politik-der-stadt-zuerich/grafik-und-foto/smartcity/Smart_City_Zurich_Strategy.pdf (accessed 28 March 2022).
90. City of Chula Vista. (2017). *City of Chula Vista Smart City Strategic Action Plan 2017.* Available online: www.chulavistaca.gov/home/showpublisheddocument/15417/636745783096200000 (accessed 28 March 2022).
91. Las Vegas City Council. (2019). *Smart Vegas: A Forward-Focused Plan.* Available online: https://files.lasvegasnevada.gov/innovate-vegas/Smart-Vegas-A-Forward-Focused-Plan.pdf (accessed 28 March 2022).
92. City of Philadelphia. (2019). *SmartCityPHL Roadmap.* Available online: www.phila.gov/media/20190204121858/SmartCityPHL-Roadmap.pdf (accessed 28 March 2022).
93. City and Council of San Francisco. (2018). *Draft Strategic Vision for Smart Cities and the Internet of Things.* Available online: https://sfcoit.org/sites/default/files/2018-02/DRAFT%20-%20Strategic%20Vision%20for%20Smart%20Cities%20and%20the%20Internet%20of%20Things.pdf (accessed 28 March 2022).

94. Cardiff Council. (2018). *Smart Cardiff: Cardiff Council's Smart City Road Map.* Available online: www.smartcardiff.co.uk/wp-content/uploads/Smart%20Cities%202 019.pdf (accessed 28 March 2022).

95. Jiang, Y. (2021). Economic development of smart city industry based on 5G network and wireless sensors. *Microprocessors and Microsystems* 80, 103563.

96. Haarstad, H. (2017). Constructing the sustainable city: Examining the role of sustainability in the 'smart city' discourse. *Journal of Environmental Policy and Planning* 19, 423–437.

97. Dizdaroglu, D., Yigitcanlar, T., Dawes, L. (2012). A micro-level indexing model for assessing urban ecosystem sustainability. *Smart and Sustainable Built Environment* 1, 291–315.

98. Jiang, H., Geertman, S., Witte, P. (2019). Smart urban governance: An urgent symbiosis? *Information Polity* 24, 245–269.

99. Golub, A., Satterfield, V., Serritella, M., Singh, J., Phillips, S. (2019). Assessing the barriers to equity in smart mobility systems: A case study of Portland, Oregon. *Case Studies on Transport Policy* 7, 689–697.

100. Sant'Ana, D., Pache, M., Borges, P., Dias, J. (2021). Accessibility and digital inclusion in Brazil and South Korea: A comparison between micro and macro territorial approach. *Sustainable Cities and Society* 64, 102524.

101. Pancholi, S., Yigitcanlar, T., Guaralda, M. (2015). Public space design of knowledge and innovation spaces: Learnings from Kelvin Grove Urban Village, Brisbane. *Journal of Open Innovation: Technology, Market, and Complexity* 1, 13.

102. Durmaz, B., Platt, S., Yigitcanlar, T. (2010). Creativity, culture tourism and placemaking: Istanbul and London film industries. *International Journal of Culture, Tourism and Hospitality Research* 4, 198–213.

103. Bibri, S. (2019). On the sustainability of smart and smarter cities in the era of big data: An interdisciplinary and transdisciplinary literature review. *Journal of Big Data* 6, 25.

104. Kitchin, R. (2014). Making sense of smart cities: Addressing present shortcomings. *Cambridge Journal of Regions, Economy and Society* 8, 131–136.

105. Yigitcanlar, T., Agdas, D., Degirmenci, K. (2022) Artificial intelligence in local governments: Perceptions of city managers on prospects, constraints and choices. *AI & Society* 38(3), 1135–1150.

106. Yigitcanlar, T., Kankanamge, N., Regona, M., Ruiz Maldonado, A., RIn, B., Ryu, A., Li, R. (2020). Artificial intelligence technologies and related urban planning and development concepts: How are they perceived and utilized in Australia? *Journal of Open Innovation: Technology, Market and Complexity* 6, 187.

107. Karvonen, A., Cugurullo, F., Caprotti, F. (2019). *Inside Smart Cities: Place, Politics and Urban Innovation.* Routledge: London, UK.

108. Calvo, P. (2020). The ethics of smart city (EoSC): Moral implications of hyperconnectivity, algorithmization and the datafication of urban digital society. *Ethics and Information Technology* 22, 141–149.

109. Kolokotsa, D. (2017). Smart cooling systems for the urban environment: Using renewable technologies to face the urban climate change. *Solar Energy* 154, 101–111.

110. Meijer, A., Bolívar, M. (2015). Governing the smart city: A review of the literature on smart urban governance. *International Review of Administrative Sciences* 82, 392–408.

111. Calvillo, C., Sánchez-Miralles, A., Villar, J. (2016). Energy management and planning in smart cities. *Renewable and Sustainable Energy Reviews* 55, 273–287.

112. Thellufsen, J., Lund, H., Sorknæs, P., Østergaard, P., Chang, M., Drysdale, D., Nielsen, S., Djørup, S., Sperling, K. (2020). Smart energy cities in a 100% renewable energy context. *Renewable and Sustainable Energy Reviews* 129, 109922.

113. Pereira, G., Parycek, P., Falco, E., Kleinhans, R. (2018). Smart governance in the context of smart cities: A literature review. *Information Polity* 23, 143–162.

114. Kitchin, R. (2013). The real-time city? Big data and smart urbanism. *GeoJournal* 79, 1–14.

115. Allam, Z., Dhunny, Z. (2019). On big data, artificial intelligence and smart cities. *Cities* 89, 80–91.

116. Macke, J., Rubim Sarate, J., De Atayde Moschen, S. (2019). Smart sustainable cities evaluation and sense of community. *Journal of Cleaner Production* 239, 118103.

117. Calzada, I., Cobo, C. (2015). Unplugging: Deconstructing the smart city. *Journal of Urban Technology* 22, 23–43.

118. Prakash, A. (2021). Smart mobility solutions for a smart city. *IEEE Potentials* 40, 24–29.

119. Butler, L., Yigitcanlar, T., Paz, A. (2021). Barriers and risks of Mobility-as-a-Service (MaaS) adoption in cities: A systematic review of the literature. *Cities* 109, 103036.

120. Kamruzzaman, M., Hine, J., Yigitcanlar, T. (2015). Investigating the link between carbon dioxide emissions and transport-related social exclusion in rural Northern Ireland. *International Journal of Environmental Science And Technology* 12, 3463–3478.

121. Yigitcanlar, T., Fabian, L., Coiacetto, E. (2008). Challenges to urban transport sustainability and smart transport in a tourist city: The Gold Coast, Australia. *Open Transportation Journal* 2, 29–46.

122. Bubelíny, O., Kubina, M. (2021). Impact of the concept smart city on public transport. *Transportation Research Procedia* 55, 1361–1367.

123. Pautasso, E., Frisiello, A., Chiesa, M., Ferro, E., Dominici, F., Tsardanidis, G., Efthymiou, I., Zgeras, G., Vlachokyriakos, V. (2021). The outreach of participatory methods in smart cities, from the co-design of public services to the evaluation: Insights from the Athens case study. *International Journal of Urban Planning: Smart Cities* 2, 59–83.

124. Li, X., Lu, R., Liang, X., Shen, X., Chen, J., Lin, X. (2011). Smart community: An internet of things application. *IEEE Communications Magazine* 49, 68–75.

125. Kolotouchkina, O., Barroso, C., Sánchez, J. (2022). Smart cities, the digital divide, and people with disabilities. *Cities* 123, 103613.

126. Wiig, A. (2015). IBM's smart city as techno-utopian policy mobility. *City* 19, 258–273.

127. Wiig, A. (2016). The empty rhetoric of the smart city: From digital inclusion to economic promotion in Philadelphia. *Urban Geography* 37, 535–553.

128. Cleveland, M., Cleveland, S. (2018). Building engaged communities: A collaborative leadership approach. *Smart Cities* 1, 9.

129. Miller, T. (2019). Imaginaries of sustainability: The techno-politics of smart cities. *Scientific Culture* 29, 1–23.

130. Van Waart, P., Mulder, I., De Bont, C. (2016). A participatory approach for envisioning a smart city. *Social Science Computer Review* 34, 708–723.

131. Masucci, M., Pearsall, H., Wiig, A. (2020). The smart city conundrum for social justice: Youth perspectives on digital technologies and urban transformations. *Annals of the American Association of Geographers* 110, 476–484.

132. Esposito, G., Clement, J., Mora, L., Crutzen, N. (2021). One size does not fit all: Framing smart city policy narratives within regional socio-economic contexts in Brussels and Wallonia. *Cities* 118, 103329.

133. Oksman, V., Raunio, M., Andreas, D. (2018). Reframing smart city in Sub-Saharan Africa: Inclusive engagement approach and co-design tools for a developing economy. *International Journal of Advanced Intelligence Systems* 11, 245–256.

134. Granier B., Kudo H. (2016). How are citizens involved in smart cities? Analysing citizen participation in Japanese Smart Communities. *Information Polity* 21, 61–76.

135. Sakuma, N., Trencher, G., Yarime, M., Onuki, M. (2021). A comparison of smart city research and practice in Sweden and Japan: Trends and opportunities identified from a literature review and co-occurrence network analysis. *Sustainability Science* 16, 1777–1796.

136. Micozzi, N., Yigitcanlar, T. (2022). Understanding smart city policy: Insights from the strategy documents of 52 local governments. *Sustainability* 14(16), 10164.

2 Policy Outcomes

2.1 Introduction

It is no surprise that the 21st century has been promoted as the "century of cities" (Carrillo et al., 2014). By 2030, 60% of the world's population is expected to live in mega-cities, by 2050, 75% of the world's population will be living in urban areas, and this figure will reach over 80% by the end of the century (Hardoy et al., 2013; Dizdaroglu & Yigitcanlar, 2014). Today, some developed nations have already exceeded this urbanisation rate. For instance, in the UK well over 80% of the population resides in urban areas. Moreover, the Anthropocene era is already upon us, which is characterised by massive human impacts on geological and ecological systems (Crutzen & Steffen, 2003).

Urban growth is a major phenomenon of the Anthropocene era, which is taking place on an unprecedented scale globally, and its impacts on society and the environment are evident (Perveen et al., 2017). Particularly, greenhouse gas (GHG) emissions, including carbon dioxide (CO_2), are major contributors to global warming (Mahbub et al., 2011; Yigitcanlar & Dizdaroglu, 2015). Climate change in this era has severe implications for the security of individuals, communities, cities, regions, and the planet (Deilami et al., 2018). Mitigating global climate change and neutralising the impacts of fossil fuel-based energy policies on the environment have emerged as the biggest challenges for the planet, threatening both natural and built systems with long-term consequences (Dur & Yigitcanlar, 2015; Arbolino et al., 2017). In recent years, a broad consensus has been established on sustainable urban development—or smart growth—as a panacea to the ills of the Anthropocene era—such as the Paris Agreement (Dizdaroglu et al., 2012; Yigitcanlar & Kamruzzaman, 2014). Consequently, the challenge to sustainable urban development has resulted in "smart cities" appearing as a hot topic of research and practice globally.

Over the past decade smart urban technologies, as part of the smart city agenda, have begun to blanket our cities with the aim of forming the backbone of a large and intelligent infrastructure (Lee et al., 2008). Along with this development, dissemination of the sustainability ideology has had a significant impact on the planning and development of our cities (Zhao, 2011; Goonetilleke et al., 2014). Today, the smart city concept is viewed as a vision, manifesto, or promise aiming to constitute the 21st century's sustainable and ideal city form. In other words, a smart city is

DOI: 10.1201/9781003403647-3

an efficient, technologically advanced, green, and socially inclusive city (Vanolo, 2014). This is to say, smart city applications place a particular technology focus at the forefront of generating solutions for ecological, societal, economic, and management challenges (Yigitcanlar, 2016). However, despite their promise to deliver sustainable outcomes with the aid of advanced technology, smart cities are heavily criticised as being just a buzz phrase that has outlived their usefulness (Kunzmann, 2014; Shelton et al., 2015).

Smart cities' primary focus mostly being exclusive to technology has been heavily criticised by a number of scholars. For instance, the darker side of smart cities—particularly the extreme dependency on technology, and on corporations dominating technology and related services—is mentioned in the literature as threatening. As stated by Kunzmann (2014, p. 17), "sooner or later society will not manage any more to live without the ICT-based services. Like addicts, or chronically sick patients who are extremely suffering from the lack of some substance, respectively the medicine they are relying on, citizens will become sick, if the access to smart ICT services will be cut-off. They will soon forget how to survive in cities, once smart ICT technologies are not available any more. The concentration processes, which characterize the global market of smart technologies, are threatening".

Smart city projects are large and expensive investments that are supposed to drive societal and environmental transformations. However, for example, after more than a decade of investment, Songdo City (Korea)—widely referred to as the world's first smart city—is still a "work in progress" project without concrete sustainable outcomes (Yigitcanlar & Lee, 2014). In contrast, Shwayri (2013) pinpoints the negative environmental externalities caused by the development of Songdo smart city.

In spite of the heavy criticisms of smart city sceptics of this type of urban form and development practice, as presented above, there is a general sense among scholars that rethinking our cities' planning and development paradigms and processes in the age of digital disruption and climate change is a good thing (Angelidou, 2017). It is, thus, imperative to clearly understand what the smart city agenda can deliver for cities before our governments heavily invest in and jump on the smart city bandwagon. However, despite the increasing popularity of the paradigms of smart and sustainable cities, measuring sustainability levels of smart cities is an under-investigated research area. Moreover, there are no empirical studies, so far, scrutinising the GHG emissions of so-called smart cities—the literature mainly focuses on the sustainable city context rather than smart cities (Coutts et al., 2010; Velasco & Roth, 2010).

Against this backdrop, this study aims to capture the big picture view on whether smart city practices have been making considerable contributions to local sustainability agendas by improving sustainable urban development outcomes. Empirically investigating sustainability achievements of smart cities is important to provide evidence on whether this new and popular smart city policy contributes to the sustainability agendas and/or accomplishments of cities. As both smart cites and sustainable urban development concepts are highly complex in nature, for practical reasons, the chapter uses proxies for these concepts: (a) the smart cities concept is characterised as city smartness; and (b) the sustainable urban development concept is characterised as CO_2 emissions. In order to address the critical issue of whether smart city policy leads to the sustainability of cities, this chapter focuses on the following two research questions:

(a) Does city smartness bring sustainability to cities in terms of CO_2 emissions?
(b) Does the impact of city smartness on CO_2 emissions change over time?

Following this introduction in Section 2.1, Section 2.2 provides a review of the literature on smart city concepts, and their potential links with urban sustainability. Next, Section 2.3 outlines the data and methods applied to address the research questions. After that, the findings of the empirical analysis are presented in Section 2.4, and discussed in policy terms. Finally, Section 2.5 concludes this chapter by highlighting the key findings of the study.

2.2 Literature Background

The adoption of technology is a global phenomenon, and the intensity of its usage is impressive all over the world. Particularly, state-of-the-art smart urban information technologies play critical roles in supporting decision-making, design, planning, development, and management operations of complex urban environments (Yigitcanlar, 2015). Their role in dealing with complexity and uncertainty and in generating sustainable and liveable urban environments has been a popular subject for many scholars (Lee et al., 2014). This has brought, with a strong push from major global technology companies—such as IBM, Cisco, Schneider Electric, Siemens, Oracle—the smart city notion and practice to the forefront of the urban agenda in many cities of the world (Alizadeh, 2017).

As stated by Goh (2015, p. 169), "visions of a kind of technology-infused smart city are becoming reality, translated from the realm of concepts into actual urban space". Particularly, the development of smart urban systems through effective use of smart urban technologies is providing an invaluable foundation for smart cities to surface. Today, more and more governments are showing interest in smart urban system investment to make cities more efficient, sustainable, and inclusive. Consequently, it is estimated that the global market for smart urban systems for transport, energy, healthcare, water, and waste will be around US$400 billion per annum by 2020 (Yigitcanlar, 2016). That is to say, smart urban systems will fast become an integral part of our lives. In recent years, many researchers have explored the most common and advanced smart urban systems, and offered examples of their adoption in contemporary cities of the world (Klauser & Albrechtslund, 2014).

Over the past decade, smart urban technologies have started to form the backbone of a large and intelligent infrastructure network in cities. Along with this development, dissemination of the sustainability ideology has had a significant impact on the planning, development, and management of our cities (Dizdaroglu & Yigitcanlar, 2016). Accordingly, the concept of smart cities, evolved from intelligent cities (Komninos, 2008), has become a popular topic, particularly for scholars, urban planners, urban administrations, urban development and real estate companies, and corporate technology firms.

Despite its popularity, so far, there is no prevalent or universally acknowledged definition of smart cities. Instead, there are numerous perspectives on what constitutes a smart city. These range from purely ecological (Lim & Liu, 2010) to technological (Townsend, 2013), and from economic (Kourtit et al., 2012) to organisational (Hollands, 2015), and societal (Deakin & Al Waer, 2012) views. The ecological perspective of smart cities focuses on getting local governments, businesses, and communities to commit to reducing GHG emissions, reversing sprawling development, increasing urban density, increasing greenspaces, encouraging polycentric development, and so on (Lazaroiu & Roscia, 2012). The technological perspective focuses on adoption of smart urban technology solutions to improve the liveability of communities and sustainability of cities—these technologies also include infrastructural ICTs that serve as the backbone, such as the internet and world wide web (Paroutis et al., 2014). The economic perspective focuses on generating an innovation economy through smart technology solution development, thus increasing the GDP and self-containment of the city (Zygiaris, 2013). The organisational perspective focuses on establishing a transparent and democratic governance model (Meijer & Bolívar, 2016). The societal perspective focuses on establishing socioeconomic equality and public participation in smart city planning and initiatives (Lara et al., 2016).

As for Kitchin (2015), the smart city symbolises a new kind of technology-led urban utopia. Utopia or not, in all the abovementioned perspectives the vision of technology and innovation is a common ground to shape our cities into a form that we want to leave to our descendants. This is to say, without a commonly agreed definition, the smart cities concept is broadly viewed as a vision, manifesto, or provocation—encompassing techno-economic, techno-societal, techno-spatial, and techno-organisational dimensions—aiming to constitute a sustainable and ideal 21st century city form (Yigitcanlar, 2016). Nevertheless, presently, there are no fully fledged smart cities (Trindade et al., 2017).

As stated by Glasmeier and Christopherson (2015, p. 4), "over 26 global cities are expected to be smart cities in 2025, with more than 50% of these smart cities from Europe and North America". Smart cities are a global phenomenon today, as there are well over 250 smart city projects underway across 178 cities around the world. The potential success of these cities triggers many more cities to follow their footsteps—for instance, it was announced in 2015 that the Smart Cities Mission of India targets the development of 100 smart cities (Praharaj et al., 2018).

At the moment, with the building or retrofitting of many of these cities underway in a large number of places around the world, smart city examples abound in both the popular media and in academic discussions. Nevertheless, in a recent study, Alizadeh (2017) highlighted the limited empirical evidence—on whether these cities will be able to keep up to their promises in forming green and inclusive urban environments—as the major shortcoming of the smart cities agenda. She raises concerns on the unjustified popularity of the concept, as there is a "limited number of in-depth empirical case studies of smart city initiatives... lack of holistic studies that compare smart city developments in different locales... and limited collaborative engagement with various stakeholders in smart cities studies" (p. 71).

Despite many cities claiming to be smart cities or at least having declared themselves as smart, for some scholars, the current hype around smart cities tends to be mostly technocratic, and beyond speculation. There is no strong evidence to suggest that a smart city can provide genuine answers to a number of complex problems that cities face today (Anthopoulos, 2017). As underlined by Mora et al. (2017, p. 20), "the knowledge necessary to understand the process of building effective smart cities in the real-world has not yet been produced, nor the tools for supporting the actors involved in this activity".

This issue brings a crucial need for further empirical studies on smart city strategies and initiatives, and forms the rationale of this study. Popularity and relatively widespread application of smart city initiatives provide us with the ability to place these cities—even though they are not developed as fully functioning smart cities—under the microscope to evaluate their performance in achieving sustainable urban outcomes.

2.3 Methodology

2.3.1 Data

This research was conducted in the context of smart cities in the UK to answer research questions. The selection of the UK as the study context is justified as: (a) it was one of the early adopter nations of the smart cities concept and practice (Caragliu et al., 2011); (b) it has the second highest city numbers (7), after the USA (9), within the top-100 smart cities of the world (IESE, 2016); and (c) it has the highest number of projects (28/148) listed in the top smart city projects of the world (Nominet, 2016). This research utilised a number of secondary sources to gather and analyse data—to address the research questions mentioned earlier—as outlined below.

2.3.1.1 CO_2 Emissions Data

The CO_2 emissions data were obtained from the Centre for Cities website (www. centreforcities.org/data-tool/su/f5fb2e6f). The website reported per capita CO_2 emissions level (tons) of 65 UK cities from 2005 to 2014. The CO_2 emissions data were originally sourced from the UK Department of Energy and Climate Change. CO_2 emissions data were used as an outcome variable in this research and regressed by city smartness data to identify their cross-sectional and impacts over time.

2.3.1.2 City Smartness Data

Some studies try to understand city smartness by considering a set of variables inside the urban system (Fistola & La Rocca, 2014). The business vision of a smart city is strongly based on the pivotal role of technology, especially the ICT (Dameri & Rosenthal-Sabroux, 2014). IESE (2016) highlights that ICT is part of the backbone of any society that wants to be called "smart". As a result, this research used two indicators of city smartness representing the ICT penetration in cities: (a) the number of websites hosted per 1,000 population, and; (b) the number of internet protocol (IP) addresses per 1,000 population. The number of websites hosted by a city indicates the quality of online services provided by the city, showing support for ICT dissemination strategies. The IP address is a unique identifier assigned to each computer and other devices (e.g., mobile phone) connected to the internet. This is a commercial indicator of the adoption of the internet by the public in a city (IESE, 2016). These two datasets were obtained from the MYIP website (https://myip.ms/browse/cities/IP_Addresses_Cities.html). They represented snapshots of the indicators in a point in time (the year 2017). This research derived a quartile classification of the data for a consistent comparison among the cities over time, given that these are real-time data and susceptible to change over time, albeit slowly.

2.3.1.3 Urban Form Characteristics

Four variables representing the urban form characteristics were obtained from the OECD websites (https://data.oecd.org). These included: (a) population density of cities (person/km^2); (b) green area (m^2 per million person)—defined as the land in metropolitan areas covered by vegetation, croplands, forests, shrubs lands, and grasslands; (c) polycentricity—the number of city cores included in a metropolitan area; and (d) the urban sprawl index (SI)—measures the evolution of sprawl over time in a metropolitan area, based on Equation (2.1) (OECD, 2016).

$$SI_i = \frac{\left[urb_{i,t+n} - \left(urb_{i,t} * \left(\frac{pop_{i,t+n}}{pop_{i,t}} \right) \right) \right]}{urb_{i,t}} * 100 \tag{2.1}$$

where, i refers to a particular metropolitan area, t refers to the initial year, $t+n$ refers to the final year, urb refers to the built-up area in km^2, and pop refers to the total population.

The SI measures the growth of the built-up area adjusted for the growth in city population. When the city population changes, the index measures the increase in the built-up area relative to a benchmark where the built-up area would have increased in line with population growth. The SI index is equal to zero when both population and built-up area are stable over time. It is larger (lower) than zero when the growth of built-up area is greater (smaller) than the growth of population, i.e., the city density has decreased (increased).

Note that the SI data were available only for the period of 2006, whereas datasets for the remaining three variables were available from 2000 to 2013 during the preparation of this manuscript. However, an initial investigation shows that the level of polycentricity has not changed over this period, meaning that this variable is also static in nature. In addition, a cross-examination between the CO_2 emissions dataset and urban form dataset shows that only 15 metropolitan areas are common in both datasets. As a result, the analysis presented in this chapter is restricted to 15 UK cities—i.e., Birmingham, Bradford, Bristol, Cardiff, Edinburgh, Glasgow, Leeds, Leicester, Liverpool, London, Manchester, Newcastle, Nottingham, Portsmouth, and Sheffield—with panel data spanning from 2005 to 2013.

2.3.1.4 Socioeconomic Data

Many prior studies have found linear relationships between per capita CO_2 emissions and per capita GDP (Du et al., 2012; Yang et al., 2015). This chapter used per capita GDP (US$, constant prices in 2010) to represent the level of socio-economic development of the selected 15 metropolitan areas.

2.3.1.5 Descriptive Summary

Table 2.1 shows descriptive statistics of the data used in this research. Given the panel nature of the variables, the summary table presents three types of variations in data (overall, between the 15 cities, and within a city over the nine-year study period). The first variable is individual city ID (identification), which is not a real variable but shows the cross-sectional dimension of the data. It varies from 1 to 15—i.e., the total number of cities (observation) analysed. The next variable is the time dimension of the data (year) and varies from 2005 to 2013 (nine years of data). These two variables are used to classify the panel nature of the data.

The CO_2 emissions variable is the main outcome variable used in this research (Kamruzzaman et al., 2015). The mean value of the CO_2 emissions data is 6.36 tons, which means that on average each person emitted 6.36 tons of CO_2 in a year. The overall standard deviation of this variable is 0.79 tons with between and within variations, respectively, being 0.51 tons and 0.62 tons. This means that there is a greater variation in the emissions levels over the periods within a city than between cities.

The research used two key exposure variables: (a) number of websites hosted per 1,000 population by the cities; and (b) number of IP addresses per 1,000 population. These are classified as quartiles, and as a result, the overall variation is shown between 1 (lowest quartile) and 4 (highest quartile). Note that the within variations in these datasets are 0 (zero), which means that these variables are time-invariant—that is the classification of the cities does not change over time. This rule applies to the two urban form variables (polycentricity and SI) because they are time-invariant as well (measured only once). In contrast to the CO_2 emissions variables, GDP, green area, and population density variables have a larger variation between the cities than within a city over time.

Table 2.1 Summary statistics of the variables

Variable name	Description	Summary	Mean	Std. Dev.	Min.	Max.	Observations
ID	ID of the case study cities	Overall			1	15	N=135
		Between			1	15	n=15
		Within			8	8	T=9
Year	Observation year	Overall			2005	2013	N=135
		Between			2009	2009	n=15
		Within			2005	2013	T=9
CO_2	Per capita CO_2 emissions (tons)	Overall	6.36	0.79	4.79	8.4	N=135
		Between		0.51	5.42	7.03	n=15
		Within		0.62	5.26	7.79	T=9
Websites	Quartile classification of the number of website hosted per 1,000 population	Overall	2.6	1.09	1	4	N=135
		Between		1.12	1	4	n=15
		Within		0	2.6	2.6	T=9
IP address	Quartile classification of the number of IP addresses per 1,000 population	Overall	2.6	1.09	1	4	N=135
		Between		1.12	1	4	n=15
		Within		0	2.6	2.6	T=9
GDP	Per capita GDP (US$, 2010)	Overall	35,986.9	7328.8	24,949.1	54,537.86	N=135
		Between		7478.48	26,762.7	53,284.92	n=15
		Within		1059.75	33,825.3	38,616.93	T=9
Green	Green area (m^2 per million person)	Overall	163.28	76.57	35.61	329.70	N=135
		Between		78.83	37.42	315.67	n=15
		Within		4.36	149.18	177.32	T=9
Density	Population density (person/km^2)	Overall	2301.06	868.57	894.85	4011.50	N=135
		Between		893.14	923.47	3815.93	n=15
		Within		65.81	2118.69	2496.63	T=9

(Continued)

Table 2.1 (Continued)

Variable name	Description	Summary	Mean	Std. Dev.	Min.	Max.	Observations
Sprawl	Sprawl index (SI)	Overall	−2.82	2.04	−6.78	0.62	N=135
		Between		2.10	−6.78	0.62	n=15
		Within		0	−2.82	−2.82	T=9
Polycentricity	Number of functional centres	Overall	1.6	1.26	1	6	N=135
		Between		1.30	1	6	n=15
		Within		0	1.6	1.6	T=9

N, population size; n, sample size.

2.3.2 Methods

As for the statistical investigation, a panel, or time series, analysis is conducted to observe sustainability-related performance figures (e.g., CO_2 emission levels) from pre-introduction (year 2005) of the smart city policy to post-policy figures (year 2013) of the selected UK cities. The panel dataset consists of both cross-sectional and time series dimensions, which are required to analyse the differences between cities and changes within cities over time. The dependent variable (CO_2 emissions) as used in this research is continuous in nature and varies over time (time-varying variable). The independent variables consist of both categorical (website and IP address) and continuous data types (GDP, population density, green area, polycentricity, and SI). Some of the independent variables vary over time (time-varying: GDP, population density, and green area), whereas the remaining independent variables are time-invariant. These complexities, particularly with the nature of the main outcome variable (CO_2 emissions) and exposure variables (website and IP address), possess unique challenges in this research to estimate a panel data model in order to answer the research questions. This research overcomes the challenges by estimating three models, as outlined below.

2.3.2.1 Pooled Regression Model

A first step in the analysis of the data could be to pool the information from all $t = 1, \ldots, 9$ panel waves for all $i = 1, \ldots, 15$ cities and treat them as though they represented independent information for $n = 9 \times 15 = 135$ cities. An ordinary least square (OLS) regression model was estimated (Equation 2.2) using this pool dataset, assuming that the residual (ε_{it}) behaves like the OLS error term.

$$y_{it} = \beta_0 + \beta_1 x_{1it} + \ldots + \beta_k x_{kit} + \gamma_1 z_{1i} + \ldots + \gamma_j z_{ji} + \varepsilon_{it} \tag{2.2}$$

where, subscript i refers to the $i = 1, \ldots, 15$ cities, which have been observed at $t = 1, \ldots, 9$ equidistant points in time; y_{it} denotes the value of the dependent variable CO_2 emissions for city i at time point t; k and j represent time-variant $(\beta_1 x_{1it} \ldots \beta_k x_{kit})$ and time-invariant $(\gamma_1 z_{1i} \ldots \gamma_1 z_{ji})$ independent variables; and $\beta_1 \ldots \beta_k$ and $\gamma_1 \ldots \gamma_j$ denote the corresponding regression coefficients to be estimated.

Previous studies have derived a logarithmic transformation of the CO_2 emissions data prior to conducting regression analysis (Du et al., 2012; Yang et al., 2015). Our analysis shows that the outcome variable is approximately normally distributed and a natural log transformation did not improve the distribution (Figure 2.1). As a result, we have used the observed CO_2 emissions score in all analyses presented in this research.

OLS is applicable to cross-sectional data if certain assumptions are met, particularly with the assumption of no serial correlation in the outcome variable. With panel data, this is at stake. Three causes of serial correlation of the dependent variable are: (a) time-constant explanatory variables that cause Y to be persistently

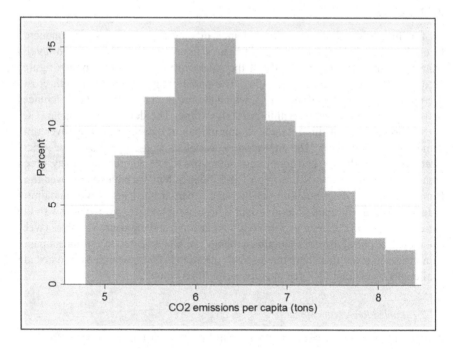

Figure 2.1 Distribution of CO_2 emissions.

above (or below) the average; (b) serially correlated time-varying explanatory variables; and (c) true state dependence of the dependent variable itself (Andreß, 2013). In relation to the first cause, the sustainability vision of a city, for instance, is a typical example of a theoretically important, but hard-to-measure explanatory factor. Different cities have different sustainability agendas, which cannot be measured and controlled in the model. If they are constant over time, this unobserved heterogeneity causes some cities to have disproportionately higher (or lower) CO_2 emissions in all years than could be expected from the independent variables in the model. Pooled OLS is only unbiased if we are ready to assume that this unobserved heterogeneity (e.g., differences with respect to sustainability vision) is independent of the explanatory variables in the model. In addition, if there is unobserved unit-specific heterogeneity that is constant over time, and even when it is uncorrelated with the variables in the model, error terms at different time points could be correlated with one another. Taking the panel structure of the dataset into account is a possible way forward to address these problems.

2.3.2.2 Two-Way Fixed Effect Panel Data Model

Apparently, pooled OLS makes unrealistic assumptions about panel data. However, the model is easily extended to account for unobserved heterogeneity at the unit level. The stochastic part of the model (ε_{it}), as presented in Equation 2.2, can be distinguished between two components ($\varepsilon_{it} = \mu_i + e_{it}$): (a) μ_i: unobserved predictors of Y that are specific to the unit and therefore time-constant; and (b) e_{it}: unobserved predictors of Y that are specific to the time point and the unit (including measurement errors). Again, depending on our assumptions about these two error terms, different estimation procedures are available. A simple starting point is the assumption that the time-varying error, e_{it}, has the same properties as the error term in OLS estimation. In other words, e_{it} is assumed to be purely random "white noise"—idiosyncratic error. Yet, the main discussion revolves around the unit-specific error, μ_i. The fixed effect (FE) model assumes that something within the city may impact or bias the predictor or outcome variables and we need to control for this. This is the rationale behind the assumption of the correlation between unit-specific error, μ_i and predictor variables. FE removes the effect of those time-invariant characteristics so we can assess the net effect of the predictors on the outcome variable. Another important assumption of the FE model is that those time-invariant characteristics are unique to the cities and should not be correlated with other city characteristics. Each city is different, and therefore, the city's error term and the constant, which capture the city's characteristics, should not be correlated with the others.

In order to account for individual fixed effects and time period fixed effects simultaneously, we constructed a two-way fixed effect model based on a generic panel data model. Additionally, FE regression—by definition—is not the technique to estimate the effects of time-constant explanatory variables Z. It should be stressed, however, that FE regression controls for all (observed and unobserved) time-constant determinants of Y, even if it does not provide numerical estimates of their effects. However, this goes against our research question to be answered: how time-constant city smartness factors influence CO_2 emissions over time. In order to overcome this limitation, we have extended the analysis by including interactions with time. Since the "year" variable has nine categories, there are eight interactions with each predictor. Note that the other time-invariant predictors (e.g., polycentricity) do not have main effects included in the model. If we had tried to include them, the software would have dropped them from the model because they have no variation within cities (unless they are also interacted with time). Our estimation function is (α_i is the city specific effect that captures all observed and unobserved heterogeneity of cities) in Equation 2.3:

$$y_{it} = \beta_0 + \beta_t.t + \beta_1 IP_i.t + \beta_2 Web_i.t + \beta_3 GDP_{it} + \beta_4 Green_{it} + \beta_5 Density_{it} + \alpha_i + \varepsilon_{it} \qquad (2.3)$$

2.3.2.3 Random Effect Panel Data Model

The fixed-effects model controls for all time-invariant differences between the cities, so the estimated coefficients of the fixed effects models cannot be biased because of omitted time-invariant characteristics such as city vision and culture. One side effect of the FE models is that they cannot be used to investigate time-invariant causes of the dependent variables. Technically, time-invariant characteristics of the cities are perfectly collinear with the city dummies, α_i. Substantively, fixed-effects models are designed to study the causes of changes within a city. A time-invariant characteristic cannot cause such a change, because it is constant for each city.

The rationale behind the random effects (RE) model is that, unlike the fixed effects model, the variation across cities is assumed to be random and uncorrelated with the predictor or independent variables included in the model. Researchers have suggested that if there is a reason to believe that differences across entities have some influence on the dependent variable, then one should use random effects (Baltagi, 2008). An advantage of random effects is that time-invariant variables (i.e., polycentricity) can be included in the model. In the fixed effects model these variables are absorbed by the intercept.

The RE model is based on the same equation that we used for the fixed effect model but including the time-constant independent variables. The crucial difference between FE and RE is that now, instead of treating α_i as a set of fixed numbers, we assume that α_i is a set of random variables with a specified probability distribution. For example, it is typical to assume that each α_i is normally distributed with a mean of 0, constant variance, and is independent of all the other variables on the right-hand side of the equation. The most apparent difference between the fixed and the random effects models is that the random effects method can include time-invariant predictors.

2.3.2.4 Choosing between RE and FE Models

In this research, we performed the Hausman test to select the appropriate model between FE and RE models, and the result indicated that the fixed effects model was better than the random effects model (chi-square = 19.56, p-value = 0.0337). However, given the requirements to answer the research questions, it is imperative to analyse the effect of time-constant variables Z on the dependent variable Y, and as a result, we have decided to present results from all three models in this research. All tests were run in Stata 13.1.

2.3.2.5 Testing for Time-Fixed Effects

We conducted an additional test (*testparm* command in Stata) to see if time fixed effects are needed when running the two-way FE model. This is a joint test to see if the dummies for all years are equal to 0. If they are 0, then no time fixed effects are needed. A statistically significant test result was found (F = 8.56, p-value = 0.000) suggesting that an inclusion of the time dummies was better than their omission from the model.

2.4 Results and Discussion

2.4.1 City Smartness and CO_2 Emissions: Descriptive Findings

The findings of the analysis (Table 2.2) suggest that: (a) some cities consistently maintained their ranking in both indicators (i.e., Bristol, Cardiff, Leeds, Liverpool,

Table 2.2 Classification of case study cities according to their smartness status

Case study cities	Quartile classification of city smartness based on:		IESW rank[a]	Huawei rank[b]
	IP address	Websites hosted		
Birmingham	2nd	3rd	118	3
Bradford	2nd	1st	–	
Bristol	4th	4th	–	2
Cardiff	1st	1st	–	
Edinburgh	4th	3rd	–	
Glasgow	4th	2nd	49	4
Leeds	2nd	2nd	156	7
Leicester	3rd	1st	–	
Liverpool	4th	4th	93	
London	2nd	4th	3	1
Manchester	3rd	4th	145	5
Newcastle	1st	3rd	–	
Nottingham	3rd	3rd	178	9
Portsmouth	1st	2nd	–	
Sheffield	3rd	2nd	–	10

[a] Ranking among the world cities based on technology dimension, lower rank corresponds to higher smartness.
[b] Ranking among the UK cities, lower rank corresponds to higher smartness.

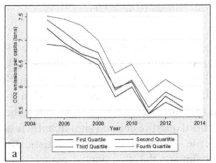 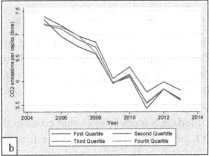

Figure 2.2 Per capita CO_2 emissions by city smartness quartiles (a) IP addresses; (b) Websites hosted

Nottingham); (b) the ranking has changed for the remaining cities justifying the need to investigate for both city smartness indicators; and (c) the use of these indicators has also been justified because external city smartness or smart city rankings seem to correspond with our ranking. For example, Bristol has been ranked second among the UK cities based on the Huawei rank. Our ranking has also consistently identified Bristol in the upper quartile.

Figure 2.2a shows the average per capita CO_2 emissions from 2005 to 2013 according to the IP address classification. From Figure 2.2a, we find that per capita

CO_2 emissions gradually declined from 2005 irrespective of the classification. The average per capita CO_2 emissions of the cities that fall within the upper quartiles of the smartness classification (according to the IP addresses) are remarkably higher than other classes throughout the period. An opposite trend is evident for the cities belonging to the second quartile. Cities in the first and third quartiles remained between these extremes over the period, with cities in the third quartile emitting slightly more than the first quartile.

A different trend in the level of CO_2 emissions was observed, when the cities are classified according to the hosted websites (Figure 2.2b). In the light of the analysis the key findings include: (a) an overall declining trend—time has an impact on the level of CO_2 emissions, perhaps cities are becoming more aware of sustainability issues and adopting policies and awareness among the city population; and (b) no clear pattern of the effect of city smartness on CO_2 emission levels—this needs to be further assessed through regression analysis.

2.4.2 Estimation Results

For each indicator, we present the results for the pooled OLS and panel models (FE and RE) in Table 2.3. The FE model includes interactions with the key exposure variables (IP addresses and websites hosted) as discussed earlier. We grouped the variables according to broader themes in Table 2.3 as urban form, socioeconomic, smartness factors, time, and interaction terms. All models were found to be statistically significant with very good explanatory powers (in terms of R^2).

2.4.2.1 City Smartness and CO_2 Emissions

The pooled OLS model shows that all else being equal, cities with more IP addresses (quartiles 3 and 4) are likely to emit a reduced level of CO_2 (Table 2.3). Findings from the RE model, however, show that only cities in the third quartile have a statistically significant association. These cities emitted a significantly lower amount of CO_2 per capita. In relation to the hosting of websites, the pooled OLS model shows that cities in the third quartile emitted significantly less CO_2 per capita than cities in the first quartile. However, this is not statistically significant in the RE model although it maintains the direction of association. Unexpectedly, the pooled OLS model shows that cities in the fourth quartile emitted a significantly higher level of CO_2 per capita which remained significant in the RE model. The interaction terms in the FE model were not found to be statistically significant, suggesting that the gaps in the CO_2 emissions levels have not been widened (or reduced) significantly between the smartness levels of the cities. That means the cities have been consistent in terms of their efforts of achieving sustainability irrespective of their smartness status. Overall, the findings show that there is a statistically significant relationship between city smartness and CO_2 emissions. However, the relationship is not linear, but tended to be U-shaped (Figure 2.3). Overall, there is not a temporal effect of the city smartness on CO_2 emissions.

Table 2.3 Estimation results

Variables	Pooled OLS model			Fixed effect model			Random effect model		
	Coefficient	t	P>|t|	Coefficient	t	P>|t|	Coefficient	z	P>|z|
Urban form characteristics									
Population density	0.0004	2.63	0.010	-0.0020	-3.04	0.003	-0.0002	-0.88	0.381
Green area	0.0136	5.86	0.000	0.0123	0.85	0.399	0.0101	2.82	0.005
Polycentricity	-0.1403	-1.68	0.095				0.0784	0.55	0.582
Sprawl index	0.3158	5.30	0.000				0.0845	0.88	0.378
Socioeconomic factor									
GDP	0.0001	4.31	0.000	0.0001	0.64	0.522	0.0001	-0.01	0.992
City smartness factor									
Websites (ref: first Q)									
Second	-0.0226	-0.10	0.924	Omitted			0.3849	0.92	0.359
Third	-0.3488	-1.81	0.073	Omitted			-0.1197	-0.32	0.746
Fourth	0.9961	2.91	0.004	Omitted			1.2451	2.12	0.034
IP addresses (ref: first Q)									
Second	0.3458	1.63	0.106	Omitted			-0.1608	-0.41	0.683
Third	-0.9345	-2.77	0.006	Omitted			-1.2095	-2.08	0.038
Fourth	-0.8177	-3.24	0.002	Omitted			0.0828	0.20	0.844
Year (ref: 2005)									
2006				-0.3955	-2.57	0.013	-0.1459	-2.76	0.006
2007				-0.5538	-3.37	0.001	-0.3450	-6.02	0.000
2008				-0.6085	-3.68	0.000	-0.5308	-9.58	0.000
2009				-1.0410	-5.98	0.000	-1.2225	-21.92	0.000
2010				-0.8702	-4.65	0.000	-1.0119	-17.28	0.000
2011				-1.5443	-7.65	0.000	-1.5951	-25.85	0.000
2012				-0.9918	-4.52	0.000	-1.2788	-19.47	0.000
2013				-1.1558	-4.86	0.000	-1.4664	-20.91	0.000

(Continued)

Table 2.3 (Continued)

Variables	Pooled OLS model			Fixed effect model			Random effect model		
	Coefficient	t	P>|t|	Coefficient	t	P>|t|	Coefficient	z	P>|z|
IP address–Year interaction									
Second Quartile#2006				0.2492	1.57	0.121			
Second Quartile#2007				0.2785	1.76	0.084			
Second Quartile#2008				0.2458	1.54	0.128			
Second Quartile#2009				0.1635	1.02	0.311			
Second Quartile#2010				0.2697	1.64	0.106			
Second Quartile#2011				0.3762	2.30	0.025			
Second Quartile#2012				0.2543	1.54	0.129			
Second Quartile#2013				0.3236	1.93	0.058			
Third Quartile#2006				0.0267	0.17	0.868			
Third Quartile#2007				-0.0102	-0.06	0.951			
Third Quartile#2008				0.0115	0.07	0.948			
Third Quartile#2009				-0.1983	-1.07	0.287			
Third Quartile#2010				-0.0998	-0.50	0.620			
Third Quartile#2011				0.0162	0.07	0.941			
Third Quartile#2012				-0.0248	-0.11	0.917			
Third Quartile#2013				0.0445	0.17	0.863			
Fourth Quartile#2006				0.1482	0.87	0.390			
Fourth Quartile#2007				0.2699	1.57	0.122			
Fourth Quartile#2008				0.1466	0.84	0.402			
Fourth Quartile#2009				0.0232	0.13	0.898			
Fourth Quartile#2010				0.1170	0.65	0.520			
Fourth Quartile#2011				0.2029	1.10	0.275			
Fourth Quartile#2012				0.1256	0.66	0.509			
Fourth Quartile#2013				0.1547	0.79	0.432			

Website–Year interaction	Coef (1)	z (1)	Coef (2)	z (2)	p (2)	Coef (3)	z (3)
Second Quartile#2006			0.1183	0.74	0.461		
Second Quartile#2007			0.0486	0.30	0.766		
Second Quartile#2008			0.0424	0.25	0.801		
Second Quartile#2009			-0.1277	-0.74	0.463		
Second Quartile#2010			-0.0841	-0.46	0.645		
Second Quartile#2011			0.0189	0.10	0.921		
Second Quartile#2012			-0.2098	-1.06	0.294		
Second Quartile#2013			-0.2185	-1.05	0.298		
Third Quartile#2006			0.2348	1.48	0.144		
Third Quartile#2007			0.1790	1.11	0.271		
Third Quartile#2008			0.1730	1.07	0.289		
Third Quartile#2009			0.0254	0.15	0.878		
Third Quartile#2010			0.0224	0.14	0.893		
Third Quartile#2011			0.0654	0.39	0.699		
Third Quartile#2012			-0.0747	-0.43	0.665		
Third Quartile#2013			-0.1093	-0.62	0.536		
Fourth Quartile#2006			0.2476	1.43	0.157		
Fourth Quartile#2007			0.2062	1.16	0.252		
Fourth Quartile#2008			0.0535	0.29	0.776		
Fourth Quartile#2009			0.0482	0.24	0.811		
Fourth Quartile#2010			0.0357	0.16	0.870		
Fourth Quartile#2011			0.0946	0.41	0.685		
Fourth Quartile#2012			0.0089	0.04	0.972		
Fourth Quartile#2013			-0.0223	-0.08	0.935		
Constant	2.295969	3.69	8.9833	2.71	0.009	6.0534	7.170
N	135		135			135	0
F/Chi^2	8.56**	0.000	42.08	0.000		2561.86	0.000
R^2 (Overall)	0.4336		0.09			0.81	
R^2 (Between)			0.03			0.56	
R^2 (Within)			0.98			0.96	

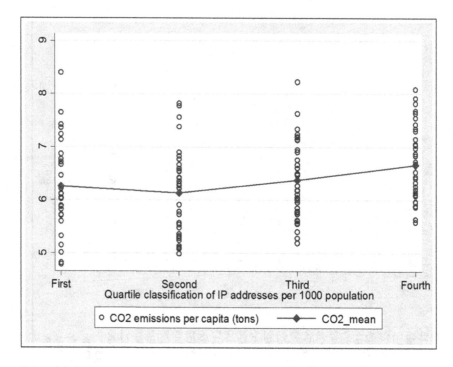

Figure 2.3 Heterogeneity in CO_2 emissions according to IP address classification.

2.4.2.2 Urban Form and CO_2 Emissions

The pooled OLS model shows that urban population density had a positive effect on per capita CO_2 emissions from cities. However, an opposite association was found in the FE and RE models, which shows that the relationship is negative—i.e., increasing population density reduces CO_2 emissions. Clearly, the findings from the pooled OLS model are contrary to most studies in Western countries (Jones & Kammen, 2014). Therefore, the findings from the FE and RE models are more consistent with the previous literature on this topic and justify the application of the panel data analytical technique for an unbiased result.

Surprisingly, a positive association between the amount of green area in a city and CO_2 emissions goes against the common wisdom on this topic. Existing knowledge suggests that green area reduces CO_2 emissions (Nowak & Craine, 2002). However, evidence started appearing that green areas emit as much CO_2 as can be found in dense urban areas (https://wattsupwiththat.com/2016/02/23/study-urban-backyards-contribute-almost-as-much-co2-as-much-as-cars-and-buildings).   The relationship is significant in the pooled OLS model and RE model but not statistically significant in the FE model. It is possible that this variable is correlated with other unobserved variables in the OLS and RE models. The FE model takes into account this unobserved relationship, and as a result, the effect became statistically insignificant. However, we believe that this is an issue that requires much broader discussion and analysis.

Two time-constant urban form variables (SI and polycentricity) were found to be statistically significant in the OLS model, but not in the RE model. As expected, the pooled OLS model shows that increasing sprawl increases CO_2 emission levels, whereas polycentricity reduces CO_2 emission levels.

2.4.2.3 Socioeconomic Effects

From the estimation results presented in Table 2.3, per capita GDP had a positive effect on per capita CO_2 emissions in all three models. However, the association is only statistically significant in the pooled OLS model.

2.4.2.4 Time Effects

In terms of the effect of time, the annual impact on per capita CO_2 emissions was negative and was highly significant for most years. More importantly, the negative effect increased annually. This means that per capita CO_2 emissions were reducing over the period and at an increasing rate after controlling for socioeconomic, urban form, and city smartness factors. This suggests that the time period captures factors that were not included in the model—it could be the policy measures that the UK government has undertaken to meet the international obligations such as the Quito Protocol.

2.5 Conclusion

In recent years, the smart cities concept has become a hot topic and a priority policy agenda for many cities in both developed and developing country contexts (Yigitcanlar, 2017). Smart city technologies are seen as being crucial for the survival of our species (Townsend, 2013). Today, many of the global cities' administrations view smart urban technology applications and systems as potential vehicles to deal with their current and future developmental challenges whether these are economic, societal, or environmental in nature. Consequently, smart cities have become a global phenomenon with over 250 smart city projects underway across 178 cities around the world.

In many instances, however, the fashionable term smart city is used for branding or marketing purposes with the lack of an integrated approach covering sustainability concerns (Söderström et al., 2014; Shelton et al., 2015; Vanolo, 2015). In other words, the fashionable term "smart" has started to replace "sustainable" in the brand of many projects—for example, China's Tianjin Eco-City is now also branded as Tianjin Smart City.

According to Ahvenniemi et al. (2017, p. 242), "the role of technologies in smart cities should be in enabling sustainable development of cities, not in the new technology as an end in itself. Ultimately, a city that is not sustainable is not really smart". There is little empirical evidence that, despite its promise, smart cities contribute to the sustainability agenda of those cities. In order to address this issue of whether a smart city really leads to sustainable outcomes, the study at hand has put cities with smart city agendas from the UK under the sustainability performance assessment microscope. Onto the best of the author's knowledge, this is the first study that has attempted to assess a causal relationship between city smartness and sustainability—by using nine waves of panel data.

The findings revealed in this study suggest that, in the investigated cities from the UK context, there is not strong evidence on: (a) a positive correlation between technology adoption and sustainable outcomes; or (b) the impact of city smartness on a change in CO_2 emissions over time. In other words, despite their promise, so far, smart city practices in UK cities have failed to make a considerable contribution to the sustainability agenda beyond the rhetoric. This finding calls for further investigation and better aligning smart city strategies to lead to concrete sustainable outcomes. In this instance, we would like to highlight the importance of prospective investigations to accurately scrutinise existing smart city projects' outcomes, and emphasising the necessity of developing smart city agendas that deliver sustainability-oriented outcomes. This would also help in maturing the smart city paradigm—as a city planning and development model and emerging urban reality—that is already in continuous transformation.

As underlined by Conroy and Berke (2004), strategically planning our cities, by adopting sustainable urban development principles, is critical to achieving sustainable outcomes—particularly by promoting planning for sustainable urban development at the local level. This in turn helps in generating ecological sustainability that is a critical element of smart cities. In order to achieve comprehensive sustainable urban future outcomes, we also need to focus on the strategic implementation of smart urban technologies rather than the smart cities concept (Taamallah et al., 2017). Moreover, Komninos (2016) highlights that in smart cities there is a need for strategy and leadership, strategic policies, and plans that will integrate bottom-up initiatives at the company or organisation level with planned projects by various stakeholders under a coherent vision for the future of the ecosystems that make up each city. The critical question here is not about implementing on-the-shelf smart city solutions, but learning to innovate with smart environments, capabilities distributed among organisations, people, and machines, and collaborative business models. This approach will better support the success of the smart cities movement, and also creating desired sustainable urban futures. That is to say, concepts of smart and sustainable—that are currently not well aligned—need to be brought together through locally designed solutions and strategic planning practices (including strategic implementation of adequate smart urban technologies) for a truly smart and sustainable urban development—hence subsequently leading to the formation of smart and sustainable cities.

In conclusion, this chapter has generated new insights and empirical evidence on whether smart city policy leads to sustainability of cities—in the case of UK cities—particularly focusing on city smartness and sustainability aspects. However, sustainable urban development is beyond technology and ecology aspects alone; a quadruple bottom line approach is critical—economic, societal, environmental, and governance (Yigitcanlar & Teriman, 2015). On this very point, Yigitcanlar (2016) suggests that for a successful: (a) *Economic development in smart cities*: we need to give our cities the capability of developing technologies unique to their own developmental problems and needs. This, in turn, contributes to the establishment of a local innovation economy and prosperity that is a central element of smart cities; (b) *Sociocultural development in smart cities*: we need to develop our cities wired with smart urban technologies not only exclusive to urban elites, but also inclusive to those unfortunate. This, in turn, helps in establishing socioeconomic equality that is an essential element of smart cities; (c) *Spatial development in smart cities*: we need to reform our cities by adopting sustainable urban development principles—e.g., minimising the urban footprint, limiting GHG emissions, establishing urban farms, and using renewable energy sources. This, in turn, helps in generating ecological sustainability that is a critical element of smart cities; and (d) *Institutional development in smart cities*: we need to equip our cities with highly dynamic mechanisms to better plan their growth and manage their day-to-day operational challenges. This, in turn, helps in performing appropriate strategic planning, development, and management practices for a coherent vision for the future of urban ecosystems of our smart cities (Yigitcanlar & Kamruzzaman, 2018).

Acknowledgements

This chapter, with permission from the copyright holder, is a reproduced version of the following journal article: Yigitcanlar, T., Kamruzzaman, M. (2018). Does smart city policy lead to sustainability of cities? *Land Use Policy, 73*, 49–58.

References

Ahvenniemi, H., Huovila, A., Pinto-Seppä, I., Airaksinen, M. (2017). What are the differences between sustainable and smart cities? *Cities, 60*(1), 234–245.

Alizadeh, T. (2017). An investigation of IBM's smarter cites challenge. *Cities, 63*(1), 70–80.

Andreß, H.J. (2013). *Applied Panel Data Analysis for Economic and Social Surveys.* Berlin: Springer.

Angelidou, M. (2017). The role of smart city characteristics in the plans of fifteen cities. *Journal of Urban Technology, 24*(4), 3–28.

Anthopoulos, L. (2017). Smart utopia vs smart reality. *Cities, 63*, 128–148.

Arbolino, R., Carlucci, F., Cira, A., Ioppolo, G., Yigitcanlar, T. (2017). Efficiency of the EU regulation on greenhouse gas emissions in Italy. *Ecological Indicators, 81*(1), 115–123.

Baltagi, B.H. (2008). *Econometric Analysis of Panel Data.* Chichester: John Wiley & Sons.

Caragliu, A., Del Bo, C., Nijkamp, P. (2011). Smart cities in Europe. *Journal of Urban Technology, 18*(2), 65–82.

Carrillo, J., Yigitcanlar, T., Garcia, B., Lonnqvist, A. (2014). *Knowledge and the City.* New York: Routledge.

Conroy, M.M., Berke, P.R. (2004). What makes a good sustainable development plan? *Environment & Planning A, 36*(8), 1381–1396.

Coutts, A., Beringer, J., Tapper, N. (2010). Changing urban climate and CO_2 emissions. *Urban Policy & Research, 28*(1), 27–47.

Crutzen, P.J., Steffen, W. (2003). How long have we been in the Anthropocene era? *Climatic Change, 61*(3), 251–257.

Dameri, R.P., Rosenthal-Sabroux, C. (2014). Smart city and value creation. In: Dameri, R.P., Rosenthal-Sabroux, C. (Eds.), *Smart city*. Berlin: Springer.

Deakin, M., Al Waer, H. (2012). *From Intelligent to Smart Cities.* New York: Routledge.

Deilami, K., Kamruzzaman, M., Yigitcanlar, T., (2018). Investigating the urban heat island effect of transit oriented development in Brisbane. *Journal of Transport Geography, 66*(1), 116–124

Dizdaroglu, D., Yigitcanlar, T. (2014). A parcel-scale assessment tool to measure sustainability through urban ecosystem components. *Ecological Indicators, 41*(1), 115–130

Dizdaroglu, D., Yigitcanlar, T. (2016). Integrating urban ecosystem sustainability assessment into policy-making. *Journal of Environmental Planning & Management, 59*(11), 1982–2006.

Dizdaroglu, D., Yigitcanlar, T., Dawes, L. (2012). A micro-level indexing model for assessing urban ecosystem sustainability. *Smart & Sustainable Built Environment, 1*(3), 291–315.

Du, L., Wei, C., Cai, S. (2012). Economic development and carbon dioxide emissions in China. *China Economic Review, 23*(1), 371–384.

Dur, F., Yigitcanlar, T. (2015). Assessing land-use and transport integration via a spatial composite indexing model. *International Journal of Environmental Science & Technology, 12*(3), 803–816.

Fistola, R., La Rocca, R.A. (2014). The sustainable city and the smart city. *WIT Transactions on Ecology & the Environment, 191*(1), 537–548.

Glasmeier, A., Christopherson, S. (2015). Thinking about smart cities. *Cambridge Journal of Regions, Economy & Society, 8*(1), 3–12.

Goh, K. (2015). Who's smart? Whose city? The sociopolitics of urban intelligence. In: Geertman, S., Ferreira, J. Goodspeed, R., Stillwell, J. (Eds.), *Planning Support Systems and Smart Cities.* Berlin: Springer, pp. 169–187.

Goonetilleke, A., Yigitcanlar, T., Ayoko, G.A., Egodawatta, P. (2014). *Sustainable Urban Water Environment.* London: Edward Elgar.

Hardoy, J.E., Mitlin, D., Satterthwaite, D. (2013). *Environmental Problems in an Urbanizing World.* New York: Routledge.

Hollands, R.G. (2015). Critical interventions into the corporate smart city. *Cambridge Journal of Regions, Economy & Society, 8*(1), 61–77.

IESE (Institute of Higher Business Studies) (2016). *IESE Cities in Motion Index.* Navarra: University of Navarra.

Jones, C., Kammen, D.M. (2014). Spatial distribution of US household carbon footprints reveals suburbanization undermines greenhouse gas benefits of urban population density. *Environmental Science & Technology, 48*(2), 895–902.

Kamruzzaman, M., Hine, J., Yigitcanlar, T., (2015). Investigating the link between carbon dioxide emissions and transport related social exclusion in rural Northern Ireland. *International Journal of Environmental Science & Technology, 12*(11), 3463–3478.

Kitchin, R. (2015). Making sense of smart cities. *Cambridge Journal of the Regions, Economy & Society, 8*(1), 131–136.

Klauser, F.R., Albrechtslund, A. (2014). From self-tracking to smart urban infrastructures, *Surveillance and Society, 12*(2), 273–286.

Komninos, N. (2008). *Intelligent Cities and Globalisation of Innovation Networks.* New York: Routledge.

Komninos, N. (2016). Smart environments and smart growth. *International Journal of Knowledge-Based Development, 7*(3), 240–263.

Kourtit, K., Nijkamp, P., Arribas, D. (2012). Smart cities in perspective. *Innovation, 25*(2), 229–246.

Kunzmann, K.R. (2014). Smart cities. *Crios, 4*(1), 9–20.

Lara, A., Costa, E., Furlani, T., Yigitcanlar, T., (2016). Smartness that matters. *Journal of Open Innovation, 2*(8), 1–13.

Lazaroiu, G.C., Roscia, M. (2012). Definition methodology for the smart cities model. *Energy, 47*(1), 326–332.

Lee, J.H., Hancock, M.G., Hu, M.C. (2014). Towards an effective framework for building smart cities, *Technological Forecasting & Social Change, 89*(1), 80–99.

Lee, S.H., Yigitcanlar, T., Han, J.H., Leem, Y.T. (2008). Ubiquitous urban infrastructure. *Innovation, 10*(2–3), 282–292.

Lim, C.J., Liu, E. (2010). *Smart-cities and Eco-warriors.* New York: Routledge.

Mahbub, P., Goonetilleke, A., Ayoko, G.A., Egodawatta, P., Yigitcanlar, T. (2011). Analysis of build-up of heavy metals and volatile organics on urban roads in Gold Coast, Australia. *Water Science & Technology, 63*(9), 2077–2085.

Meijer, A., Bolívar, M.P.R. (2016). Governing the smart city. *International Review of Administrative Sciences, 82*(2), 392–408.

Mora, L., Bolici, R., Deakin, M. (2017). The first two decades of smart-city research. *Journal of Urban Technology, 24*(1), 3–27.

Nominet (2016). *Smart city projects showcase.* Accessed on 17 April 2017 from https://nominet-prod.s3.amazonaws.com/wp-content/uploads/2016/09/nominet_smartcities_analysis.pdf

Nowak, D.J., Crane, D.E. (2002). Carbon storage and sequestration by urban trees in the USA. *Environmental Pollution, 116*(3), 381–389.

OECD (2016). *The OECD Metropolitan Areas.* Paris: OECD.

Paroutis, S., Bennett, M., Heracleous, L. (2014). A strategic view on smart city technolog. *Technological Forecasting & Social Change, 89*, 262–272.

Perveen, S., Yigitcanlar, T., Kamruzzaman, M., Hayes, J. (2017). Evaluating transport externalities of urban growth. *International Journal of Environmental Science & Technology, 14*(3), 663–678.

Praharaj, S., Han, J.H., Hawken, S. (2018). Urban innovation through policy integration. *City, Culture & Society, 12*, 35–43.

Shelton, T., Zook, M., Wiig, A. (2015). The actually existing smart city. *Cambridge Journal of the Regions, Economy & Society, 8*(1), 13–25.

Shwayri, S.T. (2013). A model Korean ubiquitous eco-city? *Journal of Urban Technology, 20*(1), 39–55.

Söderström, O., Paasche, T., Klauser, F. (2014). Smart cities as corporate storytelling. *City, 18*(3), 307–320.

Taamallah, A., Khemaja, M., Faiz, S. (2017). Strategy ontology construction and learning. *International Journal of Knowledge-Based Development, 8*(3), 206–228.

Townsend, A.M. (2013). *Smart Cities.* New York: WW Norton & Co.

Trindade, E., Hinnig, M., Costa, E., Sabatini-Marques, J., Bastos, R., Yigitcanlar, T. (2017). Sustainable development of smart cities. *Journal of Open Innovation, 3*, 11.

Velasco, E., Roth, M. (2010). Cities as net sources of CO_2. *Geography Compass, 4*(9), 1238–1259.

Vanolo, A. (2014). Smartmentality. *Urban Studies, 51*(5), 883–898.

Vanolo, A. (2015). The image of the creative city, eight years later. *Cities, 46*(1), 1–7.

Yang, W., Li, T., Cao, X. (2015). Examining the impacts of socio-economic factors, urban form and transportation development on CO_2 emissions from transportation in China. *Habitat International, 49*(1), 212–220.

Yigitcanlar, T. (2015). Smart cities. *Australian Planning, 52*(1), 27–34.

Yigitcanlar, T. (2016). *Technology and the City.* New York: Routledge.

Yigitcanlar, T. (2017). Smart cities in the making. *International Journal of Knowledge-Based Development, 8*(3), 201–205.

Yigitcanlar, T., Dizdaroglu, D. (2015). Ecological approaches in planning for sustainable cities. *Global Journal of Environmental Science & Management, 1,* 159–188.

Yigitcanlar, T., Kamruzzaman, M. (2014). Investigating the interplay between transport, land use and the environment. *International Journal of Environmental Science & Technology, 11*(8), 2121–2132.

Yigitcanlar, T., Lee, S. (2014). Korean ubiquitous-eco-city. *Technological Forecasting & Social Change, 89*(1), 100–114.

Yigitcanlar, T., Teriman, S. (2015). Rethinking sustainable urban development. *International Journal of Environmental Science & Technology, 12*(1), 341–352.

Yigitcanlar, T., & Kamruzzaman, M. (2018). Does smart city policy lead to sustainability of cities? *Land Use Policy, 73,* 49–58.

Zhao, J. (2011). *Towards Sustainable Cities in China.* Berlin: Springer.

Zygiaris, S. (2013). Smart city reference model. *Journal of the Knowledge Economy, 4*(2), 217–231.

3 Policy Acceptance

3.1 Introduction

Since the early 2000s, smart city development has been gaining global momentum. Thus, many models or concepts have been formed, adopted, and evaluated [1]. For example, the seminal smart city concept by [2] laid the basis for the formation of six smart city domains (i.e., smart economy, people, governance, mobility, environment, and living) and emphasised activities that would cultivate independent citizens. Since then, many models have been adopted and adapted from the concept of [2], such as the smart cities wheel by [3], the initiative framework of the smart city by [4], the alternative framework for smart city governance by [5], the conceptual framework for defining the smart city by [6], and the Unified Smart City Model by [7]. On the other hand, top-down smart policies that have been adopted and adapted from the work of [2] include the Hong Kong Smart City Blueprint [8] and the Malaysian Smart City Framework (MSCF) [9].

Furthermore, many studies have evaluated smart city performance. For instance, [2] developed the European medium-sized (smart) city indicators and ranking; [10] used the analytic network process (ANP) to investigate the relations between smart city domains, actors (i.e., government, industry, university, and civil society), and strategies; [11] examined the Malaysian smart city domains through the AHP; [12] developed a smart city descriptor scoring table to qualitatively compare smart city domain performances in Singapore, Korea, and Malaysia; [13] developed a smart city sharable framework to evaluate 17 smart cities in China; [14] developed a fuzzy synthetic evaluation of the challenges facing smart city development in developing countries; [15] developed a typology of smart city assessment tools and evaluated 122 cities; [16] developed the smart city index and ranking; and [17] recently developed a smart city measurement framework for inclusive growth.

Nevertheless, far less research has been conducted on evaluating smart city policy, with the exception of scholars such as [18], who made a general evaluation of smart city policy and the challenges facing five UK cities. It is crucial to evaluate each planned top-down policy, especially from the public perspective. With just internal assessments by the relevant authorities and departments, actual situations and shortfalls may be overlooked. This could result in overall failure and wasted investment and resources. Taking the case of the MSCF, launched in

DOI: 10.1201/9781003403647-4

2019, to date there have been no evaluation reports on the strategies being planned. Furthermore, the period from 2021 to 2022 was scheduled as the time to implement smart initiatives nationwide [9]. Many local authorities lack suitable references and benchmarking on the details of the smart city domains and strategies to be adopted [19]. Without reference to evaluation, authorities or officers on the ground tend to believe that a blueprint is perfect and will follow it to the letter. Thus, in this research, and given the practical knowledge gaps, the author intends to answer the following questions:

- What level of understanding do practitioners have of the smart city domains stated in MSCF?
- What level of acceptance do practitioners have of the smart city domains stated in MSCF?

Based on these research questions, this study aims to evaluate the understanding and acceptance of practitioners from various sectors who are involved in smart city development in developing countries (using Malaysia as a case study). Knowing the levels of public understanding and acceptance was intended to be the output of this study, which would thus provide guidance to governments and policymakers to improve the smart city strategies and policies so that more smart and inclusive living would be available to their citizens.

3.2 Literature Background

Understanding the basic smart city domains is mainly influenced by the six domains outlined by [2], namely the smart economy, living, environment, people, governance, and mobility.

According to [2], the smart economy component is characterised by competitiveness. Among the sub-components of the smart economy (in the case of medium-sized European city rankings) are an innovative spirit, entrepreneurship, an economic image and trademark, productivity, labour market flexibility, and international embeddedness. As the economy is a broad concept and its strategies are context-based, many scholars and agencies have suggested measuring specific components, including nineteen economic attributes in the case of India, as stated by [20]. These include promoting balanced and sustainable economic growth, making strategic investments on strategic assets, and knowing that all forms of economics function at the local level. In another case, the smart economy domain of the Hong Kong Smart City Blueprint [8] promotes sharing economy, fintech, smart tourism, and re-industrialisation.

In the case of Malaysia, the components stated in MSCF are to intensify the application of technology and digitalisation in core business functions, enhance the usage of e-payment, attract investment in high value-added industries, create a workforce to match the jobs in these industries, provide technology labs and collaborative platforms, establish incubators and accelerators, and leverage existing government assistance and funding. Supporting literature can be found in Table 3.1.

Table 3.1 Smart economy domain

Smart economy strategy	Reference
Intensify technology application and digitalisation in core business functions	[2,20–22]
Enhance the usage of e-payment	[23–25]
Attract investment in high value-added industries	[26,27]
Create workforce to match jobs in high value-added industries	[4,28,29]
Provide technology labs and collaborative platforms	[22,30,31]
Establish incubators and accelerators	[32,33]
Leverage on existing government assistance and funding	[20,30]

High value-added activities refer to the major contribution of a private industry or government sector to overall gross domestic product (GDP) [34]. Contributions to GDP include higher wages and compensation for employees, taxes on production, lower import subsidies, and a gross operating surplus [34]. The Hong Kong labour market is an example of a concentration of high value-added service industries, with 25.9% of employees working in public administration or in the social and personal services industry in 2014 [35]. However, it is challenging to transition from low to high value-added industries in developing countries. This is the case in Indonesia, where low value-added industries such as textiles are desperately fighting rising wages and seeking protection from international competition. High value-added sectors largely utilise technology in various activities, including designing products, delivering products, processing customer orders, and improving product quality [27]. Nevertheless, according to MSCF, technology disruptors in Malaysia, such as robotics and analytics, are shifting traditional services towards value-adding and non-traditional service areas. However, the author has observed that MSCF did not refer to the issues of wages and imbalanced urban–rural development. Correspondingly, the smart city policy has offered opportunities within the Fourth Industrial Revolution (Industry 4.0) mostly in developed states and urban areas, while less-developed states and rural areas, such as Sabah, are mentioned far less often.

The second domain of smart living is characterised by the quality of life. Among the sub-components found in the smart living concept outlined by [2] are cultural facilities, health conditions, individual safety, housing quality, educational facilities, touristic attractivity, and social cohesion. In the Indian case, [20] scoped smart living into 14 attributes, including promoting shared values in society, celebrating local history and culture, and opening highly accessible public spaces. In the case of Hong Kong, their strategies are in building a Wi-Fi-connected city, developing faster digital payment systems, providing free electronic identity (eID) citizenship for government and commercial online transactions, and launching a $1 billion funding scheme to support the procurement of technological products by elderly and rehabilitation service units [8].

In Malaysia, the MSCF strategies are to enhance safety and security, promote the provision of quality housing, optimise emergency responses, enhance the quality

Table 3.2 Smart living domain

Smart living strategy	Reference
Enhance safety and security	[20,36,37]
Promote quality housing	[2,38]
Optimise emergency response	[20,39]
Enhance quality of healthcare services through digital technology	[40–43]
Encourage urban farming for better living	[23,44]

of healthcare services through digital technology and encourage urban farming for better living. Supporting literature can be found in Table 3.2.

Concerning the element of enhancing safety and security, one key initiative in Malaysia is the focus on crime reduction [36,45]. For example, under the safe city initiative through the Ministry of Housing and Local Government, a safer city can be created using several strategies, such as crime prevention through environmental design (CPTED) and crime prevention through social design (CPSD) [46]. With CPTED, information and communication technology (ICT), and mechanical surveillance design initiatives are popular, including the installation of closed-circuit television (CCTV) in public spaces, IoT (Internet of Things) lighting, safety (panic button) alarms, and establishing GIS (geographic information system) mapping for crime detection [36]. In the case of the capital city, Kuala Lumpur, crime is always an important issue for the citizens and city authorities. Research has shown that the challenges to making Kuala Lumpur a safe city can be mitigated by enhancing the role of guardians (i.e., the authorities); promoting CPTED and CPSD activities; and assisting victims and offenders with psychological, financial, and family assistance [47].

The idea behind the third domain, smart environment, centres on preserving natural resources. The smart environment sub-components outlined by [2] are the attractivity of natural conditions, pollution, environmental protection efforts, and sustainable resource management. Another source of reference from India, Vinod Kumar [20], presented 22 attributes to describe the smart environment, which included protecting nature; managing water resources, water supply systems, floods, and inundations effectively; encouraging neighbourliness and a spirit of community; upgrading urban resilience to the impacts of climate change; and creating a low-carbon environment based on energy efficiency, renewable energy, and the like. In the case of Hong Kong, the strategies are focused on reducing the carbon intensity; promoting energy efficiency and conservation in the community, with a particular focus on green and intelligent buildings; reducing waste; and monitoring the air pollution and cleanliness of public spaces [8].

In Malaysia, MSCF smart environment strategies include the need to preserve green areas and enhance the management of trees in public parks; strengthen the integrated and sustainable solid waste management; strengthen the solid waste laws and policies; improve the air quality and its monitoring system; improve the water quality and its monitoring system; increase energy efficiency and promote

Table 3.3 Smart environment domain

Smart environment strategy	Reference
Preserve green area and enhance the management of trees in public parks	[2,48]
Strengthen the integrated and sustainable solid waste management	[2,48]
Strengthen the solid waste laws and policies	[49,50]
Improve the air quality and its monitoring system	[50,51]
Improve the water quality and its monitoring system	[2,50]
Increase energy efficiency and promote renewable energy sources in community	[2,20,37]
Enhance the disaster risk management by adopting advanced technology application	[52,53]
Enhance the non-revenue water management	[2,54]
Encourage the development of low carbon city concept to be adopted at local level	[48,55]

renewable energy sources in the community; enhance disaster risk management by adopting advanced technology applications; enhance non-revenue water management; and encourage the development of a low-carbon city concept that can be adopted at the local level. Supporting literature can be found in Table 3.3.

In terms of park and green area management, the reduction in size of reserved forest and the preservation of green space in development plans are continual issues in Malaysia. Although forest land may have been gazetted, new development plans have always resulted in excuses to degazette forest reserves in favour of mixed-use development. For example, the Selangor State Government has recently granted a mixed development project on 931 hectares of the Kuala Langat North Forest Reserve, which is largely a move to rescind the protected status of the remnants of a once-sprawling peat forest that has been home to four indigenous Temuan settlements. The project also threatens wildlife [56]. This is one case that demonstrates the image of the Malaysian government, which can easily override gazetted land protection with the introduction of new plans under political influence and with profitable intentions, despite concerns for the public good of civil society, climate change, and the overall environment.

In terms of community attitudes to environmental protection, much change is required in Malaysia, especially within the authority-dependence mindset. A study on the Iskandar territory, Johor, Malaysia [57], showed that residents are conscious of the need for environmental cleanliness; however, their mindsets were hindered by the belief that the cleanliness of public space is mainly the responsibility of the authorities. Thus, [57] reaffirmed that the involvement and accountability of all parties are greatly needed in caring for the natural environment.

The fourth domain of smart people is characterised by social and human capital [2]. The indicators for the case of Europe include the level of qualification, affinity with lifelong learning, social and ethnic plurality, flexibility, creativity, cosmopolitanism, open-mindedness, and participation in public life. In the case of India, "smart people" are proposed as being the fundamental building block of a smart

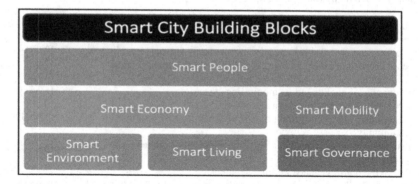

Figure 3.1 Smart city system building blocks, adapted from [20].

Table 3.4 Smart people domain

Smart people strategy	Reference
Improve moral education in schools	[58,59]
Enhance public awareness in practicing good moral and civic	[59,60]
Increase skilled and talented human capital at every level	[8,20]
Enhance public participation and community empowerment initiatives	[20,61–63]
Improve gender sensitisation and inclusivity of vulnerable groups	[52,64]
Increase the public willingness to adapt with emerging technologies	[8,20,65]

city system because, without people's active participation, a smart city system would not function effectively (Figure 3.1). Thus, [20] proposed eleven attributes of smart people by including the need to be actively involved in the city's sustainable development; excel in creativity and finding unique solutions to challenging issues; opt for lifelong learning and use e-learning models; and be cosmopolitan and open-minded and hold a multicultural perspective. In the case of Hong Kong, this focuses on nurturing young talent, innovation, and entrepreneurial culture [8].

In the case of Malaysia, the strategies are to improve moral education in schools; enhance public awareness in practicing good moral and civic duties; increase skilled and talented human capital at every level; enhance public participation and community empowerment initiatives; improve gender sensitisation and the inclusivity of vulnerable groups; and increase public willingness to adapt to emerging technologies. Supporting literature can be found in Table 3.4.

The element of cultivating skilled and talented human capital is particularly crucial, as Malaysia is determined to adopt the National Fourth Industrial Revolution Policy (Malaysian Industry 4.0 Policy), which was launched on 1 July 2021 [66]. This Industry 4.0 policy was launched with the purpose of transforming Malaysia into a high-income state through technology and digitalisation. Five fundamental technologies of the Industry 4.0 policy include artificial intelligence, the Internet of Things, blockchain, cloud computing and big data analytics, and advanced materials and technologies [67]. For the young generation to master these Industry 4.0 skills, it is crucial to plan every level of education properly. The Industry 4.0 policy is aligned with the Shared Prosperity Vision 2030, launched in 2019. The aim is to drive Malaysia towards developed nation status by 2030.

The moral and spiritual education element is considered appropriate for the majority-Muslim society in Malaysia. The moral element of cultivating smart people is comparatively silent in most Western European smart societies (refer to [2,68]). Since the early 1980s, Royal Professor Ungku Abdul Aziz bin Ungku Abdul Hamid, a well-known academician in Malaysia, has creatively interpreted a religious and moral form of development, which represents a balance between the spiritual and material world that is geared towards the needs of the local Muslim community [59]. The emphasis on the moral and spiritual element adopted in the MSCF will further strengthen the quality of Malaysian citizenship by developing a more peaceful and caring society.

Citizen participation and community empowerment are often identified as important elements in realising a citizen-centric smart city [20,62]. However, this attention should never be blinded by political actions that assume that tokenism and non-participation (refer to [61]) satisfy this type of participation. On the contrary, it is vital to involve citizens in decision-making and agenda setting in the smart city initiatives [69].

The core value of the fifth domain of smart governance is political participation. From the European perspective, [2] described smart governance using the components of participation in decision-making, public and social services, and transparent governance. The systematic literature review by [70] summarised six attributes for building a smart governance system. It should be based on ICT, external collaboration and participation, internal coordination, decision-making processes, e-administration, and outcomes. Prior research also suggests that the main outcome of smart city governance is the production of a wide range of public values through innovative collaborations [70].

From the Indian perspective, [71] suggested 12 steps to convert existing e-governance to smart governance, including an increase in city expenditure on ICT; the ease of access to e-services such as lodge complaints, claims and rights to information; and the promotion of e-democracy through e-decision-making and e-voting. From the Hong Kong perspective, smart governance is promoted through using open data for smart city innovations; building smarter city infrastructure, such as the fifth-generation (5G) mobile network; building a new big data analytics platform; data sharing among government departments; and adopting building information modelling (BIM) for major government capital work projects [8].

From the MSCF perspective, the components include increasing the scope of e-government services, increasing the quality of e-government services, elevating the use of data-sharing platforms across government agencies, and promoting information disclosure and open data from the government. Table 3.5 shows the smart governance strategies in MSCF and the related citations.

Table 3.5 Smart governance domain

Smart governance strategy	Reference
Increase the scope of e-government services	[64,71,72]
Increase the quality of e-government services	[2,40,71,73]
Elevate the use of data-sharing platform across government agencies	[26,70,74,75]
Promote information disclosure and open data from government	[8,76–79]

It is crucial to be aware of the component of elevating the use of data-sharing platforms across government agencies, as the isolated performance of government agencies was identified by the former prime minister as hindering the performance and services of government agencies [80]. In fact, this lack of efficiency, which is due to excessive bureaucracy, the reluctance of public servants to share data, and other factors, is not a new issue in the delivery of the Malaysian government system [81,82].

Concerning the sixth domain, smart mobility, the main concerns outlined by [2] were transport and ICT. The sub-components of [2] include local accessibility; (inter)national accessibility; the availability of an ICT infrastructure; and sustainable, innovative, and safe transport systems. In the case of India, [20] described smart mobility in terms of ten attributes, such as a focus on the mobility of people but not vehicles; advocating walkability and cycling; balanced transportation options such as a mass rapid transit system; and seamless mobility for differently abled people. In the Hong Kong case, the strategies are to focus on intelligent transport systems and traffic management; public transport interchanges/bus stops and parking; environmental friendliness in transport; and smart airports with facial biometric technology. These features should offer a hassle-free travel experience [8].

In the Malaysian case, the smart mobility strategies address the need to establish intelligent transport management; enhance data-sharing and digital mobility platforms; establish demand-based ridesharing services; utilise AI and the sensor-based predictive maintenance of a public transport fleet and infrastructure; enhance the dynamic smart parking infrastructure; establish an electric vehicle revolution; enhance collaboration with academia on research and development (R&D) into, and the commercialisation of, EVs and next-generation automobiles; and promote the usage of public transport applications. Table 3.6 shows the smart mobility strategies in MSCF and the related citations.

In general, all the components and strategies in various countries discussed above indicate that smart mobility is universal, regardless of whether it is introduced in the global north or south. The common item is the promotion of people-centric (rather than vehicle-centric) [83] and environmentally friendly (rather than utility convenient) transportation means [84]. The measures involved include opting to cycle and walk and to take public transport in the city rather than using a personal vehicle that produces greenhouse gas, carbon emissions, and pollution. This is predominantly important in many Asian cities; for example, Kuala Lumpur is characterised by heavy car dependence, leading to traffic congestion and delays

Table 3.6 Smart mobility domain

Smart mobility strategy	Reference
Establish intelligent transport management	[2,8,20]
Enhance data-sharing and digital mobility platform	[83,84]
Establish demand-based ride-sharing services	[8,20,85]
Utilise AI and sensor-based predictive maintenance of public transport fleet and infrastructure	[2,22,43,85,86]
Enhance dynamic smart parking infrastructure	[8,43,83]
Establish electric vehicle revolution	[85,87]
Enhance collaboration with academia on R&D and commercialisation on EVs and next-generation automobile	[83,85]
Promote the usage of public transport application	[8,83–85]

[85]. Planning for future mobility must focus less on building more highways and being car-dependent but rather on alternative ways of thinking about environmentally friendly mobility means and adoption. Considering the need for environmental protection and the preference for connecting two destination points via electronic platforms/communication, the actual physical cost of travelling could be reduced.

In addition to the above six basic domains, the author would like to discuss another emerging domain, that of smart digital infrastructure. This domain did not appear as an individual domain in [2,8,20]. Giffinger et al. [2] explicitly merged this element into the smart mobility domain. Meanwhile, in the case of Hong Kong, this digital infrastructure is explained/inserted in the smart government domain. As digital infrastructure is a frequent practice in Western and developed countries in Europe and North America, it is quite ready and more embedded into other domains. Under the New York Smart and Equitable City Plan 2015, digital infrastructure was embedded in the domains of smart buildings and infrastructure; smart transport and mobility; smart energy and environment; smart public health and safety; and smart government and community [88]. All the sectors and strategies within the smart cities concept centre on ICT infrastructure, a point on which the authors and the majority of smart city scholars agree (Figure 3.2).

However, in most private sector conceptions, due to the propagation and sale of their latest technologies, this digital infrastructure element is explicitly highlighted. In the case of Frost and Sullivan, it is even divided into two different domains: smart technology and smart infrastructure (Figure 3.3).

In MSCF, smart digital infrastructure has been designated as a separate seventh domain. The smart digital infrastructure strategies include the need to enhance the roles of service providers in developing digital infrastructure; enhance internet speed and connectivity; enhance the government's role in facilitating the development of communication infrastructure; enhance indoor and outdoor network coverage; strengthen policies related to personal data protection; and strengthen policies related to cybersecurity. Table 3.7 illustrates the strategies of the smart digital infrastructure domain and its related citations.

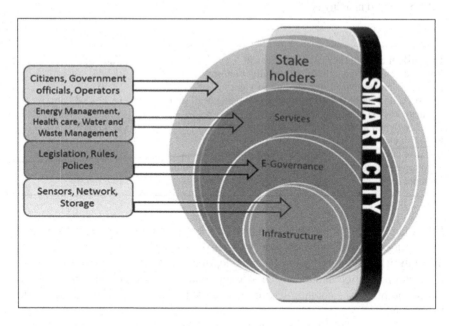

Figure 3.2 Digital infrastructure is the heart of smart city development [89].

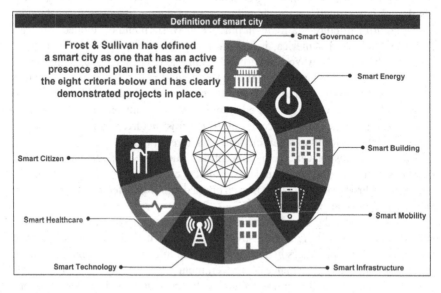

Figure 3.3 Smart city domains [90].

Table 3.7 Smart digital infrastructure domain

Smart digital infrastructure strategy	Reference
Enhance service provider's role in developing digital infrastructure	[8,37,90,91]
Enhance internet speed and connectivity	[90,92]
Enhance government's role in facilitating the development of communication infrastructure	[8,70,93]
Enhance indoor and outdoor network coverage	[2,94,95]
Strengthen policies related to personal data protection	[96–98]
Strengthen policies related to cybersecurity	[8,37,89,99,100]

One form of digital infrastructure to attract attention in smart city development is the IoT. Using the internet, the IoT is a network that interconnects ordinary physical objects, such as smartphones, with identifiable addresses to provide intelligent services [101]. In 2021, 35 billion IoT devices were expected to be installed and there were 46 billion connected devices around the world [102]. These numbers, in total, represent more than ten times the size of the global population. Therefore, it could be imagined that it is crucial to tackle the cybersecurity issues that relate to using IoT machines and to address the need for personal data protection as part of living in smart cities. In Malaysia, cybersecurity cases rose by 82.5% between 18 March and 7 April 2020 (838 cases), compared to the same timeframe in 2019 (459 cases) [103]. These cases include some form of cyberbullying; fraud or intruding into an unauthorised system such as phishing and email scams; data breaches and distributed denial of service (DDoS) attacks on local businesses; and hacking into private video conferencing chats and harassing the participants during the COVID-19 movement control period.

To tackle these cybersecurity problems in combination with promoting IoT adoption, in 2015, the National IoT Strategic Roadmap was launched by the Ministry of Science, Technology, and Innovation, with the national applied R&D centre MIMOS Bhd. as the implementation secretariat and with the support of agencies such as Cybersecurity Malaysia [104]. This roadmap targeted a contribution of RM 9.3 billion (about USD 2.2 billion) to the gross national income and the creation of more than 14,000 highly skilled employment opportunities by 2020. In addition, other policies have been initiated, such as the National Industry 4.0 policy, the National Cyber Security Policy, and the Malaysia Personal Data Protection Act 2010. MSCF mentioned the need to review and enforce stronger laws, as well as upgrade security systems and procedures in the public and private sectors. In this context, cybersecurity has been identified as a policy to be strengthened in the smart city context.

3.3 Methodology

After outlining the smart city domains and examples of smart city policies worldwide, this methodology section explains the MSCF case study, the samples of respondents, the data collection, the questionnaire design, and the data analysis method.

3.3.1   *The Case of the Malaysian Smart City Framework*

MSCF is the first top-down document to formulate the direction of smart city development in Malaysia. The document was launched in September 2019 and drafted by the Ministry of Housing and Local Government. In MSCF, smart cities are defined as "cities that use ICT and technological advancement to address urban issues, including to improve quality of life, promote economic growth, develop a sustainable and safe environment and encourage efficient urban management practices" [9]. This definition, in practice, aims to achieve the vision of "quality and smart living" [9].

In terms of planning, the implementation of smart cities nationwide is divided into three phases from 2019 to 2025. These are phase 1 (the foundation stage), from 2019 to 2020 (two years); phase 2 (the development stage), from 2021 to 2022 (two years); and phase 3 (the advanced development and monitoring stage), from 2023 to 2025 (three years). To ensure its effective implementation, understanding and acceptance among the population must also be investigated, especially for urban residents. Hence, this study focuses on the understanding and acceptance among professionals of MSCF. The study has been developed to identify the appropriateness of the outlined strategies.

As discussed previously, various components/strategies can be found in academic and grey literature under the grouping of each smart city domain, all of which depends on managing problems and challenges in local contexts. The case is the same in Malaysia, where the government had customised the domains, components, and strategies according to the local challenges. Based on the planned domains, 90 questionnaire items were designed (see Appendix 3.3A) and face validated by two smart city experts.

3.3.2   *Sampling and Data Collection*

This study employed a quantitative survey via the fuzzy Delphi method. In obtaining expert opinions using the fuzzy Delphi method, the ideal sample size is between 10 and 50 respondents [105,106]. Therefore, the authors decided to sample 40 smart city practitioners from the Kuala Lumpur Greater Valley area, including the city of Kuala Lumpur, Putrajaya, and Cyberjaya (Table 3.8).

As Table 3.8 shows, this group of practitioners consisted of those in the government, private, and self-employed sectors. They represented the middle class and various professional job roles, such as director/CEO, assistant director/senior officer, executive officer, engineer/planner/architect, and technician. Since the 1970s, the middle class has emerged as a significant group contributing to the urbanisation process in major cities in Malaysia [107]. Thus, the selection of professionals as respondents was significant given the composition of this group, the majority of whom lived in urban areas. The professionals were selected based

Table 3.8 Informant sampling

Characteristics	Quantity (N = 40)	Percentage (%)
Gender		
Male	19	47.5
Female	21	52.5
Age		
23–30 years old	1	2.5
31–40	24	60.0
41–50	13	32.5
51 years old and above	2	5.0
Race		
Malay	36	90.0
Chinese	2	5.0
Bumiputera Sabah and Sarawak	2	5.0
Academic qualification		
Bachelor's degree	26	65.0
Master's degree	8	20.0
PhD	6	15.0
Employment sector		
Government	32	80.0
Private	4	10.0
Self-employed	4	10.0
Work experience		
5 to 8 years	4	10.0
9 to 10 years	8	20.0
11 to 15 years	13	32.5
16 to 20 years	8	20.0
21 years and above	7	17.5
Job Position		
Director/CEO	12	25.5
Assistant director/Senior officer	10	21.3
Executive officer	8	17.0
Engineer/Planner/Architect	14	29.8
Technician	3	6.4

on various criteria: they had to have a minimum of five years of work experience; possess at least a bachelor's degree; and be primarily involved in the planning, design, delivery, and management of cities and their development.

The success of the fuzzy Delphi method depends on the insights and information supplied by experts. Thus, a panel of experts/respondents was identified through a purposive sampling and nomination process, rather than random selection. Later, a focus group discussion was organised, and data were collected.

3.3.3 Questionnaire Design

Through a structured questionnaire, a survey strategy of enquiry was conducted. Three sections were used in the questionnaire to obtain information from the respondents. Section one was designed to determine the respondent's background.

Section two focused on their understanding, while section three focused on their acceptance of the MSCF's domains. The questionnaire adopted a closed-ended design. The respondents were asked to rate the 90 variables based on their level of significance using a five-point Likert scale, with 5 being Strongly Agree and 1 being Strongly Disagree. For the details of the survey items, see Appendix 3.3A. Aghimien et al. [14] adopted a similar approach in their study that evaluated the challenges facing smart cities.

3.3.4 Data Analysis

In addition, the fuzzy Delphi method was chosen as the analysis technique to obtain the agreement of experts, namely the professionals, based on the study objectives. The fuzzy Delphi method is a Delphi method performed to obtain information regarding consensus on measurement variables or factors from a group of experts [108,109]. The Delphi method has been shown to be effective in publishing the best ideas/views through collective responses from expert informants [110]. With the principle of "more minds are better than a single mind", the fuzzy Delphi method is designed as a forecasting tool to gather the ideas of structured groups, which are said to be more accurate than unstructured predictions [111]. This technique allows experts to coordinate their actions systematically in addressing a particular problem or difficulty and reach a consensus.

In this study, expert consensus was evaluated based on the seven MSCF domains, namely the smart economy, smart living, smart environment, smart people, smart government, smart mobility, and smart digital infrastructure. Each of these domains has its own strategic initiatives to enable cities in Malaysia to achieve smart city status. Respondents' understanding and acceptance were analysed to achieve the objectives of the study.

Questionnaire data obtained from the focus group feedback of professionals were analysed using a formulated Microsoft Excel worksheet by [106]. The experts' score inputs were evaluated in stages. Mathematical scores—the Likert scale and the triangular fuzzy scale scores for each item—were obtained (Table 3.9) and converted into mean values. Later, the threshold value (d), the percentage of expert agreement, and the "defuzzification" process of the fuzzy score with α-cut value

Table 3.9 Triangular fuzzy number scale [106]

Likert scale	Strongly disagree		Disagree		Moderately agree		Agree		Strongly agree		
	1		2		3		4		5		
Triangular fuzzy Delphi scale	0.0	0.0 0.2	0.0	0.2 0.4	0.2	0.4 0.6	0.4	0.6 0.8	0.6	0.8	1.0

were calculated. Finally, based on the above three criteria, the ranking positions of the consensus items accepted/rejected by the expert panel were analysed.

In detail, let us say the item "I am ready to use e-payment in my daily affairs" was scored 5 (strongly agree) by an expert. The score is converted into the minimum, most plausible, and maximum values of 0.6, 0.8, and 1.0 fuzzy scores. It indicated the expert is agreeable to the item as 60%, 80%, and 100%, respectively. Then, the fuzzy scale of (0.6, 0.8, 1.0) is converted into a mean value $(\bar{m})$ among the 40 responses.

Next, according to [112], the calculation of the threshold (d) value performed was as follows:

$$d(\bar{m},\bar{n}) = \sqrt{\frac{1}{3}\left[(m_1 - n_1)^2 + (m_2 - n_2)^2 + (m_3 - n_3)^2\right]} \tag{3.1}$$

where,
d = the threshold value,
m_1 = the smallest mean value of a fuzzy number,
m_2 = the most plausible mean value of a fuzzy number,
m_3 = the maximum mean value of a fuzzy number,
n_1 = the smallest value of a fuzzy number,
n_2 = the most plausible value of a fuzzy number, and
n_3 = the maximum value of a fuzzy number.

The value of "d" (the threshold value) for all items of the questionnaire indicates expert consensus agreement for each item. According to [112], the value of "d" must be greater than or equal to 0.2 to indicate consensus agreement for each item.

For the expert agreement/consensus percentage, if the expert consensus exceeded 75%, it was considered as accepted [113,114]. Then, through the process of defuzzification or the process of determining the scores, the ranking positions of each item were determined. The formula used to determine the ranking/score for an item was as follows:

$$A_{max} = \frac{1}{3}(m_1 + m_2 + m_3) \tag{3.2}$$

After an assessment was made, if the fuzzy (A_{max}) score or α-cut value was equal to or exceeded 0.5, this indicated expert consensus to accept the item [115].

The Delphi method is a widely accepted, efficient, and effective way of bringing together experts to discuss, debate, and organise a body of information in order to develop a validated instrument, reach agreement on an issue, uncover common factors, or forecast trends [116,117]. This method is deemed particularly highly reliable when more than ten experts in the given field were employed [105,106]. Additionally, to minimise the bias, it is important to involve experts in a study that possess extensive experience, high qualifications, and knowledge in the field or the subject matter [118]. Evidently, this study meets these requirements as it has involved 40 experts with a minimum of five years of work experience, possessed at least a bachelor's degree, and involved intensively in the planning and management of smart cities in the context of Malaysia (Table 3.8). Hence, we did not employ an additional validation mechanism for the generated results of the Delphi study.

3.4 Results

In general, the understanding and acceptance of the targeted group of experts in this study were contested. This shows that the community has different perceptions of the smart city domains stated in the MSCF. This divergent phenomenon can be described in two ways. Firstly, from the domain perspective, the majority of domains (i.e., smart economy, living, people, and governance) were accepted, two domains (i.e., smart environment and digital infrastructure) were rejected, while the smart mobility domain was partially accepted. Secondly, from the objective perspective, more than half of the domains were accepted (Table 3.10).

To accept the criteria of the fuzzy Delphi analysis, the results must meet three conditions: (a) threshold value, $d \le 0.2$, (b) expert agreement percentage $\ge 75\%$, and (c) average fuzzy score $(A_{max}) \ge \alpha - $ cut value $= 0.5$. Overall, all the domains fulfilled the third criteria, with fuzzy scores equal to or exceeding 0.5. Meanwhile, the threshold value and expert agreement showed mixed results.

To provide more detail on the item results, as shown in Table 3.11, the smart economy and living had a 100% acceptance rate for the objective of Acceptance, hinting that these two domains can be implemented directly at ground level with little modification. On the other hand, the smart environment scored the lowest acceptance rates, 22.22% for the Understanding objective and 33.33% for the Acceptance objective. This result indicates that the smart environment domain has experienced great public dissensus and more refinement is needed before its implementation to avoid later failures.

In general, the results of the analysis on the smart economy, living, people, and governance domains met all three conditions of the fuzzy Delphi method in terms of Understanding and Acceptance. However, some item details must be addressed (refer to Appendix 3.3B).

First, for the Understanding objective of the smart economy, the two rejected items were items 3 (high value-added industry investment, with threshold value $d = 0.21$, and expert agreement at only 33%) and 7 (assistance to business operations, with 73% expert agreement). For the Acceptance objective of the smart economy, all the items were accepted. For the high value-added industry investment, the respondents did not arrive at a consensus. Some thought that the authorities should focus on the manufacturing sector, especially in suburban and rural areas, instead of prioritising high value-added industry, which would accelerate the existing urbanisation issues in metropolitan Malaysia, such as in Kuala Lumpur and the Klang Valley area.

Second, under smart living, the only problematic Understanding item was item 1 (crime reduction). Respondents were less able to comprehend why Malaysia was stated as having a high, instead of moderate, crime rate, since most of them lived

Table 3.10 Results of fuzzy Delphi analysis by smart city domains

Domain	Threshold (d) value		Expert agreement (%)		Average of Fuzzy score (A_{max})		Result		Ranking by the Fuzzy score	
	(U)	(A)	(U)	(A)	(U)	(A)	(U)	(A)	(U)	(A)
Smart Economy	0.142	0.139	76%	89%	0.725	0.731	Accepted	Accepted	2	2
Smart Living	0.132	0.171	75%	91%	0.719	0.700	Accepted	Accepted	4	4
Smart Environment	0.189	0.212	57%	55%	0.654	0.639	Rejected	Rejected	7	7
Smart People	0.123	0.128	80%	83%	0.745	0.743	Accepted	Accepted	1	1
Smart Government	0.188	0.184	92%	91%	0.704	0.698	Accepted	Accepted	5	5
Smart Mobility	0.164	0.245	83%	56%	0.724	0.654	Accepted	Rejected	3	6
Smart Digital Infrastructure	0.204	0.150	72%	74%	0.670	0.725	Rejected	Rejected	6	3

Note: U stands for Understanding, A stands for Acceptance. Three conditions to accept an item: threshold value $(d) \leq 0.2$, percentage of experts' consensus $\geq 75\%$, and average fuzzy score $(A_{max}) \geq \alpha - $ cut value $= 0.5$.

Table 3.11 Results of fuzzy Delphi analysis by objectives

Objective	Domain	Item	Accepted item	% of Acceptance	Rejected item	% of Rejection	Fuzzy score interval
Understanding	Economy	7	5	71.43	2	28.57	0.775 − 0.655 = 0.120
	Living	5	4	75.00	1	25.00	0.775 − 0.620 = 0.155
	Environment	9	2	22.22	7	77.78	0.745 − 0.572 = 0.173
	People	6	4	66.67	2	33.33	0.765 − 0.715 = 0.050
	Government	4	3	75.00	1	25.00	0.725 − 0.693 = 0.032
	Mobility	8	6	75.00	2	25.00	0.755 − 0.685 = 0.070
	Digital Infrastructure	6	3	50.00	3	50.00	0.735 − 0.523 = 0.212
Acceptance	Economy	7	7	100.00	0	0.00	0.770 − 0.710 = 0.060
	Living	5	5	100.00	0	0.00	0.725 − 0.670 = 0.055
	Environment	9	3	33.33	6	66.67	0.720 − 0.557 = 0.163
	People	6	4	66.67	2	33.33	0.770 − 0.720 = 0.050
	Government	4	3	75.00	1	25.00	0.715 − 0.680 = 0.035
	Mobility	8	3	37.50	5	62.50	0.700 − 0.563 = 0.137
	Digital Infrastructure	6	4	66.67	2	33.33	0.760 − 0.655 = 0.105
Total		90	54	61.36	34	38.64	

Note: Refer to Appendix 3.3B for detailed calculations.

in peaceful environments. Meanwhile, they were inclined to accept that the MSCF would be able to reduce the crime rate effectively through ICT applications, such as the installation of CCTV in public areas.

Third, for the understanding and acceptance of smart people, all four rejected items were due to the 70–73% expert agreement. For item 3, the acceptance of the education policy for human capital development, respondents were not fully confident that the restructuring of education at the tertiary level would produce innovative graduates. One respondent commented that the current graduate market indicated that graduates were able to perform at routine levels while lacking innovative thinking and solution-creation skills.

Fourth, for the understanding and acceptance of smart governance, item 3— inter-governmental data sharing—was the only item rejected as the threshold value $d = 0.224$ and 0.202. Respondent feedback suggested that they did not understand how inter-governmental data could be shared in practice, as some were still experiencing issues such as the separate performance of departments, the redundancy of providing data to particular departments, and the inability to receive valid and complete data through a single department enquiry. For example, the Department of Statistics does not provide open demographic data by city or district level so one needs to go to the particular local authorities.

The major focus of this study should be the smart environment and digital infrastructure domains because both were rejected in terms of the Understanding and Acceptance objectives. In general, for the environment, its threshold (d) construct for Acceptance (0.212) was more than 0.2 while both values of expert agreement (57% for Understanding and 55% for Acceptance) were less than 75%. For digital infrastructure, its threshold (d) construct for Understanding (0.204) was also more than 0.2, while both values of expert agreement (72% for Understanding and 74% for Acceptance) were also less than 75%. These negative results show that the public remain less likely to understand and accept the components planned in these two domains, smart environment and digital infrastructure.

In detail, for the smart environment, the three lowest-ranked Understanding items related to items 1 (park and green area management), 8 (non-revenue water management and reporting), and 9 (low-carbon city and carbon emissions). Meanwhile, the three lowest-ranked Acceptance items related to items 7 (readiness towards disaster-resilient cities), 4 (air quality monitoring), and 2 (waste segregation and recycling). From the overall perspective, the environment-related issues worrying the public are broad in scope and a cause for grave alarm. The smart environment domain faces major public understanding and acceptance issues and the authorities should prioritise improvements in this domain.

For the smart digital infrastructure, two items of interest in terms of Understanding are items 6 (cybersecurity) and 5 (personal data protection); for Acceptance, they are items 1 (roles of service providers) and 2 (internet speed). It seems that respondents lacked confidence in the authority's online system security and personal data protection, and felt they were vulnerable to cyber-attacks and personal data leaks. Attention should also be given to the respondents who did not fully accept that private service providers were solely responsible and thought that the government was too. Another important issue involved rural areas with low internet speeds of 4G and below.

For smart mobility, the result was accepted for Understanding but rejected for Acceptance. The acceptance of respondents was rejected since the threshold (d) conduct was 0.245, which is over the 0.2 required; furthermore, the expert agreement of 56% was much less than the 75% required.

Clearly, the rejection phenomenon identified for the Acceptance objective needs attention. A low level of expert agreement was observed for items 6 (electric vehicle), 1 (smart traffic management), 8 (public transport application), and 5 (smart parking infrastructure). These results showed that the respondents were worried about the traffic planning presented in the MSCF and were unconvinced by the solutions related to the issues stated above.

3.5 Discussion

3.5.1 Voicing Dissensus Opinions for Building a More Inclusive Smart City Blueprint

The findings indicate divergent expert perceptions. The different job roles and employment sectors of the respondents could be expected to produce diverse results. Figure 3.4 summarises the occurrence of three conditions.

The dissensus in the results is a finding that leaders and policymakers should be aware of. They should accept this reality and include those opinions that do not always favour the majority. For example, people were dissatisfied with the smart environment domains; for example, they did not comprehend the ineffectiveness of the authorities' park and green area management and preservation, nor did they accept that the authorities had done enough pertaining to this matter. Evidence from [2,20] showed that the smart environment covers a wide range of natural resources preservation and the resilience of human actions to the impact of climate change; thus, it is crucial to contemplate the divergent opinions of the respondents.

For smart digital infrastructure, respondents did not recognise that their personal data are protected by the Malaysia Personal Data Protect Act 2010; they felt unsafe

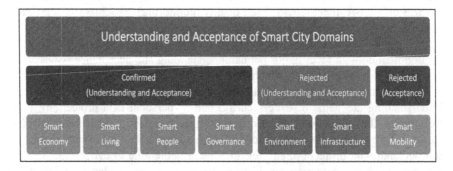

Figure 3.4 Dissensus opinions on the understanding and acceptance of smart city domains.

from cyber-attacks and were also unconvinced that the authorities would reduce cyber threats and have a positive impact by protecting online users.

For smart mobility, although most understood that this domain is important, they showed disagreement in accepting the implemented initiatives. For example, they did not express confidence in the promotion of autonomous and electric or green vehicles, smart traffic light functioning, and public transport applications. This finding is interesting from a global perspective as these measures are working elsewhere in other countries, meaning they were understood by the respondents. However, it is clear that the authorities should improve these matters to bring about greater local acceptance and avoid wasted investment. The following subsections provide various ideas for reconsidering the implementation of smart city domains in MSCF.

In the broader topic of smart city understanding and acceptance, the above result reflected a developing country's context and dynamic in practice [1,14]. The administrators should be responsive and improve the smart city domains and strategies from time to time. As for the specific scientific field, the smart environment needs more attention as climate change is real [2,20,87] and applying smart digital infrastructure with higher security [21,22,37] to counter this global issue urgently needs to be addressed.

3.5.2 Rethinking the Viability of Smart City Domains and Strategies

A smart economy tends to possess high value-added industries, so it is proposed that high value-added industrial investment promotion initiatives be reconsidered geographically as the distribution of secondary industry is unbalanced and currently heavily favours the Peninsula and urban areas [119]. Sabah and Sarawak are still heavily dependent on primary products (i.e., timber, oil, and LNG). Targeting the relocation of manufacturing sectors to less-developed areas, which would create new urban growth centres or smart cities, needs far more attention, rather than targeting high-value investment in the already mature urban and metropolitan areas. Furthermore, wages in less-developed areas need to be improved since continuing to invest in high-value industries in urban areas will further exacerbate the urbanisation issues. Malaysia could learn from India in promoting balanced and sustainable economic growth and ensuring that all economic activities work well at the local level (refer to [20]). Furthermore, Malaysia could also learn from Hong Kong in placing greater focus on sharing economic activities among regions and in the re-industrialisation of the necessary supporting primary and secondary sectors (refer to [8]).

Another point to consider is the potential of e-commerce. Online transaction expansion initiatives that are gaining a place in the hearts of consumers can be created in line with the increasingly busy lifestyles of urban citizens. A study of online purchasing practices in Malaysia by [120] found that buying online was chosen because it is a convenient and easy way to shop for necessities while avoiding long queues at the outlets. Online shopping is a trend in modern society since internet usage has increased in the last decade. It has accelerated under the stay-at-home new normality caused by the COVID-19 pandemic. Thus, considering online shopping initiatives as part of the smart economy initiative should enable improvements in the economic status of urban residents, either as traders or customers, which would enhance the lives of both parties [25].

For smart living, the experts rejected the understanding that the crime rate in Malaysia remains high compared to other countries. The respondents thought that the crime rate was at a controlled level. This opinion matches the findings of [121], whose local studies in Kuala Lumpur showed that city residents are not concerned about the crime situation. Additionally, [121] found that the perception that the crime rate was high in Malaysia actually did exist in the foreign discourse. Thus, the authorities could consider all such perspectives, turning their focus to the means of adaptation to the fear of crime, the omnipresence of police in public spaces, and assistance to prevent criminal acts in community areas [47,121].

Furthermore, in terms of smart living, voluntary and more active community involvement initiatives related to the safety, educational, and health aspects of the local community can be added to reduce the extent of dependence on government resources. According to [122], community involvement ensures that the needs and aspirations of the community are not neglected; the result is that community members will be educated and subsequently empowered. This shows that the role of the community can resolve local issues more effectively.

In terms of smart people, referring to skilled and talented human capital, the government must rethink tertiary education and determine how to actively produce digitally talented innovative graduates to suit value-added industry in the Industry 4.0 era. More structured and holistic learning opportunities within the areas of IoT devices development, telecommunications, middleware, big data analytics, and artificial intelligence are needed. This is because engineering students currently focus mainly on hardware and connectivity aspects, while computer science students learn middleware and big data analytics separately [104]. To adopt Industry 4.0 technologies in Malaysian smart city society, a radical paradigm shift in educating graduates so they transform into talented human capital should be the priority, a notion that was reaffirmed by the Prime Minister [67]. Thus, the 2013 national education policy is somewhat outdated, so rethinking how to enhance it through the Industry 4.0 perspective is crucial. Questions such as how to nurture young people so they master the fundamental Industry 4.0 technologies in stages, from primary, secondary, and tertiary education up to life-long learning for elderly community members, should become the central aim in formulating a new national education policy.

Next, moral and ethical development, as mentioned in the MSCF, is considered a good move for developing countries like Malaysia, as many Western developed countries have resolved this moral element (refer to [2]). As mentioned in the literature, Ungku Aziz's 1980s' ideas are still considered fundamental and remain relevant enough to be adopted in the current smart city development in Malaysia. Although the values of education related to moral development were stated in the National Education Blueprint 2013, the latest education plan could be enhanced based on the five principles of Maqasid Al-Syariah, namely caring for religion, caring for life, caring for intellect, caring for one's offspring, and caring for property. Maqasid Al-Syariah refers to the noble purpose of Islamic law, which is based on the principle of Maslahat and which mankind could universally obtain through the text or authority of Islamic law [123]. This universal concept is seen by all as practicable.

Another aspect to enhance in terms of smart people in Malaysia is the level of civic participation in local authority decision-making and programs [73]. Participation in decision-making differs from community empowerment: the former involves the level of citizen power and can influence agenda setting, while the latter refers to the tokenism level of service delivery stages [61]. Furthermore, in the former, people are active in decision-making and co-creating with the authorities, whereas, in the latter, people tend to be in a weaker, beneficiary, or reactive position when they are deemed to be "empowered" by the authorities. Contemplating the lower level of participation in decision-making in Malaysia, the authors argue that the implementation of the MSCF could enhance the extent of this form of participation. Although it may face dissensus of opinion, in the long term, this move will help in building more democratic spaces and independent citizenship for Malaysian nation-building [124].

On the governance issue, excessive bureaucracy, delays in approving applications and licenses, as well as a lack of information on new policies and regulations are among the main problems plaguing the government's delivery system [81,82]. Intergovernmental data sharing is another challenge due to the separate departmental practices in Malaysia. To address this, Hong Kong's initiatives can be adopted, such as building a new big data analytics platform; adopting public cloud services, which would enable real-time data transmission and sharing among government departments; and enhancing security features so that government departments can deliver efficient and agile e-services [8]. Future smart city governance should make effective use of their data assets to secure outcomes that are appropriate to citizens' needs. Investment by agencies in system-wide data capture, integration, and analytics capabilities [75] is a crucial aspect to develop.

Apart from data sharing, smart governance ultimately aims to produce public values for citizens, such as from the perspective of asset management and financial and economic sustainability [93]. To realise such public values, e-democracy must be upheld through active e-voting and e-decision-making [71], which is a major topic for Malaysian smart development advocates to deliberate. According to the Democracy Index 2020, out of 167 countries, Malaysia (ranked 39) and India (ranked 53) fell into the category of flawed democracies. Meanwhile, Hong Kong ranked 87 due to its hybrid regime of flawed democracy and authoritarian control [125]. In terms of the purpose of building independent citizens [2] within the conception that smart cities are democratic ecologies [126], Malaysia and similar places must actually strive further to achieve higher transparency and open governance. As suggested by [127], "good enough governance" for smart city societies in Malaysia should consider the cultural context of the Muslim majority, prioritise governance content that allows more scope for political participation and free speech, and cultivate the imagination and unselfishness of children.

Furthermore, it was found that the understanding and acceptance of initiatives in the smart environment is the most critical among all the domains. In this regard, announcements on smart environment initiatives must be intensified and expanded to ensure the sustainability of the existing environment. Most importantly, the author's view is that environmental accountability initiatives must be added to this component to enable each party to understand the concept and play their respective roles in caring for the environment. In the case of maintaining a clean environment, [57] found that all stakeholders should take responsibility, not solely the authorities. Efforts to maintain and preserve the environmental space relate to the question of community awareness and attitude, which, if sufficiently high, would ensure that the environment is always clean, healthy, and sustainable.

In terms of preserving parks and green spaces in urban areas, Malaysia's development control guidelines set a minimum of 10% green and open space reservation, which is considered relatively low. In comparison, the city of Wuhan, China, has launched its Wuhan Low-Carbon Urban Development Plan 2013, which reserves 28% for green areas in the city [48]. Therefore, a rethink is suggested that would impose a greater green space allocation in new development plans and, together with agencies such as PLANMalaysia, the MSCF could incorporate this higher green space allocation as one of its smart environment initiatives.

In terms of smart mobility and, in particular, electrical vehicles (EVs) in Malaysia, Putrajaya city bought 150 electric buses (each costing RM1.5 million). They operate in Putrajaya and the vicinity, the aim being to cut carbon emissions, noise pollution, and traffic congestion while improving public transport and parking systems [128]. The operation of the electric buses is calibrated by battery capacity and charging facilities and has been found to outperform conventional bus operations [129]. However, cases of the inefficiency of public transport management were identified, whereby the electric buses were found abandoned at the Depoh Putrajaya. Bus breakdowns are frequent due to lack of maintenance, unreliable and delayed bus arrival times, and reductions in bus routes [130]. Thus, although electric cars are efficient in costs and energy saving with long-term usage [84], the adoption of an EV ecosystem is required, involving features such as efficient management and the availability of efficient power charging stations.

As for privately owned electric cars, it has been found that the understanding and acceptance of the community remain low. The respondents in this study felt the costs involved in owning and maintaining a private electric vehicle were higher than those of a typical vehicle. It is true that research has shown that the cost of electric vehicle ownership in Malaysia is not yet as competitive as typical internal combustion vehicles [131]. This shows the market and society acceptance of electric cars remains low. Those involved in the MSCF should rethink the issues of EVs, along with the latest National Automotive Policy 2020, in promoting affordable new technologies. For example, incentives and funding are available under the National Automotive Policy 2020 to develop the technology and engineering required for NxGV (next-generation vehicles), autonomous vehicles, MaaS (mobility-as-a-service), and Industry 4.0 [132]. Thus, MSCF initiatives such as promoting collaboration with the private sector in developing affordable EVs could be implemented.

Last but not least, for the smart digital infrastructure, in terms of the cybersecurity and personal data protection issues, it seems that the MSCF did not provide clear direction on how to strengthen the necessary cybersecurity and personal data protection. The ranking of Malaysia as eighth out of 194 countries in the Global Cybersecurity Index 2021 [133] seems to contradict the results of this study's finding. Recently reported cyber intrusion cases [103] were over the targeted 9000– 10,000 per year [9], and the assessment of the National IoT Strategic Roadmap was also ambiguous [104]. All the supporting agencies, such as Cybersecurity Malaysia, the Department of Personal Data Protection, and the Malaysia Administrative Modernization and Management Planning Unit must work more closely together and actively provide improvements or amendments to the policies, especially more strict enforcement of the Malaysian Personal Data Protection Act 2010.

As for the issues of low internet speed and digital infrastructure coverage in less-developed states and rural areas, more MSCF initiatives could be planned in conjunction with the latest National Digital Infrastructure Plan (JENDELA), the Malaysian Industry 4.0 Policy, and the Malaysia Digital Economy Blueprint (MyDigital). For instance, the current wireless broadband coverage in Malaysia is 96.7% for 2G, 95.3% for 3G, and 91.8% for 4G coverage in populated areas, with 25 Mbps speed [134]. Therefore, MSCF initiatives could plan to achieve 100% 4G coverage in populated areas and a speed of 100 Mbps by adopting 5G.

3.6 Conclusion

First, Malaysia's experience in smart city development dates back to the 1996 Multimedia Super Corridor Malaysia initiative and the later efforts in developing research universities and integrating them with the city they are located in [135,136]—through knowledge-based urban development principles to make space and place for smart urban communities [137]. Today, with its new smart city framework, Malaysia aims to transform its cities and societies into smarter ones. This chapter aims to generate insights into how this framework is perceived with professional practitioners. In order to do so, this study conducted an empirical investigation concerning the seven smart city domains planned as part of a top-down national policy of the Malaysian Smart City Framework (MSCF). The findings disclosed that smart environment and digital infrastructure require the most attention, followed by smart mobility, governance, living, economy, and people.

Second, this study has contributed to the smart city discourse and literature particularly by examining the levels of understanding and acceptance from the multi-perspectives of practitioners from various sectors. The study is unique as it is one of the first in capturing professional practitioners' voices and perspectives on a national-level smart city policy that impacts a large portion of the population. This finding is an important insight added to the literature investigating, in detail, smart city domains in practice. The divergent and dissensus opinions from the ground are valuable references for leaders and policymakers to consider in building a more inclusive and smarter city blueprint. Furthermore, applying the fuzzy Delphi method in smart city studies is rather new. It has great potential to be explored and expanded into urban studies and planning disciplines as this method is popular in education, business, and management studies [138].

Finally, the limitations of this study are the selection of purposive sampling for the fuzzy Delphi analysis and the formulation of questionnaire items from the broader scopes of the smart city domains. Thus, based on the smart city domains and after designing two objectives of understanding and acceptance, future studies could explore other qualitative or quantitative methods to justify the results of this study. Other studies that evaluate the implementation of the smart city domain objectives could be conducted, such as using structural equation modelling to assess the implementation of smart city strategies in Greece [139] and acceptance of smart metres in Malaysia [37]. Moreover, future studies could be expanded to capture the voices and perspectives of the general public on national and local smart city strategies and initiatives. This will be the focus of our prospective study [140].

Acknowledgements

This chapter, with permission from the copyright holder, is a reproduced version of the following journal article: Lim, S., Malek, J., Yussoff, M., & Yigitcanlar, T. (2021). Understanding and acceptance of smart city policies: Practitioners' perspectives on the Malaysian smart city framework. *Sustainability*, 13(17), 9559.

Appendix 3.3A

Table 3.A1 Survey items

Domain 1: Smart economy

Item	Understanding	Acceptance
Intensify technology application and digitalisation in core business functions	I am aware that the use of technology in the services sector needs to be expanded and intensified in order to be able to compete with the use of technology in the manufacturing sector.	I am sure the application of technology and digitisation in core business functions can be implemented quickly.
Enhance the usage of e-payment	I understand that the widespread use of debit and credit cards catalyses e-payment.	I am ready to use e-payment in my daily affairs.
Attract investment in high value-added industries	I understand that investment promotion activities have been restructured to target high value-added industry investors.	I am confident that the attractiveness of high value-added investments can be increased from time to time.

Table 3.A1 (Continued)

Domain 1: Smart economy

Item	Understanding	Acceptance
Create a workforce to match jobs in high value-added industries	I am aware that computer science skills and critical thinking need to be widely disseminated as the high value-added industry sector requires creative and innovative employees.	I am sure the matching of high-income work with high value-added industries can be more efficient.
Provide technology labs and collaborative platforms	I understand that the strengthening and establishment of technology laboratories can help entrepreneurs to become more efficient in penetrating a wider market.	I am confident that the establishment of technology laboratories and collaborative platforms can enhance knowledge exchange in various fields.
Establish incubators and accelerators	I understand that incubators and drivers need to work more closely to meet market needs.	I am sure the creation of incubators and drivers can help realise new ideas to produce more competitive businesses that impact the local community and society.
Leverage existing government assistance and funding	I understand that the assistance provided by various government agencies should be used optimally to improve business operations.	I am confident that the optimal use of facilities provided by the Government can help improve business operations.

Domain 2: Smart living

Item	Understanding	Acceptance
Enhance safety and security through perspectives of crime	I understand the crime rate in Malaysia is still high compared to other countries.	I am sure the installation of analytical proactive surveillance, such as CCTV, can reduce the crime rate in Malaysia.
Promote quality housing	I understand the promotion of the smart home can improve the quality of life.	I believe that the adoption of smart home applications, such as facial recognition systems and IoT lighting, could provide better quality housing.

(Continued)

Table 3.A1 (Continued)

Domain 2: Smart living

Item	Understanding	Acceptance
Optimise emergency response	I understand that an emergency call centre can help in cases of emergency, such as fire.	I believe that the adoption of an emergency call centre with a real-time mobile rescue application is crucial when an emergency occurs.
Enhance the quality of healthcare services	I believe good healthcare can improve the quality of life.	I believe that the Smart City Framework is able to facilitate public health services.
Encourage urban farming for better living	I believe that urban farming activities can enhance the relationship between neighbours and their sense of belonging.	I am confident that through urban farming, a community can work together more closely and appreciate each other.

Domain 3: Smart environment

Item	Understanding	Acceptance
Preserve green areas and enhance the management of trees in public parks	I understand that local authorities have improved the management efficiency of public parks, such as adapting the use of smart management systems to preserve green areas (i.e., the use of RFID technology to inventory existing trees).	I gain positive effects from the use of well-managed public parks and green areas by local authorities, such as increased social interaction, peace of mind, and stress reduction.
Strengthen integrated and sustainable solid waste management	I am aware that waste segregation at source and the recycling of waste are the best solid waste management methods to maintain environmental sustainability.	I always practice waste segregation at source and the recycling of waste items at home and work.
Strengthen the solid waste laws and policies	I am of the view that the government has provided adequate laws and policies to improve solid waste management in the country.	I am confident that the laws and policies formulated by the government can improve the sustainability of the country's solid waste management.

Table 3.A1 (Continued)

Domain 3: Smart environment

Item	Understanding	Acceptance
Improve the air quality and its monitoring system	I am aware of the importance of using public transport as an initiative to reduce carbon emissions that can affect the environmental air quality.	I strive to increase my use of modes of public transportation in day-to-day affairs to help reduce carbon emissions.
Improve the water quality and its monitoring system	I understand that the government has, over time, improved the efficiency of the water monitoring system technology.	I am confident that the improvement of water monitoring system technology in urban areas by the government will provide a high-quality, clean water source for residents.
Increase energy efficiency and promote renewable energy sources	I find that efforts are being made by the government and the private sector to increase the use of renewable energy in the community.	I have applied the use of energy-efficient appliances, such as LED lighting, at home and at work to reduce the use of electricity generated from fossil fuels.
Enhance disaster risk management by adopting advanced technology applications	I understand that the government has implemented disaster risk management through the use of the latest technology, such as warning delivery systems, to facilitate the delivery of information to the public.	I participate in disaster management awareness programs organised at the community level so that I can be better prepared in the event of a disaster.
Enhance Non-Revenue Water Management	I am of the view that public understanding of the importance of non-revenue water management in water resources management has increased.	I immediately make an online report to the agency or responsible party when faced with incidents such as a burst pipe.
Encourage the development of the low-carbon city concept to be adopted at the local level	I understand that the implementation of initiatives to reduce carbon emissions from buildings and vehicles has been implemented in tandem with the urbanisation process.	I believe the development of low-carbon cities by private developers is a positive step towards reducing the carbon footprint of urban areas.

(Continued)

Table 3.A1 (Continued)

Domain 4: Smart people		
Item	Understanding	Acceptance
Improve moral education in schools	I agree that the element of moral education among the younger generation is important as it is an initial step in the formation of an ethical society.	I welcome the government's intention to improve moral education and prioritise it in the early stages of schooling.
Enhance public awareness in practicing good morals and civics	I understand and realise that the concept of a moral and ethical society is an important element in building a smart city culture.	I agree that the building of a smart city community culture can be achieved through civic awareness programs on public facilities, the environment, and the importance of community living.
Increase the volume of skilled and talented human capital at every level	I think that the formation of an educated and highly skilled generation is an important aspect of building a knowledgeable society as part of the construction of smart cities.	I am confident that the restructuring of the education policy at every level in the fields of research, science and technology will produce a generation of highly-educated, skilled and innovative people.
Enhance public participation and community empowerment initiatives	I realise that community participation, community engagement, and community empowerment are highly important in every policy formation of a country and lead to the well-being of the people.	I agree the community needs to be directly involved in the making of every government policy and initiative through a simple and fast digital platform.
Improve gender sensitization and the inclusivity of vulnerable groups	I am aware that the interests and needs of women and people with disabilities (OKU) must be taken into account in every aspect of urban development planning.	I support the idea that facilities are provided in every urban development, which through a digital medium, take into account the needs and safety of all groups, especially women and people with disabilities (OKU).
Increase public willingness to adapt to emerging technologies	I understand that the concept of the smart city formation will be formed from a skilled and efficient society and with the use of IT.	I agree that it is time for digital skills to be learned earlier in childhood and subsequently introduced into continuous learning in the community through digital billboards placed in public spaces.

Table 3.A1 (Continued)

Domain 5: Smart government

Item	Understanding	Acceptance
Increase the scope of e-government services	I understand that through the Smart City Framework, the government can widen the scope of government services to the community.	I believe that through the Smart City Framework, a wider range of government services will be available to the community.
Increase the quality of e-government services	I understand that the use of the Smart City Framework can improve the quality of e-government services.	I believe the Smart City Framework can improve e-government services to the community.
Elevate the use of data sharing platforms across government agencies	I am confident that if inter-governmental data sharing works well, there will be fewer community complaints and better-quality government/ private services.	Through inter-governmental data sharing, I have received valid and accurate data/information from government/ private organisations.
Promote the use of information disclosure and open data on behalf of the government	I understand that the dissemination of open data and authentic information can expedite the transparency of governmental services.	I agree that the accessibility of open data and information dissemination would benefit all.

Domain 6: Smart mobility

Item	Understanding	Acceptance
Establish intelligent transport management	I understand the importance of smart transportation management, such as the use of smart traffic lights, the use of sensors for traffic management, and pollution tracking.	I am satisfied with the way smart transportation management functions, such as with the use of smart traffic lights, the use of sensors for traffic management, and pollution tracking.
Enhance the use of data sharing and digital mobility platforms	I understand the importance of data sharing and digital mobility platforms.	I am willing to use data sharing and digital mobility platforms.
Establish demand-based ridesharing services	I know about on-demand ridesharing service applications for vans or shuttle buses, trains, Grab, or SOCAR.	I use on-demand ridesharing service applications for vans or shuttle buses, trains, Grab, or SOCAR services.

(Continued)

Table 3.A1 (Continued)

Domain 6: Smart mobility

Item	Understanding	Acceptance
Utilize AI and sensor-based predictive maintenance for the public transport fleet and infrastructure	I understand the use of AI (Artificial Intelligence) and sensor-based maintenance forecasting for the public transportation infrastructure and traffic.	I agree that AI and sensor-based forecast maintenance for the public transport infrastructure is required so that forecast maintenance can take place before damage and disruption occurs.
Enhance the dynamic smart parking infrastructure	I know about dynamic smart parking infrastructures, like smart parking meters and apps that provide real-time parking vacancy information.	I use smart parking infrastructure, such as smart parking meters and apps that provide real-time parking vacancy information.
Establish an electric vehicle revolution	I understand the importance and necessity of the electric vehicle revolution.	I have used electric cars/green vehicles/energy-efficient vehicles/electric buses.
Enhance collaboration with academia on R&D into, and the commercialisation of, EVs and next-generation automobile	I understand the importance of collaborating with academics and the private sector in R&D into, and the commercialisation of, next-generation electric vehicles and cars.	I am willing to work with academics and the private sector on the framework, testing, and regulation of autonomous vehicles/long-term transit planning.
Promote the usage of public transport applications	I know about applications regarding travel on public transport services such as buses, trains, or taxis.	I use applications regarding travel on public transport services such as buses, trains or taxis.

Domain 7: Smart digital infrastructure

Item	Understanding	Acceptance
Enhance the roles of service providers in developing digital infrastructure	I am confident that the infrastructure sharing policy among service providers will provide better high-speed internet services.	I understand that the role of completing the communication infrastructure of a new development project is the responsibility of the developer.

Table 3.A1 (Continued)

Domain 7: Smart digital infrastructure

Item	Understanding	Acceptance
Enhance internet speed and connectivity	I know that the government will enforce minimum internet speed standards in stages.	I am aware that most major cities in Malaysia are equipped with 4G high-speed internet facilities.
Enhance the government's role in facilitating the development of communication infrastructure	I understand that the government always assists service providers in facilitating the development of communication infrastructure.	I believe that the Malaysian Commission of Communications and Multimedia (MCMC) should enforce the appropriate standards for network services.
Enhance indoor and outdoor network coverage	I agree that development companies need to equip new development projects with fibre optic lines to support the Smart City policy.	I agree that new buildings are equipped with in-building fibre optic network access facilities.
Strengthen policies related to personal data protection	I am confident that the personal information of internet users is protected by the Personal Protection Act 2010.	I am sure that the reduction of cyber threats will have a positive impact on the government, companies and individuals.
Strengthen policies related to cybersecurity	I understand that online systems and information are safe from cyber-attacks.	I feel that policies and laws related to cybersecurity and personal data need to be updated periodically to protect consumers.

Appendix 3.3B

Table 3.A2 Fuzzy Delphi analysis results

No.	Domain 1: Smart economy (understanding)						Result	Ranking according to the Fuzzy score
	Triangular Fuzzy number		Defuzzification process					
	Threshold (d) value	Expert agreement (%)	m_1	m_2	m_3	Average of Fuzzy score		
1	0.067	88%	0.575	0.775	0.975	0.775	Accepted	1
2	0.107	78%	0.555	0.755	0.955	0.755	Accepted	2
3	0.210	33%	0.455	0.655	0.855	0.655	Rejected	7
4	0.130	78%	0.545	0.745	0.945	0.745	Accepted	3
5	0.193	88%	0.490	0.690	0.890	0.690	Accepted	6
6	0.156	98%	0.515	0.715	0.915	0.715	Accepted	5
7	0.133	73%	0.540	0.740	0.940	0.740	Rejected	4

(*Continued*)

Table 3.A1 (Continued)

No.	Domain 1: Smart economy (acceptance)						Result	Ranking according to the Fuzzy score
	Triangular Fuzzy number		Defuzzification process					
	Threshold (d) value	Expert agreement (%)	m_1	m_2	m_3	Average of Fuzzy score		
1	0.080	88%	0.570	0.770	0.970	0.770	Accepted	1
2	0.130	78%	0.545	0.745	0.945	0.745	Accepted	3
3	0.179	90%	0.510	0.710	0.910	0.710	Accepted	7
4	0.156	98%	0.515	0.715	0.915	0.715	Accepted	4
5	0.158	98%	0.510	0.710	0.910	0.710	Accepted	6
6	0.156	98%	0.515	0.715	0.915	0.715	Accepted	4
7	0.115	75%	0.550	0.750	0.950	0.750	Accepted	2

No.	Domain 2: Smart living (understanding)						Result	Ranking according to the Fuzzy score
	Triangular Fuzzy number		Defuzzification process					
	Threshold (d) value	Expert agreement (%)	m_1	m_2	m_3	Average of Fuzzy score		
1	0.206	35%	0.420	0.620	0.820	0.620	Rejected	5
2	0.101	83%	0.560	0.760	0.960	0.760	Accepted	2
3	0.171	81%	0.41	0.78	0.87	0.687	Accepted	4
4	0.113	83%	0.555	0.755	0.955	0.755	Accepted	3
5	0.069	90%	0.575	0.775	0.975	0.775	Accepted	1

No.	Domain 2: Smart living (acceptance)						Result	Ranking according to the Fuzzy score
	Triangular Fuzzy number		Defuzzification process					
	Threshold (d) value	Expert agreement (%)	m_1	m_2	m_3	Average of Fuzzy score		
1	0.179	90%	0.470	0.670	0.870	0.670	Accepted	5
2	0.183	90%	0.500	0.700	0.900	0.700	Accepted	3
3	0.165	85%	0.492	0.824	0.741	0.686	Accepted	4
4	0.155	95%	0.525	0.725	0.925	0.725	Accepted	1
5	0.172	93%	0.510	0.710	0.910	0.710	Accepted	2

Table 3.A1 (Continued)

No.	Domain 3: Smart environment (understanding)						Result	Ranking according to the Fuzzy score
	Triangular Fuzzy number		Defuzzification process					
	Threshold (d) value	Expert agreement (%)	m_1	m_2	m_3	Average of Fuzzy score		
1	0.242	35%	0.375	0.570	0.770	0.572	Rejected	9
2	0.128	70%	0.540	0.740	0.940	0.740	Rejected	2
3	0.214	35%	0.425	0.625	0.825	0.625	Rejected	5
4	0.122	73%	0.545	0.745	0.945	0.745	Rejected	1
5	0.155	93%	0.530	0.730	0.930	0.730	Accepted	3
6	0.193	90%	0.490	0.690	0.890	0.690	Accepted	4
7	0.244	23%	0.400	0.600	0.800	0.600	Rejected	6
8	0.201	48%	0.390	0.585	0.785	0.587	Rejected	8
9	0.204	45%	0.400	0.590	0.790	0.593	Rejected	7

No.	Domain 3: Smart environment (acceptance)						Result	Ranking according to the Fuzzy score
	Triangular Fuzzy number		Defuzzification process					
	Threshold (d) value	Expert agreement (%)	m_1	m_2	m_3	Average of Fuzzy score		
1	0.174	50%	0.425	0.625	0.825	0.625	Rejected	6
2	0.233	33%	0.395	0.590	0.790	0.592	Rejected	7
3	0.219	35%	0.445	0.640	0.840	0.642	Rejected	4
4	0.260	38%	0.380	0.570	0.770	0.573	Rejected	8
5	0.189	88%	0.505	0.705	0.905	0.705	Accepted	2
6	0.181	90%	0.505	0.705	0.905	0.705	Accepted	2
7	0.256	38%	0.360	0.555	0.755	0.557	Rejected	9
8	0.246	30%	0.435	0.630	0.830	0.632	Rejected	5
9	0.153	98%	0.520	0.720	0.920	0.720	Accepted	1

(Continued)

Table 3.A1 (Continued)

No.	Domain 4: Smart people (understanding)						Result	Ranking according to the Fuzzy score
	Triangular Fuzzy number		Defuzzification process					
	Threshold (d) value	Expert agreement (%)	m_1	m_2	m_3	Average of Fuzzy score		
1	0.088	83%	0.565	0.765	0.965	0.765	Accepted	1
2	0.107	78%	0.555	0.755	0.955	0.755	Accepted	2
3	0.133	73%	0.540	0.740	0.940	0.740	Rejected	5
4	0.122	73%	0.545	0.745	0.945	0.745	Rejected	4
5	0.122	80%	0.550	0.750	0.950	0.750	Accepted	3
6	0.169	93%	0.515	0.715	0.915	0.715	Accepted	6

No.	Domain 4: Smart people (acceptance)						Result	Ranking according to the Fuzzy score
	Triangular Fuzzy number		Defuzzification process					
	Threshold (d) value	Expert agreement (%)	m_1	m_2	m_3	Average of Fuzzy score		
1	0.110	80%	0.555	0.755	0.955	0.755	Accepted	2
2	0.080	88%	0.570	0.770	0.970	0.770	Accepted	1
3	0.128	70%	0.540	0.740	0.940	0.740	Rejected	3
4	0.133	73%	0.540	0.740	0.940	0.740	Rejected	3
5	0.150	95%	0.530	0.730	0.930	0.730	Accepted	5
6	0.165	93%	0.520	0.720	0.920	0.720	Accepted	6

No.	Domain 5: Smart government (understanding)						Result	Ranking according to the Fuzzy score
	Triangular Fuzzy number		Defuzzification process					
	Threshold (d) value	Expert agreement (%)	m_1	m_2	m_3	Average of Fuzzy score		
1	0.182	95%	0.505	0.700	0.900	0.702	Accepted	2
2	0.192	90%	0.495	0.695	0.895	0.695	Accepted	3
3	0.224	88%	0.500	0.690	0.890	0.693	Rejected	4
4	0.155	95%	0.525	0.725	0.925	0.725	Accepted	1

Table 3.A1 (Continued)

No.	Domain 5: Smart government (acceptance)						Result	Ranking according to the Fuzzy score
	Triangular Fuzzy number		Defuzzification process					
	Threshold (d) value	Expert agreement (%)	m_1	m_2	m_3	Average of Fuzzy score		
1	0.176	95%	0.495	0.695	0.895	0.695	Accepted	3
2	0.169	93%	0.515	0.715	0.915	0.715	Accepted	1
3	0.202	85%	0.480	0.680	0.880	0.680	Rejected	4
4	0.191	90%	0.500	0.700	0.900	0.700	Accepted	2

No.	Domain 6: Smart mobility (understanding)						Result	Ranking according to the Fuzzy score
	Triangular Fuzzy number		Defuzzification process					
	Threshold (d) value	Expert agreement (%)	m_1	m_2	m_3	Average of Fuzzy score		
1	0.137	75%	0.540	0.740	0.940	0.740	Accepted	3
2	0.130	78%	0.545	0.745	0.945	0.745	Accepted	2
3	0.113	83%	0.555	0.755	0.955	0.755	Accepted	1
4	0.209	85%	0.495	0.695	0.895	0.695	Rejected	7
5	0.147	80%	0.540	0.740	0.940	0.740	Accepted	3
6	0.220	85%	0.485	0.685	0.885	0.685	Rejected	8
7	0.175	90%	0.515	0.715	0.915	0.715	Accepted	6
8	0.177	90%	0.520	0.720	0.920	0.720	Accepted	5

No.	Domain 6: Smart mobility (acceptance)						Result	Ranking according to the Fuzzy score
	Triangular Fuzzy number		Defuzzification process					
	Threshold (d) value	Expert agreement (%)	m_1	m_2	m_3	Average of Fuzzy score		
1	0.311	20%	0.390	0.590	0.790	0.590	Rejected	7
2	0.184	90%	0.485	0.685	0.885	0.685	Accepted	4
3	0.227	80%	0.490	0.690	0.890	0.690	Rejected	3
4	0.176	93%	0.500	0.700	0.900	0.700	Accepted	1
5	0.245	25%	0.465	0.660	0.860	0.662	Rejected	5
6	0.346	25%	0.380	0.555	0.755	0.563	Rejected	8
7	0.200	93%	0.495	0.690	0.890	0.692	Accepted	2
8	0.273	20%	0.460	0.650	0.850	0.653	Rejected	6

(Continued)

(Continued)

No.	Domain 7: Smart digital infrastructure (understanding)						Result	Ranking according to the Fuzzy score
	Triangular Fuzzy number		Defuzzification process					
	Threshold (d) value	Expert agreement (%)	m_1	m_2	m_3	Average of Fuzzy score		
1	0.165	95%	0.530	0.725	0.925	0.727	Accepted	2
2	0.217	85%	0.495	0.690	0.890	0.692	Accepted	3
3	0.191	93%	0.485	0.680	0.880	0.682	Accepted	4
4	0.144	73%	0.535	0.735	0.935	0.735	Rejected	1
5	0.214	30%	0.460	0.660	0.860	0.660	Rejected	5
6	0.291	58%	0.330	0.520	0.720	0.523	Rejected	6

No.	Domain 7: Smart digital infrastructure (acceptance)						Result	Ranking according to the Fuzzy score
	Triangular Fuzzy number		Defuzzification process					
	Threshold (d) value	Expert agreement (%)	m_1	m_2	m_3	Average of Fuzzy score		
1	0.221	33%	0.455	0.655	0.855	0.655	Rejected	6
2	0.202	90%	0.490	0.690	0.890	0.690	Rejected	5
3	0.110	80%	0.555	0.755	0.955	0.755	Accepted	2
4	0.101	83%	0.560	0.760	0.960	0.760	Accepted	1
5	0.134	80%	0.545	0.745	0.945	0.745	Accepted	3
6	0.134	80%	0.545	0.745	0.945	0.745	Accepted	3

Note: Three conditions to accept an item: threshold value $(d) \leq 0.2$, percentage of experts' consensus $\geq$ 75%, and average fuzzy score $(A_{max}) \geq \alpha - $ cut value = 0.5.

References

1. De Souza, K.C., Hunter, M., Jacob, B., Yigitcanlar, T. (2020). Pathways to the making of prosperous smart cities: An exploratory study on the best practice. *Journal of Urban Technology* 27, 3–32,
2. Giffinger, R., Fertner, C., Kramar, H., Kalasek, R., Pichler, N., Meijers, E. (2007). *Smart Cities: Ranking of European Medium-Sized Cities*. TU Vienna: Wien, Austria.
3. Cohen, B. (2012). *What Exactly Is a Smart City?* Available online: www.fastcodesign.com/1680538/what-exactly-is-a-smart-city (accessed 8 August 2017).
4. Chourabi, H., Nam, T., Walker, S., Gil-Garcia, J.R., Mellouli, S., Nahon, K., Pardo, T.A., Scholl, H.J. (2012). *Understanding Smart Cities: An Integrative Framework*. In: Proceedings of the 45th Hawaii International Conference on System Sciences Understanding (ICSS), Maui, HI, USA, 4–7 January 2012; IEEE: Piscataway, NJ, USA, pp. 2289–2297.

5.   Alonso, R.G., Castro, S.L. (2016). Technology helps, people make: A smart city governance framework grounded in deliberative de-mocracy. In: *Smarter as the New Urban Agenda; A Comprehensive View of the 21st Century City*. Gil-Garcia, J.R., Pardo, T.A., Nam, T., (Eds.). Springer: Cham, Switzerland, pp. 333–347.

6.   Mosannenzadeh, F., Vettorato, D. (2014). Defining smart city. A conceptual framework based on keyword analysis. *TeMA Journal of Land Use, Mobility and Environment* 6, 683–694.

7.   Anthopoulos, L., Janssen, M., Weerakkody, V. (2016). A unified smart city model (USCM) for smart city conceptualization and benchmarking. *International Journal of Electronic Government Research* 12, 77–93.

8.   Hong Kong. (2020). *Hong Kong Smart City Blueprint*. Available online: www.smartc ity.gov.hk/doc/HongKongSmartCityBlueprint(EN).pdf (accessed 2 February 2020).

9.   Ministry of Housing and Local Government. (2019). *Malaysia Smart City Framework*. Ministry of Housing and Local Government: Putrajaya, Malaysia.

10.   Lombardi, P., Giordano, S., Farouh, H., Yousef, W. (2012). Modelling the smart city performance. *Innovation: The European Journal of Social Science Research* 25, 137–149.

11.   Tahir, Z., Malek, J.A. (2016). Main criteria in the development of smart cities determined using analytical method. *Planning Malaysia* 14, 1–14.

12.   Yasmin, M.A., Hasniyati, H., Melasutra, M.D., Md Nasir, D., Anuar, A. (2016). An initiatives-based framework for assessing smart city. *Planning Malaysia* 14, 13–22.

13.   Li, C., Dai, Z., Liu, X., Sun, W. (2020). Evaluation system: Evaluation of smart city shareable framework and its applications in China. *Sustainability* 12, 2957.

14.   Aghimien, D.O., Aigbavboa, C., Edwards, D.J., Mahamadu, A.-M., Olomolaiye, P., Nash, H., Onyia, M. (2020). A fuzzy synthetic evaluation of the challenges of smart city development in developing countries. *Smart and Sustainable Built Environment* 11(3), 405–421.

15.   Sharifi, A. (2020). A typology of smart city assessment tools and indicator sets. *Sustainable Cities and Society* 53, 101936,

16.   Institute for Management Development (IMD). (2019). *Smart City Index*. Institute for Management Development and Singapore University of Technology and Design: Singapore.

17.   OECD. (2020). *Measuring Smart Cities' Performance: Do Smart Cities Benefit Everyone?* Organisation for Economic Co-operation and Development: Paris, France.

18.   Caird, S.P., Hallett, S.H. (2019). Towards evaluation design for smart city development. *Journal of Urban Design* 24, 188–209,

19.   Lim, S.B., Malek, J.A., Hashim, N. (2021). Implementing the smart city concept in Malaysia: Contemporary challenges, strategies and opportunities in the COVID-19 era. *Malaysian Townplan Journal* 1–20.

20.   Vinod Kumar, T.M., Dahiya, B. (2017). Smart economy in smart cities. In: *Smart Economy in Smart Cities, Advances in 21st Century Human Settlements*. Vinod Kumar, T.M., (Ed.). Springer: Singapore, pp. 3–76.

21.   Deng, T., Zhang, K., Shen, Z.J. (2021). A systematic review of a digital twin city: A new pattern of urban governance toward smart cities. *Journal of Management Science and Engineering* 6, 125–134,

22.   Yigitcanlar, T., Cugurullo, F. (2020). The sustainability of artificial intelligence: An urbanistic viewpoint from the lens of smart and sustainable cities. *Sustainability* 12, 8548.

23.   British High Commission Kuala Lumpur. (2021). *Smart City Handbook Malaysia: How Technology and Data Are Shaping the Future of Malaysian Cities*. British High Commission Kuala Lumpur: Kuala Lumpur, Malaysia, 2021.

24. Centre for Liveable Cities. (2018). *ASEAN Smart Cities Network*. Centre for Liveable Cities: Singapore.

25. Low, S., Ullah, F., Shirowzhan, S., Sepasgozar, S.M.E., Lee, C.L. (2020). Smart digital marketing capabilities for sustainable property development: A case of Malaysia. *Sustainability* 12, 5402.

26. Hasibuan, A., Sulaiman, O.K. (2019). Smart city, konsep kota cerdas sebagai alternatif penyelesaian masalah perkotaan kabupat-en/kota. *Bul. Utama Tek.* 2019, 14, 127–135.

27. Oxford Business Group. (2021) *Going Strong: The Shift toward Higher-Value-Added Activities Is Creating New Challenges as well as Prospects.* Available online: https://oxfordbusinessgroup.com/overview/going-strong-shift-toward-higher-value-added-activities-creating-new-challenges-well-prospects (accessed 27 July 2021).

28. Rana, N.P., Luthra, S., Mangla, S.K., Islam, R., Roderick, S., Dwivedi, Y.K. (2019). Barriers to the development of smart cities in Indian context. *Information Systems Frontiers* 21, 503–525.

29. Firmansyah, H.S., Supangkat, S.H., Arman, A.A. (2015). Studi tentang model pengembangan kota cerdas. In: *Proceedings of the e-Indonesia Initiatives (eII-Forum)*, Bandung, Indonesia, 15–16 October 2015. Institut Teknologi Bandung: Bandung, Indonesia, pp. 42–47.

30. Eden Strategy Institute. (2018). *Top 50 Smart City Governments*. Eden Strategy Institute and Ong&Ong Pte Ltd: Singapore.

31. Diez, T. (2012). Personal fabrication: Fab labs as platforms for citizen-based innovation, from microcontrollers to cities. *Nexus Network Journal* 14, 457–468.

32. Monzon, A. (2015). Smart cities concept and challenges: Bases for the assessment of smart city projects. In: *Smartgreens 2015 and Vehits 2015, Communications in Computer and Information Science 579*; Helfert, M., Krempels, K.H., Klein, C., Donellan, B., Guiskhin, O., (Eds.). Springer: Cham, Switzerland, pp. 17–31.

33. Katz, B., Wagner, J. (2014). *The Rise of Innovation Districts: A New Geography of Innovation in America*. Brookings Metropolitan Policy Program: Washington, DC, USA.

34. BEA. (2021). *What Is Industry Value Added? Bureau of Economic Analysis, US Department of Commerce.* Available online: www.bea.gov/faq/index.cfm?faq_id=1842006 (accessed 24 July 2021).

35. Govada, S.S., Spruijt, W., Rodgers, T. (2017). Introduction to Hong Kong's development. In: *Smart Economy in Smart Cities*; Vinod Kumar, T.M., Dahiya, B., (Eds.). Springer: Singapore, pp. 171–186.

36. Lim, S.B., Yong, C.K., Malek, J.A., Jali, M.F.M., Awang, A.H., Tahir, Z. (2020). Effectiveness of fear and crime prevention strategy for sustainability of safe city. *Sustainability* 12, 10593.

37. Alkawsi, G.A., Ali, N., Mustafa, A.S., Baashar, Y., Alhussian, H., Alkahtani, A., Tiong, S.K., Ekanayake, J. (2021). A hybrid SEM-neural network method for identifying acceptance factors of the smart meters in Malaysia: Challenges perspective. *Alexandria Engineering Journal* 60, 227–240.

38. Hollands, R.G. (2016). Beyond the corporate smart city? Glimpses of other possibilities of smartness. In: *Smart Urbanism: Utopian Vision or False Dawn?* Marvin, S., Luque-Ayala, A., McFarlane, C., (Eds.). Routledge: London, UK, pp. 168–184.

39. Anttiroiko, A.-V. (2021). Successful government responses to the pandemic: Contextualizing national and urban responses to the COVID-19 outbreak in East and West. *International Journal of E-Planning Research* 10, 1–17.

40. Choi, C., Choi, J., Kim, C., Lee, D., Baek, U., Sim, Y. (2020). The smart city evolution in South Korea: Findings from big data analytics. *Journal of Asian Finance, Economics and Business* 7, 301–311.

41. Kashif, M., Samsi, S.Z.M., Awang, Z., Mohamad, M. (2016). EXQ: Measurement of healthcare experience quality in Malaysian settings. A contextualist perspective. *International Journal of Pharmacetical and Healthcare Marketing* 10, 27–47.

42. Petrova-Antonova, D., Ilieva, S. (2018). Smart cities evaluation—A survey of performance and sustainability indicators. In: *Proceedings of the 44th Euromicro Conference on Software Engineering and Advanced Application* (SEAA), Prague, Czech Republic, 29–31 August 2018; IEEE: Piscataway, NJ, USA, pp. 486–493.

43. Yigitcanlar, T., De Souza, K., Butler, L., Roozkhosh, F. (2020). Contributions and risks of artificial intelligence (AI) in building smarter cities: Insights from a systematic review of the literature. *Energies* 13, 1473.

44. Smart Selangor Delivery Unit (SSDU). (2020). *Smart Selangor Action Plan to 2025 (SSAP 2025)*. Menteri Besar Selangor Inc.: Shah Alam, Malaysia.

45. PLANMalaysia. (2010a). *Bandar Selamat 2010*. PLANMalaysia (Jabatan Perancangan Bandar dan Desa): Kuala Lumpur, Malaysia.

46. PLANMalaysia. (2010b). *Reka Bentuk Bandar Selamat: Panduan Pelaksanaan. Crime Prevention through Environmental Design (CPTED) Implementation Guide.* PLANMalaysia (Jabatan Perancangan Bandar dan Desa): Kuala Lumpur, Malaysia.

47. Lim, S.B., Yong, C.K., Rashid, M.F.A., Malek, J.A. (2020). A framework of challenges facing the safe city programme in Kuala Lumpur. *Planning Malaysia* 18, 47–61.

48. Tan-Mullins, M., Cheshmehzangi, A., Chien, S.-S., Xie, L. (2017). *Smart-Eco Cities in China: Trends and City Profiles 2016*. University of Exeter (SMART-ECO Project): Exerter, UK.

49. Valencia, S.C., Simon, D., Croese, S., Nordqvist, J., Oloko, M., Sharma, T., Buck, N.T., Versace, I. Adapting the Sustainable Development Goals and the New Urban Agenda to the city level: Initial reflections from a comparative research project. *International Journal of Urban Sustainable Development* 11, 4–23.

50. Kundu, D., Sietchiping, R., Kinyanjui, M. (Eds.) (2020). *Developing National Urban Policies: Ways Forward to Green and Smart Cities*. Springer: Singapore.

51. Yigitcanlar, T., Butler, L., Windle, E., DeSouza, K., Mehmood, R., Corchado, J. (2020). Can building "artificially intelligent cities" safeguard humanity from natural disasters, pandemics, and other catastrophes? An urban scholar's perspective. *Sensors* 20, 2988.

52. UN-Habitat. (2020). *World Cities Report 2020: The Value of Sustainable Urbanization*. United Nations Human Settlements Programme: Nairobi, Kenya.

53. Connolly, C. (2019). From resilience to multi-species flourishing: (Re)imagining urban-environmental governance in Penang, Malaysia. *Urban Studies* 57, 1485–1501.

54. Fong, V. (2018). *Smart Selangor Blueprint: Selangor Smart Cities?* Available online: www.smartcitiesasia.com/blueprint-smart-city-selangor/ (accessed 1 February 2018).

55. Yigitcanlar, T., Teriman, S. (2015). Rethinking sustainable urban development: Towards an integrated planning and development process. *International Journal of Environmental Science and Technology* 12, 341–352.

56. Qureshi, F. (2001). In: *Malaysia, the Fate of a Peat Forest Relies on a Powerful State Official*. Available online: www.eco-business.com/news/in-malaysia-the-fate-of-a-peat-forest-relies-on-a-powerful-state-official/ (accessed 25 July 2021).

57. Abdullah, M.Y.H., Pawanteh, L., Abdullah, S.M.S., Mustaffa, N. (2010). Kesedaran dan sikap komuniti dalam pengurusan perseki-taran di Wilayah Iskandar. *Jurnal Melayu.* 5, 71–86.
58. Hare, R.M. (2002). A philosophical autobiography. *Utilitas* 14, 269–305.
59. Borhannuddin, M.S. (2015). Ungku Aziz's perspective on "development". *Turkish Journal of Islamic Economics* 2, 1–15.
60. Tegos, S. (2021). Civility and politeness in early modern thought. In; *Encyclopedia of Early Modern Philosophy and the Sciences*; Jalobeanu, D., Wolfe, C.T., (Eds.). Springer: Cham, Switzerland, pp. 1–8.
61. Arnstein, S.R. (1969). A ladder of citizen participation. *Journal of the American Institute of Planners* 35, 216–224.
62. Malek, J.A., Lim, S.B., Yigitcanlar, T. (2021). Social inclusion indicators for building citizen-centric smart cities: A systematic literature review. *Sustainability* 13, 376.
63. Rotta, M.J.R., Sell, D., dos Santos Pacheco, R.C., Yigitcanlar, T. (2019). Digital commons and citizen coproduction in smart cities: Assessment of Brazilian municipal e-government platforms. *Energies* 12, 2813.
64. United Nations (UN). (2020). *E-Government Survey 2020.* Department of Economic and Social Affairs, United Nations: New York, NY, USA.
65. Yigitcanlar, T., Kankanamge, N., Vella, K. (2021). How are smart city concepts and technologies perceived and utilized? A systematic geo-Twitter analysis of smart cities in Australia. *Journal of Urban Technology* 28, 135–154.
66. Bedi, R.S. (2021). *Malaysia Embarks on Digitalisation Journey with National 4IR Policy Launch.* Available online: www.thestar.com.my/news/nation/2021/07/01/malaysia-embarks-on-digitalisation-journey-with-national-4ir-policy-launch (accessed 26 July 2021).
67. Economic Planning Unit. (2021). *National Fourth Industrial Revolution (4IR) Policy.* Economic Planning Unit, Prime Minister's Department: Putrajaya, Malaysia.
68. Caragliu, A., del Bo, C.F., Nijkamp, P. (2011). Smart cities in Europe. *Journal of Urban Technology* 18, 65–82.
69. Lim, S.B., Malek, J.A., Hussain, M.Y., Tahir, Z., Saman, N.H.M. (2021). SDGs, smart urbanisation, and politics: Stakeholder partner-ships and environmental cases in Malaysia. *Journal of Sustainability Science and Management* 16, 190–219.
70. Meijer, A., Bolívar, M.P.R. (2016). Governing the smart city: A review of the literature on smart urban governance. *International Review of Administrative. Sciences* 82, 392–408.
71. Vinod Kumar, T.M. (Ed.) (2015). E-governance for smart cities. In: *E-Governance for Smart Cities, Advances in 21st Century Human Settlements.* Springer: Singapore, pp. 1–46.
72. Johnson, P.A., Acedo, A., Robinson, P.J. (2020). Canadian smart cities: Are we wiring new citizen–local government interactions? *Canadian Geographer* 64, 402–415.
73. Lim, S.B., Malek, J.A., Hussain, M.Y., Tahir, Z. (2020). Participation in e-government services and smart city programs: A case study of Malaysian local authority. *Planning Malaysia* 18, 300–312.
74. Meijer, A. (2018). Datapolis: A public governance perspective on "smart cities." *Perspectives on Public Management and Governance* 1, 195–206.
75. Urban Tide. (2014). *Overview of the Smart Cities Maturity Model: Joining the Dots of Smart Cities.* Urban Tide and Scottish Government: Edinburgh, Scotland.
76. Komninos, N., Kakderi, C., Panori, A., Tsarchopoulos, P. (2019). Smart city planning from an evolutionary perspective. *Journal of Urban Technology* 26, 3–20.

77. Purwanto, A., Zuiderwijk, A., Janssen, M. (2020). Citizen engagement with open government data: A systematic literature review of drivers and inhibitors. *International Journal of Electronic Government Research* 16, 1–25.
78. Yigitcanlar, T., Han, H., Kamruzzaman, M., Ioppolo, G., Sabatini-Marques, J. (2019). The making of smart cities: Are Songdo, Masdar, Amsterdam, San Francisco and Brisbane the best we could build? *Land Use Policy* 88, 104187.
79. Yigitcanlar, T. (2018). Smart city policies revisited: Considerations for a truly smart and sustainable urbanism practice. *World Technopolis Review* 7, 97–112.
80. Thestar. (2021) *Smart City Players Working in Silos Hindering Development as a Whole, Says Dr M*. Available online: www.thestar.com.my/news/nation/2019/09/23/ smart-city-players-working-in-silos-hindering-development-as-a-whole-says-dr-m (accessed 2 February 2021).
81. Idrus, N.A., Ismail, S., Sanusi, F.A. (2019). Delays in Malaysian government projects: Learning from project management failure. *Jurutera* 10, 13–19.
82. Ramli, H. (2021). *Birokrasi Jejas Sistem Penyampaian*. Available online: www.mef. org.my/MEFITN/utusan070209a.pdf (accessed 20 July 2021).
83. Trombin, M., Pinna, R., Musso, M., Magnaghi, E., De Marco, M. (2020). Mobility management: From traditional to people-centric approach in the smart city. In: *Emerging Technologies for Connected Internet of Vehicles and Intelligent Transportation System Networks, Studies in Systems, Decision and Control*; Elhoseny, M., Hassanien, E., (Eds.). Springer: Cham, Switzerland, pp. 165–182.
84. Yigitcanlar, T., Kamruzzaman, M. (2019). Smart cities and mobility: Does the smartness of Australian cities lead to sustainable commuting patterns? *Journal of Urban Technology* 26, 21–46.
85. Asirvatham, D., Brohi, S.N., Xion, T.E., Theng, T.G., Fei, N.J., Kaur, S., Pillai, T.R., Sukumaran, S., Yue, W.S., Wei, G., et al. (2018). *Smart Mobility Cities: Connecting Bristol and Kuala Lumpur Project Report*. University of Bristol: Bristol, UK.
86. D'Amico, G., L'Abbate, P., Liao, W., Yigitcanlar, T., Ioppolo, G. (2020). Understanding sensor cities: Insights from technology giant company driven smart urbanism practices. *Sensors* 20, 4391.
87. Walker, A. (2020). *Safe Streets Are the Best Tool We Have to Combat Climate Change and We Need to Act Now*. Available online: www.curbed.com/2018/10/10/17957532/ climate-change-street-design-vision-zero (accessed 14 March 2020).
88. NYC Mayor's Office. (2015) *Building a Smart + Equitable City*. NYC Mayor's Office of Tech + Innovation: New York, NY, USA.
89. Sarkar, A. (2021) *Smart Cities: A Futuristic Vision*. Available online: www.thesmartcity journal.com/en/articles/1333-smart-cities-futuristic-vision (accessed 26 July 2021).
90. Frost and Sullivan. (2021). *Smart Cities—Frost & Sullivan Value Proposition*. Available online: www.frost.com/wp-content/uploads/2019/01/SmartCities.pdf (accessed 5 August 2021).
91. Dirks, S., Keeling, M. (2009). *A Vision of Smarter Cities: How Cities Can Lead Way into a Prosperous and Sustainable Future*. International Business Machines Corporation: New York, NY, USA.
92. Praharaj, S., Han, J.H., Hawken, S. (2017). Innovative civic engagement and digital urban infrastructure: Lessons from 100 smart cities mission in India. *Procedia Engineering* 180, 1423–1432.
93. Castelnovo, W., Misuraca, G., Savoldelli, A. (2016). Smart cities governance: The need for a holistic approach to assessing urban participatory policy making. *Social Science Computer Review* 34, 724–739.

94. Wilson, B., Chakraborty, A. (2019). Planning smart(er) cities: The promise of civic technology. *Journal of Urban Technology* 26, 29–51.
95. Caprotti, F., Springer, C., Harmer, N. (2015). 'Eco' for whom? Envisioning eco-urbanism in the Sino-Singapore Tianjin Eco-city, China. *International Journal of Urban and Regional Research* 39, 495–517.
96. Breuer, J., Pierson, J. (2021). The right to the city and data protection: Complementary for developing citizen-centric digital cities. *Information Communication and Society* 24, 797–812.
97. Gjermundrød, H., Dionysiou, I. (2015). A conceptual framework for configurable privacy-awareness in a citizen-centric eGovernment. *International Journal of Electronic Governance* 11, 258.
98. Banisar, D. (2011). *The Right to Information and Privacy: Balancing Rights and Managing Conflicts*. The World Bank: Washington, DC, USA.
99. Nautiyal, L., Malik, P., Agarwal, A. (2018). Cybersecurity system: An essential pillar of smart cities. In: *Smart Cities, Computer Communications and Networks*; Mahmood, Z., (Ed.). Springer: Cham, Switzerland, pp. 25–50.
100. Goodwin, C.F., Nicholas, J.P. (2014). *Developing a City Strategy for Cybersecurity: A Seven-Step Guide for Local Governments*. Microsoft: Washington, DC, USA.
101. Ma, H.D. (2011). Internet of Things: Objectives and scientific challenges. *Journal of Computer Science and Technology* 26, 919–924.
102. Nick, G. (2021). *How Many IoT Devices Are There in 2021?* Available online: https://techjury.net/blog/how-many-iot-devices-are-there/#gref (accessed 27 July 2021).
103. Devanesan, J. (2021). *Cybersecurity Is Top Concern, as Online Threats Mount in Malaysia by 82.5%*. Available online: https://techwireasia.com/2020/04/cybersecurity-is-top-concern-as-online-threats-mount-in-malaysia-by-82-5/ (accessed 27 July 2021).
104. Yun, T.Z. (2021). *Moving beyond Awareness to Adoption of IoT*. Available online: www.theedgemarkets.com/article/cover-story-moving-beyond-awareness-adoption-iot (accessed 27 July 2021).
105. Jones, H., Twiss, B.L. (1978). *Forecasting Technology for Planning Decisions*. Macmillan: New York, NY, USA.
106. Jamil, M.R.M., Noh, N.M. (2020). *Kepelbagaian Metodologi Dalam Penyelidikan: Rekab Bentuk dan Pembangunan*. Qaisar Prestige Resources: Shah Alam, Malaysia.
107. Embong, A.R. (2002). *State-Led Modernization and the New Middle Class in Malaysia*. Palgrave: New York, NY, USA.
108. Dalkey, N., Helmer, O. (1963). An experimental application of the DELPHI method to the use of experts. *Management Science* 9, 458–467.
109. Lateh, N., Yaacob, S.E., Md Rejab, S.N. (2017). Applying the fuzzy delphi method (FDM) to analyze the expert consensus values for instrument of shariah-compliant gold investment. *Pertanika Journal of Social Sciences and Humanities* 25, 165–178.
110. Ulschak, F. (1983). *Human Resource Development: The Theory and Practice of Need Assessment*. Reston Publishing Company: Reston, VA, USA.
111. Grime, M.M., Wright, G. (2016). Delphi method. In: *Wiley StatsRef Statistics Reference Online*. Balakrishnan, N., Colton, T., Everitt, B., Piegorsch, W., Ruggeri, F., Teugels, J.L., (Eds.). Wiley: Hoboken, NJ, USA, pp. 1–6.
112. Cheng, C.-H., Lin, Y. (2002) Evaluating the best main battle tank using fuzzy decision theory with linguistic criteria evaluation. *European Journal of Operational Research* 142, 174–186.

113. Chu, H.-C., Hwang, G.-J. (2008). A Delphi-based approach to developing expert systems with the cooperation of multiple experts. Expert Systems with Applications 34, 2826–2840.
114. Murry, J.W., Hammons, J.O. (1995). Delphi: A versatile methodology for conducting qualitative research. Research in Higher Education 18, 423–436.
115. Tang, C.-W., Wu, C.-T. (2010). Obtaining a picture of undergraduate education quality: A voice from inside the university. *Higher Education* 60, 269–286.
116. Esmaeilpoorarabi, N., Yigitcanlar, T., Guaralda, M., Kamruzzaman, M. (2018). Evaluating place quality in innovation districts: A Delphic hierarchy process approach. *Land Use Policy* 76, 471–486.
117. Perveen, S., Kamruzzaman, M., Yigitcanlar, T. (0107). Developing policy scenarios for sustainable urban growth management: A Delphi approach. *Sustainability* 9, 1787.
118. Sulaiman, H.F., Ismail, R., Yusoff, H.M., Anuar, N., Jamil, M.R.M., Daud, F. Validation of occupational zoonotic disease questionnaire using fuzzy Delphi method. *Journal of Agromedicine* 25, 166–172.
119. Drabble, J. (2021). *The Economic History of Malaysia*. Available online: http://eh.net/encyclopedia/economic-history-of-malaysia/ (accessed 24 July 2021).
120. Mat Arisah, F., Zainal Badari, S.A., Hashim, A.H. (2016). Amalan pembelian secara atas talian dan faktor-faktor mempengaruhi. Malaysian *Journal of the Society of Science and Humanities* 1, 111–123.
121. Lim, S.B., Malek, J.A., Kong, Y.C., Tahir, Z., Hernowo, B. (2021). Lessons from differences in the global and local discourse views on the safe city status of Kuala Lumpur, Malaysia. *Geografia-Malaysian Journal of Society and Space* 17, 143–158.
122. Malek, J.A., Lim, S.B., Tahir, Z. (2019). Understanding the issues of citizen participation. *Journal of Nusant. Studies* 4, 1–22.
123. Aziz, S.A. (2016). Maqasid Al-Syariah dalam perlembagaan persekutuan: Suatu perbahasan awal. *Kanun Journal of Undang. Malaysia* 28, 278–312.
124. Lim, S.B., Malek, J.A., Mohd Yusof, H., Tahir, Z. (2021). Malaysia Smart City Framework: A trusted framework for shaping smart Malaysian citizenship? In: *Handbook of Smart Cities*; Augusto, J.C., (Ed.). Springer, Cham, Switzerland, pp. 515–538.
125. Economist Intelligence Unit (EIU). (2020). *Democracy Index 2020: In Sickness and in Health?* Economist Intelligence Unit: London, UK.
126. Araya, D. (Ed.) (2015). *Smart Cities as Democratic Ecologies*. Palgrave Macmillan: New York, NY, USA; London, UK.
127. Lim, S., Malek, J., Yigitcanlar, T. (2021). Post-materialist values of smart city societies: International comparison of public values for good enough governance. *Future Internet* 13, 201.
128. Majid, N.A. (2021). *150 Electric Buses for Putrajaya by 2025*. Available online: www.nst.com.my/news/nation/2017/10/290305/150-electric-buses-putrajaya-2025 (accessed 25 July 2021).
129. Teoh, L.E., Khoo, H.L., Goh, S.Y., Chong, L.M. (2018). Scenario-based electric bus operation: A case study of Putrajaya, Malaysia. *International Journal of Transportation Science and Technology* 7, 10–25.
130. Alias, W.N.H.W. (2017). *Bas Awam Putrajaya Tersadai, "Merangkak"*. Available online: www.bharian.com.my/berita/nasional/2018/08/460658/bas-awam-putrajaya-tersadai-merangkak (accessed 25 July 2017).

131. Mustapa, S., Ayodele, B., Ishak, W.M., Ayodele, F. (2020). Evaluation of cost competitiveness of electric vehicles in Malaysia using life cycle cost analysis approach. *Sustainability* 12, 5303.
132. MITI. (2020). *National Automotive Policy 2020.* Ministry of International Trade and Industry: Putrajaya, Malaysia.
133. Culpan, T. (2021). *A Quiet Leader: Why Malaysia Ranks High in Global List of Cybersecurity.* Available online: www.business-standard.com/article/international/malaysia-among-top-ten-countries-in-cybersecurity-due-to-global-cooperation-121070200403_1.html (accessed 27 July 2021).
134. MCMC. (2020). *National Digital Infrastructure Lab (NDIL). Report 3 September 2020.* Malaysian Communications and Multimedia Commission: Putrajaya, Malaysia.
135. Yigitcanlar, T., Sarimin, M. (2015). Multimedia super corridor, Malaysia: Knowledge-based urban development lessons from an emerging economy. *Vine* 45, 126–147.
136. Yigitcanlar, T., Sarimin, M. (2011). The role of universities in building prosperous knowledge cities: The Malaysian experience. *Built Environment* 37, 260–280.
137. Yigitcanlar, T., Dur, F. (2013). Making space and place for knowledge communities: Lessons for Australian practice. *Australasian Journal of Regional Studies* 19, 36–63.
138. Perveen, S., Kamruzzaman, M., Yigitcanlar, T. (2019). What to assess to model the transport impacts of urban growth? A Delphi approach to examine the space–time suitability of transport indicators. *International Journal of Sustainable Transportation* 13, 597–613, https://doi.org/10.1080/15568318.2018.1491077
139. Siokas, G., Tsakanikas, A., Siokas, E. (2021). Implementing smart city strategies in Greece: Appetite for success. *Cities* 108, 102938.
140. Lim, S., Malek, J., Yussoff, M., Yigitcanlar, T. (2021). Understanding and acceptance of smart city policies: Practitioners' perspectives on the Malaysian smart city framework. *Sustainability*, 13(17), 9559.

4 Development Pathways

4.1 Introduction

Cities continue to invest significant resources in information and communication technologies (ICT) that increase their "smartness" and "intelligence" (Cosgrave et al., 2013; Angelidou, 2015). These efforts have come to define the smart city movement which, over the last decade, has become an important part of the urban agenda and discourse (Kitchin, 2015; Husar et al., 2017). As cities have continued to invest in creating smart (or smarter) cities, scholars have sought to develop an intellectual foundation for understanding this movement. There is now an extensive "smart city literature" that: (a) conceptualises and defines smart cities (Yigitcanlar et al., 2018), (b) explores its social and political implications (Rossi, 2016), and (c) examines the data that define and shape smart city efforts (Hashem et al., 2016). An important, yet understudied issue, is the way in which smart cities, actually, emerge. With a few notable exceptions, (e.g., Desouza et al., 2019; Yigitcanlar et al., 2019a), there is little in the way of a systematic examination of the pathways that lead to smart cities. Thus, while we have some sense of *what smart cities are*, we know far less about: *how they come to be?*

Much of the scholarship suggests that the emergence of smart cities is a "natural" or organic process (Husar, 2017). It represents the "conclusion" of an ongoing pattern of integrating ICT with the everyday activities of cities. While this "natural" progression represents an important part of the story of smart cities, such as path dependency, it is incomplete. It does not account for the *deliberate and intentional efforts* to create smart cities. This omission is non-trivial. The increasing awareness of urban fragility, and the need for resilience in the face of a growing population and numerous environmental challenges, create an increasing demand for cities to deliberately identify new urban efficiencies and planning approaches (Hunter et al., 2019; Desouza et al., 2019). These intentional efforts vary from city to city and, depending on the approach taken, they present different challenges for the realisation of smart city objectives. In this chapter, we consider three different types of deliberate approaches, i.e. pathways, to the creation of smart cities: (a) the development of entirely new (smart) cities—from scratch development, (b) smart city development projects within particular parts of the city—infill smart precinct/neighbourhood development, and (c) the advancement of smart cities through the

DOI: 10.1201/9781003403647-5

integration of ICT's within the city organisation—retrofitting the city with smart technologies and platforms to increase efficiencies.

To better understand the different pathways to smart cities we employ nine case examinations. It is worth noting that some of the cases in this study are considered canonical examples of smart cities. The reliance on these oft-employed examples has been met with some criticism. For example, Kitchin (2015: 133) notes that these examples may be "exceptional in nature, rather than typical." As a result, they have become "master tropes for smart cities... . [that] provide idealized visions of possible futures." That said, unlike previous case-study research on smart cities, we put these cases forward not as examples of best practices to be emulated, but rather, as examples that reflect the continuum of smart city efforts.

Following this introduction, the chapter proceeds in five parts. The first section describes our conceptualisation of "pathways to smart cities", as well as the framework we use to examine these pathways. After introducing the methodologic approach in the second section, the third section provides an overview of our cases and their relationship to the three pathways we consider. The fourth section summarises our key findings, and then lastly we offer some concluding thoughts in the final section with respect to future directions for research.

4.2 Conceptual Background

In this chapter, we are interested in understanding the different pathways taken for creating or facilitating smart cities. While scholars have yet to offer any systematic examination of these different pathways, the literature offers, fairly clear descriptions thereof. Drawing on this literature, then, we are able to conceptualise three different pathways to smart cities. As depicted in Figure 4.1, this

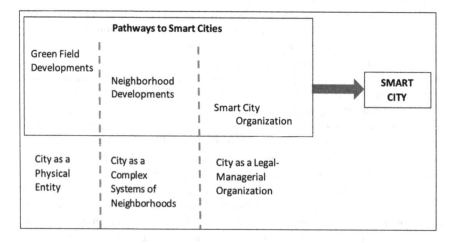

Figure 4.1 Pathways to smart cities.

conceptualisation allows for different understandings of "a city," and thus implies different types of challenges.

First, in many instances, smart cities are developed from scratch. This conceptualisation of—and operational approach to—smart cities draws upon the idea of a city as a singular physical entity. As such, it can be built "from scratch" to draw upon the economic benefits typically attributed to cities. Often referred to as *green field developments*, these new cities are created, through a series of public–private partnerships. Often as part of a federal/national government initiative, these developments are marketed in terms of their potential for solving issues regarding urbanisation, congestion, and employment. In this chapter, we examine this pathway through the following three smart city cases: Songdo, South Korea; Masdar, Abu Dhabi; and Gujarat, India.

A second, but related, pathway focuses on the development of particular neighbourhoods within a city. To some degree, this is the most challenging conceptualisation and operationalisation of a smart city. It requires "retrofitting infrastructures and systems" to existing cities. We examine this pathway, through the following two smart city cases: the Hudson Yards development project, New York; and Jurong Lake development project, Singapore.

Finally, the third pathway we consider focuses less on developing the physical space that occupies the city, but rather pursuing a smart city through the development of a technological platform that integrates data from various organisational siloes within the city. From this perspective, the city is understood in its organisational and managerial forms. The emphasis here is on the "smartness" of the city, as it relates to improved delivery of public services. We consider this pathway through the following four smart city cases: Amsterdam, Netherlands; Manchester, England; Barcelona, Spain; and Tel Aviv, Israel.

As noted above, these pathways are not wholly unique. Other scholars have described smart city cases in similar terms. The contribution that we offer in this chapter then, is to provide a side-by-side examination of these pathways. To focus our examination, we consider each of these pathways in terms of three dominant themes that comprise the smart city literature—i.e., *governance and services, integration of ICT infrastructure*, and *the role of sustainability and social capital*.

As depicted in Figure 4.2, these themes offer a lens through which we can examine the different pathways to smart cities. The themes, as we describe below, reflect key ideas about the objectives and potential outcomes of smart cities. They provide a reasonable basis, by which to then consider the different paths toward smart cities. It is worth noting, however, that while these pathways may not be entirely unrelated, our conceptualisation is not meant to reflect a sequential relationship between them. More specifically, we can examine—through our cases— how these objectives and outcomes have been, more or less, realised through different pathways.

Over the previous two decades, scholars have put forward numerous definitions of smart cities. For example, Bowerman et al. (2000: 1) defined a smart city as a place capable of monitoring the conditions of all critical infrastructure while optimising resources, planning preventative maintenance activities, and monitoring security

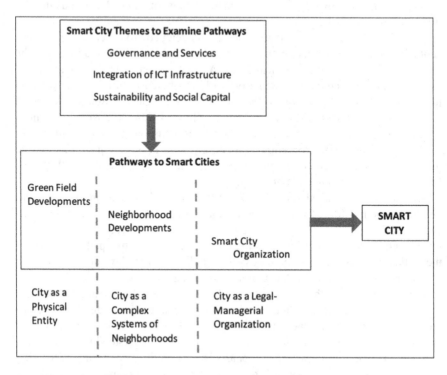

Figure 4.2 A framework for examining the pathways to smart cities.

aspects to maximise services to residents. This definition focuses on the relationship between the physical infrastructure, technology, and systems in place capable of maximising services to residents. In contrast, Rios (2008: 4) defines a smart city as "A city that gives inspiration, shares culture, knowledge, and life, a city that motivates its inhabitants to create and flourish in their own lives. An admired city, a vessel to intelligence, but ultimately an incubator of empowered spaces." While this idea is on the far side of human centred, it demonstrates the variance between "smartness" through technological means and "smartness" through human capital. Finally, a third definition focuses on governance and information systems. In particular, Piro's (2014: 169) definition denotes "A smart city is intended as an urban environment which, supported by pervasive ICT systems, is able to offer advanced and innovative services to residents to improve the overall quality of their life."

These definitions reflect the three main themes behind the smart city concept (Waart, 2016); namely, a technological theme, based on the use of infrastructures; a human theme, based on people, education, learning, and knowledge as key drivers; and an institutional theme, based on governance and policy and as a result of the importance of cooperation between stakeholders and governments (Nam and Pardo, 2011). We employ these three themes, *'governance and services'*, *'integration of ICT infrastructure'*, and *'the role of sustainability and social capital'*, in our analysis. They provide a lens through which to examine the motivations, processes, and outcomes of each case study. As an exploratory project, we seek to develop insights about how each of the pathways manifest the different outcomes described in each theme.

4.2.1 Theme One: Smart City Governance and Services

Information systems and urban policy research have launched a large body of scholarly work surrounding the intersection of technology and city governance, with a strong focus on digitalisation of services to improve residents' quality of life. For example, Liu et al. (2014) regard smart governance as a city which develops policies, strategies, and frameworks that serve the unique needs of individual residents. Dunleavy et al. (2006) describe this as digital era governance and note a transition towards a re-aggregation of public services under direct government control around the resident.

Over the past two decades this perspective has largely defined the use of ICT within public services and has been identified as having three separate phases. Liu et al. (2014) regard the first generation as a mirror of the private sector with a focus on reducing costs and increasing automation. The second generation saw government adopting market-based mechanisms to increase efficiencies, however this often resulted in increased complexity for government organisations. In the final phase, governance adopted a platform-based approach where ICT products are enablers of outcomes, with a focus on service to residents (Fishenden, 2013).

4.2.2 Theme Two: Smart City ICT/Infrastructure

Another focus of smart city research has been the movement towards technologically enhanced public infrastructure. By focusing on technological advancements, researchers have considered that efficiencies of the urban environment could be increased considerably to deal with increasing populations (Yigitcanlar et al., 2019b). Heo et al. (2014) divide a smart city into six main technological areas: (1) smart power grids, (2) structural approaches, (3) surveillance applications, (4) transportation and traffic management, (5) food, water quality and environmental monitoring, and (6) ubiquitous healthcare applications. This approach varies considerably from the digital governance focus of other researchers. This approach has a definite focus on a city's infrastructure rather than the services it can offer to residents. Thus, this theme requires that we consider how, as a city's infrastructure is improved by technological advancements, it might open the city to challenges regarding network scalability, security and privacy concerns, network communication standards, and system interoperability (Heo et al., 2014).

4.2.3 Theme Three: Smart City Sustainability and Social Capital

The concept of sustainability developed from the realisation that current social, economic, and urban development research failed to fully account for the risks of environmental disasters or social decays (Bibri, 2018). Following this, the premise of sustainability has risen as a holistic approach to aligning city practices and urban development with nature (Bibri and Krogstie, 2017). Its defining factor is that it looks at all-inclusive decisions for long-term benefits. This is a key distinction from the digital era governance approach (described above) that look towards individualised services. Instead, sustainability is based in the holistic, all-encompassing nature of future developments. As such, sustainability can be thought of as a state in which the natural and social systems are not undermined by society (Bibri, 2018).

Smart city sustainability research has largely focused on ICT enablement to support the natural environment and, as such, the common understanding of smart city sustainability tends to focus on renewable energies, waste removal, and other environmentally sustainable practices. While these practices often focus on the physical environment, researchers have begun to suggest that sustainability must also consider the social sphere in general, and social capital, in particular (Lara, 2016; Granier and Kudo, 2016).

Social capital can be understood as: "the links, shared values and understandings in society that enable individuals and groups to trust each other and so work together" (OECD, 2007: 102). Within the smart city literature, this idea has been adopted to consider the influence of information technologies to empower communication, community engagement, and co-creation. This approach to a city "smartness" is based on creating a network of communication that simultaneously shares, educates, and evolves all residents, helping the city adapt to the problems that arise. This thinking follows the idea that "human capital will transform how people live and interact with each other leading to advancements in tech innovation. Investments in communities and their learning capabilities would lead to a better yield in innovation and entrepreneurship" (Kummitha, 2017: 47).

4.3 Methodology

This research applied a "case study" method for the investigation. The method was considered appropriate for this research, because it affords us the opportunity to consider the contextual issues in each case by employing multiple sources of evidence (Yin, 2011). This research utilises both "descriptive" and "explanatory" case study methods. The descriptive analysis identifies the key characteristics of the best practice smart cities, whereas the explanatory analysis portrays cause-and-effect relationships (Yin, 2011). Both analyses follow a qualitative methodological approach for the empirical investigation.

Following Yin (2003), cases were selected at the beginning of the research study. In this study, we consider the different pathways and their relationships to the three themes that define the smart city literature through a series of case studies. Thus, the case studies we have selected each represent one of three pathways to smart cities. More specifically, the green field pathway is examined through: Songdo, South Korea; Masdar, Abu Dhabi; and Gujarat, India. The neighbourhood development pathway is examined through: Hudson Yards, New York; and Jurong Lake,

Singapore. The platform pathway is examined through: Amsterdam, Netherlands; Manchester, England; Barcelona, Spain; and Tel Aviv, Israel.

The complexity and variation between the cases limits our ability to draw direct comparisons—even within the same pathways. Nonetheless, given the exploratory nature of this study, this limitation is not particularly problematic. We employ the cases and draw insights into the relationship between the different pathways and the smart city outcomes relating to: *governance and services, integration of ICT infrastructure,* and *the role of sustainability and social capital.* To the degree that we can discern such relationships we cannot, nor do we, make any causal inference. Nonetheless, the insights provide a foundation and framework for future research into potential pathways to a smart city.

While substantively different, the cases reflect similar implementation time frames. In particular, all of the cases were implemented during the last five years (2015–2020). That said, many of these initiatives were the result of planning from the early 2000s. The data for each case were drawn from academic and grey literature and interviews. The next section describes each of the cases as they relate to their particular pathway.

4.4 Results

4.4.1 Green Field Pathway Cases

4.4.1.1 Songdo, South Korea

Envisioned as early as 2001, Songdo was born out of a political drive for low-carbon sustainable growth and a push for trade-based economic growth (Mullins, 2016). South Korea's economic development over the previous half-century has been largely driven by manufacturing and export as the country has few natural resources. As a result, South Korea imports almost the entirety of its fuel supply to maintain its manufacturing economy (Kaye, 2017). Songdo looks to lower the economic costs of importing fuel while simultaneously improving the trade network of South Korea by developing a city strategically located for trade, powered by renewable energy technology (Shwayri, 2013).

Built entirely on reclaimed land from the Yellow Sea, Songdo is situated on the tip of the Incheon Free Economic Zone positioning it roughly three and half hours from one-third of the world's population (Moser, 2013). This economic zone was first developed in the early 2000s and has been successful in attracting foreign investment (approximately 11 billion USD in the previous 15 years) (Byung-yeul, 2018). While, Songdo hopes to attract further investment to the zone with its strategic location, it is a 2-hour commute from Seoul (the nation's capital). The public generally believes that this distance is too far for a daily commute, but not far enough to recognise Songdo as its own viable economic centre. This is reflected by Songdo's 60-percent housing vacancy and 70,000 daily commuters. While 70,000 daily commuters alone appears impressive, it pales in comparison to Seoul's population of 9 million and struggles to ease the congestion faced by the capital—as was originally advertised (Poon, 2018). Songdo's current population sits at 100,000, which, while impressive for a city built from scratch, is still short of its goal of 300,000 residents.

The city offers technological benefits through providing automated waste removal directly from your apartment, smart phone-controlled temperature and lighting, traffic and temperature sensors to economise resources, and it is even planned to completely eliminate the need for cars by strategically situating public transport (Garfield, 2017). Besides, in Songdo's CBD there is the highest concentration of LEED-certified projects in the world (Poon, 2018). Songdo has partnered with different universities for the Incheon Global Campus Initiative (IGC, 2019) and is currently developing 990,000 square meters of land for medical research and investment, hoping to become the world's best Bio-Hub (Da-Sol, 2018).

While Songdo's smart city initiative is highly technology driven and offers world-class modern convenience to its residents, it may have focused too heavily on "impressive" technology and not enough on the practicalities of daily life at a local level. From the outside looking in, Songdo presents a high standard for utilising technology to improve the community lifestyle. A closer examination, however, suggests that the city still struggles to garner enough interest to consider the city a success. Songdo's development strongly aligns with Smart City 1.0 research (Cohen, 2015; Bowerman, 2000; Heo et al., 2014), which is a top-down technology-based approach to smart city development, where cities are developed with a focus on technologically advanced solutions typical of traditional smart city discourse. This top-down approach that Songdo has adopted is criticised by urban scholars—as without the involvement of all stakeholders, achieving the desired outcomes of a smart city is not possible (Yigitcanlar and Lee, 2014). Furthermore, the top-down policymaking practice generates technocratic solutions only for smart cities that are built from scratch—such as Songdo (Yigitcanlar et al., 2019a).

The Songdo case demonstrates the limits of development that do not include residents in the decision-making process, especially in a city built from scratch. Songdo's current technology and infrastructure is impressive, however there is widely held criticism that it lacks any sense of community (Poon, 2018).

4.4.1.2 Masdar City, Abu Dhabi, UAE

Masdar City began as an incredibly ambitious project hoping to be the world's first zero-carbon city (Cugurullo, 2013). First established in 2006, Abu Dhabi looked towards developing an economic, social, and environmental sustainability blueprint of a city that would help the nation's economy diversify away from its traditionally non-renewable assets (fossil fuels, including oil). Its aim was to develop large-scale renewable energy projects, become a clean-tech hub, provide homes for 50,000 people and facilities for 1,500 businesses, and develop a new Masdar Institute of Science and Technology (MIST) (Masdar, 2019).

Still in development, Masdar City has faced numerous challenges due to its location and its initial sustainability projections. This project has been considered extremely ambitious due to the severe desert weather conditions, the aims for complete sustainability, the research, development, and implementation of renewable technology, and its overall greenfield nature. This project is located 17 km southeast of Abu Dhabi City and is strategically placed alongside Abu Dhabi International Airport. The desert conditions noticeably affected the construction of the city, with shifting sands adding difficulty to the initial foundations and extreme temperatures affecting workers (Malone, 2016). This directly affected the budget, which in turn had a negative impact on Masdar City as an economically sustainable project. As a result, its initial carbon-free scheme has changed to carbon neutral, and only two of its 1,500 planned transport stations are currently active (Cugurullo, 2013). Masdar has been built from scratch, using a top-down approach that has struggled to garner interest from United Arab Emirates (UAE) residents, with its current population sitting close to just 3,000 people, mostly students (Goldenberg, 2016).

Within the last decade Masdar City has begun to establish numerous global partnerships and multi-national clean-tech projects (Masdar, 2019). After 13 years since its initial conceptualisation, the research and development of renewable energy technology has become a commodity that Masdar City can now profit from. The UAE's initial economic drive to diversify assets is now realised through clean energy projects involving Masdar City technology. Where harsh weather conditions initially provided challenges for Masdar City, they now offer a marketable point to other municipalities due to the capabilities of its wind and solar technology. Masdar City hosts the Middle East's largest sustainability gathering, known as Abu Dhabi Sustainability Week (ADSW). ADSW acts as a platform for 850 companies, 170 countries, and numerous policy makers and technology specialists to collaborate and educate each other on the future of sustainability. While advertised as a platform to facilitate discussion, the ADSW also offers numerous sustainability prizes and hosts sustainability forums to bring together UAE research institutes. Through ADSW launching their "We Are Committed" campaign, the group not only discusses its commitment to sustainability, it also considers how sustainability makes business sense and can be used as a means of business competition.

Masdar, like Songdo, has also adopted a top-down planning and design approach, and so far, the city has performed best in the environmental domain of sustainable urban development. However, the Masdar project has faced struggles economically. The project heavily capitalises on environmental concerns to generate profit (Cugurullo, 2016). Nevertheless, the project has not been able to attract as many innovative industries as was hoped, along with the impacts of the global financial crisis which has forced Masdar to scale back its budget and ambitions (Yigitcanlar et al., 2019a).

While its population is currently limited, Masdar City's global impact within the clean-tech sector is offering continued economic and environmental sustainability to Abu Dhabi that strongly aligns with the initial intentions of the development. ADSW alone claimed to have 10.5 billion USD worth of deals announced at its last conference (Gulfnews, 2019), and the economic return from a range of global clean energy projects which will continue to prove beneficial (Masdar Projects, 2019). While the city itself is still considered "empty", its ability to transfer renewable technology research into an economically viable source of income is apparent. This proposes an interesting point for economic growth as a driving force behind smart city initiatives. The result of this being that Masdar City has been able to demonstrate benefits and successes to the greater Abu Dhabi community and economy, regardless of its small population and without receiving public criticism.

4.4.1.3 Gujarat International Finance Tec-City, India

As part of India's 100 Smart City Program (Smart Cities Mission, 2019) Gujarat International Finance Tec-City (GIFT) has been conceptualised as a vehicle to help adapt to the community and economic needs of India's future. With 70 percent of Indians projected to be living in cities by 2050 and roughly 500 million moving to urban areas, GIFT looks to develop an economic hub within the Indian Economic Zone capable of housing large numbers of multinational companies and scaling into a business capital of the world (GIFT-City, 2019).

GIFT began development in 2011, although it was not until the launch of the 100 smart cities program in 2015 that it became recognised as a viable project nationally (Charles, 2015). GIFT's early stages of development were marked as its most difficult. The city struggled to garner investment or interest nationally or globally (Abhirup and Jain, 2019). Initially, it was expected to construct over 100 skyscrapers capable of supporting 1 million jobs within its first decade. Nonetheless, it was not until 2014 that Prime Minister Modi introduced a clear regulatory framework regarding the city's overarching goals, and it was not until 2016 that the Modi government set up favourable tax initiatives for finance and technology firms looking to invest in GIFT. Also, it is often argued that foreign businesses are more likely to operate out of Mumbai due to its pre-existing talent pool (Abhirup and Jain, 2019).

GIFT utilises smart city technologies such as automated waste disposal, renewable energy infrastructure, and real-time monitoring of city life to aid in the national development of sustainability and environmental norms against the growing population crisis (Hunter et al., 2019). To this end, GIFT aims to move most of its infrastructure underground, with power, water, waste, and fire hydrant services built into two different wet or dry sections of a utility tunnel plan (GIFT-City, 2019). These large service trenches aim to provide the council with access to all important city infrastructure without the need for digging or resurfacing, allowing for a well-designed and uninterrupted urban transport plan on the surface. Its current power system demonstrates 99.9 percent reliability, with roughly 5.3 minutes of outage per annum, and the efficiency of its waste disposal system is four times the national standard (GIFT City, 2019).

During Phase 1, the GIFT city-group focused largely on marketing the city as India's next financial hub. Initially, this focus demonstrated limited returns, but over the past two years it has begun to demonstrate a greater return on investment. GIFT was recently named in the top three emerging business hubs in the world (Venkataraman, 2018) and in late 2018 the city announced a collaboration with Bloomberg aimed at incentivising foreign interest through best practice, transparent frameworks, and secure data/technology infrastructure (Bloomberg, 2018). Currently, over 200 companies are operational in GIFT city including Oracle, State Bank of India, and the Indian International Exchange.

Operating as a 50/50 joint venture between the state government (GUDC, 2019) and private enterprise (Indianix, 2019), GIFT's construction was initially slow with only six commercial towers developed. Ramakant Jha, CEO of the GIFT city-group, described the smart city concept as "a hub for a specific economic activity where each smart city will have to be customized keeping the end user industry in mind" (Bhatnarga, 2015: para. 5). This industry-focused approach is reminiscent of Smart City 1.0 discourse, which develops high-class infrastructure with few notable improvements for residents and liveability (Cohen, 2015).

4.4.2 Neighbourhood Development Pathway

4.4.2.1 Hudson Yards, New York, USA

The Hudson Yards development was conceptualised as early as 2001. It was originally born out of the desire to host the 2012 Olympic Games and a need for further urban space within Manhattan (Plitt, 2019). To create this urban space, the Hudson Yards project looked at developing an entire district on top of a major rail centre and transport hub. This extremely ambitious project has been considered the most expensive private development in US history, budgeted at roughly 25 billion USD (Tyler and Bendix, 2018).

The development was first advertised as New York's smartest new neighbourhood, with sensor technology delivering data-driven updates, allowing the developers to repeatedly improve the quality of life of residents (Anuta, 2014). In a bid to become America's first "quantified community", Hudson Yards advertised sensors that would monitor air quality, noise levels, temperature, and pedestrian traffic, alongside technology typical of the smart city movement. Pneumatic waste disposal chutes would automate waste collection, micro-grid and gas-fired turbines would reduce greenhouse gases, and even more sensors would monitor resource efficiency and reduce downtime (Anuta, 2014).

Its highly sought-after location garnered interest from numerous multinationals, with investment from HSBC, Bank of China, and Deutsche Bank, and current commercial renting from SAP, BCG, Warner Media, and L'Oréal (Nolan, 2019). This development's promised technology to improve the quality of life within Manhattan but has been met with its own criticisms. Hudson Yards is currently perceived as a space only available to those who can afford it, with only limited "public space." As such, it appears that the original anticipated benefits have yet to be realised (Nolan, 2019).

The primary private developer for the Hudson yards project, Related, initially advertised Hudson Yards as a technologically improved urban area due to its use of data analytics to improve resource efficiency. They have since noted that data technology has changed rapidly, and as such, increased complications regarding privacy and analytics (Nonko, 2019). The physical construction of Hudson Yards has since taken priority over technology and social capital enhancements, as it provides a more tangible economic return. A recent analysis published by the developer suggests the project will employ 7,000 construction workers annually until 2025, and companies operating out of the completed towers will contribute 19 billion USD to the city's gross domestic product (GDP) (Goldenberg, 2016). Additionally, it is believed that the project will generate 500 million USD annually in taxes (Hudson Yards, 2016). Unfortunately, this has steered Hudson Yards away from its "quantified community approach," limiting the benefits that were to be gained from a fully instrumented urban data science platform on the rest of the city. While various elected officials have argued that there is a positive influence from attracting large businesses, namely the economic growth and new jobs, residents have been critical that the development is ostensibly an enclave for the ultra-wealthy. Residential apartments are priced in the millions of dollars (or US$9,000 a month to rent) and residents consider themselves spectators of the development, rather than participants.

This case raises the issue around the challenges associated with the private development approach to smart city initiatives. In this case, the primary developer of the Hudson Yards realised the issues surrounding data-driven initiatives as too complex and costly, and instead focused its attention towards the physical development of the neighbourhood. This has resulted in an incredibly impressive urban transformation, but without a demonstrated benefit to the greater residents of New York. What was originally planned as a test-lab for smart city technology has become something closer to a modern commercial and economic hub. Without the data processing Hudson Yards first advertised, it is impossible for it to deliver on the promise to monitor or improve the quality of daily life for residents. In 2015, the development advertised "harnessing big data to innovate, optimize enhance and personalize the experience" (Hudson Yards, 2016). While technology has been implemented for waste management and renewable power, the sensors and data required to properly monitor these technologies have not.

Interestingly, the positive influence on Greater Manhattan has come from local government, where in response to the Hudson Yards development major upgrades to public transport took place. Rail and subway lines were improved to increase the flow of congestion within the area. It could be argued that this infrastructure is in itself enough of an improvement to residents city-wide to avoid the backlash of other economically driven private developments, although the tax incentives and breaks received by Hudson Yards were actually greater than those offered to Amazon (Haag, 2019). With 5.4 billion USD taxpayer dollars spent on the Hudson Yards development; the local government has made a substantial investment on the public's behalf for the future of the Manhattan area. For a project advertised as a smart city initiative, its current benefits do not offer replicable intelligent solutions to other city-wide issues. In the meantime, this development demonstrates more benefit to the private enterprise involved than it does to the greater Manhattan area.

4.4.2.2 Jurong Lake District, Singapore

Singapore's Jurong Lake District (JLD) is a small-scale smart city project looking at developing 160 hectares of West Singapore into 45 hectares of transit, 20,000 new homes, and 10,000 new jobs. This project is taking an interesting approach, relative to the other development cases examined in this chapter, as it has been marketed as a *bottom-up* scheme. The government looks to facilitate relationships between public agencies, industry partners, and residents to co-create holistic solutions. In 2008, the Urban Development Authority unveiled a masterplan that looked to elevate JLD to a second Singapore Central Business District (CBD) with infrastructure projects and an integrated transport strategy being the major focus. Singapore has been ranked high within numerous smart city rankings since due to its implementation of disruptive technologies and undertaking of planning towards further innovation (Drubin, 2018).

JLD demonstrates an interesting middle point for the smart city initiatives on this list, where it aims to deliver infrastructure similar to that of greenfield smart city projects, but within a pre-existing population and with a bottom-up approach. The role of government in this situation seems to be not only as a facilitator, but also a demonstrator of government strategy and its benefits to residents. The government argument for JLD is both geographically and economically based. JLD believes it can tap into an already existent talent pool within West Singapore's population estimated at 1 million, 70 percent of whom work in the current Singapore CBD.

To support this approach, JLD is located at the end of China's Belt and Road initiative (Goh and Reilly, 2017). This initiative looks to develop economic cooperation through five corridors out of China, including land routes to Europe, the Middle East, and South East Asia, and sea routes to the South Pacific and Southern Europe (Wade, 2017). In this case, Singapore is hoping to connect a high-speed rail with Kuala Lumpur and eventually the rest of Asia. JLD will develop the high-speed rail terminus at the end of this massive initiative, and, as such, city planners believe it will be physically and symbolically important for companies to have their headquarters at the end of the network (Au-Yong, 2017). While the JLD initiative should provide an excellent centre for business and economic growth, there has been criticism that it relies too heavily on the success of other global projects (Au-Yong, 2017). Singapore's ability to connect to the Belt and Road initiative is entirely dependent on whether Malaysia has the capacity to develop its own rail infrastructure and enable its own economic stability towards the project.

In addition, JLD is also situated within a "tech corridor" made up of the National University of Singapore, Jurong Innovation District, and numerous other think-tanks and major industry players. Jurong Innovation District promises some of the bottom-up approach that JLD is looking to implement through the development of a high-tech manufacturing district. Nanyang Technological University has been situated next to a manufacturing campus to develop "synergistic partnerships to rapidly evolve manufacturing trends" according to the former chairman of ASTAR, Mr. Lim Chuan Poh (ASTAR, 2017, para. 11). This district will capitalise on JLD's academic strengths to foster innovation and garner external investment within the area (JTC, 2019).

Nevertheless, JLD has yet to move beyond the master-planning phases and currently is looking towards a 2050 horizon for its full development (Au-yong, 2017), which introduces entirely new issues regarding an ageing population. This issue has been crucial for other successful bottom-up initiatives. While it may be too early to tell in this case, lessons learned from other projects in this list demonstrate a need for the government and resident strategies to be aligned. Currently, JLD seems to demonstrate a top-down economic strategy, with little bottom-up collaboration and a heavy reliance on external investment and co-operation. Singapore's previous ability to leverage itself as a centre for economic interest (Zarroli, 2015) demonstrates hope for the financial feasibility of the project, however a need to understand the residents of the next few decades is crucial in ensuring success overall.

4.4.3 Platform Development Cases

4.4.3.1 Amsterdam, The Netherlands

Amsterdam's Smart City Initiative has adopted and further promotes a European trend in smart city development by designing a technology platform with which residents of the community can engage (Mora et al., 2019). This approach has found success throughout European municipalities as a non-intrusive way to promote a smart city initiative to a community and has, generally, demonstrated greater buy-in from residents (Mancebo, 2019). Rather than a direct upgrade to physical infrastructure, local government has utilised technology to launch an open innovation platform that promotes community-based suggestions for improving liveability in urban areas (Lawrence, 2017). The platform operates in a Twitter-esque fashion, in that members of the community can post their thoughts on one of the issues the initiative is promoting, and other members can engage, communicate, or direct the community to more information regarding the topic. This creates a network effect of innovation, where residents who have not previously met can engage with each other around the topics of interest and form inter-disciplinary partnerships that were previously impossible (Menny, 2018; Choque et al., 2018).

The municipality also promotes extremely clear strategic goals for the city regarding sustainability and improvement, and utilises technology as a way to encourage community engagement and participation. Overarching sustainability goals look towards 45 percent less CO_2 emissions by 2025, as well as 65 percent household waste separated by 2020 (European Commission, 2019). Amsterdam has been able to collect large amounts of data regarding what is important to the community and therefore worthwhile to improve by focusing on the implementation of technology that allows the community to engage. As a result, the positive impacts of the approach include the initial startup costs and sustained techno-literacy of the population (Mancebo, 2019). The development of this platform cost 4 million Euro initially and won another 950,000 Euro through Europe's Capital of Innovation award (iAmsterdam, 2019). A 5 million Euro budget is considerably cheaper than the billion-dollar costs of aforementioned smart city infrastructure development projects.

Furthermore, establishing a technology platform that is familiar and inclusive of residents allows the smart city premise to be viewed in a positive light (SmartCities World, 2018). Amsterdam Smart City Initiative offers numerous tours of the Marineterrein Innovation District that encourage resident feedback alongside a digital social media style website that houses the community and continuously prompts for suggestions and requests from the public. One such example, is the Amsterdam Smart Citizens Lab (Amsterdam Smart Citizens Lab, 2016). This lab deals with themes ranging from air quality to noise pollution and has developed numerous low-cost open-source sensors for communities to engage in environmental action, thanks to its partnerships with local Amsterdam tech-business SenseMakers, and its greater support from Amsterdam's Economic Board (Amsterdam Smart Citizens Lab, 2016). The group has over 1,000 members and meets regularly to discuss the challenges relevant to the community and Amsterdam's sustainability goals (Meetup, 2019). This approach encourages residents to engage digitally. Thereby improving the digital education of the populace and cultivating data on residents' behaviours in a transparent and voluntary way.

Amsterdam adopted a retrofitting approach in its efforts to develop the Amsterdam Metropolitan Area into a flourishing smart city. It has successfully integrated both environmental and societal goals with economic and technologic ones (Yigitcanlar et al., 2019a). As a result, the Amsterdam Smart City Initiative has been considered a major success, with its innovation platform housing 5,500 innovators, Internet of Things (IoT) labs, sustainable housing projects, innovation arenas, and more (iAmsterdam, 2019). This demonstrates an interesting role for government within a smart city initiative given their role in creating the necessary infrastructure and facilitating the use of ICT. This approach aligns itself with the Smart City 3.0 approach through promoting the initiatives of residents, companies, and institutions (van den Bosch, 2018). As the project continues, there will be ongoing costs for upgrading necessary connectivity infrastructure or funding of larger projects, but these projects will already have much greater public approval as they have been processed through the platform.

The Amsterdam Smart City does not offer a large urban transformation directly, compared to other initiatives, however, it offers a platform where government, business, and community can directly collaborate. This approach argues that the "smartness" of a city does not come directly from technology, instead it comes from the use of technology to facilitate and democratise the decision-making process (Lara, 2016). With government playing a facilitative role, the Amsterdam Smart City Chief Technology Officer (CTO) puts direct importance on data, stating that correct private sector and public data are imperative in a city's ability to manage expectations, consider resident input, and facilitate change (Macpherson, 2017). Taking a data inventory is considered to be the fundamental first step to a bottom-up initiative like this, followed closely by a clear and transparent demonstration of the overarching city goals (Fitzgerald, 2016).

4.4.3.2 *CityVerve, Manchester City, UK*

With the help of InnovateUK, Cisco, Siemens, Manchester Metro University, and Manchester City Council were part of the UK's first attempt to develop a smart city blueprint (ANS, 2018). Intended as a demonstrator for other smart city projects within the UK and across the globe, CityVerve implemented IoT technology and a community platform to improve the city across numerous sectors including transport, energy, health, and culture.

With a budget of approximately 16 million pounds, Manchester City developed a smart city platform similar to other European municipalities. CISCO CityVerve representative Peter Shearman, placed a priority on capturing clean data from the community and also designing organisational processes capable of supporting this goal. As such, Manchester developed a social media style platform and forum in which residents can engage and suggest improvements to the city initiative. CISCO CityVerve's aim was to allow for the collection of information from anywhere in the city, while being accessible from a single point. For the public sector, this would provide a clear picture of the entire city in one place. Additionally, the platform looks to host new applications that can be developed by the community or through business partnerships (Blackman, 2018). Similar to Amsterdam, this allows for the CityVerve project to be the facilitator of numerous projects and collate the data at a single analytical point. The council believes a smarter city is based on community engagement, participation, and the generation of data based on these interactions.

To properly utilise the aforementioned technology, CityVerve was largely implemented by CISCO, who were capable of the implementation of sensor technology and complex network architecture. The benefits of an experienced private enterprise allowed for the CityVerve initiative to be developed within just two years, however, the ownership of the initiative's model remains with CISCO. As such, after the project's completion, CISCO are looking at the replicability of this initiative across other municipalities (Blackman, 2018).

While this initiative is still largely beneficial to Manchester City, it could be argued that if the city was able to retain ownership of the blueprint, the government could largely benefit from its replicable value. In a landscape where cities are looking to digital transformation, and only 33 percent of Western cities are currently optimised (McKinsey, 2018), the value of a smart city blueprint is extremely high and could offer new forms of revenue to councils such as Manchester City.

CityVerve believes these data would be extremely valuable if commercialised. As other cities look towards smart city solutions, datasets regarding transport and shared city issues like congestion will increase in value. Discovering ways in which governments can begin to market these data to other municipalities will develop new sources of revenue for smart city initiatives, essentially re-creating a digital version of Masdar City's research and development resale. Nevertheless, CityVerve has noted that complex governance, procedure, and procurement can be problematic for these initiatives and interfacing with the community on such a large scale requires process efficiency and clean management of data as its foundations to succeed.

The lessons learned throughout CityVerve's implementation were more internal than external, with CISCO analysis claiming an importance on innovating government processes (Ismail, 2018). Essentially, the implementation of innovative technology cannot be the sole transformation in a smart city initiative; government processes must evolve with the technology. Processes should be identified and mapped out in the beginning so the technological concept can align with them. These initiatives often include public–private partnerships and community engagement. Therefore, processes must be identified as early as possible so that collaboration between each partner is most effective. Nonetheless, Manchester City's urban transformation has been widely regarded as a success through providing new knowledge for data-driven technologies and demonstrating how they can be implemented within a community.

4.4.3.3 Barcelona, Spain

Barcelona's smart city transformation began in 2011 and as it looked towards innovating energy usage and mobility, it began with a technological upgrade to infrastructure (Bakici, 2013). By 2014, Barcelona was recognised as a "smart city" by the European Union (European Commission, 2014). During this time, Barcelona had implemented a massive number of sensors for everything from parking to streetlights and transport systems. To ensure these sensors were connected, the city also implemented connectivity infrastructure upgrades. These upgrades not only allowed for the successful communication of technologies, but also sparked Barcelona to become the mobile capital of the world (Otgaar, 2016). The government took advantage of this by developing applications that would allow residents to interface with these technologies through their smartphone devices.

Mancebo (2019) highlights Barcelona as one example where the smart city strategy was deeply rooted in heavy infrastructure development, but with the intention of developing a new urban model "La ciudad autosuficiente" (self-sustaining city). Similarly, existing urban developments may look towards digitalising services for individuals but again with the long-term goal of building social capital and improving innovation. Barcelona's latest initiative demonstrates a reflection on their previous approaches and highlights the progression of the role of governments within smart city development. Barcelona considers itself at the forefront of a Smart City 3.0 ideology, where publicly available data allow residents to develop community-based solutions (Hernandez, 2018). CTO Francesca Bria believes the fairest way for technology to advance is for local communities to be included in its development and rewarded by clear evidence of how it can improve their lives (Albers, 2018). This is further supported by Barcelona's strategy for digital sovereignty (Barcelona, 2016). This strategy is highly data-driven and highlights the importance of data as a part of urban infrastructure. Establishing the ownership, control, and management of city data allows for a more educated public and a more empirically sound decision-making process (Berrone et al., 2016; Albers, 2018).

These technological upgrades have led to Barcelona being widely considered the world's smartest city and a golden standard for smart city development (Centre de Formacio, 2015). Barcelona's push for a more open and connected data strategy is based on the lessons learned from implementing numerous different privately owned hardware solutions across the city. Each of these products offers its own dashboard and operates within its own silo. Sensors in the pavement were not able to communicate with sensors in the lighting due to separate vendors vertical business models, leaving the city with numerous interoperability issues. These hardware or business issues mean government must focus more on the interoperability of technology, and less on the demonstrated use of this technology for residents (Forster, 2018). This results in added complexity for the transformation due to the duplication of government and technological silos.

By standardising the way governments can analyse and interact with data, governments can effectively turn data into intelligence for the city. Bria (2018) argues this is the most important step for the future of smart city projects. While Bria (2018) does not deny that implementing more efficient energy or waste disposal technology will serve as a strong return on investment, it is argued that without the proper interoperability of these technologies, the returns are short term and arguably diminishing (Bria, 2018). To resolve this, Barcelona's new initiative looks to a CityOS approach where the entirety of the smart city projects can be analysed through a single dashboard.

As a result, Barcelona is the world's leading smart city as its current strategy highlights a redevelopment of the basic structure for which a smart city should be built (Yigitcanlar and Inkinen, 2019). Following the introduction of numerous technologies, Barcelona is essentially learning from a costly lesson by restructuring its internal processes to properly capture the smartness this technology brings. To avoid future challenges, other cities should utilise the lessons learned here and recognise the importance of a standardised data methodology and community engagement platform. Similar to Barcelona's transformation, smart city strategies should focus on resident needs and policy goals. Where driven by data, internal processes and interoperability must be considered before implementation of solutions.

4.4.3.4 Tel Aviv, Israel

Tel Aviv was the 2014 winner of the "World's Best Smart City" (SmartCityExpo, 2014), however its tech-focus as a populace largely predates popular smart city discourse. During the 1980s, Tel Aviv experienced an influx of immigration to which the government responded by developing small business subsidies (Garber, 1991). This encouraged entrepreneurship that is arguably responsible for Tel Aviv's title as "Start Up Capital of the World" (Cooper, 2017). Outside of Silicon Valley, Tel Aviv has the most start-ups per capita in the world. The rise in start-ups has been coupled with advancing technology in the previous decade, and so Tel Aviv's trajectory towards smart city initiatives was inevitable. In 2008 the city began to conceptualise a smart city plan and Tel Aviv's government has largely played the role of facilitator ever since.

As such, this entrepreneurial culture has also embedded itself within Tel Aviv's identity where it now markets itself as a non-stop city with a competitive identity (Telaviv.gov, 2019). An entrepreneurial nature seems to translate into benefits for other aspects of the city as well. Tel Aviv's transfer of academic knowledge into industry products is amongst the highest in the world (Dodd, 2017; Cluer, 2019). Tel Aviv University's research budget sits at close to 90 million USD, whereas Massachusetts Institute of Technology (MIT) sits at 1.5 billion USD.

Tel Aviv's greatest push is on the techno-literacy of its residents and the digitalisation of their lifestyle. Its most successful concept is "Digi-tel", a digital community platform that provides residents with individually tailored information, that allows them to complete all government-based tasks and further contribute to the digital ecosystem (Oliveira, 2017). All data are open source and lay the foundations for continued effective innovation generated by the digitally literate community. Furthermore, the platform offers numerous rewards to subscribed residents to incentivise continued participation, such as discounted tickets to cultural events and further access to contribute to the municipality's decision-making process. Having a platform such as Digi-tel allows a way for Tel Aviv government to interface with its residents on many issues, encouraging trust and transparency among residents and easier facilitation of overall community goals.

Tel-Aviv's implementation of the Digi-tel platform offers residents individually tailored city information on their mobile device, but also offers an open-source platform that tech-savvy residents can utilise to develop their own additions to the platform. This allows for an initial benefit to resident services aligned with a long-term goal of raising the techno-literacy of all residents utilising the platform.

This platform was developed using Microsoft's CityNext services to essentially create a city-wide Customer Relationship Management platform. Tel Aviv utilised this software for its own development which allowed the city to retain control and maintain ownership compared to contracting development by a third party. While data play a part in this ecosystem, most of the lessons learned from this initiative are regarding the facilitation of dialogue between government and residents, encouraging internal collaboration within government, driven by an understanding of what residents need. The community platform allows the government to gather feedback from its residents, and ensures this feedback is utilised most effectively (G Press, 2018). Utilising residents as a resource to develop new solutions allows for a cheaper and more community-driven digital transformation, ensuring higher engagement towards urban change. Furthermore, by retaining government ownership of this transformation, Tel Aviv is afforded a product for consultation to other cities beginning their transformation journey.

4.5 Findings and Discussion

Our objective, in this chapter, is to begin to develop some insights into the different pathways that lead to the creation of thriving smart cities. In particular, we sought to understand how the pathways differed (or not) with respect to achieving key outcomes that define smart cities; notably *governance and services, integration of ICT infrastructure,* and *the role of sustainability and social capital.* In this section, we summarise the key insights from our case examinations for each of these outcomes. Table 4.1 provides a summary of the key smart city case study findings.

Table 4.1 Summary of the key smart city case study findings

Case study	Description	Lessons learned	Timeframe	Budget	Research Theme	Smart City Phase
Songdo, South Korea	Built on reclaimed land from the Yellow Sea, Songdo looks to create a new economic centre for Korea while simultaneously demonstrating the improvements of sustainability-based technology	A focus on external investment and ICT infrastructure has led to a currently under-populated and under-utilised development. Impressive technologically, but largely regarded as a ghost town by locals	2022	$4 billion USD	ICT/infrastructure and sustainability	1.0–2.0
Hudson Yards, NYC	Developed on top of an urban transport hub, the most expensive development in US history looked to bring smart city technologies to an inner-city New York block	As a hugely commercial development, the private partners are yet to deliver on a large amount of the technology promised initially. However, construction of the development has been successful and acts as mostly a tourist attraction then a "smart" contribution to the city	2025	$25 billion USD	ICT/infrastructure and sustainability	1.0–2.0

Masdar City, Abu Dhabi	An extremely ambitious project undertaken by Abu Dhabi with the plans to create a blueprint for a truly sustainable city, both economically and environmentally	Similar to Songdo, this initiative has struggled significantly to gather a substantial population. However, Masdar City now serves in numerous global partnerships making commercially viable the previous investment spent on researching sustainable infrastructure projects	2025	$19.8 billion USD	Sustainability, ICT/infrastructure	1.0–2.0
Gujarat International Finance Tec-City, India	As a part of India's 100 smart cities program, GIFT city looks to develop a financial centre to aid in India's population crisis and act as a global business centre. A large investment in infrastructure and marketing so far has led to similar outcomes as the above projects	Yet to be finished and extremely under-populated, GIFT has struggled in its initial development. Over time however, it has gained interest from the business world, thanks to a large push on city marketing. It is yet to be known whether investment from Bloomberg and other large business will help the city	2025	$20 billion USD	ICT/infrastructure and sustainability	1.0–2.0

(Continued)

Table 4.1 (Continued)

Case study	Description	Lessons learned	Timeframe	Budget	Research Theme	Smart City Phase
Amsterdam Smart City, The Netherlands	Amsterdam is known for innovation across Europe, winning numerous awards for its smart city initiative. This initiative focuses on community engagement and increasing social capital. A platform has been developed to educate and incentivise public–private partnerships related to issues raised within the platform	So far largely successful, Amsterdam's creation of an innovation platform has helped the transfer of knowledge amongst important public and private sectors within Amsterdam. This low-cost platform has allowed for the leveraging of resident data to undertake projects relevant to the residents of the city	2025	5 million Euro	Smart governance/ services, sustainability	2.0–3.0
CityVerve Manchester, UK	CityVerve began as an attempt to develop a blueprint for smart city initiatives across the UK. It aimed to utilise IoT hardware and resident engagement to develop a holistic approach to improving a community	CityVerve has been deemed successful by the UK and the partners involved, however it is yet to be fully analysed. CISCO retains the rights to the blueprint of the initiative, and as such looks to replicating this throughout the UK and Europe. This blueprint is very valuable, however it is not owned by the city it was built for	2019	16 million pounds	ICT/infrastructure and smart governance/ services	2.0–3.0

Smart City Barcelona, Spain	Widely regarded as a pinnacle for smart city development, Barcelona has been a focus for much research regarding smart cities. In this case, we consider the most recent lessons learned and criticisms from within Barcelona government. Directly related to the silos of technology vendors and government departments, and the issues this creates for smart city data	Barcelona has struggled with the implementation of numerous ICT silos due to private hardware vendors and a rushed uptake of IoT solutions. The previous year Barcelona noted the importance of developing an open data strategy and restructuring the way the council interacts with all solutions, to ensure a mitigation of silos and much better interoperability. Furthermore, they have aimed this at being inclusive of residents	2022	2 billion Euro	ICT/infrastructure, smart governance/ services and sustainability/ social capital	2.0–3.0
Jurong Lake District, Singapore	Jurong Lake District has been in planning since 2008, however it is yet to begin proper construction. The masterplan looks as far as 2040–2050 for development. The plan looks towards massive infrastructure upgrades to develop new economic and innovation centres alongside massive transport and logistic hubs	At this stage, JLD have not been able to continue their plan due to Malaysia postponing their contribution to the belt and road initiative. It is yet to be properly analysed, but JLD seems to be marketing a holistic resident-inclusive initiative while developing an externally focused infrastructure upgrade	2040	25 billion USD estimate	ICT/infrastructure, sustainability/ social capital	2.0–3.0

(Continued)

Table 4.1 (Continued)

Case study	Description	Lessons learned	Timeframe	Budget	Research Theme	Smart City Phase
Tel Aviv, Israel	Tel-Aviv has received as much praise as Barcelona in previous years for the development of its digital platform Digi-tel. This platform allows residents to perform numerous digital services within one application, and has been revered as a successful way to deliver services to residents and simultaneously improve their techno-literacy	Similar to CityVerve in some ways, Tel-Aviv utilised Microsoft technology to develop their Digi-tel platform, however it retains ownership of the platform itself. This allows for city-based modifications and effective use of the data generated by the platform. Tel-Aviv appears to be successful in navigating the issues of other smart cities like Barcelona. However, Tel-Aviv does not demonstrate any major infrastructure upgrades specifically	On-going	4 billion USD	Smart governance/ services, sustainability	2.0–3.0

First, at the core of the *governance and services* theme is a question of the provision of public services. That is, how is the adoption of ICTs facilitating government services? It may not be surprising, but the two development pathways—green field and neighbourhood development—seem less successful than the platform pathway in enhancing public service delivery. This insight, however, may be somewhat premature. The primary objective of the development pathways is to establish a new physical infrastructure—which these development projects have, more or less, achieved. The question of how these infrastructure efforts have effectively met the needs of residents remains something of an open question. In contrast, the platform-based pathway, perhaps predictably, is more quickly and effectively enhancing the service provision for local residents. For example, Tel-Aviv's population has seen a large improvement in technological capabilities from the Digi-tel platform, noting residents are even developing their own improvements to the software. This technologically educated population provides an attractive talent pool for business and investment and allows residents to engage further with the co-creation of solutions to numerous urban challenges. Additionally, to the degree that "transparency" is an objective of public sector service provision, the platform pathway far exceeds the two development pathways. For example, in the smart city initiatives in both Amsterdam and Barcelona, the government enhanced transparency towards the community by publishing documents and websites that clearly outline the goals of the initiative. Rather than attempting to reach these goals independently, the council launched a platform where the community can contribute and become a part of the discussion.

The second theme, *integration of ICT infrastructure*, shifts the emphasis from service delivery to infrastructure development. As one might anticipate, both development pathways are clearly more successful at integrating ICTs with their physical infrastructure than the platform-based approach. That said, these development pathways face multiple challenges in terms of achieving "smartness." That is to say, projects have demonstrated varying levels of success, partly due to the complexity, duration, and scale of the transformation. For example, green-field developments like Masdar City show little success in terms of population, but large success in terms of global partnerships and economic returns. Also, Hudson Yards is one such example that has received public criticism due to its failure to so far deliver on the advanced data and sensor technology it promised. The physical construction has been successful, but without delivering on some of the initial "smart city" deliverables, the development has been interpreted as purely an exercise for commercial investment, without a clear benefit for the greater public. What these examples demonstrate is that even as the physical infrastructure is developed, one of the most difficult challenges with these development projects—both greenfield and neighbourhood—is in aligning the development processes with the socio-economic and political conditions in which they operate. Often, the most impressive infrastructure upgrades have been left underutilised due to a lack of public interest, or the political conditions change before the project's completion.

In our final theme, *the role of sustainability and social capital*, we find some unique findings. At the heart of this theme is the idea that smart communities are both environmentally and socially sustainable—where social sustainability is understood in terms of resident engagement and connectedness. Interestingly, the platform pathway has provided a far greater reported level of engagement and connectedness. This is somewhat surprising. Because the development pathways occur in the physical space of the city and are, typically, part of a public development approval process, one might expect to see more resident engagement than in smart cities created through the platform pathway. Conversely, we found the opposite. For example, a noticeable trend across the European smart city landscape; Amsterdam, Barcelona, and Manchester have all focused on the development of a platform that allows residents to participate within the urban transformation conversation. At the outset, these initiatives are cheaper and tend to result in greater buy-in from the public. Less examples of public criticism can be found within these initiatives as the public is a present actor within the transformation. These initiatives tend to align with the transformation of existing areas and the integration of ICT systems to enable the resident–government conversation. Relative to the development pathways, the platform pathways are, in some ways, developed and implemented through a more engaged and "bottom-up" approach. That said, both development pathways are, clearly, far more complex undertakings. As a result, more "top-down" approaches may seem to be the more expedient way forward. However, to pursue smart city developments from this perspective presents clear limits on the ability to fully develop a city's "smartness."

4.6 Conclusion

Transforming urban areas into prosperous, liveable, and sustainable settlements is a longstanding goal for local governments. Today, countless urban settlements across the globe have embraced the smart city idea to achieve this goal. Under the smart city agenda, many government agencies are attempting to engineer an urban transformation to tackle urban issues mostly through technology solutions (Yigitcanlar et al., 2020a). Nevertheless, there is limited understanding on what smart cities really are, how they emerge, and how prosperous and sustainable, smart cities can be erected. This chapter sought to shed light on this understudied area and generate insights to assist cities and their administrations.

Our exploratory study allowed us to develop insights into the making of thriving smart cities. The investigation revealed that we are at the beginning of a new era that technology and the city are converging; but at the same time the traditional tools of urban policymaking and planning—such as stakeholder/community engagement, placemaking, participatory design, urban metabolism approach—are still highly relevant. A healthy mix of contemporary and traditional tools and approaches is critical in the development of prosperous and sustainable smart cities. That is to say, while smart technology is critical (Yigitcanlar et al., 2020b), technology alone cannot create smart cities, as it takes more than just the state-of-the-art technological solutions to transform cities into truly smart and sustainable ones.

Additionally, as the study reveals, different approaches are followed in different corners of the globe for the development and practice of smart cities. This finding has helped us to conceptualise three distinctive pathways for smart cities. These pathways to the making of prosperous smart cities are: (a) the development of entirely new (smart) cities—from scratch development, (b) smart city development projects within particular parts of the city—infill smart precinct/neighbourhood development, and (c) the advancement of smart cities through the integration of ICTs within the city organisation—retrofitting the city with smart technologies and platforms to increase efficiencies.

Next, while each of the abovementioned pathways has their strengths and weaknesses, and are suitable for certain country contexts, they shed light on the future research studies that will focus on the development of new and consolidated pathways. Nevertheless, it should not be forgotten that the making of prosperous smart cities highly depends on adequately linking the guiding principles (such as having a system of systems approach, adopting a quadruple-bottom-line sustainable urban development perspective, and mainstreaming the urban metabolism approach) and traditional policymaking and planning methods with technological advancements and the needs of societies (Yigitcanlar et al., 2019c). This rule applies to all of the distinctive pathways this study has introduced, and the prospective ones yet to be formed.

Future research is needed to build on our work. First, while our cases have revealed critical patterns in smart city development trajectories, further work is needed to understand and validate the various socio-economic and political factors that impact development trajectories. Second, research should examine how planners and policymakers can design more sustainable pathways to develop new smart cities and retrofit existing cities. Third, as noted in our cases, the use of public finance, the design and governance of public–private partnerships, and the management of mega-scale projects impact the success of smart city development efforts. Future research is desperately needed on these issues to improve our track record on smart city development efforts (Desouza et al., 2020).

Acknowledgements

This chapter, with permission from the copyright holder, is a reproduced version of the following journal article: Desouza, K., Hunter, M., Jacob, B., Yigitcanlar, T. (2020). Pathways to the making of prosperous smart cities: An exploratory study on the best practice. *Journal of Urban Technology* 27(3), 3–32.

References

Abhirup, R., Jain, R. (2019). *India's Jobs Deficit: Project in Gujarat Struggling to Create Employment*. USA: Reuters. www.reuters.com/article/us-india-election-giftcity-insight/indias-jobs-deficit-project-in-gujarat-struggling-to-create-employment-idUSKCN1SU04Y (accessed 24 May 2019).

Albers, E. (2018). *Using Free Software to Build a More Democratic, Inclusive and Sustainable Digital Society*. ES: Free Software Foundation Europe. https://fsfe.org/news/2018/news-20180705-01.en.html (accessed 12 June 2019).

Albino, V., Berardi, U., Dangelico, R. (2015). Smart cities: Definitions, dimensions, performance, and initiatives. *Journal of Urban Technology, 22*(1), 3–21.

Amsterdam Smart Citizens Lab. (2016). *Citizen Science – The Bottom Up Way*. Amsterdam, NL: Amsterdam Smart Citizens Lab. https://amsterdamsmartcity.com/projects/amsterdam-smart-citizens-lab-3901oh7g (accessed 28 May 2019).

Angelidou, M. (2017). The role of smart city characteristics in the plans of fifteen cities. *Journal of Urban Technology, 24*(4), 3–28.

ANS. (2018). *Creating the 1st blueprint for UK smart cities – ANS means business.* Manchester, UK: ANS. www.ans.co.uk/case-studies/cityverve/ (accessed 11 June 2019).

Anuta, J. (2014). *Hudson Yards to be First 'Quantified 'Community'*. New York, NY: Crains New York Business. www.crainsnewyork.com/article/20140414/REAL_ESTATE/140419932/hudson-yards-to-be-first-quantified-community – Anuta 2014 (accessed 12 May 2019).

ASTAR. (2017). *Opening Address by Chairman of A*STAR, Mr. Lim Chuan Poh, at the Future of Manufacturing Summit Singapore on 5 September 2017 at Resorts World Sentosa.* Singapore, SG: ASTAR. www.a-star.edu.sg/News-and-Events/News/Speeches/ID/5671 (accessed 20 June 2019).

Au-Yong, R. (2017). *The Story of Jurong Lake District – From the Boondocks to Boom-Town and Beyond.* Singapore, SG: The Straits Times. www.straitstimes.com/singapore/from-the-boondocks-to-boom-town-and-beyond (accessed 18 June 2019).

Bakici, T., Almirall, E., Wareham, J. (2013). A smart city initiative: the case of Barcelona. *Journal of the Knowledge Economy, 4*(2), 135–148.

Barcelona City Council. (2016). *General Principles of Technological Sovereignty.* Barcelona, EG: Barcelona Government. www.barcelona.cat/digitalstandards/en/tech-sovereignty/0.1/general-principles (accessed 25 May 2019).

Berrone, P., Ricart, J., Carrasco, C. (2016). The open kimono: Toward a general framework for open data initiatives in Cities. *California Management Review, 59*(1), 39–70.

Bhatnarga, J. (2016). *Gujarat International Finance Tec-city: A Smart GIFT"*. India: Financial Express. www.financialexpress.com/economy/gujarat-international-finance-tec-city-a-smart-gift/53955/ (accessed 15 October 2019).

Bhattacharya, T., Bhattacharya, A., McLellan, B., Tezuka, T. (2018). Sustainable smart city development framework for developing countries. *Urban Research & Practice, 13*(2), 180–212.

Bibri, S. (2018). *Smart Sustainable Cities of the Future The Untapped Potential of Big Data Analytics and Context–Aware Computing for Advancing Sustainability.* Springer Cham.

Bibri, S., Krogstie, J. (2017). Smart sustainable cities of the future: An extensive interdisciplinary literature review. *Sustainable Cities and Society, 31*, 183–212.

Blackman, J. (2018). *We Will Seriously 'Productize' CityVerve.* United Kingdom, UK: Internet of Things Enterprise. https://enterpriseiotinsights.com/20180620/channels/news/we-will-productise-cityverve-says-cisco-tag40 (accessed 21 June 2019).

Bloomberg (2018). *Gujarat International Finance Tec-City and Bloomberg Collaborate to Advance India's International Financial Services Center to Global Investors.* United States of America, US: Bloomberg Professional Services. www.bloomberg.com/company/press/gujarat-international-finance-tec-city-gift-city-bloomberg-collaborate-advance-indias-international-financial-services-centre-ifsc-global-investors/ (accessed 10 June 2019).

Bouzguenda, I., Alalouch, C., Fava, N. (2019). Towards smart sustainable cities: A review of the role digital citizen participation could play in advancing social sustainability. *Sustainable Cities and Society, 50*, 101627.

Bowerman, B., Braverman, J., Taylor, J., Todosow, H., Wimmersperg, U. (2000). *The Vision of a Smart City*, paper presented at 2nd International Life Extension Technology Workshop. Paris, September 28, 2000.

Byung-yeul, B. (2018). *Incheon FEZ Becomes Global Business Hub*. Korea, KOR: The Korea Times. www.koreatimes.co.kr/www/tech/2018/12/693_259369.html (accessed 14 June 2019).

Capdevila, I., Zarlenga, M. (2015). Smart city or smart citizens? The Barcelona case. *Journal of Strategy and Management, 8*(3), 266–282.

Centre de Formacio. (2015). *Juniper Research Ranked BCN as the Number One Smart City this Year*. Barcelona, ES: Centre De Formacio. http://blog.barcelonaguidebur eau.com/juniper-research-ranked-bcn-as-the-no-1-smart-city-this-year/ (accessed 12 June 2019).

Charles, A. (2015). *How can India make Smart Cities a Reality?* Davos, CH, World Economic Forum. www.weforum.org/agenda/2015/11/how-can-india-make-smart-cit ies-a-reality/ (accessed 24 May 2019).

Choque, J., Medela, A., Echevarria, J., Diez, L., Munoz, L. (2018). *Enabling Incentivization and Citizen Engagement in the Smart-City Co-creation Paradigm*, paper presented at 2018 Global Internet of Things Summit, June 4–7, Bilbao.

CISCO. (2017). *CISCO Announces $1 Billion Program for Smart Cities*. Manchester, UK: CISCO. https://newsroom.cisco.com/press-release-content?type=webcontent& articleId=1895705 (accessed 15 June 2019).

CISCO. (2019). *Public Sector Digital Transformation Map – CISCO Case Studies*. Manchester, UK: CISCO. www.cisco.com/c/m/en_us/solutions/industries/smart-connected-communities/digital-transformation-map.html (accessed 15 June 2019).

Cluer, J. (2019). *Top Five: Israel's Innovation Centre*. Western Australia, AUS: Australia-Israel – Chamber of Commerce WA Inc. www.aiccwa.org.au/Profiles/aiccwa/Assets/ClientData/Images/Events/Israels_Innovation_Culture.pdf (accessed 2 July 2019).

Cohen, B. (2015). *The Three Generations of Smart Cities*. New York, NY: Fast Company. www.fastcompany.com/3047795/the-3-generations-of-smart-cities (accessed 15 September 2015).

Cooper, C. (2017). *How Israel Became a Start-up Nation*. Melbourne, AU: InTheBlack – Economics. www.intheblack.com/articles/2017/11/01/israel-start-up-nation (accessed 2 July 2019).

Cosgrave, E., Arbuthnot, K., Tryfonas, T. (2013). Living labs, innovation districts and information marketplaces: A systems approach for smart cities. *Procedia Computer Science, 16*(C), 668–677.

Cugurullo, F. (2013). How to build a sandcastle: An analysis of the genesis and development of Masdar City. *Journal of Urban Technology, 20*(1), 23–37.

Cugurullo, F. (2016). Urban eco-modernisation and the policy context of new eco-city projects: Where Masdar City fails and why. *Urban Studies, 11*(53), 2417–2433.

Dameri, R. (2013). Searching for smart city definition: A comprehensive proposal. *International Journal of Computers and Technology, 11*(5), 2544–2551.

Da-sol, K. (2018). *IEFZ Unveils Plans to Make Songdo World-class Bio Industry Hub*. Korea, KOR: The Korea Times. www.koreaherald.com/view.php?ud=20180424000 721 (accessed 2 July 2019).

Desouza, K., Bhagwatwar, A. (2012). Citizen apps to solve complex urban problems. *Journal of Urban Technology, 19*(3), 107–136.

Desouza, K., Bhagwatwar, A. (2014). Technology-enabled participatory platforms for civic engagement: The case of US Cities. *Journal of Urban Technology, 21*(4), 25–50.

Desouza, K., Hunter, M., Yigitcanlar, T. (2019). Under the hood: A look at techno-centric smart city development. *Public Management, 101*(11), 30–35.

Desouza, K., Flanery, T. (2013). Designing, planning, and managing resilient cities: A conceptual framework. *Cities, 35*, 89–99.

Desouza, K., M. Hunter, B. Jacob, T. Yigitcanlar (2020). Pathways to the making of prosperous smart cities: An exploratory study on the best practice. *Journal of Urban Technology, 27*(3), 3–32.

Dodd, T. (2017). *Hebrew University of Jerusalem earned US20b Revenue from Commercializing its Research.* Australia, AUS: Australian Financial Review. www.afr.com/work-and-careers/management/hebrew-university-of-jerusalem-earns-us20b-from-commercialising-its-research-20170713-gxaqb9 (accessed 4 July 2019).

Drubin, C. (2018). Singapore tops in smart city rankings. *Microwave Journal, 61*, 6.

Dunleavy, P., Margetts, H., Bastow, S., Tinkler, J. (2006). New public management is dead—Long live digital-era governance. *Journal of Public Administration Research and Theory, 16*(3), 467–494.

European Commission. (2014). *Amsterdam Smart City.* Amsterdam, NL: European Commission. https://ec.europa.eu/regional_policy/en/projects/best-practices/netherlands/2115 (accessed 2 June 2019).

Fishenden, J., Thompson, M. (2013). Digital government, open architecture, and innovation: Why public sector IT will never be the same again. *Journal of Public Administration Research and Theory, 23*(4), 977–1004.

Fitzgerald, M. (2016). *Data Driven City Management.* Cambridge, MA: MIT Sloan Management Review. https://sloanreview.mit.edu/case-study/data-driven-city-management/ (accessed 18 May 2019).

Forster, R. (2018). How Barcelona's Smart City Strategy Is Giving 'Power to the People'. *Cities Today* https://cities-today.com/power-to-the-people/ (accessed 23 June 2019).

Garber, B. (1991). *Israel Opens Labor Force for Russians.* Boston, MA: Jewish Advocate. https://gateway.library.qut.edu.au/login?url=https://search.proquest.com/docview/205159350?accountid=13380 (accessed 11 June 2019).

Garfield, L. (2017). *South Korea is Building a $40 Billion City Designed to Eliminate the Need for Cars.* AUS: The Business Insider. www.businessinsider.com.au/songdo-south-korea-design-2017-11?r=US&IR=T (accessed 12 June 2019).

Gascó-Hernandez, M. (2018). Building a smart city: Lessons from Barcelona. *Communications of the ACM, 61*(4), 50–57.

GIFT-City. (2019). *GIFT Special Economic Zone.* India: Gujarat International Financial Services Centre. www.giftgujarat.in/gift-sez (accessed 25 May 2019).

Goh, E., Reilly, J. (2017). China's belt and road initiative. *East Asia Forum Quarterly, 9*(4), 33–34.

Goldenberg, S. (2016). *Analysis shows Hudson Yard's Impact of City's Economy.* NY: Politico. www.related.com/sites/default/files/2019-03/acquiadam-assets/relatedcorporate-news-05-2017-Politico-HudsonYards-economic-impact.pdf (accessed 2 June 2019).

Goldenberg, S. (2016). *Masdar's Zero-carbon Dream could become World's First Green Ghost Town.* AUS: The Guardian. www.theguardian.com/environment/2016/feb/16/masdars-zero-carbon-dream-could-become-worlds-first-green-ghost-town (accessed 17 February 2016).

Granier, B., & Kudo, H. (2016). How are citizens involved in smart cities? Analysing citizen participation in Japanese "smart communities". *Information Polity, 21*(1), 61–76.

GUDC. (2019). *About Us.* India: Gujarat Urban Development Company. www.gudcltd.com/ (accessed 3 June 2019).

GulfNews. (2019). 10.5 billion worth of deals reach at energy summit in Abu Dhabi. UAE: Gulf News – Energy. https://gulfnews.com/business/energy/105-billion-worth-of-deals-reached-at-energy-summit-in-abu-dhabi-1.1548070371434 (accessed 15 May 2019).

Haag, M., (2019). *Amazon's Tax Breaks and Incentives Were Big. Hudson Yards are Bigger.* New York, NY: The New York Times. www.nytimes.com/2019/03/09/nyregion/hudson-yards-new-york-tax-breaks.html (accessed 9 March 2019).

Hammer, S., Kamal-Chaoui, L., Robert, A., Plouin, M. (2011). Cities and green growth: A conceptual framework. *OECD Regional Development Working Papers,* OECD Publishing, 08.

Hanifan, L.J. (1916). The rural school community centre. *Annals of the American Academy of Political and Social Sciences, 67,* 130–138.

Hashem, I.A., Chang, V., Anuar, N.B., Adewole, K., Yaqoob, I., Gani, A., Chiroma, H. (2016). The role of big data in smart city. *International Journal of Information Management, 36*(5), 748–758.

Heo, T., Kim, K., Kim, H., Lee, C., Ryu, J., Leem, Y., Ko, J. (2014). Escaping from Ancient Rome! Applications and challenges for designing smart cities. *Transactions on Emerging Telecommunications Technologies, 25*(1), 109–119.

Hollands, R. (2008). Will the real smart city please stand up?: Intelligent, progressive or entrepreneurial? *City, 12*(3), 303–320.

Hudson Yards (2016). *New Report Details Substantial Economic Impact of Hudson Yards Development.* New York, NY: Hudson Yards – Press Releases. www.hudsonyardsnewyork.com/press-media/press-releases/new-report-details-substantial-economic-impact-hudson-yards-development (accessed 14 June 2019).

Hunter, M., Selby, J.D., Desouza, K.C. (2019). *Cities Are Surprisingly Fragile.* Scientific American. https://blogs.scientificamerican.com/observations/cities-are-surprisingly-fragile/ (accessed 3 June 2019).

Husár, M., Ondrejička, V., Variş, S. (2017). Smart cities and the idea of smartness in urban development – A critical review. *IOP Conference Series: Materials Science and Engineering, 245*(8), 082008/1–082008/8.

iAmsterdam (2019). *Amsterdam: Capital of Innovation.* Amsterdam, NL: Amsterdam and Partners Foundation. www.iamsterdam.com/en/business/news-and-insights/capital-of-innovation (accessed 28 May 2019).

IMD. (2019). *IMD and SUTD Unique Ranking Shows Importance of Citizens' Needs in Policy Making.* IMD Smart City Index. www.imd.org/smart-city-observatory/smart-city-index/ (accessed 8 June 2019).

Incheon Global Campus. (2019). *About.* IGC, KOR: Incheon Global Campus. www.igc.or.kr/en/index.do (accessed 11 June 2019).

India ICT. (2019). *Digitel – Tel Aviv, Israel. Case Study.* India: ICT Enabled Integration for Green Growth Project. http://icities4greengrowth.in/casestudy/digitel-tel-aviv-israel (accessed 3 June 2019).

Indianix. (2019). *Services, About Us.* India: International Financial Services Centre. www.indiainx.com/static/ifsc.aspx (accessed 4 June 2019).

Ismail, N. (2018). *3 Smart City Lessons from Manchester and the UK's Smart City IoT demonstrator, City Verve. Information Age, Topics, Smart Cities.* UK: Information Age. www.information-age.com/smart-city-lessons-123474272/ (accessed 4 June 2019).

JTC Corporation. (2019). *Jurong Innovation District.* SG: JTC – Projects and Properties. www.jtc.gov.sg/industrial-land-and-space/Pages/jurong-innovation-district.aspx (accessed 11 June 2019).

Kaye, L. (2017). *Pushing the Low Carbon Boundaries: South Korea's Smart Grid Initiative.* Australia, AUS: The Guardian. www.theguardian.com/sustainable-business/south-korea-smart-grid-low-carbon (accessed 24 May 2019).

Khare, V. (2019). *India Election 2019: Have '100 smart cities' been built?* London, UK: BBC News. www.bbc.com/news/world-asia-india-47025472 (accessed 16 June 2019).

Kitchin, R. (2015). Making sense of smart cities: Addressing present shortcomings. *Cambridge Journal of Regions, Economy and Society, 8*(1), 131–136.

Komninos, N., Kakderi, C., Panori, A., Tsarchopoulos, P. (2019). Smart city planning from an evolutionary perspective. *Journal of Urban Technology, 26*(2), 3–20.

Kummitha, R., Crutzen, N. (2017). How do we understand smart cities? An evolutionary perspective. *Cities, 67*, 43–52.

Lara, A., Moreira Da Costa, E., Furlani, T., Yigitcanlar, T. (2016). Smartness that matters: Towards a comprehensive and human-centered characterisation of smart cities. *Journal of Open Innovation: Technology, Market, and Complexity, 2*(1), 1–13.

Lawrence, C. (2017). *Why Smart City Amsterdam is the Home of Innovation.* IoT Zone. https://dzone.com/articles/why-smart-city-amsterdam-is-the-home-of-innovation (accessed 8 June 2019).

Liu, N., Gavino, A., Purao, S. (2014). A method for designing value-infused citizen services in smart cities. *Proceedings of the 15th Annual International Conference on Digital Government Research*, 34–43.

Macpherson, L. (2017). *8 Years on, Amsterdam is still leading the way as a Smart City.* Towards Data Science. https://towardsdatascience.com/8-years-on-amsterdam-is-still-leading-the-way-as-a-smart-city-79bd91c7ac13 (accessed 10 June 2019).

Malone, D. (2016). *Despite Troubled Development, Masdar City Forges Ahead.* BCD Network, Urban Planning. www.bdcnetwork.com/despite-troubled-development-masdar-city-forges-ahead (accessed 17 June 2019).

Mancebo, F. (2019). Smart city strategies: Time to involve people. Comparing Amsterdam, Barcelona and Paris. *Journal of Urbanism: International Research on Placemaking and Urban Sustainability, 13*(2), 133–152.

MASDAR. (2019). *Clean Energy – Projects.* UAE: Masdar City Website – The City. https://masdar.ae/en/masdar-city/the-city/sustainability (accessed 16 June 2019).

MASDAR. (2019). *Sustainability.* UAE: Masdar City Website – The City. https://masdar.ae/en/masdar-city/the-city/sustainability (accessed 16 June 2019).

McKinsey. (2018). *Smart Cities: Digital Solutions for a more Livable Future.* McKinsey Global Institute. www.mckinsey.com/~/media/mckinsey/industries/capital%20projects%20and%20infrastructure/our%20insights/smart%20cities%20digital%20solutions%20for%20a%20more%20livable%20future/mgi-smart-cities-full-report.ashx (accessed 2 July 2019).

Meetup.com. (2019). *Amsterdam Smart Citizens Lab.* Meetup.com. www.meetup.com/Amsterdam-Smart-Citizens-Lab/events/

Menny, M., Palgan, Y., McCormick, K. (2018). Urban living labs and the role of users in co-creation. *Gaia, 27*(S1), 68–77.

Microsoft. (2018). *Microsoft Driving Intelligent, Connected Smart Cities.* Microsoft in Government, Industry Blogs. https://cloudblogs.microsoft.com/industry-blog/government/2018/11/12/microsoft-driving-intelligent-connected-smart-cities/ (accessed 1 July 2019).

Microsoft. (2019). *Welcome to Microsoft CityNext.* Partner Network, Microsoft. https://partner.microsoft.com/en-us/solutions/citynext (accessed 23 June 2019).

Mora, L., Deakin, M., Reid, A. (2019). Strategic principles for smart city development: A multiple case study analysis of European best practices. *Technological Forecasting and Social Change, 142*, 70–97.

Moser, S. (2013). New cities: Opportunities, visions and challenges: Summary and analysis report. *Cityquest – KAEC Forum.*

Mullins, P., Shwayri, S. (2016). Green cities and "IT839": A new paradigm for economic growth in South Korea. *Journal of Urban Technology, 23*(2), 47–64.

Nam, T., Pardo, T.A. (2011). Conceptualizing smart city with dimensions of technology, people, and institutions. *12th Annual International Digital Government Research Conference: Digital Government Innovation in Challenging Times,* 282–291.

Newton, P. (2012). Liveable *and* sustainable? Socio-technical challenges for twenty-first-century cities. *Journal of Urban Technology, 19*(1), 81–102.

Nolan, H. (2019). *New York's Hudson Yards is an ultra-capitalist Forbidden City.* New York, NY: The Guardian. www.theguardian.com/commentisfree/2019/mar/13/new-york-hudson-yards-ultra-capitalist (accessed 8 June 2019).

Nonko, E. (2019). *Hudson Yards promised a High-Tech Neighborhood – It was a Greater Challenge than Expected.* Metropolis Magazine. www.metropolismag.com/cities/hudson-yards-technology-urbanism/ (accessed 8 June 2019).

OECD Insights. (2007). The bigger picture. Human capital: How what you know shapes your life. *OECD Insights, 6*, 102–105.

Oliveira, E. (2017). Review of citizen empowerment and innovation in the data-rich city. *Journal of Urban Technology, 24*(2), 111–114.

Otgaar, A., Carvalho, L. (2016). Mobile world capital (Barcelona). In: *Delivering Sustainable Competitiveness: Revisiting the Organising Capacity of Cities,* 92–107.

Pereira, G., Cunha, M., Lampoltshammer, T., Parycek, P., Testa, M. (2017). Increasing collaboration and participation in smart city governance: A cross-case analysis of smart city initiatives. *Information Technology for Development, 23*(3), 526–553.

Piro, G., Cianci, I., Grieco, L.A., Boggia, G., Camarda, P. (2014). Information centric services in smart cities. *Journal of Systems and Software, 88*(1), 169–188.

Plitt, A. (2019). *Hudson Yards Opening: Timeline of the Megaproject's Major Moments.* New York, NY: Curbed New York – NYC Development News. https://ny.curbed.com/2019/3/13/18252323/hudson-yards-new-york-construction-timeline (accessed 25 June 2019).

Poon, L. (2018). *Sleepy in Songdo, Korea's Smartest City.* Korea, KOR: Citylab. www.citylab.com/life/2018/06/sleepy-in-songdo-koreas-smartest-city/561374/ (accessed 4 June 2019).

G Press. (2018). *6 Lessons From Tel-Aviv For Successful Digital Transformation Of Smart Cities.* Forbes, Enterprise and Cloud. www.forbes.com/sites/gilpress/2018/03/22/6-lessons-from-tel-aviv-for-successful-digital-transformation-of-smart-cities/#351873965330 (accessed 2 June 2019).

PR Newswire. (2018). *A Record-breaking Edition of Smart City Expo Will Focus on Building More Liveable Cities.* New York, NY: PR Newswire. http://search.proquest.com/docview/2132240521/ (accessed 23 June 2019).

Reboredo, R. (2019). *What a Failed Johannesburg Project Tells Us about Mega Cities in Africa.* Australia, AUS: The Conversation. http://theconversation.com/what-a-failed-johannesburg-project-tells-us-about-mega-cities-in-africa-112420 (accessed 11 June 2019).

Rios, P. (2008). *Creating "the Smart City".* Detroit: University of Detroit Mercy.

Rojc, P. (2019). *Promised Data-Driven Infrastructure on Hold at Hudson Yards.* USA: Planetizen. www.planetizen.com/news/2019/02/103015-promised-data-driven-infrastructure-hold-hudson-yards (accessed 25 May 2019).

Rossi, U. (2016). The variegated economics and the potential politics of the smart city. *Territory, Politics, Governance, 4*(3), 337–353.

Shwayri, S. (2013). A model Korean ubiquitous eco-city? The politics of making Songdo. *Journal of Urban Technology, 20*(1), 39–55.

SmartCities. (2016). *Smart Cities Mission.* India: Ministry of Housing and Urban Affairs, Government of India. http://smartcities.gov.in/content/ (accessed 23 June 23 2019).

SmartCities World. (2018). *Citizen Engagement is the Key to Smart City Success.* Smart Cities World. www.smartcitiesworld.net/news/news/citizen-engagement-is-key-to-smart-city-success-2685 (accessed 19 June 2019).

SmartCity.com. (2019). *Oslo – A Smart City with a Pioneering Thinking Against Climate Change. Environment, Climate Change, Europe, Smart City Press.* Smart City Press. www.smartcity.press/climate-change-in-oslo/ (accessed 13 June 2019).

SmartCityExpo. (2014). *SCEWC 2014 Report. Change The World.* Smart City Expo, World Congress. www.smartcityexpo.com/the-event/past-editions-2014 (accessed 19 June 2019).

Soyata, T., Habibzadeh, H., Ekenna, C., Nussbaum, B., Lozano, J. (2019). Smart city in crisis: Technology and policy concerns. *Sustainable Cities and Society, 50,* 101566.

Telaviv.gov. (2019). *Tel-Aviv Startup City.* Tel Aviv, IL: Tel Aviv Non Stop City. www.tel-aviv.gov.il/en/WorkAndStudy/Pages/StartupCity.aspx (accessed 20 June 2019).

Tieman, R. (2017). *Barcelona: Smart City Revolution in Progress.* Financial Times. www.ft.com/content/6d2fe2a8-722c-11e7-93ff-99f383b09ff9 (accessed 23 May 2019).

Tyler, J., Bendix, A. (2018). *Hudson Yards is the most Expensive Real-estate Development in the US History. Here's what it's like Inside the $25 Billion Neighbourhood.* AUS: Business Insider. www.businessinsider.com.au/hudson-yards-tour-of-most-expensive-development-in-us-history-2018-9?r=US&IR=T (accessed 23 May 2019).

United Nations. (2008). *World Urbanization Prospects: The 2007 Revision Population Database.* UN. http://esa.un.org/unup/ (accessed 3 June 2019).

van den Bosch, H. (2018) *Smart Beyond Technology Push. Smart City Hub, Technology and Innovation.* Smart City Hub. http://smartcityhub.com/technology-innnovation/smart-beyond-technology-push/ (accessed 11 June 2019).

van Waart, P., I. Mulder, I., de Bont, C., Bolívar, M., Meijer, A., Gil-Garcia, J. (2016). A participatory approach for envisioning a smart city. *Social Science Computer Review, 34*(6), 708–723.

Venkataraman, P. (2018). *Gujarat's GIFT City named among Top Three Emerging Business Hubs in the World.* News18. www.news18.com/news/business/gujarats-gift-city-named-among-top-three-emerging-business-hubs-in-world-1876885.html (accessed 16 June 2019).

Wade, G. (2017). *China's 'One Belt, One Road' Initiative.* AUS: Foreign Affairs, Defence and Security. Parliament of Australia. www.aph.gov.au/About_Parliament/Parliamentary_Departments/Parliamentary_Library/pubs/BriefingBook45p/ChinasRoad (accessed 8 June 2019).

Yigitcanlar, T. (2011). Moving towards a knowledge city?: Brisbane's experience in knowledge-based urban development. *International Journal of Knowledge-Based Organizations (IJKBO), 1*(3), 22–38.

Yigitcanlar, T. (2016). *Technology and the City: Systems, Applications and Implications.* Routledge: Taylor & Francis Group.

Yigitcanlar, T., Hoon, M., Kamruzzaman, M., Ioppolo, G., Sabatini-Marques, J. (2019a). The making of smart cities: Are Songdo, Masdar, Amsterdam, San Francisco and Brisbane the best we could build? *Land Use Policy, 88,* 104187.

Yigitcanlar, T., Kamruzzaman, M., Foth, M., Sabatini-Marques, J., Costa, E., Ioppolo, G. (2019b). Can cities become smart without being sustainable? A systematic review of the literature. *Sustainable Cities and Society, 45,* 348–365.

Yigitcanlar, T., Foth, M., Kamruzzaman, M. (2019c). Towards post-anthropocentric cities: Reconceptualising smart cities to evade urban ecocide. *Journal of Urban Technology, 26*(2), 147–152.

Yigitcanlar, T., Han, H., Kamruzzaman, M. (2019d). Approaches, advances, and applications in the sustainable development of smart cities: A commentary from the guest editors. *Energies, 12*(23), 4554.

Yigitcanlar, T., Desouza, K., Butler, L., Roozkhosh, F. (2020a). Contributions and risks of artificial intelligence (AI) in building smarter cities: Insights from a systematic review of the literature. *Energies, 13*(6), 1473.

Yigitcanlar, T., Butler, L., Windle, E., Desouza, K., Mehmood, R., Corchado, J. (2020b). Can building 'artificially intelligent cities' protect humanity from natural disasters, pandemics and other catastrophes? An urban scholar's perspective. *Sensors, 20*(10), 2988.

Yigitcanlar, T., Kamruzzaman, M., Buys, L., Ioppolo, G., Sabatini-Marques, J., Costa, E., Yun, J. (2018). Understanding 'smart cities': Intertwining development drivers with desired outcomes in a multidimensional framework. *Cities, 81,* 145–160.

Yigitcanlar, T., Lee, S. (2014). Korean ubiquitous-eco-city: A smart-sustainable urban form or a branding hoax? *Technological Forecasting and Social Change, 89,* 100–114.

Yin, R.K. (2003). *Case Study Research, Design and Methods.* Newbury Park: Sage.

Yin, R.K. (2011). *Qualitative Research from Start to Finish.* Guilford Press: London.

Zarroli, J. (2015). *How Singapore Became One of the Richest Places on Earth.* SG: Weekend Edition Sunday. NPR. www.npr.org/2015/03/29/395811510/how-singapore-became-one-of-the-richest-places-on-earth (accessed 27 May 2019).

Zhang, X. (2019). *Remaking Sustainable Urbanism Space, Scale and Governance in the New Urban Era.* Palgrave Macmillan.

5 Best Practice

5.1 Introduction

The number of urban dwellers has been growing at a rate of around 60 million people annually over the last few decades (Goonetilleke et al., 2014). This trend, day by day, is turning our planet into an exceedingly urbanised one. The worst side of this growth is that it is largely unplanned or informal and sprawling in nature. This urbanisation practice—in the Anthropocene, a geological era of human domination of Earth's resources—leads to many complex problems, with the most important one being the climate emergency (Dizdaroglu et al., 2012). Over the last few years, various solutions have been put forward to combat the consequential problems of unsustainable urbanism. These include adopting new paradigms to make cities more sustainable, resilient, and smarter—and as a consequence to generate prosperity, liveability, and wellbeing for citizens, and making cities more environmentally friendly (Yigitcanlar, 2009; Albino et al., 2015).

These solutions, however, have not found large-scale application across the globe. Problems caused by rapid urbanisation—and also dependency on fossil fuel—have thus remained catastrophic. In most parts of the world, city administrations are being challenged to provide essential services to the urban population such as accessibility, safety and security, healthy built and natural environments, social equity, clean energy, affordable shelter, and amenities—let alone addressing the sustainability problem adequately (Gilbert et al., 2013; Konys, 2018). This issue has led to seeking smarter solutions for the delivery of urban services—through innovative services, efficient mechanisms, and smart and sustainable infrastructures (Yigitcanlar, 2015).

The notion of the smart city has been introduced at the early 2000s (Lara et al., 2016). It was initially conceptualised as technology-assisted—through sensors, surveillance cameras, control centres, autonomous driving, and connected infrastructure and communities—and was assumed to result in increased productivity, efficiency, innovation, and safety (Trindade et al., 2017; Zawieska & Pieriegud, 2018; Faisal et al., 2019). In other words, the main objective of smart cities is to provide a way of improving quality of life through the deployment and use of smart urban technologies (Yigitcanlar & Kamruzzaman, 2018, 2019). Another objective concerns boosting urban innovation and economic productivity through

DOI: 10.1201/9781003403647-6

sustainable industrial ecosystem development (Ioppolo et al., 2016; Arbolino et al., 2018; Aldieri et al., 2019c). The concept of sustainability was generally used as an ancillary goal, which, so far, has not been adequately incorporated into smart city practice (Han & Hawken, 2018; Martin et al., 2018). Conversely, it is essential for a smart city to generate high-quality, sustainable, and liveable places for all—rather than to offer cutting-edge digital technology services for the urban elite (Leem et al., 2019).

Despite its abovementioned practice limitations, the smart city movement has gone viral globally during the last decade. This is a result of technology—aggressively promoted by the global technology, construction, and consultancy companies—being seen as a remedy to urbanisation problems (Chang et al., 2018). While a massive consumption society is an integral contributor of the experienced problems, the existing smart city agenda has a negligible focus on consumption behaviour change. The reason for that is technology is a commodity—constantly producing new versions, and making earlier ones redundant—and its materialism is profitable for the technology companies that drive the (corporate) smart city agenda (Hollands, 2015). For example, some scholars perceive innovation/technology as a vehicle to conquer the growth limits of capitalism (Yun, 2015).

This mostly consumerist, corporate, and technology-centric perspective, however, has become subject to heavy criticism among some scholars. These criticisms include: (a) the notion of smart city being ambiguous; (b) the existence of only limited conceptual frameworks to help cities and their administrations understand the grand challenge of this new paradigm; and (c) current efforts not being able to address the climate emergency—which is the single biggest problem of our time (Stanley et al., 2009; Ersoy, 2017).

Against this backdrop, this chapter focuses on investigating and shedding light on the unclear aspects of the making of smart cities, and providing a thorough critique of and insights into the smart city paradigm and practice. This investigation is done by reviewing the literature, elaborating the smart city notion through a multidimensional conceptual framework, placing global smart city best practices—i.e., Songdo, Masdar, Amsterdam, San Francisco, Brisbane—under the microscope. The findings of this study disclose the limitations of the smart city practice in incorporating sustainable development principles.

5.2 Literature Background

Thanks to advances in science, engineering, and technology, today we live much longer and more prosperous lives than ever before. It is also predicted that the average global life expectancy will rise 4.4 years by 2040 (Forman et al., 2018). We have made huge advances to create conditions for better health for billions of people. Nevertheless, this progress is taking a heavy toll on the planet's natural systems—e.g., ecological and climate emergencies. Consequently, the damages caused to natural systems have started to affect dramatically not only our quality of life, but also wellbeing—along with other species on the planet (Albouy et al., 2016). Climate change is the prevailing outcome of the damages made. We are entering a new era—the era of disasters—as the world warms 2°C beyond pre-industrial levels. As stated by Glasser (2019: 3), "across the globe of record-breaking heatwaves, prolonged droughts, massive bushfires, torrential flooding, and record-setting storms" are being observed.

Advancing technology has created a (false) hope to ease, if not to cure, the damages made in the natural systems. The idea of technology as the saviour is promoted by the large technology, construction, start-up, and consultancy companies globally (Paroutis et al., 2014). Consequently, a new ideology is formed to address our malpractice urbanisation and incorrect energy resource choices with technological solutions (Buuse & Kolk, 2019). This ideology firstly gave birth to the intelligent city, and then the smart city concept. Today, smart cities are widely seen as urban settlements that adopt state-of-the-art technologies to address various urbanisation challenges. For instance, as stated by Mora et al. (2019: 90), "[t]ransforming urban areas into smart cities is an ambition that local and regional governments are trying to realise by developing strategies that make it possible to tackle urban sustainability by means of ICT solutions."

Although the notion is widespread, smart cities are in their infancy. According to Harrison and Donnelly (2011, p. 6), "the current ad hoc approaches of smart cities to the improvement of cities are reminiscent of pre-scientific medicine. They may do well, but we have little detailed understanding of why. Smart city is a field in want of a good theoretical base". Smart city optimists argue that through time the concept and its practice will eventually evolve and mature (Yadav et al., 2019). However, Yigitcanlar et al. (2018, p. 156) emphasise that "the delay in the conceptualisation will highly likely result in inefficient policies, poor investment decisions, and not being able to address the urbanisation challenges properly in a timely and adequate manner".

Time is, unfortunately, something that we do not have much of. The 2018 Special Report of Intergovernmental Panel on Climate Change (IPCC) on the significant impacts expected from 1.5°C of global warming—the aspirational limit that countries adopted in the Paris Agreement—generated widespread and deep concerns. Moreover, the report revealed that we have only limited time left to act on climate change (IPCC, 2018). Responding to climate emergency at the global scale is a major task given that there is limited time and still no clear intergovernmental agreement on the required actions (Harris, 2018). The recent global school strikes for climate action (a.k.a. Fridays for Future)—initiated by Nobel Peace Prize nominee environmental teen activist Great Thunberg—evidence that scientists and youth are pressuring politicians to get on-board before it is too late.

In their current conceptual and practical foci, there is no evidence that smart cities actually have the capacity, and hence will generate, genuine solutions to unsustainable urbanisation problems—including the climate emergency. Mora et al. (2017, p. 20) remind us that, "the knowledge necessary to understand the process of building effective smart cities in the real-world has not yet been produced, nor the tools for supporting the actors involved in this activity". Having said that, the whole planning process of smart cities needs to be revisited.

Particularly, a crosscheck is required that smart city projects will actually be creating the desired outcomes targeted at the beginning of the planning stage. While this is all good and well in theory, the issue is that most of the smart city initiatives are not integrated with the urban planning mechanisms of that city; besides, their fit in the planning process is not clearly stated in these projects' reports (Caragliu & Del Bo, 2019). The main reasons for this are the non-existence of a sound framework to link the smart city concept with urban planning/development processes, and the lack of clarity on the expected outcomes from these projects—such as clear metrics on what the desired sustainability targets are (Yigitcanlar et al., 2019b).

In support of the abovementioned limitations, Mora et al. (2017) indicate that the smart cities notion has not been conceptualised adequately to deliver sustainable urbanism outputs. One reason for this is that cities are not taking advantage of the environmental innovation efforts for sustainable urban development (Szopik-Depczyńska et al., 2018; Aldieri et al., 2019a, 2019b).

On that note, it is useful to share the views of Caragliu et al. (2011, p. 67) on what makes a city smart: "(a) The utilisation of networked infrastructure to improve economic and political efficiency and enable social, cultural and urban development; (b) An underlying emphasis on business-led urban development; (c) A strong focus on the aim of achieving the social inclusion of various urban residents in public services; (d) A stress on the crucial role of high-tech and creative industries in long-run urban growth; € Profound attention to the role of social and relational capital in urban development, and; (f) Social and environmental sustainability as a major strategic component for smart cities".

There are significant limits to the currently available smart city frameworks. For instance, the lack of a "system of systems" view (McLoughlin, 1969), and the development drivers are not lucidly intertwined with desired outcomes. The urgency for a consolidated theorisation of the smart city notion comes from the lack of incorporation of the sustainable development theory (Ingrao et al., 2018; Ioppolo et al., 2019). This has led to the development of new conceptual frameworks in recent years. One of these frameworks, by Yigitcanlar (2018), aims to establish the missing link between smart city development frameworks and the sustainable urban planning and development processes. This conceptual framework is illustrated in Figure 5.1, and elaborated below.

The conceptual framework (Figure 5.1) bases itself on an input-process-output-impact model—that also contains a "system of systems" view—that is a widely used model in urban and regional planning (Fincher, 1972; Chadwick, 2013). The assets of a city are the main inputs of that city's smart urbanism endeavours. These assets are put into use through various processes. These processes include the key drivers of technology, community, and policy. Various desired outputs are expected to be realised, in the case of assets and drivers theses are to be successfully operationalised. The procedure is to generate sustainable and knowledge-based development outputs—i.e., in the economic, societal, environmental, institutional development domains—to achieve desired outcomes. Given the ampleness of the desired outcomes—i.e., productivity, innovation, liveability, wellbeing,

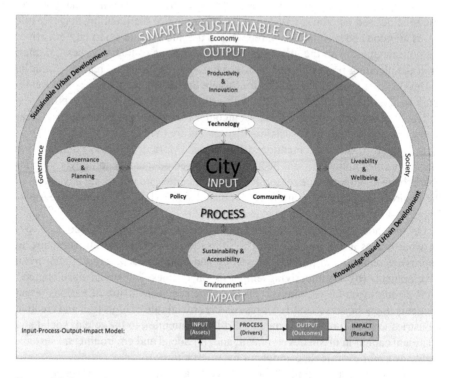

Figure 5.1 Smart city conceptual framework (derived from Yigitcanlar, 2018).

sustainability, accessibility, governance, planning—the resulting impacts transform the city into a smarter one.

The inner workings of the framework have been discussed in the literature (Yigitcanlar et al., 2018, 2019a). Instead of repeating these, we highlight that the framework perceives urban *technology* only as a "mean" or an "enabler" to an end—that is to achieve desired urban outcomes. This perspective is in line with Kanter and Litow's (2009, p. 2) view of "a smart city as an organic whole of a network and a linked urban system". Additionally, this framework emphasises the role of the wider urban *community* as users and developers of the smart city they live in. This is in line with Hughes and Spray's (2002) view of providing necessary technology to engage the community in local smart city projects. Furthermore, the framework places urban *policy* at the heart of smart city development as a process that is critical to get it right—where technology is only one of the integral elements. This is in line with Aurigi's (2006) view of strategies for the selection and adoption of technology or relevant solutions in appropriate ways.

In sum, this conceptual framework establishes a consolidated notion of smart cities, and seeks ways for achieving desired urban outcomes for an effective and efficient smart city transformation. While doing so, the framework also offers the following consolidated definition of what smart cities are: "Smart city is an urban locality functioning as a healthy system of systems with sustainable and balanced practices of economic, societal, environmental and governance activities generating desired outcomes and futures for all humans and non-humans" (Yigitcanlar, 2018, p. 108).

5.3 Methodology

The overall methodological approach of this study is fourfold. Firstly, the study undertakes a thorough review of the literature on smart cities and its environmental sustainability dimension. This review is undertaken with the aim of providing a clearer picture of the concept, and showing the limited understanding on the interpretation of the smart city notion by practitioners.

Secondly, following the review of the academic literature, the study introduces one of the conceptual smart city frameworks that provides a comprehensive view of smart cities from the angle of the input-process-output-impact model (presented in Figure 5.1).

Thirdly, the study evaluates the global best smart city practices using the introduced smart city conceptual framework as a lens (Figure 5.1). Due to the limitations of detailed data collection on the investigated smart city case studies, the research uses available academic and grey literature and the research team's extensive personal knowledge on these cases as the main data sources. Due to the challenges of obtaining detailed data for analysis, the study only uses the core part of the smart city conceptual framework (Figure 5.1) that contains the following smart city foundations: (a) technology; (b) community; and (c) policy. These three foundational elements are adopted in this study as the indicators of the global smart city best practice analysis.

Finally, the study provides an analysis of the findings from the five smart city case studies—i.e., Songdo (Korea), Masdar (UAE), Amsterdam (The Netherlands), San Francisco (USA), and Brisbane (Australia). These smart city practices are selected as they are widely referred to as the best practices in the literature (Albino et al., 2015; Ching & Ferreira, 2015; Russo et al., 2016; Angelidou, 2017). In this study, we limit the case study numbers from each major region of the world—i.e., Asia, America, Europe, Middle East, Oceania—to one.

The following methodological limitations should be noted when interpreting the study findings: (a) the study undertook a review of the literature on the best practice smart cities; (b) the study relied on the judgements of the research team, consisting of five smart city experts, in interpreting the findings; (c) the study only scrutinised five case study smart city best practices; and (d) the study adopted a particular smart city conceptual framework and its three core elements—i.e., technology, community, policy—as the lenses to evaluate smart city lessons of the selected case cities.

5.4 The Practice of Smart Cities

There are no best practices yet in line with the consolidated notion of smart cities discussed in the earlier section. There are, however, some promising initiatives (these are referred to in the literature as good or best practices) that help us understand the current status of smart city practice. This chapter investigates some of these best practices—namely Songdo (Korea), Masdar (UAE), Amsterdam (The Netherlands), San Francisco (USA), and Brisbane (Australia). These cities are selected from the five different regions of the world, and they have distinctive smart city characteristics and visions. Focusing on their strengths and weaknesses, in the light of the technology, community, and policy smart city foundations, could help generate insights into where we are currently with smart city practice, and where we want to be.

5.4.1 Songdo, Korea

Background: Songdo is an exemplar new city development from Korea based on the smart city concept (Lee et al., 2008; Shwayri, 2013). Initially inspired by Dubai, Songdo is a master-planned international business hub developed on sea-reclaimed land, located near the Incheon international airport. The smart city development is planned to be fully completed in 2020, and will house about 65,000 residents and 300,000 workers. Songdo is referred to as the most progressive large-scale greenfield-based smart city project in the world (Kim, 2010).

Technology: Songdo is the outcome of joint work among real-estate developers, corporate technology companies, and national- and local-level governments for building an urban centre from scratch that is filled with cutting-edge technologically enhanced infrastructure and services. In Songdo, all of the state-of-the-art technology-wired high-rise towers have received green building ratings, neighbourhoods are smartly designed, an urban oasis is created modelled on the Central Park of New York, a robust public transit system is in place, an effective water recycling system is installed, and the city is wired with ubiquitous broadband internet connections (Strickland, 2011). The city aims to excel particularly in bio-, nano-, information, and ubiquitous technologies, and become a prosperous global hub for innovation and technology development (Carvalho, 2012). Many leading international and Korean technology companies have located their research and development (R&D) facilities in the city. For Townsend (2013), these investments are turning Songdo into a testbed for radio frequency identification (RFID) and a centre for R&D in its crucial smart urban technologies.

Community: Yigitcanlar and Lee (2014) offer a comprehensive appraisal of Songdo from the angle of economic, societal, spatial, and governance perspectives. The top-down development strategy in Songdo has been found to be problematic, as without involvement of all stakeholders—including local communities—achieving desired outcomes is not possible. For instance, socio-cultural infrastructures have been neglected, as the city's focus is more on international businesses rather than catering for the socio-cultural needs of the residents/workers (Millar & Ju-Choi, 2010). The primary reason for this omission is that the smart city planning process does not involve wide community participation in Korea (Lee et al., 2008). Nevertheless, with the high-cost technology, innovative building material, and infrastructure investment, the city can only serve those who can afford it and it is

Figure 5.2 A view from the footpaths of Songdo, 2019. A copyright free photo by Hon Kim on Unsplash: https://tinyurl.com/y6xrauzu

becoming a city for the affluent class only. Figure 5.2 is a snapshot from an urban scene of Songdo, with two creative classes of knowledge workers commuting to work on foot—a reference to the walkability and highly efficient clientele politics of the city (Benedikt, 2016).

Policy: As stated by Shwayri (2013, p. 52), Songdo's master plan is "based on a combination of sustainable design principles, such as sustainable modes of transport and a mix of open and green spaces, which received the Sustainable City Award in 2008". However, it is contradictory that the city is located on sea-reclaimed land and caused the destruction of precious wetlands, home to some of the rarest species on the planet. In Songdo, cutting-edge urban technologies linked with sustainable urban design practices are targeting the creation of a utopian future city and lifestyle. However, the top-down policymaking practice generates only technocratic solutions for smart cities that are built from scratch—such as Songdo. The smart city policy in Korea should be expanded to the retrofitting of existing cities, as building new smart cities is not a sustainable approach—increasing the urban footprint—while existing cities need upgrades to become more sustainable.

Global implications: This city is widely considered to be a role model of the Southeast Asian smart city (Strickland, 2011; Angelidou, 2014). The development of a ubiquitous urban environment is in fast progress in Songdo, and the ambitious smart city initiative provides an optimistic view for establishing the smart cities of our time—but only in the case that we favour techno-centric smartness over a collective one (technology-community-policy smartness). Today, it is widely accepted that Songdo has created a new development path for and is setting the benchmark high for smart urbanism (Kolotouchkina & Seisdedos, 2018). Nevertheless, it is not clear how much hope the Songdo project generates in terms of truly sustainable urbanism.

5.4.2 Masdar, UAE

Background: Masdar is a planned smart city project situated in a desert location near Abu Dhabi. The Masdar smart city development project was initiated in 2006, in line with Abu Dhabi's Vision 2030. Masdar smart city is designed as a living laboratory for sustainable urban technologies, and one of the first projects in the Middle East aiming towards a master-planned, zero-carbon, sustainable, and smart settlement form (Cugurullo, 2013). The city is widely viewed as a role model of the Middle Eastern smart city (De Jong et al., 2019). The first stage of development was completed in 2011, and soon after its opening Masdar claimed to be the largest planned development in the world that solely uses renewable energy sources. Today, the city is seen as an emerging global clean-technology cluster located on one of the world's most challenging geographies fighting for sustainable urban development powered by renewable energy. As outlined by Sgouridis and Kennedy (2010), when the development is completed in 2025, it will have 50,000 residents, 1,500 clean-tech companies, start-ups staffed by 10,000 new employees, a research university, and 60,000 daily commuting workers. Figure 5.3 is a snapshot from the solar energy fields of Abu Dhabi— the world's largest single-site solar project with a capacity of 1.177 gigawatts (Kennedy, 2019).

Technology: According to the plans, residents' transport needs will be addressed with high-technology smart and active mobility solutions—which include an autonomous and electrified public transport system, and walking and cycling network. The power for the city is supplied by a 22-hectare field designated for solar panels. Additionally, the rooftops of buildings are also covered with solar panels. Shared autonomous electric vehicles are planned to replace cars in the city. The design of the walls of the buildings reduces the demand for air conditioning by 55%. All buildings have movement sensors that cut electricity consumption by 51% and water usage by 55% (Hopwood, 2010). Technology and innovation sectors are also planned to be the primary economic activities of the city. Despite the desert climate, Masdar encourages walkability through using smart solutions. Smart innovations in comfortable walkability include: smart wind towers, sheds, shelters, bus stops, street furniture, and pavements (Kamel, 2013).

Community: At the conception stage of the Masdar project, challenges were mostly economy-driven. However, today these challenges have expanded to include natural resource depletion, population growth, climate emergency, and the Arab Spring (Cugurullo, 2016). At present, Masdar is a location for the affluent to reside, and workers of the city commute by private motor vehicles. In the urban

Figure 5.3 A view from the photovoltaic fields of Abu Dhabi, 2019. A copyright free photo
by David Mark on Pixabay: https://tinyurl.com/yyj98uxm

plan of the Masdar city only 20% of the accommodation areas are assigned to low-
income workers—due to the planning code requirements (De Jong et al., 2019). In
spite of the social sustainability in the vision of Masdar, the city is largely occupied
by an affluent population, pointing to exclusiveness of the city (Cugurullo, 2013).
Moreover, Mezher et al. (2010, p. 757) suggest that "in order to ensure social prosperity in Abu Dhabi, all stakeholders must be engaged in direct coordination and
collaboration to develop the right energy policies, incentives to invest in projects,
ensure the funding is available for R&D, put in place the needed market mechanisms
for diffusing renewable energy technologies, and build public awareness".

    Policy: Masdar adopted a top-down planning and design approach, and so far,
the city has performed best in the environmental domain of sustainable urban
development. As much as smart urban technology utilisation, another reason for
the success was replicating the traditional Arabic urban form—such as the city's
shape, orientation of streets, windcatchers, courtyards, the pattern of streets, and
density and mixed use. Hassan et al. (2016) compared urban form attributes of
medieval Cairo with modern Masdar, and revealed that the success of Masdar lies
in pursuing, learning, and including characteristics of a traditional city. As a consequence of the planning strategy, unlike the other iconic cities of the region—such
as Doha and Dubai—Masdar does not accommodated any high-rise buildings. As

for the environmental sustainability policy, as highlighted by Cugurullo (2016), in Masdar, sustainability strongly links environmentalism with consumerism. Although Masdar is one of the first attempts in constructing carbon-neutral cities, it creates hope for the development of a sustainable smart city. However, the Masdar project is not economically feasible. The project heavily capitalises on environmental concerns to generate profit (Cugurullo, 2016). Nevertheless, the project not being able to attract as much innovative industries as hoped for, along with the impacts of the global financial crisis, has forced Masdar to scale back its budget and ambitions (Mezher et al., 2011).

Global implications: Although most of the ideas to develop Masdar into a truly smart and sustainable city were innovative and ambitious, not many of them have found application on the ground at the city scale. For instance, the autonomous electric public transit system, which is the flagship feature of Masdar's car-free strategy, has been discarded due to the technology not being able to meet the city's transport needs. There also have been delays in the development of the planned light rail network and metro system. Additionally, it is realised that the construction of large solar panels would be less effective than anticipated due to local dust storms, which reduce the solar power output by at least 40% (Crot, 2013). Similarly, the hydrogen power plant project in Abu Dhabi was placed on hold due to a lack of resources and change in the project priorities. These downgrades, due to either technology miscalculations or the economic downturn, have forced the city administration to change the city brand from "zero-carbon" to "carbon-neutral" (Mezher et al., 2010). Similarly to Songdo, Masdar also has been a pioneer testbed to trial smart urbanism concepts due to the bold steps of the national administration. While this attempt is commendable and provided lessons of what works and what does not, the Masdar project has not managed to showcase a successful smart and sustainable urbanism practice. Both Songdo and Masdar bring important questions to mind: Should we focus on transforming cities step by step into smart ones, rather than building new ones from scratch at scale? Furthermore, another key question to consider is: How can the near bankruptcy of major smart city development fantasies, such as Middle Eastern smart cities, be avoided?

5.4.3 Amsterdam, The Netherlands

Background: The City of Amsterdam, Amsterdam Economic Board, and internet operators jointly initiated the Smart City Amsterdam project in 2009. Smart City Amsterdam aims to turn itself into a more sustainable city by working along two principles to: (a) enable stakeholders to apply innovative technologies and (b) stimulate behavioural change in end-users (Sauer, 2012). The starting point of the project, thus, was not merely providing technical solutions, but the collaboration, co-creation, and partnership between stakeholders within the city for moving towards sustainable and smart solutions. The project, hence, was developed in a quadruple-helix partnership model between the public sector, private sector, academia, and community. The operational aim of the smart city project was to help achieve the ambitious sustainability targets set in Europe (Manville et al., 2014).

Technology: Different to the previously presented Songdo and Masdar cases, technology is not central to Amsterdam's smart city approach, although the testing and implementation of smart city technologies has been integrated into most projects (Van Winden et al., 2016). However, the smart city initiative of Amsterdam is still famous not only for engaging technology solutions for a smart city development, but also using the smart city living labs to engage local communities to determine in a bottom-up manner solutions to the city and its residents. According to Van Winden et al. (2016, p. 12), in the roll-out of a smart city initiative, "a technology or solution that was successfully tested and developed in the pilot project is commercialised/brought to the market, widely applied in an organisation, or rolled out across the city. Possibilities for rollout largely emerge from living lab projects (such as Climate street and WeGo), where companies can test beta versions of new products/solutions" within a local community. Figure 5.4 is a snapshot from one of Amsterdam's canals in which self-driving/autonomous boats—so-called "roboats"—are being trialled (Vincent, 2016).

Community: In 2013, the smart city platform of Amsterdam established partnerships with over 80 partners that are engaged in a number of smart city initiatives. These initiatives focused on a variety of areas including over 40 projects on smart living, smart working, smart mobility, smart public space, and open data themes. These projects particularly aimed at supporting sustainable real-estate development, company energy consumption improvement, and employee awareness to work in a smarter manner. In addition, the following initiatives that

Figure 5.4 A view from one of Amsterdam's canals, 2019. A copyright free photo by Ethan Hu on Unsplash: https://tinyurl.com/y5ja88y6

deployed solutions in the Smart City Amsterdam are worth pointing out: Climate Street, Ship-to-grid, Smart building management systems, and Health Lab (Dameri, 2014). The initial smart city project was top-down in nature, but later, community input and involvement were also considered and became an integral part of the smart city initiative—such as the earlier mentioned living lab programmes. The Amsterdam Smart City platform is an important connector in this respect as it has evolved into a facilitator of the smart city community in the Amsterdam region (Van Winden et al., 2016).

Policy: Planners expect to boost the local economy through high-tech infrastructure investment that also would cut emissions by 40% by 2025, which would also convert Amsterdam into a smart city (Dameri, 2014). The Amsterdam smart city project also established and maintained strong linkages with a number of other European smart city initiatives, including NiCE, Citadel, Digital cities, Open cities, and Common4EU (Manville et al., 2014). Amsterdam shares data openly with the wider community and provides critical information on transport, environment, and so on through a dedicated city dashboard—similar to many other European smart cities, e.g., Birmingham, Dublin, and London. Furthermore, Amsterdam is one of the most walkable and cyclable cities in the world (Lehmann, 2016). The smart city policy ensures increased green and active transport options in the city.

Global implications: As in most European smart city projects, Amsterdam also adopted a retrofitting approach in its efforts for developing the Amsterdam Metropolitan Area into a flourishing smart city. It has successfully integrated both environmental and societal goals with economic and technologic ones. Hence, this city could be considered as a role model European smart city. This smart city development is managed to embed all kinds of digital infrastructure and networks, devices, sensors, and actuators; as a result, the volume of data produced has grown exponentially. Smart city data managers need to pay special attention to this issue as stated by Kitchin (2014), this may create a concern with the data quality, fidelity, security, management, and validity of analytics that are interpreted and acted upon. Furthermore, as underlined by Townsend (2013), even though Amsterdam is widely recognised as a global leader in smart solutions for sustainable urban outcomes, emissions generated from the city are still rising at 1% annually. This brings down the issue to the non-renewable energy use, and not addressing the climate emergency seriously.

5.4.4 San Francisco, USA

Background: San Francisco sees smart city strategies as an important method to build its sustainable urban future. In recent years, many Silicon Valley-based companies have made a move to base their headquarters in San Francisco, due to the high quality of life and place offerings for companies' talented staff, along with affordability and tax benefits. Today, the city is home to a large number of internet-based companies. San Francisco offers a large number of free Wi-Fi hotspots in various public locations. For example, on a main road downtown, there is about a five-kilometre-long free Wi-Fi zone (Hudson, 2010; Zhu et al.,

Figure 5.5 A view from San Francisco's Lombard Street, 2019. A copyright free photo by Brandon Nelson on Unsplash: https://tinyurl.com/y3j4ykhp

2017). Figure 5.5 is a snapshot of San Francisco's famously twisty Lombard Street, which is a symbol of smart solutions the city generates—the crookedest street in the world was built in 1922 in its unusual form to reduce the slope to allow driving (Leadbeater, 2019).

Technology: San Francisco is renowned amongst the global trendsetters when it comes to smart urban technology initiatives. San Francisco has an ambitious goal of becoming a carbon-free city by 2030. The city has implemented a number of incentive programmes that involve smart technology applications. For example, "SF Energy Map" is a tool that tracks the solar and wind energy potentials of locations across the city. With this application, residents and businesses can check their solar potential. Similarly, "Energy Use Challenge" is an application for sharing energy bill data, where these data can be used to enhance energy efficiency programmes. Likewise, "Honest Buildings" is a software platform that focuses on buildings to help buildings save energy (Dahlquist & Fell, 2015). Moreover, "SF Park" is an application to improve parking in the city through real-time parking information. This way traffic congestion can be avoided or eased, less energy is consumed, and consequently fewer pollutants are released to the atmosphere. Additionally, "ChargePoint" is an application to help track the usage and functional status of electric vehicle charging stations. The app provides real-time status of the chargers, and generates long-term reports. Furthermore, today, San Francisco is 41% renewable energy powered, and the city houses over 300 LEED-certified buildings (Scheer, 2012). San Francisco has been upgrading transport services through smart mobility technologies that have advanced urban policy aims in the arena of transport governance for sustainability (Davis, 2018). This has resulted in increased public transport service quality and efficiency in the city/region. San Francisco is the home of ride hailing service companies such as Uber and Lyft, and a trial city for shared autonomous vehicle projects (Yigitcanlar et al., 2019c).

Community: Primarily, San Francisco's high concentration of talent base, strong entrepreneurial culture, and close proximity to the world's most innovative technology cluster contributes to the establishment of an urban ecosystem in the city that accelerates smart and sustainable urban outcomes. A number of apps use the open data source provided through Data SF, and "Metro San Francisco", "Transit Bay", and "Walkonomics" are among the apps that are used widely by local residents to improve their mobility in the region (Brown et al., 2011). One of the big smart city challenges of the city is the provision of affordable housing to its residents. The popularity of the city has attracted technology companies and talented workers, and in consequence property prices have sky rocketed in the city—leading to social problems (Palm & Niemeier, 2017).

Policy: The city is widely acknowledged as a leader in embracing sustainability and smart urban development policy and practice as it excels in smart and sustainability initiatives. San Francisco has an ambitious goal of achieving zero-waste by 2020. In order to achieve the zero-waste goal, the city introduced various smart city initiatives. For instance, "RecycleWhere" is an online tool that provides residents with recycling, reuse, and disposal options. Similarly, "Zero Waster Signmaker" is another online tool that residents and business owners can use to create compost, recycling, and landfill signs for their homes and businesses. Because of these initiatives, the city has reached an 80% waste diversion rate (Kaufman et al., 2010). Another important development that supports the smart city formation of San Francisco is the open data legislation that was passed in 2009. This pioneering legislation has made all city departments have to provide public access for all nonconfidential datasets through the city's e-government portal.

Global implications: San Francisco is considered to be one of the greenest cities and the clean-technology capital of North America. The city has various smart city support mechanisms for its clean-technology and innovation firms that contribute to the city's economic development, neighbourhood revitalisation, and sustainable operations. For example, the "living innovation zones" project helps businesses use city assets to demonstrate new and emerging technologies. Likewise, "smart grid" and "LED street-light conversion" projects help the city save energy (Lee et al., 2014). A critical evaluation of the functions and effectiveness of the smart city framework of San Francisco by Lee et al. (2014, p. 84) indicates the following key characteristics and issues of the city's twist on smart urban technology utilisation: "Urban openness; Service innovation; Partnership formation; Urban proactiveness; Smart city infrastructure integration; Smart city governance". The city, henceforth, could be considered as a role model North American smart city.

San Francisco showcases a successful model of urban transformation; however, it comes with social costs that require further attention and solid policies to tackle.

5.4.5 Brisbane, Australia

Background: Brisbane was one of the early adopters of the smart city concept. Queensland's 1998 Smart State Strategy underlines the importance of Brisbane's, the capital city of the state, transformation into a smart city. The smart cities policy, initiated in 2007, was an applied economic development and land use macro plan for Brisbane as the nucleus for smart state development (Yigitcanlar et al., 2012). The smart cities policy recommended various strategies to turn Brisbane into a prosperous smart city. These were: (a) creating a legible structure plan; (b) uniting disparate precincts; (c) creating definitive pedestrian spines; (d) linking the city centre by mass transit; (e) defining a knowledge corridor; (f) investing in sustainability; (g) developing effective planning processes; and (h) developing a smart city model (Hortz, 2016). These strategies also resulted in the development of Brisbane's knowledge corridor—a milestone project that connects all key innovative institutes of the city physically. Today, the knowledge corridor is highly active and Brisbane's global innovation districts are gaining international recognition, turning the city into a prosperous smart city (Pancholi et al., 2015a; Esmaeilpoorarabi et al., 2018).

Technology: The city invested in improving its road infrastructure, as well as its public transport system, by developing a number of tunnels to ease rush-hour traffic congestion (Dur & Yigitcanlar, 2015). In these projects, high-technology smart traffic systems are utilised, including digital message signs, CCTV cameras, and Bluetooth sensor devices to deliver notifications to motorists and improve the road intelligence. Brisbane also adopted Sydney's Coordinated Adaptive Transport System to manage traffic signals, and installed pedestrian countdown timers. Additionally, Brisbane has installed numerous way-finding devices for people with vision impairment. Furthermore, free Wi-Fi systems are installed in the major city parks, libraries, shopping malls, and suburban shopping strips, and this was followed by the erection of smart poles in the major public spaces for big data collection (Hamstead et al., 2018). Figure 5.6 is a snapshot of a target smart pole location—to collect data on pedestrian and cyclist traffic, construction and traffic noise levels, flood levels, and air quality, among other potential uses including hosting CCTV cameras, and free Wi-Fi/5G and USB charging points (Stone, 2019).

Community: Brisbane pursues an effective smart city vision with its sustainable brand of smart urbanism (Hollands, 2008). Brisbane is amongst the limited cities that have committed to economic growth and environmental sustainability simultaneously, while developing mechanisms for community involvement in major urban policy decisions. For instance, Brisbane has utilised the smart label in conjunction with notions of the "sustainable city" with regards to its smart water, water recycling, draught-combatting measures, resilient infrastructure, and subtropical building and urban design programmes (Pancholi et al., 2015b). While at the sustainable urbanism front, the city has gone a long way, in terms of smart urban

Figure 5.6 A view from a target smart pole location from Brisbane, 2019. A copyright free
photo by Michael on Unsplash: https://tinyurl.com/y2rudeel

technology development, adoption and deployment in the city remains behind most
of the cities in other countries claiming the smart city title (Berger, 2019). As for
the community programmes, the city has been committed to the smart community
development programme (Alizadeh, 2015).

Policy: Following the success of the smart cities policy, in 2009 Brisbane City
Council launched "CitySmart" to help make Brisbane Australia's most sustainable city. Unlike the previous policy attempts, CitySmart is financially supported
to deliver projects. Major CitySmart projects include: (a) Australia's first district
cooling energy system to provide cheaper/more efficient air conditioning for CBD
buildings; (b) "Reduce Your Juice", an energy-efficiency programme tailored specifically for the city's low-income young adults; (c) "Queensland Watt Savers",
which supplied more than 300 SMEs easy-to-use tools and expertise to reduce
energy consumption and related expenses; (d) "EzyGreen", a residential energy-
reduction programme, which engaged 61,000 Brisbane households to save over
$10 million in annual energy costs; and (e) the city's first electric vehicle charging
station (Muriuki et al., 2016).

Global implications: Brisbane, with its long history of smart and sustainable
city initiatives, could be seen as a role model Oceanian smart city. The city, today,
is capable of collecting and analysing real-time data to improve liveability, in

the case the city puts more efforts in investing in the technological architecture and collaborates with businesses to realise its potential. On this front, presently Brisbane is following the European information-sharing model—a popular smart city practice (e.g., Amsterdam, Birmingham, Dublin, London) to share information through city dashboards and digital public displays—by adopting a citywide dashboard to enable the monitoring of weather, energy consumption, and traffic flow. There is no fully fledged statutory smart city policy in the city yet. However, Brisbane developed a brief smart city agenda policy in 2017—"Smart, Connected Brisbane"—a first step toward an umbrella smart city strategy for Brisbane (BCC, 2017). Despite Brisbane being a policy-rich/obsessive city, it lacks a clear overarching smart city strategy to guide the transformation of the city into a smart and sustainable one.

5.5 Discussion and Conclusion

The smart city literature and investigated best practices—i.e., Songdo, Masdar, Amsterdam, San Francisco, Brisbane—have shown that we are at the beginning of a new era in which technology and the city are converging (Stimmel, 2016). At present, the smart city is a highly popular topic in urban policy circles/debates in many cities around the world. However, our knowledge on smart cities is greatly limited, and our expectations from them are unrealistic and full of speculation. This brings serious criticism and scepticism to the smart city discourse. In line with the views of Vanolo (2012), there are some underlying issues associated with smart cities, as they are increasingly becoming an idealised development paradigm, without proper critical debates and politics.

The notion of the smart city, despite some promising attempts, has not been conceptualised adequately yet. This lack of conceptualisation is mainly due to perceiving the "smart" in smart cities as technological smartness rather than human/ decision smartness. This is evident in some of the investigated case studies, e.g., Masdar, Songdo. They present, in general, the development and application of advanced technology much more than the development and implementation of correct decisions or policies. This issue has resulted in so far not being able to build a truly smart city.

As the study findings reveal, different approaches are followed in different corners of the globe for the conceptualisation and practice of smart cities. In Southeast Asia, smart cities are used as a vehicle to create national identity, boost economy through technological innovation, and test and implement technologies on large-scale urban development projects. On the contrary, in Europe, North America, and Oceania, the smart cities model is mostly adopted to improve the urban and household quality of living, along with the establishment of a more sustainable urban future—but generally in relatively small-scale projects.

One of the critical issues behind the limited large-scale application of smart city projects is the reservations towards how the smart city model is perceived. Today there are a number of self-claimed smart cities (Hollands, 2008) based only on the fact that they are using technology tools. While *smart technology* is critical, technology alone cannot create smart cities, as it takes more than just the state-of-the-art technological solutions to transform cities into truly smart and sustainable ones.

Moving away from a heavily smart technology-centric view to a smart decision or *smart policy* view may change the reserved attitudes towards these projects. As identified by Yigitcanlar and Lee (2014), current failures in the development of smart cities will help us to not make the same mistakes, and plan, design, develop, and manage the next generation of cities much better than we have done before. However, we might not have the luxury of time for too many trials and errors in the era of climate emergency.

We will, hence, have to establish a consolidated smart city paradigm as soon as possible to form a role model for the cities of the future—such as the post-Anthropocene city that provides quadruple-bottom-line sustainability for all humans and non-humans (Yigitcanlar et al., 2019b). In other words, in line with the views of Ratti and Townsend (2011), more than smart systems that improve efficiency in the city, what is needed is to make the city itself "smart"—which includes its people, in other words a *smart community*.

The making of successful smart cities highly depends on adequately linking conceptual developments in the field with sustainable practices. So far, as Wiig (2015) indicates, the smart city practice is a techno-utopian policy in motion, its results are in the outward self-promotion of cities in attracting multinational corporations that are selling urban and technology products.

This chapter advocates the adoption of a comprehensive view on smart city conceptualisation to inform policymaking and urban planning and development practices. As deliberated by Yigitcanlar et al. (2019b), the renewed smart city approach carries high potential to become an ideal model to address the climate emergency and build the cities of the future. However, realisation of this potential depends on the adoption of three critical guiding principles. These principles are, the smart city notion to: (a) contain a system of systems approach; (b) adopt a balanced quadruple-bottom-line sustainable urban development perspective; and (c) mainstream the urban metabolism approach (Kennedy & Hoornweg, 2012; Ioppolo et al., 2014).

Based on the conducted literature review and investigated smart city best practices, we compile the following insights into the making of successful smart cities.

First, in terms of economic development in smart cities (*smart economy*), we need to give our cities the capability of developing technologies unique to their own developmental problems and needs. This, in turn, contributes to the establishment of a local innovation economy and prosperity that is a central element of smart cities.

Second, in terms of sociocultural development in smart cities (*smart society*), we need to develop our cities wired with appropriate, affordable, and effective smart urban technologies not only exclusive to urban elites, but also inclusive to those less fortunate, in other words to all. This in turn helps in establishing socioeconomic equality—and the formation of smart communities—that is an essential element of smart cities.

Third, in terms of spatial development in smart cities (*smart environment*), we need to reform our cities by adopting sustainable urban development principles— e.g., minimising urban footprint, limiting emissions, encouraging active and green transport use, establishing urban farms, and addressing the urban waste problem. This in turn helps in generating ecological sustainability which is a critical element of smart cities.

Fourth, in terms of institutional development in smart cities (*smart governance*), we need to equip our cities with highly dynamic mechanisms to better plan their growth and manage their day-to-day operational challenges. This, in turn, helps in performing appropriate planning, development, and management practices that are a core element of smart cities.

Last, but not least, as discussed earlier, a balance between the four development domains of cities is critical to building successful smart cities, and performing smart urbanism practices. The fundamental drivers of such developments include: (a) community (a knowledgeable, conscious, forward-thinking, engaged, united despite differences, and active community); (b) technology (a locally developed, affordable, appropriate, energy-efficient, and effective technology); and (c) policy (a strategic, comprehensive, long-term, dynamic, well-intended, inclusive, and effective public/urban policy).

In sum, the study at hand has disclosed some lessons from the best practice smart cities, and at the same time revealed their limitations in building truly smart and sustainable cities. Insights generated from the study point to a more comprehensive and consolidated view on what smart cities are or should be. In a quest to determine "how a truly smart and sustainable urbanism practice can be realised", further research efforts are needed to advance our understanding, particularly on the development of effective local government smart city policies. In that perspective, the following research questions are worth considering in prospective research concerning the role of local government and policy in the smart city transformation (Yigitcanlar et al., 2019d):

a) What are the most common local government smart city policy characteristics across the globe, and how effective are they in delivering the desired outcomes?
b) What are the conceptual differences in smart city policy adaptation in local governments across the globe, and what is the impact of the local context?
c) What are the most needed government policy mechanisms to produce effective smart city practice that delivers the desired outcomes?
d) How can a comprehensive local government smart city policy framework be developed to guide effective smart city policy development?
e) How can such a policy framework assist smart city transformation and support local governments and practice while achieving the desired outcomes?

Acknowledgements

This chapter, with permission from the copyright holder, is a reproduced version of the following journal article: Yigitcanlar, T., Han, H., Kamruzzaman, M., Ioppolo,

G., & Sabatini-Marques, J. (2019). The making of smart cities: Are Songdo, Masdar, Amsterdam, San Francisco and Brisbane the best we could build? *Land Use Policy* 88, 104187.

References

Albino, V., Berardi, U., Dangelico, R.M. (2015). Smart cities: definitions, dimensions, performance, and initiatives. *Journal of Urban Technology, 22*(1), 3–21.

Albouy, D., Graf, W., Kellogg, R., Wolff, H. (2016). Climate amenities, climate change, and American quality of life. *Journal of the Association of Environmental and Resource Economists, 3*(1), 205–246.

Aldieri, L., Carlucci, F., Cirà, A., Ioppolo, G., Vinci, C.P. (2019a). Is green innovation an opportunity or a threat to employment? An empirical analysis of three main industrialized areas: the USA, Japan and Europe. *Journal of Cleaner Production, 214*, 758–766.

Aldieri, L., Ioppolo, G., Vinci, C.P., Yigitcanlar, T. (2019b). Waste recycling patents and environmental innovations: an economic analysis of policy instruments in the USA, Japan and Europe. *Waste Management, 95*, 612–619.

Aldieri, L., Carlucci, F., Vinci, C., Yigitcanlar, T. (2019c). Environmental innovation, knowledge spillovers and policy implications: a systematic review of the economic effects literature. *Journal of Cleaner Production, 239*, 118051.

Alizadeh, T. (2015). A policy analysis of digital strategies: Brisbane vs. Vancouver. *International Journal of Knowledge-Based Development, 6*(2), 85–103.

Angelidou, M. (2014). Smart city policies: a spatial approach. *Cities, 41*, S3–S11.

Angelidou, M. (2017). Smart city planning and development shortcomings. *Journal of Land Use, Mobility and Environment, 10*(1), 77–94.

Arbolino, R., Simone, L., Carlucci, F., Yigitcanlar, T., Ioppolo, G. (2018). Towards a sustainable industrial ecology: implementation of a novel approach in the performance evaluation of Italian regions. *Journal of Cleaner Production, 178*(1), 220–236.

Aurigi, A. (2006). New technologies, yet same dilemmas? Policy and design issues for the augmented city. *Journal of Urban Technology, 13*(3), 5–28.

BCC (2017). *Smart, Connected Brisbane*. Brisbane City Council (BCC).

Benedikt, O. (2016). The valuable citizens of smart cities: the case of Songdo City. *Graduate Journal of Social Science, 12*(1), 17–36.

Berger, R. (2019). *Smart City Breakaway: How a Small Group of Leading Digital Cities is Outpacing the Rest*. Roland Berger.

Brown, B., Chui, M., Manyika, J. (2011). Are you ready for the era of big data? *McKinsey Quarterly, 4*(1), 24–35.

Buuse, D.V., Kolk, A. (2019). An exploration of smart city approaches by international ICT firms. *Technological Forecasting and Social Change, 142*(1), 220–234.

Caragliu, A., Del Bo, C., Nijkamp, P. (2011). Smart cities in Europe. *Journal of Urban Technology, 18*(2), 65–82.

Caragliu, A., Del Bo, C.F. (2019). Smart innovative cities: the impact of smart city policies on urban innovation. *Technological Forecasting and Social Change, 142*, 373–383.

Carvalho, L. (2012). Urban competitiveness, u-city strategies and the development of technological niches in Songdo, South Korea. In: *Regional Development: Concepts, Methodologies, Tools, and Applications* (pp. 833–852). IGI Global.

Chadwick, G. (2013). *A Systems View of Planning: Towards a Theory of the Urban and Regional Planning Process*. Elsevier.

Chang, D.L., Sabatini-Marques, J., da Costa, E.M., Selig, P.M., Yigitcanlar, T. (2018). Knowledge-based, smart and sustainable cities: a provocation for a conceptual framework. *Journal of Open Innovation: Technology, Market, and Complexity, 4*, 5.

Ching, T.Y., Ferreira, J. (2015). Smart cities: concepts, perceptions and lessons for planners. In: *Planning Support Systems and Smart Cities* (pp. 145–168). Springer.

Crot, L. (2013). Planning for sustainability in non-democratic polities: the case of Masdar city. *Urban Studies, 50*(13), 2809–2825.

Cugurullo, F. (2013). How to build a sandcastle: an analysis of the genesis and development of Masdar City. *Journal of Urban Technology, 20*(1), 23–37.

Cugurullo, F. (2016). Urban eco-modernisation and the policy context of new eco-city projects: where Masdar City fails and why. *Urban Studies, 53*(11), 2417–2433.

Dahlquist, E., Fell, T. (2015). Smart cities. In: *Handbook of Clean Energy Systems* (pp. 1–12). John Wiley & Sons.

Dameri, R.P. (2014). Comparing smart and digital city: initiatives and strategies in Amsterdam and Genoa. Are they digital and/or smart? In: *Smart City* (pp. 45–88). Springer.

Davis, D.E. (2018). Governmental capacity and the smart mobility transition. In: *Governance of the Smart Mobility Transition* (pp. 105–122). Emerald Publishing.

De Jong, M., Hoppe, T., Noori, N. (2019). City branding, sustainable urban development and the rentier state: how do Qatar, Abu Dhabi and Dubai present themselves in the age of post oil and global warming? *Energies, 12*(9), 1657.

Dizdaroglu, D., Yigitcanlar, T., Dawes, L. (2012). A micro-level indexing model for assessing urban ecosystem sustainability. *Smart and Sustainable Built Environment, 1*(3), 291–315.

Dur, F., Yigitcanlar, T. (2015). Assessing land-use and transport integration via a spatial composite indexing model. *International Journal of Environmental Science and Technology, 12*(3), 803–816.

Ersoy, A. (2017). Smart cities as a mechanism towards a broader understanding of infrastructure interdependencies. *Regional Studies, Regional Science, 4*(1), 26–31.

Esmaeilpoorarabi, N., Yigitcanlar, T., Guaralda, M., Kamruzzaman, M. (2018). Does place quality matter for innovation districts? Determining the essential place characteristics from Brisbane's knowledge precincts. *Land Use Policy, 79*, 734–747.

Faisal, A., Yigitcanlar, T., Kamruzzaman, M., Currie, G. (2019). Understanding autonomous vehicles: a systematic literature review on capability, impact, planning and policy. *Journal of Transport and Land Use, 12*(1), 45–72.

Fincher, C. (1972). Planning models and paradigms in higher education. *The Journal of Higher Education, 43*(9), 754–767.

Foreman, K., Marquez, N., Dolgert, A., Fukutaki, K., Fullman, N., McGaughey, M. (2018). Forecasting life expectancy, years of life lost, and all-cause and cause-specific mortality for 250 causes of death. *The Lancet, 392*(10159), 2052–2090.

Gilbert, R., Stevenson, D., Girardet, H., Stren, R. (2013). *Making Cities Work: Role of Local Authorities in the Urban Environment.* Routledge.

Glasser, R. (2019). *Preparing for the Era of Disasters.* Australian Strategic Policy Institute.

Goonetilleke, A., Yigitcanlar, T., Ayoko, G.A., Egodawatta, P. (2014). *Sustainable Urban Water Environment: Climate, Pollution and Adaptation.* Edward Elgar.

Hamstead, Z.A., Fisher, D., Ilieva, R.T., Wood, S.A., McPhearson, T., Kremer, P. (2018). Geolocated social media as a rapid indicator of park visitation and equitable park access. *Computers, Environment and Urban Systems, 72*, 38–50.

Han, H., Hawken, S. (2018). Introduction: innovation and identity in next-generation smart cities. *City, Culture and Society, 12*, 1–4.

Harris, P.G. (2018). Climate change: science, international cooperation and global environmental politics. In: *Global Environmental Politics* (pp. 133–152). Routledge.

Harrison, C., Donnelly, I.A. (2011). A theory of smart cities. In: *Proceedings of the 55th Annual Meeting of the ISSS-2011*, UK.

Hassan, A.M., Lee, H., Yoo, U. (2016). From medieval Cairo to modern Masdar City: lessons learned through a comparative study. *Architectural Science Review, 59*(1), 39–52.

Hollands, R.G. (2008). Will the real smart city please stand up? *City, 12*(3), 303–320.

Hollands, R.G. (2015). Critical interventions into the corporate smart city. *Cambridge Journal of Regions, Economy and Society, 8*(1), 61–77.

Hopwood, D. (2010). Abu Dhabi's Masdar plan takes shape. *Renewable Energy Focus, 11*(1), 18–23.

Hortz, T. (2016). The smart state test: a critical review of the smart state strategy 2005–2015's knowledge-based urban development. *International Journal of Knowledge-Based Development, 7*(1), 75–101.

Hudson, H.E. (2010). Municipal wireless broadband: lessons from San Francisco and Silicon Valley. *Telematics and Informatics, 27*(1), 1–9.

Hughes, C., Spray, R. (2002). Smart communities and smart growth-maximising benefits for the corporation. *Journal of Corporate Real Estate, 4*(3), 207–214.

Ingrao, C., Messineo, A., Beltramo, R., Yigitcanlar, T., Ioppolo, G. (2018). How can life cycle thinking support sustainability of buildings? Investigating life cycle assessment applications for energy efficiency and environmental performance. *Journal of Cleaner Production, 201*(1), 556–569.

Ioppolo, G., Cucurachi, S., Salomone, R., Shi, L., Yigitcanlar, T. (2019). Strategic environmental assessment and material flow accounting: a novel approach for moving towards sustainable urban futures. *International Journal of Life Cycle Assessment, 24*(7), 1269–1284.

Ioppolo, G., Heijungs, R., Cucurachi, S., Salomone, R., Kleijn, R. (2014). Urban metabolism: many open questions for future answers. In: *Pathways to Environmental Sustainability*, (pp. 23–32). Springer.

Ioppolo, G., Szopik-Depczyńska, K., Stajniak, M., Konecka, S. (2016). Supply chain and innovation activity in transport related enterprises in Eastern Poland. *LogForum,* 12(4), 227–236.IPCC (2018). *Special Report on Global Warming of 1.5°C.* Intergovernmental Panel on Climate Change (IPCC).

Kamel, M. (2013). Encouraging walkability in GCC cities: smart urban solutions. *Smart and Sustainable Built Environment, 2*(3), 288–310.

Kanter, R., & Litow, S.S. (2009). *Informed and Interconnected: A Manifesto for Smarter Cities*. Harvard Business School.

Kaufman, S.M., Krishnan, N., Themelis, N.J. (2010). A screening life cycle metric to benchmark the environmental sustainability of waste management systems. *Environmental Science & Technology, 44*(15), 5949–5955.

Kennedy, C., Hoornweg, D. (2012). Mainstreaming urban metabolism. *Journal of Industrial Ecology, 16*(6), 780–782.

Kennedy, M. (2019). *Abu Dhabi Throws the Switch on World's Largest Single-Site Solar Project*. Accessed on 12 July 2019 from https://newatlas.com/abu-dhabi-worlds-largest-single-site-solar-project/60463

Kim, C. (2010). Place promotion and symbolic characterization of new Songdo City, South Korea. *Cities, 27*(1), 13–19.

Kitchin, R. (2014). The real-time city? Big data and smart urbanism. *GeoJournal,* *79*(1), 1–14.

Kolotouchkina, O., Seisdedos, G. (2018). Place branding strategies in the context of new smart cities: Songdo IBD, Masdar and Skolkovo. *Place Branding and Public Diplomacy, 14,* 115–124.

Konys, A. (2018). An ontology-based knowledge modelling for a sustainability assessment domain. *Sustainability, 10*(2), 300.

Lara, A.P., da Costa, E.M., Furlani, T.Z., Yigitcanlar, T. (2016). Smartness that matters: towards a comprehensive and human-centred characterisation of smart cities. *Journal of Open Innovation: Technology, Market, and Complexity, 2,* 1–13.

Leadbeater, C. (2019). *The Curious Case of Lombard Street, San Francisco's Overcrowded Oddity.* Accessed on 12 July 2019 from www.telegraph.co.uk/travel/destinations/north-america/united-states/california/articles/taking-a-toll-lombard-street-san-francisco-california

Lee, J.H., Hancock, M.G., Hu, M.C. (2014). Towards an effective framework for building smart cities: lessons from Seoul and San Francisco. *Technological Forecasting and Social Change, 89,* 80–99.

Lee, S.H., Yigitcanlar, T., Han, J.H., Leem, Y.T. (2008). Ubiquitous urban infrastructure: infrastructure planning and development in Korea. *Innovation, 10*(2–3), 282–292.

Leem, Y., Han, H., & Lee, S. (2019). Sejong smart city: on the road to be a city of the future. In: *Computational Urban Planning and Management for Smart Cities* (pp. 17–33). Springer.

Lehmann, S. (2016). Advocacy for the compact, mixed-use and walkable city: designing smart and climate resilient places. *International Journal of Environment and Sustainability, 5*(2), 1–11.

Manville, C., Cochrane, G., Cave, J., Millard, J., Pederson, J.K., Thaarup, R.K., Kotterink, B. (2014). *Mapping Smart Cities in the EU.* European Union.

Martin, C.J., Evans, J., Karvonen, A. (2018). Smart and sustainable? Five tensions in the visions and practices of the smart-sustainable city in Europe and North America. *Technological Forecasting and Social Change, 133,* 269–278.

McLoughlin, J.B. (1969). *Urban and Regional Planning: A Systems Approach.* Faber & Faber.

Mezher, T., Goldsmith, D., Choucri, N. (2011). Renewable energy in Abu Dhabi: opportunities and challenges. *Journal of Energy Engineering, 137*(4), 169–176.

Mezher, T., Tabbara, S., Al-Hosany, N. (2010). An overview of CSR in the renewable energy sector: examples from the Masdar Initiative in Abu Dhabi. *Management of Environmental Quality, 21*(6), 744–760.

Millar, C.C., Ju-Choi, C. (2010). Development and knowledge resources: a conceptual analysis. *Journal of Knowledge Management, 14*(5), 759–776.

Mora, L., Bolici, R., Deakin, M. (2017). The first two decades of smart-city research: a bibliometric analysis. *Journal of Urban Technology, 24*(1), 3–27.

Mora, L., Deakin, M., Reid, A., Angelidou, M. (2019). How to overcome the dichotomous nature of smart city research: proposed methodology and results of a pilot study. *Journal of Urban Technology, 26*(2), 89–128.

Muriuki, G., Dowd, A.M., Ashworth, P. (2016). Urban sustainability: a segmentation study of Greater Brisbane, Australia. *Journal of Environmental Planning and Management, 59*(3), 414–435.

Palm, M., Niemeier, D. (2017). Achieving regional housing planning objectives: directing affordable housing to jobs-rich neighborhoods in the San Francisco bay area. *Journal of the American Planning Association, 83*(4), 377–388.

Pancholi, S., Yigitcanlar, T., Guaralda, M. (2015a). Place making facilitators of knowledge and innovation spaces: insights from European best practices. *International Journal of Knowledge-Based Development, 6*(3), 215–240.

Pancholi, S., Yigitcanlar, T., Guaralda, M. (2015b). Public space design of knowledge and innovation spaces: learnings from Kelvin Grove Urban Village, Brisbane. *Journal of Open Innovation: Technology, Market, and Complexity, 1*, 13.

Paroutis, S., Bennett, M., Heracleous, L. (2014). A strategic view on smart city technology: the case of IBM smarter cities during a recession. *Technological Forecasting and Social Change, 89*, 262–272.

Ratti, C., Townsend, A. (2011). The social nexus. *Scientific American, 305*(3), 42–48.

Russo, F., Rindone, C., Panuccio, P. (2016). European plans for the smart city: from theories and rules to logistics test case. *European Planning Studies, 24*(9), 1709–1726.

Sauer, S. (2012). Do smart cities produce smart entrepreneurs? *Journal of Theoretical and Applied Electronic Commerce Research, 7*(3), 63–73.

Scheer, H. (2012). *Energy Autonomy: The Economic, Social and Technological case for renewable energy*. Routledge.

Sgouridis, S., Kennedy, S. (2010). Tangible and fungible energy: hybrid energy market and currency system for total energy management—a Masdar City case study. *Energy Policy, 38*(4), 1749–1758.

Shwayri, S.T. (2013). A model Korean ubiquitous eco-city? The politics of making Songdo. *Journal of Urban Technology, 20*(1), 39–55.

Stanley, J., Loy, D.R., Dorje, G. (2009). *A Buddhist Response to the Climate Emergency*. Simon and Schuster.

Stimmel, C. (2016). *Building Smart Cities: Analytics, ICT, and Design Thinking*. CRC Press.Stone, L. (2019). *Smart Poles to Collect City Data for Brisbane City Council*. Accessed on 12 July 2019 from www.brisbanetimes.com.au/national/queensland/smart-poles-to-collect-city-data-for-brisbane-city-council-20190514-p51n9f.html

Strickland, E. (2011). Cisco bets on South Korean smart city. *IEEE Spectrum, 48*(8), 11–12.

Szopik-Depczyńska, K., Kędzierska-Szczepaniak, A., Szczepaniak, K., Cheba, K., Gajda, W., Ioppolo, G. (2018). Innovation in sustainable development: an investigation of the EU context using 2030 agenda indicators. *Land Use Policy, 79*, 251–262.

Townsend, A.M. (2013). *Smart Cities: Big Data, Civic Hackers, and the Quest for a New Utopia*. WW Norton & Company.

Trindade, E.P., Hinnig, M.P., da Costa, E.M., Marques, J.S., Bastos, R.C., Yigitcanlar, T. (2017). Sustainable development of smart cities: a systematic review of the literature. *Journal of Open Innovation: Technology, Market, and Complexity, 3*, 11.

Van Winden, W., Oskam, I., Van den Buuse, D., Schrama, W., Van Dijck, E.J. (2016). *Organising Smart City Projects: Lessons from Amsterdam*. Amsterdam University of Applied Sciences.

Vanolo, A. (2014). Smartmentality: the smart city as disciplinary strategy. *Urban Studies, 51*(5), 883–898.

Vincent, X. (2016). *Self-Driving Boats Will be Tested on Amsterdam's Canals Next Year*. Accessed on 12 July 2019 from www.theverge.com/2016/9/19/12968420/amsterdam-self-driving-boats-roboat

Wiig, A. (2015). IBM's smart city as techno-utopian policy mobility. *City, 19*(2–3), 258–273.

Yadav, G., Mangla, S.K., Luthra, S., Rai, D.P. (2019). Developing a sustainable smart city framework for developing economies: an Indian context. *Sustainable Cities and Society, 47*, 101462.

Yigitcanlar, T. (2009). Planning for smart urban ecosystems: information technology applications for capacity building in environmental decision making. *Theoretical and Empirical Researches in Urban Management, 4*(3), 5–21.

Yigitcanlar, T. (2015). Smart cities: an effective urban development and management model? *Australian Planner, 52*(1), 27–34.

Yigitcanlar, T. (2018). Smart city policies revisited: considerations for a truly smart and sustainable urbanism practice. *World Technopolis Review, 7*(2), 97–112.

Yigitcanlar, T., Kamruzzaman, M. (2018). Does smart city policy lead to sustainability of cities? *Land Use Policy, 73*(1), 49–58.

Yigitcanlar, T., Kamruzzaman, M. (2019). Smart cities and mobility: does the smartness of Australian cities lead to sustainable commuting patterns? *Journal of Urban Technology, 26*(2), 21–46.

Yigitcanlar, T., Kamruzzaman, M., Buys, L., Ioppolo, G., Sabatini-Marques, J., da Costa, E., Yun, J. (2018). Understanding 'smart cities': intertwining development drivers with desired outcomes in a multidimensional framework. *Cities, 81*(1), 145–160.

Yigitcanlar, T., Kamruzzaman, M., Foth, M., Sabatini-Marques, J., Costa, E., Ioppolo, G. (2019a). Can cities become smart without being sustainable? A systematic review of the literature. *Sustainable Cities and Society, 45*(1), 348–365.

Yigitcanlar, T., Foth, M., Kamruzzaman, M. (2019b). Towards post-anthropocentric cities: reconceptualising smart cities to evade urban ecocide. *Journal of Urban Technology, 26*(2), 147–152.

Yigitcanlar, T., Wilson, M., Kamruzzaman, M. (2019c). Disruptive impacts of automated driving systems on the built environment and land use: an urban planners' perspective. *Journal of Open Innovation: Technology, Market, and Complexity, 5*, 24.

Yigitcanlar, T., Lee, S.H. (2014). Korean ubiquitous-eco-city: a smart-sustainable urban form or a branding hoax? *Technological Forecasting and Social Change, 89*, 100–114.

Yigitcanlar, T., Metaxiotis, K., Carrillo, F.J. (2012). *Building Prosperous Knowledge Cities: Policies, Plans and Metrics*. Edward Elgar.

Yigitcanlar, T., Han, H., Kamruzzaman, M., Ioppolo, G., Sabatini-Marques, J. (2019d). The making of smart cities: Are Songdo, Masdar, Amsterdam, San Francisco and Brisbane the best we could build? *Land Use Policy, 88*, 104187.

Yun, J.J. (2015). How do we conquer the growth limits of capitalism? Schumpeterian Dynamics of Open Innovation. *Journal of Open Innovation: Technology, Market, and Complexity, 1*, 17.

Zawieska, J., Pieriegud, J. (2018). Smart city as a tool for sustainable mobility and transport decarbonisation. *Transport Policy, 63*(1), 39–50.

Zhu, C., Zhou, H., Leung, V.C., Wang, K., Zhang, Y., Yang, L.T. (2017). Toward big data in green city. *IEEE Communications Magazine, 55*(11), 14–18.

Part 2

Smart City Community

This part of the book concentrates on providing a clear understanding on the community dimension of smart city practice. The part offers lessons from the examples on digital commons, participatory governance, good enough governance, augmenting community engagement, and alleviating community disadvantage.

DOI: 10.1201/9781003403647-7

6 Digital Commons

6.1 Introduction

When applied to cities, "smartness" refers to efficient use of human, social, natural, and technological resources towards sustainable urban living. There is an intrinsic connection between such challenges and the notion of "smart government" as public digital spaces with both authorities and citizenship participation, based on public (good) governance and efficient electronic government (eGov) [1,2]. In smart eGov platforms, public services are not only delivered by government, but include citizen participation supported by modern information technology [3]. In this sense, in developing initiatives and projects related to eGov, public administration can use a more humanistic approach, using the principles of the "new public service" (NPS)—the focus of which is the public interest and the coproduction of the common good, and the public servants at the service of all citizens [4].

In the context of eGov and NPS, coproduction is an essential requirement for the provision of public good and quality services in a network, presupposing the engagement of citizens, government, and organisations. From this perspective, citizens are the main element to define "what" should be produced and "how", and participate in the elaboration, evaluation, and accountability of the process, through the networks of state and non-state actors. Such flexibility to change according to the citizens' interests and needs, by the use of technologies as enablers to connect and engage government and citizens, is described by Marsh [5] as the "humane smart city". In the "commons theory", platforms that support such coproduction can be referred to as digital commons [6]. This can be the case of smart eGov platforms. Such platforms are public digital commons when they contribute to transparency, participation, accountability, effectiveness, and other open governance principles.

According to Ostrom [7], commons are goods of collective use shared by individuals, and subject to social conflicts, and by: (a) emphasis on social interaction; (b) common objectives, rules, and standards; (c) practices of sharing and distribution of power relations; (d) institutions for decision-making; and (e) governance [8,9]. In turn, the concept of commons has advanced, and has become richer and more diversified, as is the case of collective and collaborative production of content mediated by digital and open resources—such as Wikipedia or Linux [10]. This has become a recurring practice in certain organisations, thus contributing to the

DOI: 10.1201/9781003403647-8

creation of a collective and adaptive creative intelligence [11]. These collaborative efforts and practices can be characterised as digital commons [6,12].

To complement this understanding, it is useful to refer to Pacheco's [13] view—particularly when considering knowledge as a type of commons involved in information and communication technologies (ICTs). He describes a new type of commons. That is the digital common, which is defined as follows: "digital commons is a resource based on information and communication technology, shared by groups and integrated in a value chain, under principles of equity, coproduction and sustainability".

In fact, through eGov platforms or portals, public administration presents its identity, purpose, and achievements, provides services and information, providing access and interaction with citizens, as well as understanding their needs, and increasing transparency and the participation of society in government actions [14]. In addition, eGov platforms can be considered tools to promote knowledge sharing, providing users with resources to promote the dissemination of knowledge and interaction between different actors and government [15]. In this sense, the importance of knowledge management is recognised in public administration, since it deals with information and knowledge about citizens, companies, markets, laws, and policy. Such deliverables and the level of government-to-society relationship can be analysed according to the maturity level that eGov platforms present.

Maturity models for eGov platforms, in turn, are structured in stages (from basic to advanced). These models provide a way to classify eGov platforms (according to the services, features, and functionalities offered), and can be used as a guide to help public administrations improve the quality and efficiency of their eGov portals [16]. In spite of the existence of approaches for the evaluation of different characteristics of eGov platforms [17,18], there is a need for means to evaluate elements that may characterise such platforms as digital commons and, more specifically, to assess their potential of promoting social commons. In recent years, we have developed the Municipal eGov Platform Assessment Model (MEPA) that is a model to assess eGov platforms as digital commons [18]. MEPA allows the identification and evaluation of several factors related to digital commons principles.

In this chapter, we present MEPA and its application in the evaluation of 903 official websites of Brazilian cities, and discuss its potential to help public managers to use eGov as integral smart cities instruments. The results of this research underline the limitations in the municipal eGov platforms in Brazil. Only a few municipalities effectively manage to provide services so that the population can fulfil its role of participation and coproduction. From the sample surveyed, in approximately 7% of the municipality platforms, it was possible to verify a higher maturity level for the feasibility of the commons offered by the government, since the highest levels of maturity (fifth, fourth, and third levels) were identified in only 66 Brazilian municipalities. The vast majority of Brazilian eGov platforms still offer simple, easy-to-access information or services, or just online transactions, remaining at the first and second maturity levels. Therefore, eGov's actions and projects need to be rethought in Brazil, in terms of services, infrastructure, governance, and financial resources, to achieve higher levels of eGov maturity.

6.2 Methodology

The MEPA model was developed by empirical research, based on the "design science research" (DSR) method [19], according to the following steps: (1) identify the problem and motivate; (2) define the objectives of a solution; (3) design and development; (4) demonstration; (5) evaluation; and (6) communication. In the following sections the development stages of the model according to the DSR are presented.

6.2.1 Problem Identification and Motivation

Ostrom [7] describes eight principles that are fundamental to the sustainable management of commons. These are delimitation, context appropriation, participation, monitoring, proportionate sanctions, affordable conflict resolution, autonomy, and adhocracy. These principles were originally formulated by the author from an examination and analysis of more than 5000 case studies, through which it was possible to verify why some communities or individuals organise themselves successfully to manage the commons, and others do not.

Based on these general principles, there is a need to establish the means to evaluate its presence on eGov platforms of Brazilian municipalities. The platforms offer different services in terms of scope, quality, influenced interaction between stakeholders and government, knowledge sharing, and the possibility of coproducing the public good in a sustainable manner, according to the level of their maturity.

Therefore, the research problem presented in this chapter seeks to answer the following questions: (1) How to relate the maturity of eGov platforms with the instrumentation of commons promotion? and (2) What is the situation of eGov platforms in Brazilian municipalities, in relation to their potential for promoting commons principles?

The MEPA problem and motivation are, hence, contextualised in multiple domains. Citizen coproduction and public governance are public management subjects. Electronic government platforms and human smart cities are contemporaneous multidisciplinary fields, and commons are a general theory suitable as a reference to several complex community-based problems. Our first step was to establish a reference concept table, with the main research construct. The result is presented in Table 6.1.

Our research problem was to check municipal websites' maturity regarding the promotion of commons and citizen participation. In order to do so, we have combined the seven conceptual multidisciplinary constructs presented in Figure 6.1.

As can be seen in Figure 6.1, the research problem combines the notions of municipal websites as eGov solutions, that can potentially help public managers to foster citizen participation by means (or towards) digital commons. Besides the

Table 6.1 Conceptual references of MEPA

Construct	Definition	Authors
Humane smart city	It is a place flexible to change according to its citizens' wishes, interests, and needs, through the use of technologies as enablers to connect and engage government and citizens, aiming to rebuild, recreate, and motivate urban communities, stimulating and supporting their collaboration activities, leading to a general increase in social well-being	Marsh (2013)
Citizen participation	Interaction of citizens and administrators, concerned with public policy decisions and public services	Ostrom (1978)
Public governance	Formal and informal arrangements that determine how public decisions are made and how public actions are carried out	OECD (2018)
New public service	A paradigm of public management that focuses on the public interest, the coproduction of the common good, transparency, accountability, and the participation of society	Denhardt (2012)
Knowledge management	Involving the means by which public administration mainly promotes the sharing and dissemination of knowledge through eGov platforms	Nah et al. (2005)
e-Government (eGov)	It is the use of information technology to produce and distribute customer-oriented, more cost-effective, differentiated, and better public services	Holmes (2001)
eGov maturity assessment	It is an assessment model composed of at least four high-level eGov applications requirements: (a) current state of maturity and capability identification; (b) benchmark with other eGov applications; (c) innovation roadmap; and (d) discretion as to whether or not to follow	Valdés et al. (2011)
Commons	Resource shared by a group of people attempting to solve social problems	Fisher & Fortmann (2010)
Digital commons	Resources available in information and communication technology platforms (i.e., digital), shared by a group (i.e., commons), integrated in a value chain (i.e., intangible asset) and performed by agents, either as a content or as a process, valuable on a given domain (i.e., knowledge)	Pacheco (2014)

specific constructs presented in Table 6.1 and illustrated in Figure 6.1, the MEPA design was based on both commons principles [20] and NPS elements [4], as indicated in Table 6.2.

Although the relations in Table 6.2 are not linear (i.e., a commons principle can be related to more than one NPS element, and vice-versa), they help to relate eGov platform services to both public commons and public decision-making. By relating commons principles to NPS elements, the MEPA model opens the possibility

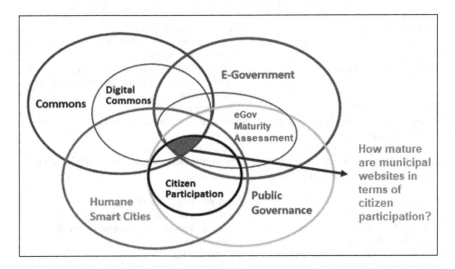

Figure 6.1 Research problem and conceptual constructs.

of eGov platform assessment in both views, first as digital commons potential promoters and, second as an instrument to support contemporaneous public management. Particularly for NPS, the MEPA analysis is concerned with:

1. Transparency and publicity: The concern of municipalities to comply with current legislation, through the publication and dissemination of information, guidelines, recommendations, and open data;
2. Civic engagement: Resources to interested parties, so that they can develop activities in their communities or workplaces through social networks and media, or the services offered, seeking to assert their interests, to provide or receive common goods, or to participate in some level of the political decision-making process;
3. Inclusion and access: Services to help, including citizens, or public or private bodies in life in society, reducing differences;
4. Shared responsibility: Municipalities' efforts to build a collective and shared notion of common, economic, and socially viable good;
5. Reaffirmation of values of democracy and citizenship, power decentralisation, coproduction, and accountability: Services and functionalities for the concrete involvement of all stakeholders, in the definition and active participation of the decision on how the public service will be delivered, and, ultimately, how the common good will be coproduced.

Additionally, MEPA has also a conceptual relationship between the commons theory and eGov maturity assessment, as illustrated in Table 6.3.

Table 6.2 Commons principles and new public service elements (derived from [4,20])

Commons principles	New public service elements
Delimitation	Inclusion and access
Define clear boundaries	Access information based on education, open government, free communication, and open discussion
Adequacy of context	Civic engagement
Match rules governing commons use to local needs and conditions	Serve citizens, not customers
Participation and coproduction	Coproduction
Ensure that the ones affected by the rules can participate in regulatory changes	Promote collective efforts and collaborative processes
Monitoring	Transparency and publicity
Develop a system carried out by community members for monitoring member's behaviour	Greater participation responds to call for greater transparency and accountability in government
Proportionate sanctions and rewards	Accountability
Use graduated sanctions for rule violators	Public servants must attend to law, community values, political norms, professional standards, and citizen interests
Resolubility	Shared responsibility
Provide accessible and low-cost means for dispute resolution	Create shared interests and shared responsibility
Autonomy	Reaffirmation of values of democracy/ citizenship
Make sure that rule-making rights are respected by outside authorities	
Adhocracy	Decentralisation of power
Governing the common resource is based on nested tiers from the lowest level up to the entire interconnected system	Collaborative structures with leadership shared internally and externally

Table 6.3 Relationship between eGov maturity levels and commons principles

eGov maturity level	Description	Commons principles
First level	The portal offers easy access to simple information and services	Delimitation and monitoring
Second level	The portal enables online transactions	Adequacy of context
Third level	The portal allows access to different sites and services, with only one authentication	Resolubility
Fourth level	The portal enables interoperability between government systems and sites	Adhocracy
Fifth level	The portal allows the personalisation of the services offered to users	Proportionate sanctions and rewards, autonomy, participation, and coproduction

The notion of a citizen as a client was proposed by "new public management". In the NPS framework, as proposed by Robert and Jane Denhardt [4], the fourth principle sets "serve citizens not customers".

We have developed MEPA considering coproduction as an essential process to do so. Citizens should participate in the creation, development, and evolution of the services promoted by the public administration. In order to do so, the channels of communication and interaction must be effectively provided, so that citizens have an active and independent role. They should be able to comment, request, evaluate, and vote for public services satisfaction as well as on the effectiveness of the electronic platform they are using.

In this view, citizens no longer play a secondary role, such as a solicitor at the mercy of the public administration, or as a customer who will "consume" the products and services of a menu, but rather of a co-producer, who participates and collaborates dynamically and actively in the evolution of the products and services that it is receiving from the public administration.

In summary, MEPA design was achieved by the conceptual and practical alignment of principles and procedures from commons, NPS, and eGov maturity analysis. Its ultimate goal is to allow the verification of the eGov platform maturity in relation to the common good, according to different levels of instrumentation and services. MEPA evaluations aim to help public managers to promote commons through eGov solutions.

6.2.2 Objectives of Finding a Solution

Municipal websites are, first, eGov solutions and, as such, subjected to maturity assessment. The proposal solution, however, should go further than eGov common maturity analysis. More than checking for technological and public services effectiveness, the maturity assessment should also reveal the potential of municipal websites promoting citizen participation. To this end, the instrument should enable the analysis of the commons' principles present in eGov platforms of Brazilian municipalities, also considering elements of NPS and knowledge management, with emphasis on how platforms promote participation and sharing between the different actors in society.

6.2.3 Design and Development

Different approaches are proposed in the literature for the analysis of eGov platforms in order to characterise their level of maturity [11,15,17,21–28]. In common, such approaches cover the breadth of the services assembled by the platform and the level of sophistication of delivery [16,29,30] and the government's relationship with different stakeholders in society [31].

During the research into other models of maturity of e-Government platforms, we found other models that presented some level of similarity with MEPA, as is the case of the methodology presented by Fietkiewicz, Mainka, and Stock [32]. Indeed, there is some similarity in the points of contact between the two models. However, each model proposes to conduct a different analysis. The methodology presented by Fietkiewicz, Mainka, and Stock [32], measures the maturity of e-Government and the usability of the navigation systems, and investigates the boundary documents available on the governmental websites.

The MEPA model, in turn, proposes to investigate the maturity of the municipal electronic government platforms in smart cities, considering the digital commons and citizens coproduction. MEPA was elaborated considering the following aspects: (1) analyse the new service public [4] and knowledge sharing as factors of relationship between eGov maturity and commons principles, according to Ostrom [7]; (2) establish a comparative framework between dimensions and maturity factors of electronic government (eGov), based on Holmes [17] and the principles of commons [7]; (3) create a maturity assessment tool of Brazilian municipal e-Government platforms, as commons promoters; (4) apply the maturity assessment tool to Brazilian municipalities; and (5) analyse the results obtained, under the lens of participation and coproduction. The MEPA model does not use, primarily, criteria such as usability navigation systems, or documents that are transacted and made available between municipal sites. The two models apply two different approaches.

In this research, we have established an eGov maturity assessment including factors regarding citizen participation. This was developed based on commons general principles and by the adaptation of eGov maturity questionnaires to include checking for citizen participation-related factors. The development of the work was carried out according to the following steps:

1. Systematic review of the literature for the composition of the preliminary evaluation instrument;
2. Evaluation of the preliminary version of the data collection instrument with specialists;
3. Application of the revised instrument in the pre-test stage;
4. Validation of intermediate analysis of the results achieved and of the data collection instrument with the support of specialists in the construction of items and measures;
5. Application of the evaluation instrument.

In the first step, in order to define the items that should compose the evaluation instrument, a systematic review of the literature was carried out, looking for elements in the literature that could characterise the relationship between open government data, coproduction, commons, governance, electronic government, and knowledge management. Therefore, the terms "open government", "commons", "governance", "eGov*" or "electronic government", "knowledge management", and "co*production" were combined to search the main journal bases. The search was performed on the ISI-Web of Knowledge/Web of Science databases; Scopus; Ebsco; Compendex, and ProQuest, and Google Scholar. Of the total of 54 articles found, 35 were selected after reading them and used to support the elaboration of the data collection instrument.

The literature review resulted in the definition of 56 items that formed the initial evaluation instrument. The initial instrument was evaluated by specialists and applied in the evaluation of 264 electronic platforms of Brazilian municipalities in the pre-test phase. The final version of the instrument is composed of 41 items and was configured considering the feedback from the pre-test phase. The 41 items were organised into groups by their affinity (in terms of functionality or characteristics), in order to make the filling of the questionnaire simpler and more intuitive. Table 6.4 presents nine groups created as well as their definitions.

In Table 6.5 we list the items of the evaluation instrument. Each item was evaluated by means of an application instrument including the response possibilities: 1 for "has the characteristic" and 0 for "does not have the characteristic".

Table 6.4 Item groups and their description

Group	Description
1. Open data, information, and public services are freely available to users	Citizens have the right to free access to public services and information, to exercise their participation, to improve service delivery, to monitor administration, and to expand democracy [11]
2. The platform offers open data, institutional and transparency information, and other topics	The digital environment provides greater transparency, facilitating access to information for citizens, allowing the monitoring of government actions, projects, and decisions [12]
3. The platform offers features for interaction with other users or with those responsible for the platform	Citizens should be aware of the communication channels available to contact the public administration, and have access in an easy, accessible, and low-cost way [33]
4. The platform provides resources for users to vote or make recommendations	Public administration should provide channels of communication, based on citizen participation, together with the assumptions of democratic decision-making processes in society [34]
5. The platform offers capabilities for downloading data (in various formats, machine-readable)	Open data must be reachable and can be physically accessed by download [35]
6. The platform provides open search/search capabilities	It should be possible to conduct research by various means to assist users in finding relevant open data [36]
7. The platform is accessible in mobile version	Citizens have the right to access public services and information, freely using ICT resources to access electronic platforms—desktop, mobile, or tablet [37]
8. Quality of data and information offered by the platform	Well-informed citizens can better combat corruption, nepotism, and government inaccuracy. On the other hand, without accurate information, it is difficult to achieve effective citizen involvement in decision-making processes [38]
9. The platform provides tools for knowledge management	The GC is essential for the success of e-Government initiatives [39]

Table 6.5 Evaluation instrument items

Item	Commons principles
1. Does the platform require no prior registration of users?	Delimitation
2. Does the platform identify the services available to each stakeholder?	Delimitation
3. Does the platform provide stakeholders with guidelines for services usage?	Delimitation
4. Does the platform have terms of use for the services, informing the rights and responsibilities of stakeholders?	Sanctions and rewards
5. Does the platform present terms of use for the services, informing penalties in case of noncompliance?	Sanctions and rewards
6. Does the platform disclose at least an index of use of the services provided?	Monitoring
7. Does the platform provide updated news about the municipality?	Monitoring
8. Does the platform provide additional information (economic, cultural, tourist, historical, geographic, ethnic, according to location or region)?	Monitoring
9. Does the platform provide digital media—employing at least one of the following services? Podcast, interactive maps, videos, digital documents, web radio?	Context and adequacy
10. Does the platform provide relevant legislation to the municipality? (It may be any type of legislation, as follows: Laws, Master Plan, Urban Zoning, Code of Works, Taxpayer's Manual, normative instructions, decree, ordinances, opinions, resolutions, etc.)	Monitoring
11. Does the platform provide access to the Official Gazette?	Monitoring
12. Does the platform provide access to the municipality's financial information (availability of government documents for collection, movement of the treasury and financial application of public resources—balance sheets, financial statements)?	Monitoring
13. Does the platform provide content related to digital inclusion?	Delimitation
14. Does the platform provide access to the municipality's transparency information?	Monitoring
15. Does the platform provide access to procurement and bidding by the municipality?	Monitoring
16. Does the platform provide access to at least one municipal office's website/portal?	Adhocracy
17. Does the platform provide access to at least one website/portal of a municipal body?	Adhocracy
18. Does the platform provide access to at least one website or portal of the municipality's attorney general's office?	Adhocracy
19. Does the platform provide open data?	Autonomy
20. Are open data available in at least one of the following formats: JSON, XML, CSV, ODS or RDF?	Context and adequacy
21. Can the open data available on the portal be downloaded?	Context and adequacy
22. Does the platform provide information about open data? (example: usage policies, category, identification, description, update frequency, etc.)	Delimitation

Table 6.5 (Continued)

Item	Commons principles
23. Does the platform provide open data search?	Context and adequacy
24. Does the platform provide a list of frequently asked questions (FAQs)?	Resolubility
25. Does the platform provide at least one communication channel for complaints, questions, criticisms, or compliments (example: Ombudsman)?	Resolubility
26. Does the platform provide an instant online service (via chat or similar tool)?	Resolubility
27. Does the platform allow integration with social networks (made up of groups that share common interests)?	Resolubility
28. Does the platform provide collaborative virtual spaces (facilitates the meeting and interaction between people who are not physically together)?	Participation and coproduction
29. Does the platform provide blogs or microblogs (example *Twitter*)?	Participation and coproduction
30. Does the platform allow the formation of communities of practice (e.g., to create and share common skills, knowledge, and experiences)?	Autonomy
31. Does the platform allow you to choose the most relevant services (which may be due to the functionality of the platform, or through network resources or social media)?	Autonomy
32. Can stakeholders use the network or social media features offered by the platform?	Delimitation
33. Does the platform offer features for electronic voting?	Autonomy
34. Does the platform provide services for the composition of the decision-making agenda involving population participation?	Autonomy
35. Does the platform provide features for recommending open data?	Participation and coproduction
36. Does the platform offer resources for recommending services?	Participation and coproduction
37. Does the platform provide resources for voting on what are the best open data?	Participation and coproduction
38. Does the platform provide resources for voting on which are the best services?	Participation and coproduction
39. Is the platform accessible in mobile version?	Context and adequacy
40. Does the platform provide tools for knowledge management (such as thesauri, classification schemes, taxonomies and ontologies, knowledge maps, and mailing lists)?	Context and adequacy
41. Does the platform provide up-to-date knowledge resources (such as lessons learned, good working practices, etc.)?	Participation and coproduction

6.2.4 Demonstration

In this phase the DSR method requires the presentation of a proof of concept in order to demonstrate the efficacy of the proposal to solve the problem. The MEPA model was built under simplicity and ease-of-use guidelines. The items that compose the MEPA questionnaire were developed considering the principles of the commons [7] and the NPS [4].

In order to evaluate the criteria in all digital commons' maturity dimensions, the MEPA model has a questionnaire, with questions about the eGov platform and the municipal website. MEPA's questions were structured in Google Forms, used by the data researchers to register the answers they uncovered when checking a particular municipal website. Hence, each research data registered their answers manually, after assessing the municipal website, checking whether or not the electronic platform has the characteristic under analysis. This method of collecting data on websites is based on [40–43].

The application of the MEPA model was performed only on the websites (electronic platforms) of the municipal public administration. Nevertheless, several items of the questionnaire aim to analyse whether the website allows the integration, interaction, voting, and publication of references in relation to the services provided, through social media. It also verifies whether the website can be accessed and used on mobile devices.

After completing the data collection, the answers are organised in data sheets. MEPA researchers perform data processing (via descriptive statistics), calculate the frequency of occurrence and draw graphs, classify them into categories of analysis (by "size", geographical region, and municipality size), and highlight the results (findings), revealing municipality digital commons maturity rankings. For the effective application of the MEPA, the researchers underwent training, so that everyone had knowledge of how to access the questionnaire online (using Google Forms); later, we defined a set of electronic municipal platforms for the researchers; in turn, each researcher, using the online questionnaire, accessed the municipal platforms they were responsible for, filling in the answers, and reporting findings that they considered relevant. This way, we were able to evaluate 903 electronic Brazilian municipal platforms, following the same standards and criteria of analysis, in a short period of time, with a high degree of reliability.

6.2.5 Evaluation

In this DSR phase we analysed how well the proposed model provides solutions to the research problem by comparing the eGov maturity assessment pursued with MEPA results. The strategy was based on a comparison between expert's opinion, literature findings, and MEPA results. MEPA metrics and techniques of analysis, and the way the evaluation was conducted, led to results similar to cities' websites situations described in the literature, as well as by the empirical observations of the researchers.

An example is the ninth publication of the eGov development benchmarking from the United Nations Department of Economic and Social Affairs (UNDESA)

[44]. In this survey, Brazil is in 51st position for better eGov services. The country stands out in the basic indicators, such as the existence of a web page of the main public agencies, data supply, and indicators on government websites. However, it has unsatisfactory levels of online eGov services.

According to the MEPA survey, municipal Brazilian eGov services offer little citizen participation in public policy decision-making over the Internet, but are well positioned to provide information in consultations (93 out of 100). A large number of the municipalities visited have an available electronic platform, data supply, and indicators in governmental sites, at some level. However, unsatisfactory levels were identified in the offer of online services, and in the actions for digital inclusion. Comparing the results of the "online participation" carried out by the UN research with MEPA results, the eGov platforms of the Brazilian municipalities offer few services for citizen participation in decisions, but they provide diverse information and news.

6.2.6 Communication

In this phase of the DSR method, the researchers should communicate the problem, its relevance, and how their proposal offers a novel solution. The MEPA model was fully described in a PhD dissertation [18]. MEPA was discussed not only in the academic forum, its application also has been considered beyond the municipal sphere, including the state and federal spheres in Brazil. Recently, the model was the basis of a discussion within the Court of Accounts of the State of Santa Catarina, when it served as the basis for the discussion of the electronic government model for the municipalities of that state.

6.3 Application of the Model to Brazilian Municipalities

As described earlier, the MEPA model was developed based on different theoretical foundations and knowledge fields. In this section, we present the application of the MEPA model to Brazilian municipalities.

6.3.1 Brazilian Municipalities and Large-Scale Model Application

According to the Brazilian official National Institute of Geography and Statistics (IBGE), the country has 5,570 cities. We have applied the MEPA model in 903 municipal websites (i.e., 16.2% of total municipalities), in cities from all five Brazilian regions, as indicated in Table 6.6.

6.3.2 MEPA Positive Responses in the Evaluated Brazilian Municipalities

The total 903 municipal websites that were analysed are from large (291), medium (453), and small cities (159). These websites were checked in all eight digital common maturity dimensions. In Table 6.7, the percentages of positive answers are presented, according to each digital commons' maturity.

Table 6.6 Population and sample—large-scale application

Brazilian region	Quantity of municipalities
South	300
Southeast	300
Midwest	91
Northeast	111
North	101
Total	903

Table 6.7 Dimensions and frequency of positive responses

Region	Frequency (%)
Monitoring	82.77
Context adequacy	72.04
Delimitation	61.26
Resolubility	59.86
Autonomy	25.20
Adhocracy	22.22
Participation and coproduction	21.96
Sanctioning and rewards	10.96

As can be seen in Table 6.7, around 82% of the municipal websites have positive Monitoring and 72% are adequate to its context. These positive results are followed by good Delimitation in about 61%, and good Resolubility in almost 60% of the evaluated municipal websites.

The investigation revealed that the evaluated municipal eGov platforms offer the following information services: (a) updated news, information on history, economy, tourism, and other relevant facts, using digital media; (b) monitoring of public agents, through services aimed at the dissemination and publicity of information on transparency and open data of the municipality in question, including municipal budget, laws and projects, purchases, bids and contracts, official gazette; and (c) communication channels with the ombudsman of the municipality.

The results presented in Table 6.7 reveal a low commitment to commons principles. The evaluated municipal websites offer low level of services related to Autonomy (25.20%), Adhocracy (22.22%), Participation and Coproduction (21.96%), and Sanctioning and Rewards (10.96%).

Therefore, fewer than one-quarter of the evaluated municipal platforms provide services related to civic engagement, platform inclusion and assessment, shared accountability, regulation participation, and decentralised power. This is coherent with low levels of Autonomy (i.e., the website is limited to eGov national or regional legislation) and Adhocracy (i.e., rules and commitment is limited to eGov public owners). Additionally, a low level of sanctioning and rewarding about how

Table 6.8 Brazilian municipal eGov regarding commons and NPS principles

Commons principles	NPS elements	Frequency (%)
Monitoring	Transparency and publicity	82.77
Adequacy of context	Civic engagement	72.04
Delimitation	Inclusion and access	61.26
Resolubility	Shared responsibility	59.86
Autonomy	Democracy/citizenship values	25.20
Adhocracy	Decentralisation of power	22.22
Participation and coproduction	Coproduction	21.96
Proportionate sanctions and rewards	Accountability	25.20

parties use the platforms reveals the lack of incentives for good use or punishment when users break rules.

From the results obtained, it was possible to perceive that the electronic platforms of large municipalities presented a higher frequency of positive responses, mainly those located in the south and southeast regions of Brazil, with higher GDP and human development index (HDI) indices.

In the MEPA model, e-Gov platforms can be verified as potential instruments to promote commons and support public management. This is done by classifying MEPA answers according to commons and NPS principles. In Table 6.8 we present the results of the 903 evaluated Brazilian municipalities.

According to the results in Table 6.8, the vast majority of Brazilian municipal eGov have transparency and publicity services (82.77%). This is related to monitoring services, often related to authorities' concerns about constitutional principles and laws that obligate government to open and disseminate public data, information, guidelines, and recommendations. Around 72% of all Brazilian municipal eGov analysed have services that help to promote civic engagement. In fact, most platforms use web, social media, or other services to allow users to identify and/or develop activities in their communities or places of work. In time, by attending to citizen interests, an eGov platforms will accumulate data and information useful to support political decision-making or even to provide/or receive common goods.

Another important finding was the fact that 61.26% of municipal eGov websites have services related to inclusion and access to all citizens. Besides being recommended by law, digital inclusion can reduce differences between social classes, educational levels, ages, gender, disability, social prejudice, or racial group. Six out of 10 (59.86%) of the Brazilian municipal eGov platforms analysed have services related to share responsibility and conflict resolution. These services help municipalities to build a collective and shared notion of common, economically and socially viable good. This includes citizens, companies, elected representatives, and administrators in a broader system of governance, aimed at promoting citizenship and serving the public interest.

The lowest rates of commons and NPS principles are in services that help to promote democracy and citizenship values (25.20%), power decentralisation (22.22%), coproduction (21.96%), and accountability (10.96%). Brazilian municipal governments provide an insufficient number of services and functionalities for the concrete involvement of all stakeholders. Municipal platforms can do more to engage citizens in defining and participating in decision-making on how public services will be delivered. This requires a focus on deliberative democracy based on citizen participation, and shared responsibilities at all levels of government and public governance.

6.3.3 Brazilian Municipalities' Common Ranking

One of MEPA model goals is to allow public managers to compare different eGov municipalities regarding their potential to promote commons. This is done by comparing commons principle eGov rates, calculated by weighted scales, where the highest levels mean more citizen participation and coproduction, as shown in Table 6.9.

Each municipal eGov reaches a specific score calculated as follows: by summing the responses to the 41 items (positive response = 1 and negative response = 0), multiplied by the weight of the respective principle item (according to Table 6.9). In addition, knowing the weights assigned to each commons principle, and the number of items per level, it is possible to establish ranges for each level (as shown in Table 6.8). In Table 6.10, we present the rank results, according to each MEPA maturity level.

Almost half of the Brazilian cities (439 or 48.62% of the evaluated platforms) are still in the first level of maturity, offering simple information or services, and are easy to access. Another significant number of cities (398 platforms or 44.08%) are in the second level of maturity, including users having the possibility to perform online transactions. Only 48 of the evaluated municipal platforms (5.32%) are in the third level of maturity, adding access to different sites and services, with a single authentication. There are 14 platforms (1.55%) at the fourth level, enabling

Table 6.9 MEPA commons dimension weights and maturity levels

Maturity level	Commons principles	Weight	Qty items	Range
First level	Delimitation Monitoring	1	14	1–41
Second level	Adequacy of context	2	6	42–59
Third level	Resolubility	3	4	60–70
Fourth level	Adhocracy	4	3	71–79
Fifth level	Proportionate sanctions and rewards Autonomy Participation and coproduction	5	14	80–120

Table 6.10 Number of municipalities by level of maturity

Maturity level	Quantity of municipalities	Percentage (%)
First level	4	0.44
Second level	14	1.55
Third level	48	5.32
Fourth level	398	44.08
Fifth level	439	48.62
Total	903	

interoperability between systems and sites other than government. Additionally, only four platforms (0.44%) are in the fifth level of maturity, including personalisation of the services offered to users.

In summary, among the 903 municipal eGov platforms analysed in Brazil, 837 (92.7%) are at the basic levels of maturity. Only a few cities provide effective services to promote citizen participation and coproduction. Brazilian municipal eGov platforms do not yet include the population, and do not provide enough means for the interested parties to participate in the elaboration and coproduction of laws, projects, and budgets, as well as the services themselves and features offered by the platform, being at the mercy of the services offered by the exclusive initiative of public agencies.

In many of the platforms visited, no evidence was found to demonstrate compliance with basic requirements, such as the availability of up-to-date information and online services. For example, in terms of transparency and open data, many municipalities simply provide information that is required by legislation, that is often incomplete, unstructured, or difficult to understand, and that does not strictly and effectively promote the transparency and publicity of actions undertaken in the public sector. The absence of services and information, or difficulty in finding and understanding them, distances citizens from the public administration, and prevents manifestations, requests, criticisms, suggestions, or compliments. The lack of inclusion of stakeholders and low understanding of the functioning, organisation, and execution of the actions of public services undermine citizen participation and public co-production.

6.3.4 *International Benchmarking*

The MEPA benchmark is conducted by comparing eGov municipalities' results with municipal eGov that fully comply with the commons principles proposed in its data collection instrument. We have found two eGov platforms that meet all MEPA criteria with maximum excellence grade: London/UK (see www.london. gov.uk/) and Singapore (see www.gov.sg/). By comparing the evaluated Brazilian platforms with these two international references, it is possible to recommend the following eGov good practices to improve MEPA grades:

1. Interface: Apply a well-structured and elaborated interface, facilitating access to the services of interest of the user;
2. Tutorial: Offer guidelines and easy identification of available services, based on user profiles of the interested party (citizen, company, server, tourist, etc.);
3. Content: Caveats about the services, informing rights, responsibilities, and penalties to the interested parties;
4. Content: Offer municipality up-to-date news/information (economic, cultural, tourist, historical, geographic, ethnic);
5. Social eGov: Digital media (e.g., podcasts, interactive maps, videos, digital documents, web radio);
6. Openness: Provide services for government transparency;
7. Openness: Apply open government practices, providing open data, with the possibility of downloading and readable by machine;
8. Interoperability: Provide access to other government agencies;
9. Communication: Channels to interact with stakeholders (e.g., ombudsman), with registration, follow-up, and closing of the request;
10. Readiness: Provide instant online services;
11. Social eGov: Allow the integration and use of social networks;
12. Interface: Allow the choice or recommendation of more relevant services;
13. Mobile eGov: Be accessible in a mobile version;
14. Knowledge management: Include resources for management and knowledge sharing.

6.4 Conclusion

Smart cities (particularly humane smart cities) call for new governance models where public authorities and citizens build sustainable relationships [45]. Both commons and NPS principles relate sustainable public relations with collective governance based on citizen participation and coproduction. Additionally, smart cities also call for efficient use of information technologies, this is also a requirement for mature eGov platforms. In this study, we have presented the MEPA model to accurately assess eGov platforms' performance in terms of citizen participation and coproduction to offer high-quality public services. In other words, by using numerous criteria, MEPA verifies eGov platforms regarding the commons, NPS, and maturity of electronic government dimensions.

In the smart cities practice, by assessing eGov platforms as common promoters, MEPA can be a highly useful tool to evaluate the levels of citizens empowerment, collective co-creation, and public authorities' commitment to use digital technologies to develop a social sense of belonging and identity. The large-scale application of MEPA in 903 Brazilian municipalities reveals the general outcome of city eGov platforms as digital commons promoters being immature/underdeveloped. There are only a few eGov municipal platforms that are in higher grades of maturity; and these are from cities with higher budgets and from more developed regions of Brazil. An international benchmark indicated several points to help public authorities to foster eGov platforms towards a higher level of commons maturity.

The MEPA model and its large-scale application indicate that in order to develop digital commons promoters, eGov platforms' authorities have to: (a) enable citizens, public and private agencies, and government at large taking into account their respective roles and responsibilities; (b) develop effective mechanisms for conflict resolution (i.e., fast, affordable, and proportionate sanctioning); (c) develop sustainable and perennial initiatives, appropriate to the context to which they refer; (d) adopt coproduction and citizen participation as guiding principles; (e) understand that the assets of society, more than public, are collective goods and responsibilities; and (f) define clear and effective rules to monitor and govern the interaction of diffuse and collective interests, considering that different communities can share the same common good.

As part of our prospective work, the MEPA model research will be expanded to its application to other levels of government (including the legislative and judicial branches). Moreover, we will adopt/develop a longitudinal data collection and analysis method to the evaluated Brazilian cities. Furthermore, we will adapt and apply the model in other countries (particularly to compare developed and developing country practices), and include eGov cross-referencing indicators such as the quantity and frequency of stakeholders' eGov access. Lastly, particularly focusing on smart cities, we will relate the MEPA model with smart/knowledge-based city models (such as smart and knowledge-based urban development) [27,45–48]. This will not only add another dimension to digital commons maturity analysis, but also will contribute to relating eGov platform maturity with smart cities requirements, e.g., smart governance [49].

Acknowledgements

This chapter, with permission from the copyright holder, is a reproduced version of the following journal article: Rotta, M., Sell, D., Santos Pacheco, R., & Yigitcanlar, T. (2019). Digital commons and citizen coproduction in smart cities: Assessment of Brazilian municipal e-government platforms. *Energies* 12(14), 2813.

References

1. Bart'h, J., Fietkiewicz, K.J., Gremm, J., Hartmann, S., Ilhan, A., Mainka, A., Meschede, C., Stock, W.G. (2017). *Informational urbanism, A Conceptual Framework of Smart Cities*. In: Proceedings of the 50th Hawaii International Conference on System Sciences, Waikoloa Village, HI, USA, 4–7 January 2017; IEEE Computer Society: Washington, DC, USA, pp. 2814–2823.
2. Caragliu, A., Del Bo, C., Nijkamp, P. (2011). Smart cities in Europe. *Journal of Urban Technology* 18, 65–82.
3. Anttiroiko, A.V., Valkama, P., Bailey, S.J. (2014). Smart cities in the new service economy: building platforms for smart services. *AI & Society* 29, 323–334.
4. Denhardt, J.V., Denhardt, R.B. (2003). *The New Public Service: Serving, Not Steering*; M.E.Sharpe: London, UK; New York, NY, USA, 2003. Available online: https://epdf. pub/the-new-public-service-serving-not-steering.html (accessed 12 July 2019).

5. Marsh, J. (2013). *The Human Smart Cities Cookbook.* Available online: www.periphe ria.eu (accessed 12 July 2019).
6. Hess, C., Ostrom, E. (2005). *A Framework for Analyzing the Knowledge Commons: A chapter from Understanding Knowledge as a Commons: From Theory to Practice.* Available online: https://surface.syr.edu/sul/21 (accessed 12 July 2019).
7. Ostrom, E. (1990). *Governing the Commons: The Evolution of Institutions for Collective Action.* Cambridge University Press: Cambridge, UK.
8. Hardt, M., Negri, A. (2009). *Commonwealth.* Harvard University Press: Cambridge, MA, USA.
9. Chourabi, H., Nam, T., Walker, S., Gil-Garcia, J.R., Mellouli, S., Nahon, K., Scholl, H.J. (2012). Understanding Smart Cities: An Integrative Framework. In: *Proceedings of the 45th Hawaii International Conference on System Sciences,* Maui, HI, USA, 4–7 January 2012; pp. 2289–2297.
10. Nam, T., Pardo, T. (2011). Conceptualizing smart city with dimensions of technology, people, and institutions. In: *Proceedings of the 12th Annual International Digital Government Research Conference.* Digital Government Innovation in Challenging Times, College Park, MD, USA, 12–15 June 2011; ACM: New York, NY, USA, pp. 282–291.
11. West, D.M. (2004). E-government and the transformation of service delivery and citizen attitudes. *Public Administration* Review 64, 15–27.
12. Bollier, D. (2007). *The Growth of the Commons Paradigm. Understanding Knowledge as a Commons,* p. 27. Available online: http://dlc.dlib.indiana.edu/dlc/bitstream/handle/10535/4975/GrowthofCommonsParadigm.pdf?sequence=1&isAllowed=y (accessed 12 July 2019).
13. Pacheco, C.S.R. (2016). Coprodução em Ciência, Tecnologia e Inovação: Fundamentos e visões. In: *Interdisciplinaridade: Universidade e Inovação Social e Tecnológica,* 1st ed.; CRV Editora: Curitiba, Brazil, pp. 21–62. Available online: www.researchgate.net/publ ication/307977522_Coproducao_em_Ciencia_Tecnologia_e_Inovacao_fundament os_e_visoes?amp%3BenrichSource=Y292ZXJQYWdlOzMwNzk3NzUyMjtBUzo0 MDUxNDExNzQ5MzE0NjddAMTQ3MzYwNDU5MTg4Ng%3D%3D&amp%3Bel= 1_x_3&amp%3B_esc=publicationCoverPdf (accessed 12 July 2019).
14. Pinho, J.A.G.D. (2008). Investigando portais de governo eletrônico de estados no Brasil: Muita tecnologia, pouca democracia. *RAP Revista de Administração Pública– Rio de Janeiro* 42, 471–493.
15. Hassan, B., Alireza, I., Majideh, S. (2012). E-government portals: A knowledge man- agement study. *Electronic Library* 30, 89–102.
16. Fath-Allah, A., Cheikhi, L., Al-Qutaish, R.E., Idri, A. (2014). e-Government maturity models: A comparative study. *International Journal of Software Engineering and its Applications* 5, 71.
17. Holmes, D. (2001). *eGov: eBusiness Strategies for Government.* Nicholas Brealey Publishing: Boston, MA, USA, 2001.
18. Rotta, M.J.R. (2018). *As Plataformas de Governo Eletrônico e seu Potencial para a Promoção dos Princípios dos Commons: O caso dos Municípios Brasileiros.* Doutorado em Engenharia e Gestão do Conhecimento; Universidade Federal de Santa Catarina, UFSC: Trindade, Brazil 2018. Available online: http://btd.egc.ufsc.br/wp-content/uplo ads/2018/12/Maur%C3%ADcio-Rotta.pdf (accessed 12 July 2019).
19. Hevner, A., Chateerjee, S. (2012). *Design Research in Information Systems Theory and Practice Forewords.* Springer: New York, NY, USA.

20. Ostrom, E. (1978). Citizen participation and policing: What Do We Know? *Journal of Voluntary Action Research* 7, 102–108.
21. Layne, K., Lee, J. (2001). Developing fully functional e-government: A four stage model. *Government Information Quarterly* 18, 122–136.
22. Andersen, K.V., Henriksen, H.Z. (2006). e-Government maturity models: Extension of the Layne and Lee model. *Government Information Quarterly* 23, 236–248.
23. United Nations (UN). *UN E-Government Survey 2012: E-Government for the People.* Available online: http://unpan1.un.org/intradoc/groups/public/documents/un/unpa n048065.pdf (accessed 12 July 2019).
24. Alonso-Muñoz, L. (2007). *Transparency and Political Monitoring in the Digital Environment: Towards a Typology of Citizen-Driven Platforms.* Available online: www. ull.es/publicaciones/latina/072paper/1223/73en.html (accessed 12 July 2019).
25. Almazan, R.S., Gil-Garcia, J.R. (2008). E-*Government Portals in Mexico.* University at Albany: New York, NY, USA.
26. Baum, C., Maio, A.D. (2000). *Gartner's Four Phases of e-Government Model.* Gartner Group Inc.; Stamford, CO, USA.
27. Moon, J. (2002). The evolution of e-government among municipalities: Rhetoric or reality? *Public Administration Review* 62, 424–433.
28. Toasaki, Y. (2003). e-*Government from A User's Perspective.* APEC Telecommunication and Information Working Group: Taipei, Taiwan.
29. Valdés, G., Solar, M., Astudillo, H., Iribarren, M., Concha, G., Visconti, M. (2011). Conception, development and implementation of an e-Government maturity model in public agencies. *Government Information Quarterly* 28, 176–187.
30. Cresswell, A.M., Pardo, T.A., Hassan, S. (2007). Assessing capability for justice information sharing. In: *Proceedings of the 8th Annual International Conference on Digital Government Research*, Los Angeles, CA, USA, 20–23 May 2007; pp. 122–130.
31. Alves, A.A., Moreira, J.M. (2004). *Cidadania Digital e Democratização Electrónica.* Porto: SPI. Available online: www.spi.pt/documents/books/inovacao_autarquia/docs/ Manual_IV.pdf (accessed 12 July 2019).
32. Fietkiewicz, K.J., Mainka, M., Stock, W.G. (2017). eGovernment in cities of the knowledge society. An empirical investigation of Smart Cities' governmental websites. *Government Information Quarterly* 34, 75–83.
33. Bollier, D. (2011). The commons, short and sweet. *Bollier Organization.* Available online: http://eco-literacy.net/wp- content/uploads/sites/4/2017/05/introduction-to-the-commons.pdf (accessed 12 July 2019).
34. Gomes, W. (2005). A Democracia Digital e o Problema da Participação Civil Na Decisão Política. *Fronteiras-Estudos Midiáticos* 7, 214–222.
35. Welle Donker, F., Van Loenen, B. (2017). How to assess the success of the open data ecosystem? *International Journal of Digital Earth* 10, 284–306.
36. Máchová, R., Lnénicka, M. (2017). Evaluating the quality of open data portals on the national level. *Journal of Theoretical and Applied Electronic Commerce Research* 12, 21–41.
37. Brazil Ministério do Planejamento. (2015). *Orçamento e Gestão.* Resolução CGPAR 05, de 29 de Setembro de 2015. Available online: www.planejamento.gov.br/assuntos/ empresas-estatais/legislacao/resolucoes/rescgpar_05.pdf (accessed 12 July 2019).
38. Abdullah, N.N., Rahman, M.F.A. (2015). Access to government information in public policy making process: A case study of Kurdistan. *International Information Institutions* 18, 8, 3447.

39. Gupta, R., Singh, J. (2014). Knowledge management and innovation in (e) government. *International Journal of Information & Computer Technology* 4, 1637–1645.
40. Pinterits, A., Treiblmaier, H., Pollach, I. (2006). Environmental websites: An empirical investigation of functionality and accessibility. *International Journal of Technology, Policy and Management* 6, 2006.
41. Al-Khalifa, H.S. (2010). The accessibility of Saudi Arabia government web sites: An exploratory study. *University Access in the Information Society* 10.
42. Stepchenkova, S., Tang, L., Jang, S.S., Kirilenko, A.P., Morrison, A.M. (2010). Benchmarking CVB website performance: Spatial and structural patterns. *Tourism Management* 31, 611–620.
43. Tezza, R., Bornia, A.C., Andrade, D.F. (2011). Measuring web usability using item response theory: Principles, features and opportunities. *Interactive Computing* 23, 167–175.
44. United Nations (UN). (2016). *United Nations E-Government Survey 2016: E-Government in Support of Sustainable Development.* United Nations: New York, NY, USA. Available online: http://workspace.unpan.org/sites/Internet/Documents/UNP AN96407.pdf (accessed 12 July 2019).
45. Yigitcanlar, T., Metaxiotis, K., Carrillo, F.J. (2012). *Building Prosperous Knowledge Cities: Policies, Plans and Metrics.* Edward Elgar Publishing: Cheltenham, UK.
46. Yigitcanlar, T., Kamruzzaman, M., Buys, L., Ioppolo, G., Sabatini-Marques, J., da Costa, E.M., Yun, J.J. (2018). Understanding 'smart cities': Intertwining development drivers with desired outcomes in a multidimensional framework. *Cities* 81, 145–160.
47. Yigitcanlar, T. (2014). Position paper: Benchmarking the performance of global and emerging knowledge cities. *Expert Systems with Applications* 41, 5549–5559.
48. Trindade, E.P., Hinnig, M.P.F., Moreira da Costa, E., Marques, J., Bastos, R., Yigitcanlar, T. (2017). Sustainable development of smart cities: A systematic review of the literature. *Journal of Open Innovation: Technology, Market, and Complexity* 3, 11.
49. Rotta, M., Sell, D., Santos Pacheco, R., Yigitcanlar, T. (2019). Digital commons and citizen coproduction in smart cities: Assessment of Brazilian municipal e-government platforms. *Energies* 12(14), 2813.

7 Participatory Governance

7.1 Introduction

With the global trend of the development of smart sustainable cities, participatory governance has played a substantial role in achieving the smart state [1,2]. This is evident in the definition of realising a smart city given by [3], that "a city [becomes] smart when investments in human and social capital and traditional (transport) and modern (ICT) communication infrastructure fuel sustainable economic growth and a high quality of life, with a wise management of natural resources, through participatory governance". Furthermore, in the seminal work of [4], smart governance mainly refers to participatory governance, which emphasises participation in decision-making and transparency through new communication channels for the citizen to use, i.e., e-government.

In the conception of [5], e-government consists of delivering online services to citizens, the readiness of telecommunications infrastructure, and human capital development. In particular, to provide online services, e-government needs to activate and facilitate its citizens' participation in e-platforms such as websites, mobile applications, social media, and other Internet-of-Things (IoT) platforms [6,7]. The design of e-platforms through e-participation must consider three levels, namely e-decision-making, e-consultation, and e-information [5]. In this chapter, e-participation serves as a proxy to inquire about participatory governance. The smart city concept has become an ideal scenario where the dynamics of participatory governance has evolved [4,8]. The overall concept of participatory governance vis-à-vis e-government in city management lies within the scope of realising the smart city and, from a wider perspective, sustainable city development that benefits the current and future populations (Figure 7.1).

In recent scholarly studies, assessments of e-participation platforms have been limited to the levels of e-information and e-consultation, and have generally assessed governmental website portals [10–12]. A cross-country comparison study [13] revealed that the governmental portals of both Lisbon (Portugal) and Brasilia (Brazil) demonstrated the intensive provision of information and online searches but less on the human and responsiveness dimensions. Another study of the e-participation portal [14], specifically the case of Estonia's Osale.ee, found that this e-platform lacked democratic participation, failed to attract people to join, and

DOI: 10.1201/9781003403647-9

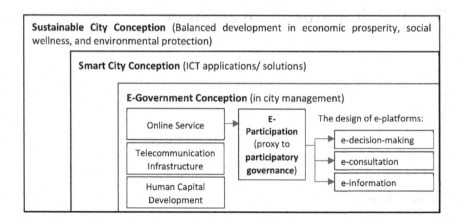

Figure 7.1 The relational conceptions of e-participation, e-government, smart and sustainable city, derived from [4,5,9].

had regulatory limitation and ambiguity in integrating people's ideas/comments into policy-making processes.

In Malaysia, the Malaysia Digital Economy Corporation has assessed governmental websites through the Provider-Based Evaluation (ProBE). As the latest ProBE assessment from 2016 shows, of the 622 participating websites from federal and local government departments and agencies, the item of "presence of e-decision-making: publish outcomes of citizen feedback on services/national strategy/policy" ranked last among the 64 items assessed. Only 5% of the 622 websites complied with this item [15]. Another observation from the Malaysian Administrative Modernization and Management Planning Unit (MAMPU) [16] and agencies such as Malaysia Competition Commission (MyCC) [17] is that explanations for e-participation policies are overly focused on providing various types of e-information and conducting surveys for e-consultation, with only ambiguous details given about how public voices may influence e-decision-making. In fact, all three processes together actually comprise a complete definition of e-participation [5], as explained above.

Meanwhile, the availability of information and communication technology (ICT) infrastructure provisions, such as internet readiness and computer facilities, is sometimes ambiguously perceived as civic e-participation (see [18]). In fact, too few scholarly studies in Malaysia have evaluated e-participation. For instance, the e-service tools provided, like opinion polls, complaints, and feedback, as well as social media pages (such as on Facebook), generally failed to function effectively [18–20]. This is aligned with [15]'s summary that although most portals and websites include some forms of e-participation, there is a lack of innovative platforms that incorporate citizens' voices. A tool offering such a depth of e-participation, involving the injection of technology into government electronic service platforms that facilitate greater citizen involvement in political deliberation and the policy decision-making process (PMPs), is a myth under representative democracy [11,21]. Furthermore, no academic study was found to link e-participation and participatory governance to smart cities development in Malaysia.

Given the abovementioned issues surrounding authentic participatory governance and e-participation, this study asks, "What is the status of participatory governance in smart cities through e-participation platforms?" Thus, taking the cases of Putrajaya and Petaling Jaya smart cities from Malaysia, this study aims to examine the status of participatory governance from the angle of e-participation platforms, such as websites and mobile applications, and from a broader scope, linking e-platforms to the implementation of smart city initiatives. These two cities were selected based on their leading roles in implementing smart cities in Malaysia.

Following this introduction, the next section reviews the literature on participatory governance and how it links to e-participation and smart city initiatives. The sections after that explain the multiple case study methodology, results, discussion, and conclusion.

7.2 Literature Background

Governance is a broad concept covering all aspects of the way a country is governed, including its economic policies, regulatory framework, and adherence to the rule of law. In traditional discussions, governance mostly relates to power [10,22]. Power can be divided into several types, such as monarchy, democracy, oligarchy, authoritarianism, and totalitarianism. In today's smart city discourse, scholars focus on how the democratic type of government contrasts or conflicts with authoritarianism [23]. The categorisation of democratic government types, as shown in the Democracy Index 2020 [24], reveals four forms of regime: full democracy, flawed democracy, hybrid regime, and authoritarian regime. Currently, the majority of countries fall into the first three categories, with about one-third under authoritarian control. A developing country like Malaysia is categorised as a flawed democracy [25]. It is ranked 39th out of 167 countries and has basic civil liberties in place; however, in other aspects of democracy, it exhibits weaknesses, such as governance problems [26].

Most countries worldwide, regardless of whether they are located in the global north or south, have adopted the smart cities development policy [27,28]. However, which conditions indicate a democratic governance style is considered smart? From the literature, [4] mentioned that "smart governance comprises aspects of political participation, services for citizens, as well as the functioning of the administration." For [29], institutional factors (or smart government) are drawn from the discussion of smart community or smart growth initiatives. Regarding the corporate sector, IBM argued that smart government will do more than simply regulate economic and societal systems' outputs; thus, it will interconnect dynamically with citizens [30,31]. In the review of [32], the authors summarised six attributes of a smart governance system, which must be based on ICT, external collaboration and participation, internal coordination, the decision-making process, e-administration, and outcomes. Then, in [3], smart governance is referred to as a type of participatory governance.

While participatory governance is a relatively recent practice in the context of smart city or smart governance, collaborative and participatory governing principles are not [33]. The Nordic and Baltic countries such as Sweden passed legislation to allow citizens to access the government process and public data since 1766; Estonia shaped the Public Information Act in 2000; and Denmark launched a healthcare reform program in 2002 to allow citizens to choose between different solutions [14,34,35]. Even before the smart city concept became popular in the early 2010s [36], cases of utilising technology in assisting participatory governance were recorded, such as the 1970s' idea of democratic dialogue via teleconferencing, the Minerva Communications Tree which was introduced in the US; and the 1980s ICT-enabled deliberation among "mini-populi" (i.e., a deliberative citizen forum/ mini-publics) in Europe and the US [37–39]. Participatory governance strengthens local democracy by allowing citizens to participate in new contexts [40]. Participatory governance is defined as the genuine participation of citizens and other organisations in the formulation of policies and strategies, the public sector's decision-making process, and the implementation of those decisions [35].

In smart city literature, participatory governance is incorporated into the practice of smart governance and moving towards the user/citizen-centric approach, in that the e-participation of citizens in decision-making is emphasised, alongside co-creation with citizens in city services [2,4,41]. In this chapter, participatory governance in smart cities is examined through the proxy of the e-participation concept. This approach was also similarly adopted by [13].

e-Participation comprises of three main elements, namely e-information, e-consultation, and e-decision-making. According to [5], e-information is defined as enabling participation by providing citizens with public information and access to information without obstacles or upon demand, e-consultation means engaging citizens in contributions to and deliberation on public policies and services, while e-decision-making refers to empowering citizens through the co-design of policy options and the co-production of service components and delivery modalities. Thus, to measure citizens' e-participation in e-platforms such as government websites and mobile applications, in this study, the authors adopted in full the definition given by [5]. As concluded by many studies, e-participation can be easily confused by referring to e-information distribution on e-spaces and e-consultation through surveys and opinion seeking. The impact of e-platforms using new technologies, such as big data analytics and artificial intelligence as part of the Fourth Industrial Revolution, remains unclear in terms of how its multiplication has translated into broader or deeper citizen participation [10,42,43].

A useful global example of fostering deeper citizen participation in a smart city is the e-platform "Decide Madrid", introduced by Madrid City Council in Spain. This engagement platform is effective and, through its open-source software Consul, has been utilised in more than 33 countries [10]. This engagement system contains four major elements, namely debates, proposals, participatory budgets, and voting [44,45]. "Debates" is an e-space where anyone can open threads on any subject and debate on the proposed topic. Next, another e-space, "Proposals", allows citizens to create proposals and seek supports. Proposals which receive support from at least 1% of the adult population (age 16 and above) will be voted on and considered by the authority. The "Participatory Budgeting" e-space allows citizens to continuously suggest the budget to spend on selected proposals. Finally, the "Voting" e-space offers a voting system, whereby people can vote for or against motions and provide additional comments. Based on the above democratic processes, the authority will evaluate the legal, competence, and economic feasibility of an initiative and decide whether to adopt or reject the proposal [46].

7.3 Methodology

The multiple case study approach was selected as the main methodological approach in this study. This approach applies more than one instrument as it uses bounded cases and examines the topic through multiple data collection methods [47,48].

In this study, two civic authority cases were evaluated: the Putrajaya Corporation and Petaling Jaya City Council from Malaysia. These two authorities were selected based on their leading roles in implementing smart cities in Malaysia. Putrajaya is one of the country's first intelligent cities since the Multimedia Super Corridor development in 1990s [46]. As the federal government administration centre, Putrajaya has been identified as a pioneer in Malaysia for publishing its city-level blueprint—the Putrajaya Smart City Blueprint (PSCB)—in 2019 and launching the Putrajaya Mobile Application (PMA) in 2016 [33,34]. Meanwhile, Petaling Jaya, a satellite township next to Kuala Lumpur, followed the steps taken by the Smart Selangor state and became the first city council to launch a smart command centre [41,49]. Petaling Jaya also launched a unique community engagement e-platform, PJKita, to gauge citizens' input and accumulate community volunteers to co-produce its vision as a smart sustainable city.

For multiple data collection methods, this study collected data from e-government platforms, namely the PJKita and the Putrajaya Mobile App, as well as related e-governmental websites and blueprint. Data collected from the e-platforms include the details of developers, dates of publications, contents of the platforms, and interactions from the platform users. Meanwhile, for the blueprint, data of the types of smart city initiatives, achievement status, and timeline of initiatives related to e-platforms were gathered. The e-platform and blueprint observations were performed between December 2020 and August 2021. Besides, a number of site visits to, and participatory observations of, Putrajaya and Petaling Jaya cities, and casual interviews of a few informants were undertaken between 2017 and 2020.

To answer the study objectives, the analyses were done mainly on the qualitative observations and supported by quantitative descriptive statistics. Firstly, to examine the status of participatory governance in smart cities through the proxy of e-participation (this approach was also adopted by [13]), the e-government platforms were qualitatively observed from the angle of e-information, e-consultation, and e-decision-making, as conceptualised in [5]. As explained in the literature review section, e-information was analysed through variability and accessibility of information to the public without obstacles or upon demand. e-Consultation was examined through signs and responsiveness of engaging citizens in contributions to and deliberation on public policies and services, i.e., surveys and opinion seeking. At the same time, e-decision-making was scrutinised through the availability of co-design of policy options and the co-production of service components and delivery modalities such as debates, proposals, participatory budgets, and voting [5,44–46]. Secondly, from the broader scope of linking e-platforms to a smart city blueprint, the achievement of planned initiatives was quantitatively examined through descriptive statistics and qualitative comparisons.

7.4 Results

7.4.1 The e-Platforms of the Putrajaya Mobile App, the PJKita Website, and Others

At first sight, the Putrajaya Mobile App e-platform is attractive and presentable (Figure 7.2). The only official Putrajaya Mobile App, it was developed by a private company—Touchpoint International—and is administered by the Putrajaya ICT internal department. There are currently about 5000 downloads of the Putrajaya Mobile App. This figure accounts for about only 5% of the total population of Putrajaya, which is 100,000.

For the purposes of e-information analysis, the Putrajaya Mobile App was launched in 2016 and currently displays eight events to explore. Among these, five of them were functioning, namely the News, Events, Points of Interest, Public Amenities, and Putrajaya Tracer. Meanwhile, the status of each of the other three—Business, Parking,

Figure 7.2 The user interface of the Putrajaya Mobile App.

and Tours—was "coming soon". No activities were displayed under the "Latest (happening) in Putrajaya". At the foot of the user interface, users could obtain an event "Ticket" from the app, "Panic" call an emergency contact (the user must insert his/her contacts' details, such as those of their spouse), use "Feedback" for feedback, or link to a GPS location, which could be useful for the user to lodge complaints.

Furthermore, from the author's observation on 9 December 2020, from the seven news items displayed, one used the standard template, and the others were old activities dating back to 2018 or 2019 (Table 7.1). Overall, the app lacks a "search" button for users to meet their needs immediately. The information displayed on the Putrajaya Mobile App is quite extensive. However, it challenges the user's patience as they must search manually for what they need. This design is considered less user-friendly and hardly encourages frequent visits from existing users. Furthermore, as declared in the "About Us" section, the Putrajaya Mobile App is designed "to enhance the cities relationship with its citizens, provides a

Table 7.1 E-information displayed in Putrajaya Mobile App

Information	Observation as of 9 January 2021
The Putrajaya News section: Seven news items were uploaded on 22 July 2019 on Local Community Activities: 1. Kelas Kemahiran (Khat, English, Islam) Hujung Minggu, activity date: March–May 2018 2. More Putrajaya News (template) 3. Kursus Penternakan Kelulut, activity date: 24 Apr 2018 4. Putrajaya Drum Circle (no date) 5. Jom Bayar Kompaun/Saman, activity date: 14 Aug–30 Sep 2018 6. Pertandingan Melukis dan Mewarna, activity date: 17 Feb 2019 7. Car Free Day Putrajaya (no date)	All the news items were considered "old" because the activities displayed were dated back to 2018 or 2019
The Events section: One upcoming event shown: Light and Motion Putrajaya (LAMPU) from 30 December 2020 to 2 January 2021 39 past events displayed, for example, royal FLORIA Putrajaya, marathon events, etc.	Only one upcoming event was displayed, and most past events just stated the date, without further information or a picture gallery
The Points of Interest section: Many points of interest were displayed, including parks and landscapes, bridges, shopping facilities, hotels and resorts, mosques, sport, and recreation centres, Sisiran Putrajaya (a walkway), Persiaran Perdana (a boulevard), the Tasik Putrajaya cruise, Melawati Palace, PICC, floral landscaping, the Natural History Museum, National Heroes Square and government offices	This section is supposedly designed for tourists. However, the authors observed that users had hardly left any comments. Little user interaction was observed, and the frequency of visits by visitors/users was not recorded either

smarter transportation and mobility experience, a smarter community to leverage profitable business opportunities and smarter infrastructure to increase security reassurance". Yet, observations revealed that there was a lack of transportation or mobility information provided.

For the purposes of e-consultation analysis, only 46 users left comments concerning the downloads, and the average rating was 3.1 (Figure 7.3). These

Figure 7.3 Reviews of the Putrajaya Mobile App.

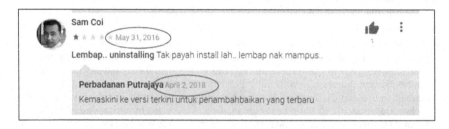

Figure 7.4 Example of official response from the Putrajaya Mobile App.

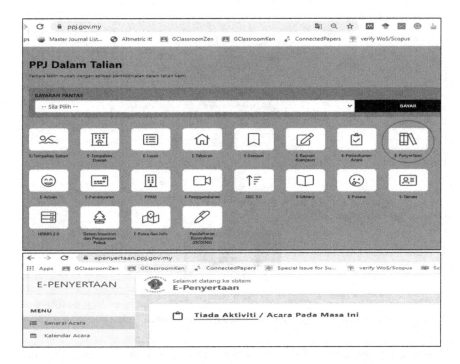

Figure 7.5 Inactive element of e-participation shown in the Putrajaya official website.

public reviews related to the issues of attractiveness (i.e., "not attractive"), usefulness (i.e., "complaint form is not easy"; "not helpful at all"), stability (i.e., "keep crashing"), and expectation (i.e., "expect there will be more features"), thus identifying the areas for potential improvements.

From the responsiveness perspective, the author observed that the administrative response of the Putrajaya Mobile App to public comments was poor, and a typical answer was to ask users to wait for the updated version. The latest administrative response was at least a year old (dated 2 April 2018) and responded to a comment made on 31 May 2016 (Figure 7.4).

An analysis of e-decision-making revealed that no elements of debates, proposals, participatory budgets, or voting were shown on the Putrajaya Mobile App.

Further e-platform analysis of the Putrajaya official website (www.ppj.gov.my) revealed an element of e-participation. However, unfortunately, when clicking into it, no activity was displayed (Figure 7.5). This observation by the author was made on 9 December 2020 and again on 23 August 2021.

Moving on to assess Petaling Jaya City Council, it had no unified Petaling Jaya City Mobile App, as Putrajaya does. Its public services were separately channelled through various e-platforms that had been designed by multiple parties. For instance, the reporting platform—Site Report MBPJ—had been created by a

Figure 7.6 Various mobile apps from Petaling Jaya City Council.

private company, Ultrack Technology Sdn. Bhd.; the Bazar platform—Bazar@ PJKita—and the public city bus service—PJ City Bus—had been designed by the internal ICT MBPJ department, among others (Figure 7.6).

This analysis focuses on the engagement platform, namely the PJKita website (www.pjkita2u.org). This website was established in 2018. Fifteen functions are available: Join Us, Q&A, Surveys, Message, Service, Support, Contacts, SDG, Community, Ideas, D.4.C, Rewards, Job Post, Funding and City Index; there is also a PJ Interactive Map (Figure 7.7).

As of 10 February 2021, the total number of visitors recorded was 2,624. This figure accounted for only 4% of the population of Petaling Jaya, which is 620,000. The authors found that this website had an interesting homepage user interface. However, the authors noticed an unpleasant user experience, finding many idle/ non-functional buttons or pages under construction, i.e., Surveys, Rewards and City Index, Service Projects, Critical Contacts, and Job Posts.

For the purposes of e-information analysis, this engagement platform provided information on topics such as Sustainable Development Goals (SDGs); it also mapped existing situations (such as floods or dengue cases) in various communities by administrative zones. Besides, this engagement platform applied the inclusivity concept, whereby under the D.4.C (data for change—engaging and supporting the vulnerable through crowd-sourced data), it allowed disabled individuals, single mothers, and senior citizens to register themselves.

For the purposes of e-consultation analysis, this engagement website was unique as it allowed community users to register themselves as local champions

Figure 7.7 An engagement platform by Petaling Jaya City Council.

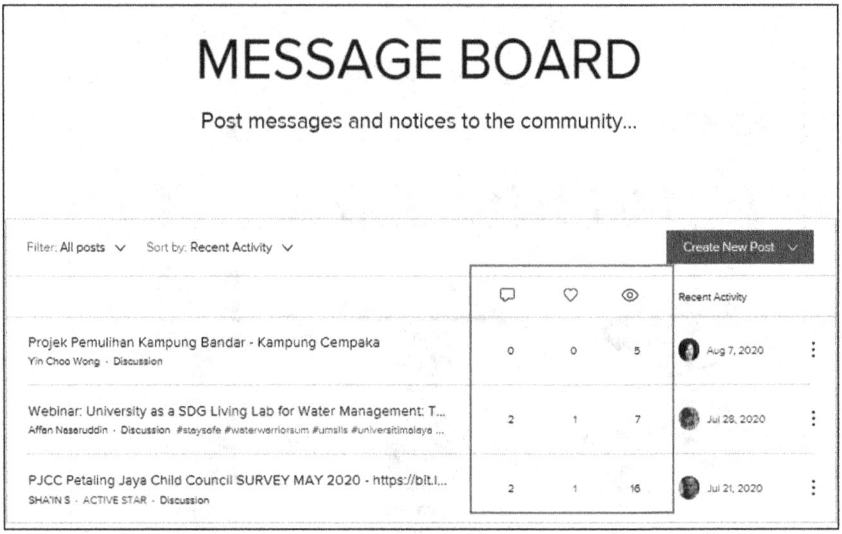

Figure 7.8 Availability of community posting under the PJKita website.

and post updates and projects. At the time of writing, not many updates had been posted, while the viewer and response numbers were low (Figure 7.8). However, in the authors' opinion, if well maintained, this post could engage citizens effectively and increase the sense of belonging to the community and city. In addition, the website had a survey button, which listed a happiness index survey, a public transportation survey, a citizen insights survey, and a parks and recreation survey. Unfortunately, these surveys were still under construction and could not be clicked on.

In terms of the e-decision-making analysis, some elements appear to cultivate co-decision-making with the community, for example, the availability of the Idea Bank and Funding buttons. However, at the time of writing, only one idea had been posted, namely "Gearing up for an ageing society". This had been posted on 25 September 2020 and had eight views, zero comments, and no response from the authority (Figure 7.9). As for Available Funding and Grants for Projects and Initiatives within the City, there was also one post, with 13 views and no response from the authority. Other than the proposals, the elements of debates, participatory budgeting, and voting were unavailable.

Besides the engagement platform, the Petaling Jaya City Council had created many other websites. These included the official portal (www.mbpj.gov.my), which serves as the master portal for the individual links alongside other new domains. It features customer relations (embpj.mbpj.gov.my) and e-complaints (eaduan. mbpj.gov.my) systems. The official website provided extensive e-information for citizens, businesses, and visitors; however, it lacked e-participation mentions.

Figure 7.9 The only available community posting under the Idea section of the PJKita website.

This shortfall could be addressed with a new customer relations system and an e-complaint website. At the time of writing, e-consultation was demonstrated through the availability of lodging complaints and surveys. There was still a lack of a clear sign that public proposals, debates, participatory budgeting, or voting would be available.

7.4.2 The Linkage between the Putrajaya Mobile App and the Putrajaya Command Centre Compared to the Putrajaya Smart City Initiatives

In terms of producing a smart city blueprint, Putrajaya has published its Putrajaya Smart City Blueprint 2019. Meanwhile Petaling Jaya, as an early satellite township to Kuala Lumpur capital city since the 1950s, has published many development plans that are constantly updating the city towards becoming "a dynamic world-class metropolis". The vision stated under the Petaling Jaya Strategic Plan 2016–2026 is "Petaling Jaya—a leading, dynamic and sustainable city". The Petaling Jaya City Council is committed to driving this metropolis in line with the concept of sustainability, smartness, and resilience [47]. Thus, "smart" is one of the strategies demonstrated under Governance—one of the four main thrusts of the Strategic Plan [47]. The initiatives planned under the Strategic Plan were general, and the City Council has yet to issue any particular smart city blueprint. An interview from a City Council officer revealed that the new Petaling Jaya Smart, Sustainable and Resilient City Blueprint is in drafting status and will be published soon. Thus, this subsection only discusses the case of Putrajaya.

The authors used the Putrajaya Mobile App and the Putrajaya Control Centre to assess the initiatives planned under the Putrajaya Smart City Blueprint 2019. Under the Blueprint, 92 initiatives were being designed. These initiatives were

Table 7.2 The status and timeline of initiatives

Initiatives	Quick win	Short term	Medium term	Long term	Total
Existing (#)	19	17	11	6	51
(%)	35.8%	32.1%	20.8%	11.3%	100.0%
Future (#)	4	5	19	11	41
(%)	10.3%	12.8%	48.7%	28.2%	100.0%
Total (#)	23	22	30	17	92
(%)	25.0%	23.9%	32.6%	18.5%	100.0%

Note: Quick win (initiatives to be launched in less than one year of 2018); short term (1–2 years; 2018–2020); medium term (3–4 years; 2018–2022) and long term (more than 5 years; 2018–2025).

Table 7.3 Quick win, short term Putrajaya in terms of integration/related to Putrajaya Mobile App and Putrajaya Command Centre, evaluated as of 10 December 2020

	Quick win			Short term		
	Existing	Future	Total	Existing	Future	Total
(a) Quantity of initiative	19	4	23	17	5	22
(b) Percentage related to e-platforms of (a)	47.4% (9)	50% (2)	47.8% (11)	70.6% (12)	40% (2)	63.6% (14)
(c) Achieved rate of (b)	22.2% (2)	50% (1)	27.3% (3)	41.7% (5)	50% (1)	42.9% (6)

Note: Quick win (initiatives to be launched in less than one year of 2018); short term (1–2 years; 2018–2020); figures in brackets show the number of related initiatives.

classified into three categories, namely quick win (initiatives to be launched in less than one year, starting in 2018); short-term (1–2 years; 2018–2020); medium-term (3–4 years; 2018–2022) and long-term (more than 5 years; 2018–2025).

Among the 92 initiatives, 55% (51) were existing initiatives that were to be expanded or enhanced, while 45% (41) were new or for the future. Table 7.2 shows that among the existing initiatives, the quick win type accounted for the highest percentage, with 35.8%, while long-term initiatives comprised the lowest, with 11.3%. Compared to the existing initiatives, the pattern of future initiatives is different, whereby the medium-term type was the highest with 48.7%, and the quick win type of initiative was the lowest, with 10.3%.

As shown in Table 7.3, for the quick win category, less than half (47.8%) of the items related to e-platforms, based on the evaluation of the Putrajaya Mobile App and Putrajaya Command Centre. Of these 11 initiatives, only 27.3% had been achieved, meaning that the implementation of more than two-thirds was not progressing or not executed as planned. It is also important to highlight the existing initiatives of the quick win; the achieved rate of 22.2% is lower than the average of the quick win initiatives.

For the short-term category, the percentages related to e-platforms (63.6%) and achieved rate (42.9%) were higher than those of the quick win initiatives. This means short-term projects targeted for completion at the end of the year 2020 were acceptably close to the average rate and were far more successful than quick wins.

Overall, the efficiency of governance in terms of initiative implementation was below the average value. For the quick win existing initiatives, for example, the authors found that many features had not been integrated into the Putrajaya Mobile App. These included automation ticketing and the cashless bus fare payment system, the supervisory control and data acquisition (SCADA) for pollution prevention control, land inventory and cadastral data, and online licensing and facilities booking. As for the short-term existing initiatives, the API environmental monitoring index (measuring air quality values), lake water and wetland management, e-wallet and e-kiosk, smart application for business promotion, healthy diet information and education, information for dengue hotspots, and non-smoking areas were in pending status in terms of their integration into the Putrajaya Mobile App. On the other hand, the most notable achievement to date had been the Putrajaya

Table 7.4 Evaluation of quick win and short-term initiatives related to e-platforms in Putrajaya: (a) quick win existing initiatives; (b) quick win future initiatives; (c) short-term existing initiatives; (d) short-term future initiatives.

No	Initiative	Implementation objective	Status	Achievement as of Dec 2020
(a)				
1	1.2.2 Automation ticketing and payment system	Integrate with the Putrajaya Mobile	Pending	To date, it is not integrated with the Putrajaya Mobile App
2	1.2.3 Cashless bus fare payment system (i.e., e-wallet)	Integrate with the Putrajaya Mobile App	Pending	To date, it is not integrated with the Putrajaya Mobile App
3	2.1.3 Supervisory control and data acquisition (SCADA) for pollution prevention control	Citizens can access API value information 24 h a day	Pending	The Putrajaya Mobile App only shows a simple air quality API figure, not a detailed SCADA system
4	3.2.1 Putrajaya Mobile App	Create a more efficient management and maintenance regime	Achieved	The Putrajaya Mobile App was released on 15 Apr 2016 on Google Playstore. The current version is 2.6, updated on 3 Sept 2020, maintained by Touchpoint International Sdn Bhd

(Continued)

Table 7.4 (Continued)

No	Initiative	Implementation objective	Status	Achievement as of Dec 2020
5	3.4.1 Digitalisation of land inventory and cadastral data (land use governance)	Integrate all the applications into the Putrajaya Mobile App	Pending	To date, it is not integrated with the Putrajaya Mobile App
6	3.4.4 Complaints online	Integrate with the Putrajaya Mobile App	Achieved	Termed 'feedback' and organised into categories such as noise, lost and found, and illegal parking
7	3.4.6 Online licence application	Integrate with the Putrajaya Mobile App	Pending	To date, it is not integrated with the Putrajaya Mobile App
8	3.4.7 Online booking of venues	Integrate with the Putrajaya Mobile App	Pending	To date, it is not integrated with the Putrajaya Mobile App

(b)

No	Initiative	Implementation objective	Status	Achievement as of Dec 2020
1	1.1.2 Mobile apps for parking guidance	Integrate Putrajaya Mobile App and Putrajaya Park by Phone (directions to parking facilities)	Pending	To date, it is not integrated with the Putrajaya Mobile App. The Putrajaya Park by Phone app cannot be found on Google Playstore
2	7.4.1 City YouTube Channel	Offer live updates on YouTube and social media like Facebook and Instagram related to every event in Putrajaya, such as ceremonies, sporting events or carnivals	Achieved	Strange to put this as a future initiative as many videos had been uploaded since 25 Feb 2010 (https://youtube.com/c/perbadananputrajaya). However, achieving the target of updating "every ceremony" is a challenging KPI to achieve

(c)

No	Initiative	Implementation objective	Status	Achievement as of Dec 2020
1	2.1.2 Air quality monitoring	Citizens can access API value information 24 h a day	Achieved	The temperature, weather and air quality API values are shown on the Putrajaya Mobile App homepage

Table 7.4 (Continued)

No	Initiative	Implementation objective	Status	Achievement as of Dec 2020
2	2.1.4 Putrajaya lake and wetland management operational system (PLWMOS)— lake water quality, flora and fauna	Citizens can access information on lake water quality, wetland management and API values	Pending	To date, it is not integrated with the Putrajaya Mobile App
3	3.1.1 Putrajaya Command Centre (monitoring)	Provide the basic infrastructure needed to upgrade the city's capabilities and capacities in working towards Smart City status	Achieved	The Command Centre is functioning
4	3.4.5 Payment online/application	Integrate with the Putrajaya Mobile App	Pending	To date, it is not integrated with the Putrajaya Mobile App
5	5.1.1 Panic Buttons	Integrate with the Putrajaya Mobile App	Achieved	The designed panic alert was linked to a predetermined close contact person named by the user
6	5.1.2 Putrajaya Command Centre (emergency response)	Provide an infrastructure for emergencies	Achieved	The Command Centre is linked to the police, the fire rescue service, Hospital Putrajaya and the Civil Service Department
7	6.1.1 E-Wallet and E-Kiosk	Integrate with the Putrajaya Mobile App	Pending	To date, it is not integrated with the Putrajaya Mobile App
8	6.2.1 Smart application for city attractions	Integrate with the Putrajaya Mobile App	Achieved	City attractions were shown in the app. However, the lack of a "search button" meant the experience was not as user-friendly as the results of a Google search
9	6.4.2 Smart application for business promotion	Integrate with the Putrajaya Mobile App	Pending	"Coming soon" status found on the Putrajaya Mobile App
10	7.3.3 Healthy diet information and education	Integrate the MyNutri App with the Putrajaya Mobile App	Pending	To date, it is not integrated with the Putrajaya Mobile App
11	7.3.4 Information on dengue hotspot areas	Integrate iDenggi with the Putrajaya Mobile App	Pending	To date, it is not integrated with the Putrajaya Mobile App

(*Continued*)

Table 7.4 (Continued)

No	Initiative	Implementation objective	Status	Achievement as of Dec 2020
12	7.3.5 Putrajaya Bebas Asap Rokok (PBAR)	Integrate non-smoking area information with the Putrajaya Mobile App	Pending	To date, it is not integrated with the Putrajaya Mobile App
(d)				
1	3.4.8 Online registration system (forum/ workshop/ training)	Integrate with the Putrajaya Mobile App	Pending	To date, it is not integrated with the Putrajaya Mobile App
2	6.2.3 Tourism feedback (visitors to rate the sites and services)	Create an apps platform for collecting tourist feedback data and integrate this with the Putrajaya Mobile App	Achieved	The rating and comment system are available. However, very few ratings were found

Command Centre for traffic, safety, and emergency response and monitoring. For a detailed evaluation of the initiatives, refer to Table 7.4.

7.5 Discussion

7.5.1 *Underdeveloped Political Culture of e-Decision-Making on the e-Platforms*

The findings above allowed the author to observe that both e-participation cases—Putrajaya and Petaling Jaya smart cities—are ready to provide e-information to the public, given the mechanism of surveys and e-consultation to satisfy public complaints, although e-decision-making has somehow been ignored. The theme of e-democracy in these Malaysian smart cities remains in an immature condition, which was reflected in the unpleasant e-participation experience [41]. More precisely, this would be termed a "flawed democracy" by the 2020 democracy index survey [24]. Basic civil liberties are respected in Malaysia, whereby the public can access government services information and channels for complaints and surveys. However, there are significant weaknesses in other aspects of democracy, such as the underdeveloped political culture and the low levels of political participation in e-decision-making.

The current e-platforms offered by Malaysia's two leading smart cities have demonstrated that citizens influencing the top-down agenda are immature and that there is great scope for improvement. The author suggests that the urban policymakers in Malaysia learn from those "full democracies", such as Spain, whose e-platforms have effective e-decision-making systems. The city of Madrid has been identified as one of the top Spanish smart cities and is regularly ranked above the average in e-government empirical studies among European Union members [50,51]. The Madrid City Council's leading initiative in terms of public participation is the award-winning portal Decide Madrid [52,53]. This is an e-platform powered by an open source that allows Madrid's citizens to engage with the local government in four ways, namely to initiate debates, create proposals, plan for participatory budgets, and vote for the adoption of proposals [10,44]. The system is a true bottom-up approach that fulfils citizens' needs and co-produces together with them. The Decide Madrid e-participation platform has an ideal design. To succeed in practical terms, such a platform needs high participation from citizens, the readiness of the e-platform design, and an anticipated authority willing to allow this e-democracy realm to happen [46].

Using the Decide Madrid e-platform as a template, the author would like to make suggestions for the existing Putrajaya Mobile App and PJKita website. The Putrajaya Mobile App was primarily designed as an e-information platform to provide information to residents and tourists, but it is lacking in e-consultation and e-decision-making facilities. Thus, the whole app needs a revamp by improving the e-consultation space and adding an e-decision-making space. The PJKita is slightly better. It was mainly designed as a community engagement platform with e-information and e-consultation spaces to provide the public with information and gather local champions. The current e-spaces could be altered to suit the four main elements of Decide Madrid. Detailed suggestions are presented in Table 7.5.

7.5.2 Participatory Governance at a Crossroads in terms of Realising Smart Cities

The second finding in this study was that the smart initiatives planned under the Putrajaya Smart City Blueprint had only achieved a below-average rate, where the Putrajaya Mobile App and Putrajaya Command Centre e-platforms are considered. The initiatives designed under the quick win (which ended in 2018) and short-term period (which was to end in 2020) were considered a booster, mainly to obtain public confidence and demonstrate the administrators' capability to govern and involve multiple stakeholders. However, these initiatives were partially achieved, which creates doubts that the Putrajaya government could advance towards the participatory style by employing ICT-related e-platforms.

The reason could be insufficient budgetary support, a lack of ICT expertise within the internal departments, political influence, or the inefficiency of the governance in terms of daily operations and planning. However, since Putrajaya, as the federal government administration centre, is strongly backed by federal government funding, and the ICT department also has the highest number of staff employed [54], the authors postulate that the latter factors—political influence and operational efficiency—were more likely to have hindered the progress of the initiatives related to e-platforms. In an interview with a Putrajaya Mobile App developer, the informant hinted that the mobile app user interface and design have

Table 7.5 The suggestion to improve e-decision-making in Malaysian smart cities e-platforms design system

Element	Malaysian smart cities E-platforms	
The element of E-Decision-Making	Putrajaya Mobile App, Putrajaya	PJKita website, Petaling Jaya
Debates	Not Available	Not Available
Proposals	Not Available	Not Available
Participatory Budgets	Not Available	Not Available
Voting	Not Available	Not Available for particular budget proposals
Scope to improve for E-Decision-Making	All the current contents were not related to e-decision-making and needed to be redesigned.	Can be improved accordingly: -Ideas (improve to Debates) -Message Board (improve to Proposals) -Funding (improve to Participatory budgets) -Community (improve to voting)
Scope not related and proposed to exclude/ modify in the new design platform; or depends on stakeholders' demand	-News -Events -Points of Interest -Public Amenities -Putrajaya Tracer (for COVID-19) -Business (idle button) -Parking (idle button) -Tours (idle button)	-Join Us -Q&A (1 posting) -Survey -Messages -Service (zero postings) -Support (1 posting) -Contact (zero postings) -SDG Projects -D.4.C (Date for change) -Job Post (zero postings) -Rewards (idle button) -City Index (idle button)

some problems. The real problem, the sluggish development, could be due to the mobile app internal operations and frequent changes in the top-down management of the Putrajaya Corporation. Technological (i.e., e-platforms), institutional (i.e., governance), and human (i.e., citizens) factors are essential in achieving the vision of a smart city [29,55], so the efficiency of governance and political interest is hugely important. If the initiatives were implemented as planned, they would surely gain greater public acceptance and confidence. For example, in the case of Osale.ee in Estonia and governmental portals of smart cities of both Lisbon (Portugal) and Brasilia (Brazil), the citizens want to see efficient and transparent governments that consider the citizens' voices in smart cities developments [2,13,33,56].

On the other hand, the smartness of the e-platforms of both Putrajaya and Petaling Jaya cases were questionable (i.e., the e-platforms lacked a lot of functionality, and the numbers of civil participants/users were also very limited). The smart city of Madrid, with an effective e-participation platform of Decide Madrid and the embedded activities of aware and active citizens, is developing its (smart) participatory governance stably [46,53]. For both Putrajaya and Petaling Jaya, the authors argue that being administratively self-congratulatory as the country's leading smart cities and yet, limited in upholding the culture of participatory governance, serves as a lesson to other countries/cities in the world: that the smart cities vision will hardly be achieved if the institutional factor of participatory governance is tokenised [13,57,58].

For this reason, the authors suggest that governors of smart cities, rather than making self-claims or overly lauding projects as smart city initiatives, should focus on building the foundations of smart government, in this case, the participatory governance element [32], which is the aspect which needs to be enhanced. An authoritarian or tokenised governance style involving superficial levels of e-participation, i.e., providing abundant e-information and creating non-feedback surveys on e-consultation, is incompatible with smart urbanism. Conversely, a smart government should incorporate the advice of institutions and scholars, such as [4,10,32], to adopt the participatory governance style. This includes motivating citizens to participate, as well as genuinely sharing agenda setting and decision-making power, which thus allows greater e-democracy spaces for citizens to propose and vote for initiatives.

7.6 Conclusion

Smart cities are scenarios of government management reform [8,59]. The future of smart cities is essentially technocratic, requiring knowledge in algorithms for procurement and participation, as well as democratic, allowing residents to participate in the shared enterprise of city-making [33,60,61]. The topics of participatory governance and smart city are inseparable, as they are deemed central to future development debates [62–67]. This study has thoroughly examined the status of participatory governance through e-platforms that are mainly utilised in reliable realisations of smart cities. Through two cases in a developing country, namely Putrajaya and Petaling Jaya smart cities in Malaysia, this study has found that the political culture of e-decision-making is underdeveloped. Meanwhile, for Putrajaya, the implementation of smart initiatives relating to e-platforms is also sub-standard. These findings are evidence of the flawed democratic state of Malaysia, and attention from policymakers is greatly needed to rethink and realise higher levels of e-democracy as part of smart city planning and development.

There are a few limitations to this study. Firstly, the Petaling Jaya City Council has yet to publish a specific smart city blueprint like Putrajaya. A future comparative study could be carried out as the new Petaling Jaya Smart, Sustainable and Resilient City Blueprint will be published in the coming year. Secondly, the authors selected the e-platforms of mobile applications and websites. The variety of e-platforms is large and keeps developing for city solutions. In future research, scholars could expand the e-platforms subject to include official social media, Internet-of-Things (IoT) platforms, or digital twins platforms that are developed using Industrial Revolution 4.0 technologies [68–71]. In brief, this study has contributed a case report on a developing country's smart cities, covering the participatory issues from the angle of e-participation and e-platforms. Furthermore, the evidence and suggestions given in this study may serve as a benchmark for other developing countries interested in the greater application of participatory governance, hence building greater e-democracy spaces for its citizens to allow them to fulfil their roles as smarter citizens [72].

Acknowledgements

This chapter, with permission from the copyright holder, is a reproduced version of the following journal article: Lim, S., & Yigitcanlar, T. (2022). Participatory governance of smart cities: Insights from e-participation of Putrajaya and Petaling Jaya, Malaysia. *Smart Cities* 5(1), 71–89.

References

1. Tenney, M., Garnett, R., Wylie, B. (2020). A theatre of machines: Automata circuses and digital bread in the smart city of Toronto. *The Canadian Geographer* 64, 388–401.
2. Malek, J.A., Lim, S.B., Yigitcanlar, T. (2021). Social inclusion indicators for building citizen-centric smart cities: A systematic literature review. *Sustainability* 13, 376.
3. Caragliu, A., Del Bo, C., Nijkamp, P. (2011). Smart cities in Europe. *Journal of Urban Technology* 18(2), 65–82.
4. Giffinger, R., Fertner, C., Kramar, H., Kalasek, R., Pichler, N., Meijers, E. (2007). *Smart Cities: Ranking of European Medium-Sized Cities*. TU Vienna: Wien, Austria.
5. United Nations (UN). (2020). *E-Government Survey 2020*. Department of Economic and Social Affairs, United Nations: New York, NY, USA.
6. Calzada, I. (2021). *Smart City Citizenship*. Elsevier: Amsterdam, The Netherlands.
7. Cardullo, P., Kitchin, R. (2019). Being a 'citizen' in the smart city: Up and down the scaffold of smart citizen participation in Dublin, Ireland. *GeoJournal* 84, 1–13.
8. Bolívar, M.P.R., Cediel, M.E.C. (2020). *Digital Government and Achieving E-Public Participation: Emerging Research and Opportunities*. IGI Global: Hershey, PA, USA.
9. Bibri, S.E. (2018). A foundational framework for smart sustainable city development: Theoretical, disciplinary, and discursive dimensions and their synergies. *Sustainable Cities and Society* 38, 758–794.
10. Le Blanc, D. (2020). *E-Participation: A Quick Overview of Recent Qualitative Trends*. DESA Working Paper No. 163; Department of Economic and Social Affairs, United Nations: New York, NY, USA.
11. Chadwick, A. (2009). Web 2.0: New challenges for the study of e-democracy in an era of informational exuberance. *I/S: A Journal of Law Policy for the Information Society* 5, 9–41.
12. Ostling, A. (2010). ICT in politics: From peaks of inflated expectations to voids of disillusionment. *European Journal of ePractice* 9, 49–56.
13. Bernardes, M.B., De Andrade, F.P., Novais, P., Lopes, N.V. (2018). Participatory governance of smart cities: A study upon Portuguese and Brazilian government portals. In: *Proceedings of the 11th International Conference on Theory and Practice of Electronic Governance*. ICEGOV'18, Galway, Ireland, 4–6 April 2018; pp. 526–536.
14. Toots, M. (2019). Why e-participation systems fail: The case of Estonia's Osale.ee. *Government Information Quarterly* 36, 546–559.

15. Malaysia Digital Economy Corporation (MDEC). (2017). *ProBE: Provider-Based Evaluation Annual Report 2016.* Malaysia Digital Economy Corporation: Cyberjaya, Malaysia.
16. Malaysian Administrative Modernisation and Management Planning Unit (MAMPU). (2021). *e-Participation Policy.* Available online: www.malaysia.gov.my/portal/cont ent/30042 (accessed 23 August 2021).
17. Malaysia Competition Commission (MyCC). (2021). *E-Participation.* Available online: www.mycc.gov.my/e-participation (accessed 1 February 2021).
18. Khadzali, N.R., Zan, Z.M. (2019). Exploring e-participation policy and initiatives in Malaysia. *International Journal of Law and Government Communication* 4, 10–25.
19. Salamat, M.A., Hassan, S., Muhammad, M.S. (2011). Electronic participation in Malaysia. *Journal of e-Government Studies and Best Practice* 2011, 270543.
20. Masrom, M., Ling, E.L.A., Din, S. (2015). E-participation behavioral in e-government in Malaysia. In: *Public Affairs and Administration: Concepts, Methodologies, Tools, and Applications.* Information Resources Management Association, (Eds.). IGI Global: Hershey, PA, USA, pp. 1490–1505.
21. Kubicek, H., Aichholzer, G. (2016). Closing the evaluation gap in e-participation research and practice. In: *Evaluating e-Participation, Public Administration and Information Technology*; Aichholzer, G., Kubicek, H., Torres, L., (Eds.). Springer: Cham, Switzerland, Volume 19, pp. 11–45.
22. Foucault, M. (1997). *Ethics: Subjectivity and Truth; The Essential Works of Michel Foucault, 1954–1984*; Volume 1. New Press: New York, NY, USA.
23. Alizadeh, T. (2021). *Global Trends of Smart Cities: A Comparative Analysis of Geography, City Size, Governance, and Urban Planning.* Elsevier: Amsterdam, The Netherlands.
24. Economist Intelligence Unit (EIU). (2020). *Democracy Index 2020: In Sickness and In Health?* Economist Intelligence Unit (EIU): London, UK.
25. Lim, S.B., Malek, J.A., Yigitcanlar, T. (2021). Post-materialist values of smart city societies: International comparison of public values for good enough governance. *Future Internet* 13, 201.
26. Lim, I. (2021). *Malaysia Reaches New Peak in World Democracy Ladder Despite Political Instability since Dr Mahathir's Resignation.* Available online: www.malaym ail.com/news/malaysia/2021/02/03/malaysia-reaches-new-peak-in-world-democracy-ladder-despite-political-insta/1946509 (accessed 8 February 2021).
27. Zhao, F., Fashola, O.I., Olarewaju, T.I., Onwumere, I. (2021). Smart city research: A holistic and state-of-the-art literature review. *Cities* 119, 103406.
28. Yigitcanlar, T. (2018). Smart city policies revisited: Considerations for a truly smart and sustainable urbanism practice. *World Technopolis Review* 7, 97–112.
29. Nam, T., Pardo, T. (2011). Conceptualizing smart city with dimensions of technology, people & institutions. In: *Proceedings of the 12th Annual International Conference on Digital Government Research*, College Park, MD, USA, 12–15 June 2011; pp. 282–291.
30. Alizadeh, T. (2017). An investigation of IBM's smarter cities challenge: What do participating cities want? *Cities* 63, 70–80.
31. Yigitcanlar, T., Cugurullo, F. (2020). The sustainability of artificial intelligence: An urbanistic viewpoint from the lens of smart and sustainable cities. *Sustainability* 12, 8548.
32. Bolivar, M.P.R., Meijer, A.J. (2016). Smart governance: Using a literature review and empirical analysis to build a research model. *Social Science Computer Review* 34, 673–692.

33. Shadowen, N., Lodato, T., Loi, D. (2020). Participatory governance in smart cities: Future scenarios and opportunities. In: *Distributed, Ambient and Pervasive Interactions; HCII 2020. Lecture Notes in Computer Science*; Streitz, N., Konomi, S., Eds.; Springer: Cham, Switzerland, Volume 12203, pp. 443–463.

34. Fischer, F. (2012). Participatory governance: From theory to practice. In: *The Oxford Handbook of Governance*; Levi-Faur, D., (Ed.). Oxford University Press: Oxford, UK, pp. 457–471.

35. Aurelia, S., Mocanu, M., Eugeniu, T. (2007). Participatory governance in the public healthcare systems of the Scandinavian and Baltic countries. *Annals of Financial Economics* 1, 625–631.

36. Mora, L., Bolici, R., Deakin, M. (2017). The first two decades of smart-city research: A bibliometric analysis. *Journal of Urban Technology* 24, 3–27.

37. Dahl, R.A. (1989). *Democracy and Its Critics*. Yale University Press: New Haven, CT, USA; London, UK.

38. Setälä, M. (2017). Connecting deliberative mini-publics to representative decision making. *European Journal of Political Research* 56, 846–863.

39. Gastil, J. (2019). A comparison of deliberative designs and policy impact in the EU and across the globe. In: *Is Europe Listening to Us?*; Kies, R., Nanz, P., Eds.; Ashgate: Farnham, UK, pp.217–237.

40. Peris, J., Acebillo-Baqué, M., Calabuig, C. (2001). Scrutinizing the link between participatory governance and urban environment management. The experience in Arequipa during 2003–2006. *Habitat International* 35, 84–92.

41 Lim, S.B., Malek, J.A., Hussain, M.Y., Tahir, Z. (2020). Participation in e-government services and smart city programs: A case study of Malaysian local authority. *Planning Malaysia Journal* 18, 300–312.

42. Yigitcanlar, T., Desouza, K.C., Butler, L., Roozkhosh, F. (2020). Contributions and risks of Artificial Intelligence (AI) in building smarter cities: Insights from a systematic review of the literature. *Energies* 13, 1473.

43. Yigitcanlar, T., Butler, L., Windle, E., Desouza, K.C., Mehmood, R., Corchado, J.M. (2020). Can building "artificially intelligent cities" safeguard humanity from natural disasters, pandemics, and other catastrophes? An urban scholar's perspective. *Sensors* 20, 2988.

44. Consul. (2021). *Consul: Free Software for Citizen Participation*. Available online: https://consulproject.org/en/ (accessed 8 January 2021).

45. Organization for Economic Co-operation and Development (OECD). (2021). *Consul Project*. Available online: https://oecd-opsi.org/innovations/consul-project/ (accessed 24 May 2021).

46. Royo, S., Pina, V., Garcia-Rayado, J. (2020). Decide Madrid: A critical analysis of an award-winning e-participation initiative. *Sustainability* 12, 1674.

47. Mills, A.J., Durepos, G., Wiebe, E. (2010). Multiple-case designs. In: *Encyclopedia of Case Study Research*; Mills, A.J., (Ed.). Sage: Thousand Oaks, CA, USA, pp. 583–584.

48. Yin, R.K. (2018). *Case Study Research and Applications: Design and Methods*, 6th ed. Sage: Thousand Oaks, CA, USA.

49. Lim, S.B., Malek, J.A., Hussain, M.Y., Tahir, Z., Saman, N.H.M. (2021). SDGs, smart urbanisation, and politics: Stakeholder partnerships and environmental cases in Malaysia. *Journal of Sustainability Science and Management* 16, 190–219.

50. Veem. (2021). *Top 3 Spanish Smart Cities*. Available online: www.veem.com/library/top-3-spanish-smart-cities/ (accessed 25 December 2021).

51. Pina, V., Torres, L., Royo, S. (2007). Are ICTs improving transparency and account-ability in the EU regional and local governments? An empirical study. *Public Administration* 85, 449–472.

52. Madrid City Council. (2021). *Decide Madrid: Citizen Participation Portal of the Madrid City Council*. Available online: https://decide.madrid.es/ (accessed 23 August 2021).

53. De Luna, A.B.M., Kolotouchkina, O. (2020). Smart place making through digital com-munication and citizen engagement: London and Madrid. In: *Digital Government and Achieving E-Public Participation: Emerging Research and Opportunities*; Bolívar, M.P.R., Cediel, M.E.C., (Eds.). IGI Global: Hershey, PA, USA, pp. 206–228.

54. Lim, S.B., Malek, J.A., Hashim, N. (2022). Implementing the smart city concept in Malaysia: Contemporary challenges, strategies and opportunities facing local author-ities in the post-COVID-19 era. *Malaysian Townplan Journal* 1, 43–56.

55. Jiang, H., Geertman, S., Witte, P. (2020). Smart urban governance: An alternative to technocratic "smartness." *GeoJournal* 87, 1639–1655.

56. Del-Real, C., Ward, C., Sartipi, M. (2023). What do people want in a smart city? Exploring the stakeholders' opinions, priorities and perceived barriers in a medium-sized city in the United States. *International Journal of Urban Sciences* 27, 50–74.

57. Allwinkle, S., Cruickshank, P. (2011). Creating smart-er cities: An overview. *Journal of Urban Technology* 18, 1–16.

58. Hollands, R.G. (2008). Will the real smart city please stand up? *City* 12, 303–320.

59. Cruz, C.O., Sarmento, J.M. (2017). Reforming traditional PPP models to cope with the challenges of smart cities. *Competition and Regulation in Network Industries* 18, 94–114.

60. Vestergaard, L.S., Fernandes, J., Presser, M.A. (2015). Towards smart city democracy. *Geoforum Perspektiv* 14, 25.

61. Lee, J.Y., Woods, O., Kong, L. (2020). Towards more inclusive smart cities: Reconciling the divergent realities of data and discourse at the margins. *Geography Compass* 14, e12504.

62. Durmaz, B., Platt, S., Yigitcanlar, T. (2010). Creativity, culture tourism and place-making: Istanbul and London film industries. *International Journal of Culture, Tourism and Hospitality Research* 4, 198–213.

63. Yigitcanlar, T., Velibeyoglu, K., Baum, S. (2008). *Creative Urban Regions: Harnessing Urban Technologies to Support Knowledge City Initiatives*. IGI Global: Hersey, PA, USA.

64. Effing, R., Groot, B.P. (2016). Social smart city: Introducing digital and social strat-egies for participatory governance in smart cities. In: *Electronic Government 2016; Lecture Note Computer Science*. Scholl, H.J., Glassey, O., Janssen, M., Klievink, B., Lindgren, I., Parycek, P., Tambouris, E., Wimmer, M.A., Janowski, T., Sá Soares, D., (Eds.). Springer: Cham, Switzerland, Volume 9820, pp. 241–252.

65. Yigitcanlar, T., Bulu, M. (2015). Dubaization of Istanbul: Insights from the knowledge-based urban development journey of an emerging local economy. *Environmental Planning A* 47, 89–107.

66. Esmaeilpoorarabi, N., Yigitcanlar, T., Guaralda, M. (2018). Place quality in innov-ation clusters: An empirical analysis of global best practices from Singapore, Helsinki, New York, and Sydney. *Cities* 74, 156–168.

67. Sarimin, M., Yigitcanlar, T. (2012). Towards a comprehensive and integrated knowledge-based urban development model: Status quo and directions. *International Journal of Knowledge Based Development* 3, 175–192.

68. Yigitcanlar, T., Kankanamge, N., Vella, K. (2021). How are smart city concepts and technologies perceived and utilized? A systematic geo-Twitter analysis of smart cities in Australia. *Journal of Urban Technology* 28, 135–154.

69. Deng, T., Zhang, K., Shen, Z.J.M. (2021). A systematic review of a digital twin city: A new pattern of urban governance toward smart cities. *Journal of Management Science and Engineering* 6, 125–134.

70. Yigitcanlar, T., Kamruzzaman, M. (2019). Smart cities and mobility: Does the smartness of Australian cities lead to sustainable commuting patterns? *Journal of Urban Technology* 26, 21–46.

71. Singh, S., Sharma, P.K., Yoon, B., Shojafar, M., Cho, G.H., Ra, I.H. (2020). Convergence of blockchain and artificial intelligence in IoT network for the sustainable smart city. *Sustainable Cities and Society* 63, 102364.

72. Lim, S., Yigitcanlar, T. (2022). Participatory governance of smart cities: Insights from e-participation of Putrajaya and Petaling Jaya, Malaysia. *Smart Cities* 5(1), 71–89.

8 Good Governance

8.1 Introduction

At the beginning of the 21st century, a new mould of society has been undergoing a silent revolution by promoting worldwide smart and sustainable city development [1]. This technology-method driven smart city trend depends on the pervasive application of information and communication technology (ICT), big data, artificial intelligence, the Internet of Things (IoTs), algorithms, and automation to allow utopian solutions to urban problems and better urban governance [2–4]. This type of urban governance often results in panoptic surveillance, predictive profiling, and social sorting of technocratic governance [5,6].

Under this technocratic governance, "smart" societies and citizens have the potential to engineer the Collective Adaptive System (CAS) [7]. This CAS operates on the social-technical combination of hybrid computing (i.e., how people and machines working together create new types of problem-solving capability), adaptivity (i.e., bringing the appropriate sub-collective to bear to solve a particular problem), and learning (i.e., accreting knowledge of how the system responds to different circumstances) [7]. Examples of these include simple cases like the Waze mobile application for traffic navigation, which utilises the wisdom of the crowd and the everyday use of a mobile connection to data, algorithms, and social networks [8]. A more complex example is the sophisticated Rio de Janeiro city command centre, which manages the daily data of more than 30 municipalities, state agencies, and citizens, interconnects to the control room, and provides intelligent solutions to the city, such as crime reduction strategies [9,10].

The CAS undoubtedly solves issues in urban society by providing a resource pool to enable a collective to develop a range of responses to a situation. However, the CAS also collectively produces friction and contention, as well as significant social and ethical issues, including disputes over the ownership of the pooled data, the privacy of personal data contribution, and accountability for the effects of the CAS should things go wrong [7]. The problems it has solved are mostly materialist, such as the order of city traffic, property protection, cost reduction, and economic gains. On the other hand, the post-materialist values of building a smart city society

DOI: 10.1201/9781003403647-10

have arguably become a secondary priority. Examples include the post-material process (enhancing citizen participation and free speech) and post-material ends (environmental sustainability) [11].

Meijer and Bolívar [11] observed that academic debates on the post-materialist values of a smart city society are focused on forming desirables for a "good society", but less so on the issues of a political struggle. This political struggle is evident in the "good governance" framework proposed by the World Bank [12], with a long list of targets that includes 114 strategies which are often criticised as difficult for governments to decide on and implement [13]. Further to "good governance", [13,14] extended the discussion to the principle of "good enough governance", the main idea of which is to prioritise development strategies based on the specific cultural context of change and queries on intervention content. However, to the limited knowledge of the present authors, there is a lack of discussion linking good enough governance and smart city society. Premat [15] has attempted to analyse the Swedish smart city agenda and urged that urban governance should correlate with emerging post-materialist values. Otherwise, the authors identified a lack of research on good governance and on dissecting post-materialist values in the context of developing countries such as Malaysia.

Most literature on smart city society in Malaysia focuses on applying ICT solutions in urban governance. Various discussions explore the roles of ICT and IoT applications in Malaysia in solving materialist issues such as mobility, energy, and economic gains [16–18]. Several scholars have discussed non-materialist issues in Malaysia, such as citizen participation [19–23], freedom of speech and expression [24], and environmental sustainability and politics [25]. The availability of discussions on such post-materialist values are positive signs and can be viewed as a rising alternative trend in the human-driven method of smart city development [4]. However, these discussions were not fully linked to the political struggle from the governance perspective, nor did they outline the importance of post-materialist values governing the future of the smart city society.

Thus, from the above intertwining research problems, the following question arose: How can good enough governance promote the smart city society under the emerging post-materialist values? Based on this main research question, the authors attempted to identify the status of materialist and post-materialist values as possessed by societies. Furthermore, once such value propositions were understood, the authors projected the application of the framework of good enough governance that might potentially form the smart city society. In another words, this study aims to analyse the application of good enough governance in considering the citizens' value propositions that shape smart city societies.

Hence, three operational research questions (RQ) were formulated:

RQ 1: What values are important in life?
RQ 2: What qualities are children encouraged to develop in shaping such values in life?
RQ 3: What are the materialist and post-materialist values of society?

8.2 Methodology

This study employed a quantitative method with cross-country comparisons. As Malaysia is undergoing the implementation stage of nationwide smart cities development, researching the governance directions for smart societies' value propositions is a timely factor. Thus, Malaysia was selected as the main case for this study and compared to Indonesia and another eight countries worldwide. The country comparisons were dissected according to the geographical location, majority religion, and economic status (Table 8.1).

Both Malaysia and Indonesia have similar backgrounds, as they are located in South-East Asia, Islam is the official religion possessed by the majority, and the economic status is upper-middle income. For Malaysia, the gross national income (GNI) per capita was USD 11,230 in 2019 and its aim is to achieve high-income status by 2030 [26]. Meanwhile, Indonesia just celebrated its milestone of moving into the group of upper-middle-income countries from its previous lower-middle-income status. Its GNI per capita reached USD 4,050 in 2019, slightly above the USD 4,046 threshold for the category [27]. Iran, Pakistan, and Nigeria represented samples from Islamic countries located outside South-East Asia. On the other hand, Brazil, the United States, Germany, and Australia represented Christian-majority countries in different parts of the world. As for China, it has the world's greatest population, an irreligious population, and a "world share" that influences the global economy [28,29]. Although China's society has deep religious traditions, decades of communist rule have installed widespread atheistic materialism [30].

Table 8.1 Studied countries [26]

Country	Geographical location	Majority religion	Economic status
Indonesia	South-East Asia	Islam	Upper-middle income
Malaysia	South-East Asia	Islam	Upper-middle income
Iran	Middle East	Islam	Upper-middle income
Pakistan	South Asia	Islam	Lower-middle income
Nigeria	Africa	Islam	Lower-middle income
Brazil	Latin America	Christians (Catholics and Protestants)	Upper-middle income
China	East Asia	Chinese Buddhism and Folk Religions	Upper-middle income
United States	North America	Christians (Protestants and Catholics)	High-income
Germany	Europe	Christians (Protestants and Catholics)	High-income
Australia	Asia Pacific	Christians (Catholic and others)	High-income

Table 8.2 Population, sample size, and year of survey [26,29,31]

Country	Population 2020 (mil.)	Density (ppl/km²)	Urban population (%)	Survey sample size	Year of survey	Mode of data collection	Mode of survey length (min.)	Urban sampling (%)
Indonesia	274	151	56	3,200	2018, June–Aug	CAPI	–	29.5
Malaysia	32	99	78	1,313	2018, Apr–May	CAWI	–	63.0
Iran	84	52	76	1,499	2020, May–Apr	PAPI	86–120	74.0
Pakistan	221	587	35	1,995	2018, Nov–Dec	CAPI	46–65	33.3
Nigeria	206	226	52	1,237	2017, Dec–2018, Jan	CAPI	66–85	49.0
Brazil	212	25	88	1,762	2018	CAPI	–	–
China	1,439	153	61	3,036	2018, Jul–Oct	PAPI	46–65	61.1
United States	331	36	83	2,596	2017, Apr–May	CAWI	Up to 45	88.4
Germany	84	240	76	1,528	2017, Oct–2018, May	CAPI	46–65	89.9
Australia	25	3	86	1,813	2018, Apr–Aug	Mail/Post	Up to 45	78.5
Total	–	–	–	19,979	–	–	–	–

CAPI: computer-assisted personal interviews; CAWI, computer-assisted web interviewing; PAPI, pen-and-paper personal interviews.)

This study did not conduct an on-site survey. Instead, the country samples were derived from the raw data files from the World Values Survey 2017–2020 [31]. In order to address the research questions, the sample size of the World Values Survey for each country was large enough to represent a confidence level of 99% and a margin of error of 3.5% [32] (Table 8.2).

The method of data collection randomly covered the major areas, ethics, and religious groups of each country. Details were openly accessed through the World Values Survey website [31]. Since its inception in 1981 and conducted globally every 5 years, the World Values Survey has currently come to its seventh wave covering 120 countries representing 94.5% of the world's population. To date, there are over 30,000 publications and researches that use the World Values Survey— value orientations to explain important political phenomena [31,33]. Examples of these include [34–38]. Especially, Curini et al. [39] selected 40 countries from the World Values Survey based on the criteria of those countries covering both established and new democracies. In contrast, this study has set 10 countries based on geographical, religious, and economic status for comparison purposes.

From the 290 questions asked in the World Values Survey, the authors selected suitable items to answer the research questions. Table 8.3 shows the selected items and scales.

Table 8.3 Selected items and scales from World Values Survey in matching the research questions, derived from [31]

Research question	Item	Scale
RQ 1	Q1–6 Important in Life: Family, Friend, Leisure Time, Politics, Work, and Religion	Question: For each of the following aspects, indicate how important it is in your life Scale: Very Important, Rather Important, Not Very Important, Not at all
RQ 2	Q7–17 Qualities to develop: Good manners, Tolerance and respect for other people, Feeling of responsibility, Independence, Religious and faith, Hard work, Obedience, Determination, Unselfishness, Thrift saving money and things, and Imagination	Question: Here is a list of qualities that children can be encouraged to learn at home. Which, if any, do you consider to be especially important? Please choose up to five Scale: Important, Not mentioned
RQ 3	Q154 Materialist Vs Post-Materialist values	Question: If you had to choose, which one of the things on this card would you say is most important? Scale: Maintaining order in the nation; Giving people more say in important government decisions; Fighting rising prices; and Protecting freedom of speech

8.3 Results

8.3.1 Important Values in Life

In these 10 countries, the most important value was agreed to be Religion (98.89%), which reached nearly 100 percent agreement in all cases, followed by Work (89.61%) and Friendship (89.49%). The least important value was agreed to be Politics (52.81%), which made up about half of the survey cases, followed by Religion (70.84%) and Leisure Time (84.42%) (Figure 8.1). Indonesia and Malaysia shared similar patterns, whereby Religion (99.9% and 91.1%, respectively) was higher than the average of the countries surveyed. On the other hand, Politics (44.2%, 51.2%) in these countries had lower importance than the overall average.

Further analysis of geographical location shows that respondents in the Asia and Oceania region countries agreed that Family and Friends are important, while Politics was the least important (Figure 8.2). Respondents in the non-Asian regions agreed that Family and Leisure Time were more important than other items. Leisure

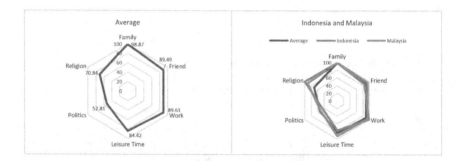

Figure 8.1 Important values in life by Indonesia and Malaysia.

Note: The average value is counted from 10 countries, i.e., Indonesia, Malaysia, Iran, Pakistan, Nigeria, Brazil, China, United States, Germany, and Australia. All values are in percentages.

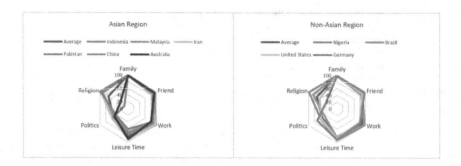

Figure 8.2 Important values in life by Asian and non-Asian regions.

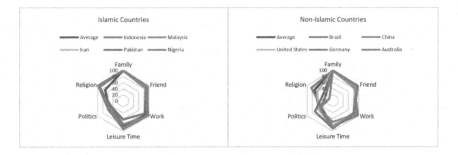

Figure 8.3 Important values in life by Islamic and non-Islamic countries.

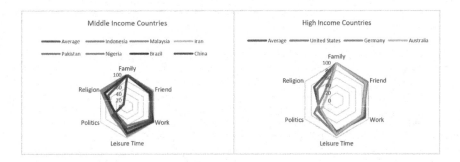

Figure 8.4 Important values in life by middle-income and high-income countries.

Time represents an aspect of the desire for freedom, and people in non-Asian countries, such as Nigeria, Brazil, the United States, and Germany, all place higher than average value on this aspect.

For Islamic countries, a clear pattern showed that Islam is above average in value (Figure 8.3). On the other hand, no clear distinction can be found in non-Islamic countries.

In middle-income countries, most were found to value religion more highly, with the exception being China (Figure 8.4). In all high-income countries, i.e., the United States, Germany, and Australia, people rank lower than average the values of Religion and Work. In countries such as the United States and Germany, respondents have higher Politics values than average.

8.3.2 Qualities to Develop

From the analysis, the five most chosen qualities were Good Manners (74.81%), Responsibility (63.23%), Tolerance (61.52%), Hard Work (51.03%), and Independence (47.65%) (Figure 8.5). Both Indonesians and Malaysians place higher than average value on the qualities of Good Manners, Responsibility,

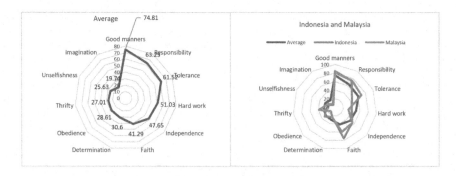

Figure 8.5 Qualities to develop for the future generation in Indonesia and Malaysia.

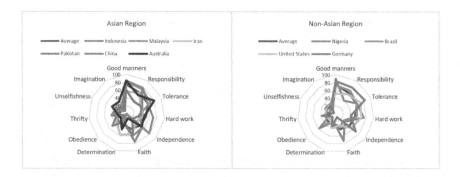

Figure 8.6 Qualities to develop for the future generation by Asian and non-Asian regions.

Independence, and Faith. In terms of Islamic Faith, Indonesia (75.2%) and Malaysia (59.7%), and Nigeria (72.5%) are among the top three highest countries with high levels of Faith. On the other hand, Malaysia and Indonesia demonstrate lower than average values in qualities such as Imagination, Unselfishness, Determination, and Hard Work. Furthermore, both countries also showed the lowest values placed on Imagination (7.3% and 9.3%, respectively), compared to the other eight countries.

Next, analysing the Asian and non-Asian regions, no patterns of particular import were observed (Figure 8.6); hence, cultivating qualities for a future generation does not significantly depend on the geographical location.

A comparative analysis of Islamic and non-Islamic countries suggests that Islamic countries demonstrated that they placed higher value on the qualities of teaching children to have religious faith (Figure 8.7). As for Imagination, all Islamic countries except Iran showed lower than average values. In non-Islamic countries, the quality of Tolerance ranked higher than or near to the average. Furthermore, all non-Islamic countries placed lower than average value in the quality of Faith. For Obedience, all non-Islamic countries except Brazil placed a lower value.

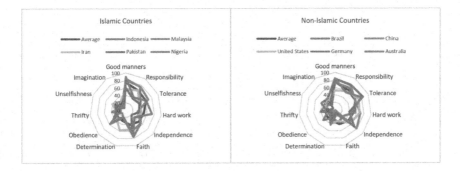

Figure 8.7 Qualities to develop for future generation by Islamic and non-Islamic countries.

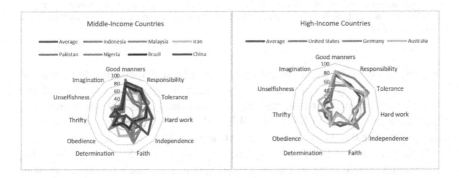

Figure 8.8 Qualities to develop for the future generation by economic status.

Conversely, Brazil was the only country to rank the quality of Imagination of low value, compared to the other four, China, the United States, Germany, and Australia.

The final analysis involved economic status. For the middle-income countries, no particular pattern was found (Figure 8.8). However, for high-income countries, the qualities of Tolerance, Independence, Determination, and Imagination were ranked higher than average. This means that Malaysia and Indonesia can learn how parents in high-income countries teach their children about qualities such as Tolerance, Independence, Determination, and Imagination. On the other hand, the high-income societies showed lower Obedience values than average.

8.3.3 Materialist vs. Post-Materialist Values

Overall, all respondents indicated that materialist values (Order and Economic Security) (58.88%) were more important than post-materialist values (Political Participation and Free Speech) (39.64%), with a ratio of 1.5:1. Malaysia and Indonesia had slightly higher ratios than average of 1.9:1 and 2.9:1, respectively.

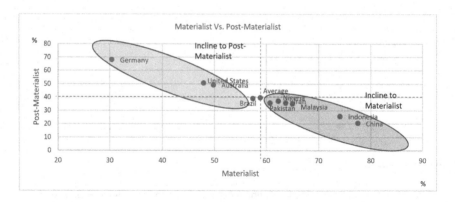

Figure 8.9 Materialist vs. post-materialist for the selected countries.

Note: Following the analysis by Inglehart [40,41], Order and Economic Security are paired to represent the value of Materialist, while Political Participation and Free Speech are paired to represent the value of Post-Materialist.

Free Speech was the least important value chosen by all respondents. In Figure 8.9, Indonesia and Malaysia are inclined to the materialist grouping, together with the other Islamic countries of Iran, Nigeria, and Pakistan. In this materialist grouping, China tops the chart, which is compatible with the Pew Research Center analysis that the Chinese top the list of the materialism poll [30].

High-income countries, such as Germany, the United States, and Australia, are inclined toward the post-materialist grouping. This result is compatible with the analyses of Inglehart [40,41]. First, all countries were previously dominated by citizens with materialist values who desired basic physical and survival needs and economic security in the post-World War II era. Moreover, Western countries, through the achievements of the Industrial Revolution, have gained faster prosperity and better lifestyles than most Eastern countries. Thus, when their basic needs and security have been fulfilled, people tend to look for freedom in life, such as free speech and greater participation in political decision-making. Through Inglehart's analyses, it can be seen that the younger cohort has a higher rate of support for post-materialist values than the older cohort, thus gradually building a contemporary society that largely subscribes to the post-materialist values of Western countries such as the United States and Germany. Figure 8.10 shows how post-materialist values changed in nine Western countries between 1970 and 2000.

Further evidence given by Inglehart [41] shows that, regardless of geographical location (Europe or Latin America) and religious background (Muslim-majority countries), the younger cohort of citizens subscribes to higher post-materialist values than the older generations (Figure 8.11).

Another finding is that the younger cohort in high-income countries tends to subscribe to higher post-materialist values (self-expression) than those in developing countries. In addition, the gap of the younger cohort is more significant than the

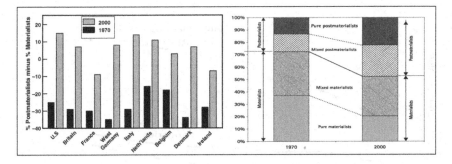

Figure 8.10 A shift toward post-materialist values among the publics of nine Western societies, 1970 and 2000 [42].

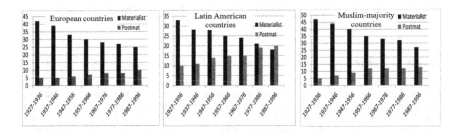

Figure 8.11 Similar materialist vs. post-materialist values across Europe, Latin American, and Muslim-majority countries, by age cohort [41].

Note: European countries include Bulgaria, Croatia, Czech Republic, Estonia, Hungary, Latvia, Lithuania, Poland, Romania, Slovakia, and Slovenia, in 2008–2012; Latin American countries include Argentina, Brazil, Chile, Colombia, Guatemala, Mexico, Peru, Uruguay, in 2005–2012; and Muslim-majority countries include Morocco, Algeria, Tunisia, Libya, Palestine, Jordan, Turkey, Albania and Indonesia, in 2007–2013.

older age cohort in comparing the high-income countries with developing countries (Figure 8.12).

In terms of the analysis from a cultural perspective, again, Protestant Europe (i.e., Germany) and the English-speaking groupings (i.e., the United States and Australia) showed a higher level of subscription to post-materialist values, while the African-Islamic grouping (i.e., Malaysia, Indonesia, Nigeria, and Pakistan) showed the lowest level of post-materialist values (Figure 8.13).

8.4 Findings and Discussion

From the above findings, three aspects are worthy of discussion: (a) political participation values through good enough governance, (b) dichotomous challenges in building citizen qualities, and (c) possibilities for building a post-materialist society.

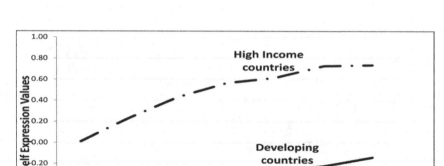

Figure 8.12 Age-related differences on survival/self-expression values, 1981–2014 [41].

Note: High-income countries (as of 1992): Andorra, Australia, Austria, Belgium, Canada, Cyprus, Denmark, Finland, France, Germany, Great Britain, Iceland, Ireland, Israel, Italy, Japan, Luxembourg, Netherlands, New Zealand, Northern Ireland, Norway, Singapore, Spain, Sweden, Switzerland, Taiwan, United States. Developing countries (as of 1992): Algeria, Argentina, Bangladesh, Brazil, Burkina Faso, Chile, China, Colombia, Dominican Republic, Ecuador, Egypt, Ethiopia, Ghana, Greece, Guatemala, India, Indonesia, Jordan, Malaysia, Mali, Malta, Mexico, Morocco, Nigeria, Pakistan, Peru, Philippines, Portugal, Rwanda, South Africa, South Korea, Tanzania, Thailand, Trinidad & Tobago, Turkey, Uganda, Uruguay, Venezuela, Vietnam, Zambia, Zimbabwe.

8.4.1 Political Participation Values to Prioritise under the Principle of Long-Term Good Enough Governance to Realise the Smart City Society

From the findings, political participation is the most necessary improvement to make when considering all the important values in life. The political participation value is an important means of creating a smarter society with a higher degree of citizen involvement in smart city initiatives [19,43,44]. Although big data and ICT are centred on smart city development, they should always be identified as part of the means and not the ultimate end of sustainable development [45]. In other words, smart city solutions should be attainable with the help of technology but not reducible to technology [46]. Thus, to apply the good enough governance concept and use technology to promote democracy and equity, the city governments of Malaysia and Indonesia should reassess their local contexts and contents in order to match their actions to their citizens' needs and allow more political participation in decision-making. It is predicted that, considering the post-materialist values analysis, this participation value will increase in the future [41].

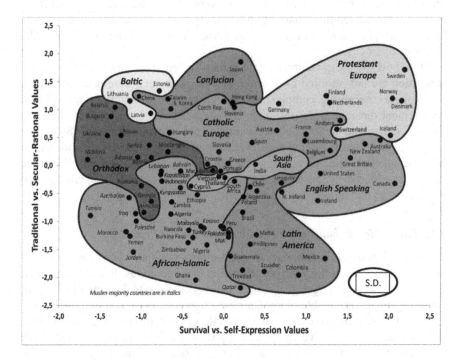

Figure 8.13 Global cultural map, 2008–2014 [41].

Note: The size of the mean standard deviation within a given country is shown on the lower left. The names of Muslim-majority societies are in italics.

The governments must prepare for, and move toward, a greater participatory form of governance that would effectively assist cities to innovate faster and allow cooperation in solving urban problems. This opinion is compatible with Meijer and Bolivar [11], whose study pointed out that it is possible to regard smart cities as outcomes of a wider move toward more effective governance, and one that emphasises a twin focus. The first focus is on different values, the most important factor being the inclusion of wealth and sustainability. The second focus is on a more democratic form of government, the most important feature being the inclusion of both representation and direct citizen participation.

8.4.2 Dichotomous Challenges in Building Qualities of Future Smart Citizens and Society

From the findings, the qualities of responsibility and independence can potentially be developed among future generations throughout the world, as well as in Indonesia and Malaysia. However, the qualities of creativity (imagination) and volunteering (unselfishness) are challenging qualities on which to focus. This showed the dichotomous state in terms of nurturing the future generation. Giffinger et al. [47] mentioned that smart city needs independent and aware citizens; while Malek et al. [19] mentioned responsible citizens and those who volunteer as the pillars of smart cities.

Thus, how can the government build a smart society if the qualities of the future generation are not nurtured to develop their creativity and unselfishness? Urban problems are becoming complex, and the co-creation of solutions with citizen involvement directed at, for example, the energy sector, is seen as an important strategy, rather than the sole reliance on limited government resources [48,49]. The authors believe that moulding such creative and unselfish citizens is a long-term process, but there must be a strong sense of priority and political will. From the short-term economic gains angle, this undoubtedly represents a huge challenge to the Malaysian and Indonesian governments.

8.4.3 Possibilities for Building the Post-Materialist Smart City Society

The analysis of trends in this study shows that post-materialist values are receiving greater attention from the younger generation in all countries. In the future smart city society, these younger generations will become the main support pillar for achieving smart sustainable cities. Currently, however, citizens in middle-income and Muslim-majority countries, such as Malaysia and Indonesia, should rethink the traditional conservative values that appear to confront openness values, such as obedience set against creativity and faith set against unselfishness. These countries should see how important it is to dare and be free to express ideas, be inclusive regardless of race and religion, and see the country and even the world as one entity. This would allow more openness and the chance for capable people to lead the country. These are some areas in which the culture and identity of the Malaysian and Indonesian majority might be contested.

In short, in building the emerging post-materialist society, options like advancing rapidly and upholding the values of openness and inclusiveness or moving slowly and steadily with a limited range of people able to share the benefits of development should be taken into account as possibilities or barriers in the minds of current and future leaders.

In search of a political struggle, good enough governance promotes the smart city society in Malaysia. This study has identified society's important values in life, qualities for children to develop, and the overall subscriptions to materialist and post-materialist values. The good enough governance framework focuses on two elements: (a) the cultural context of change and (b) queries on intervention content. First, the context of Malaysia is a country approaching high-income status [13,14]. Citizens of Malaysia and other Muslim-majority countries like Indonesia possess family and religion as preferable important values and view politics less favourably. They tend to teach their children to have good faith but place less emphasis on cultivating imagination and unselfishness. The overall ratio of materialists to post-materialists is 2:1, but post-materialist values are emerging in the younger generation. Second, based on the above cultural contexts, the query on intervention content should repeatedly ask a series of questions such as what needs to be done, when it needs to be done, and how it needs to be done [13].

Therefore, given the trend toward an affluent and emerging post-materialist society, now is the right time for the government of Malaysia to suggest this prioritisation of post-materialist values. This would include: (a) adopting participatory governance that allows more space for citizens to become involved in political decision-making, as well as freedom of speech and self-expression; and (b) ensuring that the design and implementation of technology promote democratic values and achieve social equity goals. Today's post-industrial society is no longer one that tends to obey orders, nor one of perseverance; the smart generation relies on collective human and machine intelligence in everyday life [7]. The government should prioritise cultivating in future smart citizens certain qualities such as having a good imagination, creativity, unselfishness, and volunteerism. These smart citizen qualities have been identified by scholars [19,47] as supporting the co-creation of better urban solutions with creative grassroots input from citizens and the involvement of large groups of volunteers, rather than solely relying on the government or private-sector resources.

8.5 Conclusion

This study has attempted to analyse and explain the application of good enough governance with the aim being to consider the citizens' value propositions that shape the smart city society. In addressing the main research question, these post-materialist value propositions for the governors to consider include the cultural content of the religious majority, allowing more space for political participation and free speech, and cultivating children in terms of imagination and unselfishness.

The advantage of this chapter is that it can become a policy reference for Muslim-majority countries such as Malaysia and Indonesia in building future smart citizens and societies, and in arriving at a balanced state of economic, social, and environmental sustainability. On the other hand, this study is limited as it provides a macro overview linking the political struggle, the smart city concept, and the CAS of smart society development and citizens' value propositions. Good enough governance queries involving content such as "when" and "how" need to be conducted in detail on the specific cultural contexts of cities and societies: this is one suggestion for further study. Future micro studies can delve into case studies of a particular city or society with a qualitative, quantitative, or mixed methodology, and the results could be compared to the global perspective of geographical location, majority religion, and economic status. Overall, this study contributes an empirical assessment on resolving doubts over the role of the political struggle in applying the concept of good enough governance to govern the emerging smart city societies from the perspective of changes in citizens' value propositions. The generated insights underline the critical role that smart societies play in establishing smart cities [50–52].

Acknowledgements

This chapter, with permission from the copyright holder, is a reproduced version of the following journal article: Lim, S., Malek, J., & Yigitcanlar, T. (2021). Post-materialist values of smart city societies: International comparison of public values for good enough governance. *Future Internet* 13(8), 201.

References

1. Yigitcanlar, T., Han, H., Kamruzzaman, M., Ioppolo, G., Sabatini-Marques, J. (2019). The making of smart cities: Are Songdo, Masdar, Amsterdam, San Francisco and Brisbane the best we could build? *Land Use Policy* 88, 104187.
2. Komninos, N., Panori, A., Kakderi, C. (2019). Smart cities beyond algorithmic logic: Digital platforms, user engagement and data science. In: *Smart Cities in the Post-Algorithmic Era: Integrating Technologies, Platforms and Governance*; Komninos, N. and Kakderi, C., (Eds.). Edward Elgar: Northampton, USA, pp. 1–15.
3. Zheng, C., Yuan, J., Zhu, L., Zhang, Y., Shao, Q. (2020). From digital to sustainable: A scientometric review of smart city literature between 1990 and 2019. *Journal of Cleaner Production* 258, 120689.
4. Kummitha, R.K.R., Crutzen, N. (2017). How do we understand smart cities? An evolutionary perspective. *Cities* 67, 43–52.
5. Kitchin, R., Lauriault, T.P., Mcardle, G. (2016). Smart cities and the politics of urban data. In: *Smart Urbanism: Utopian Vision or False Dawn?*; Marvin, S., Luque-Ayala, A., and McFarlane, C., (Eds.). Routledge: London, pp. 16–33.
6. Yigitcanlar, T., Corchado, J.M., Mehmood, R., Li, R.Y.M., Mossberger, K., Desouza, K. (2021). Responsible urban innovation with local government artificial intelligence (AI): A conceptual framework and research agenda. *Journal of Open Innovation: Technology, Market and Complexity* 7, 71.
7. Hartswood, M., Grimpe, B., Jirotka, M., Anderson, S. (2014). Towards the ethical governance of smart society. In: *Social Collective Intelligence*; D. Miorandi et al., (Eds.). Springer: Switzerland, 3–30.
8. Staletić, N., Labus, A., Bogdanović, Z., Despotović-Zrakić, M., & Radenković, B. (2020). Citizens' readiness to crowdsource smart city services: A developing country perspective. *Cities* 107, 102883.
9. Mckinsey Global Institute. (2018). *Smart Cities: Digital Solutions for a More Livable Future*. Mckinsey & Company: New York.
10. Rotta, M.J.R., Sell, D., dos Santos Pacheco, R.C., Yigitcanlar, T. (2019). Digital commons and citizen coproduction in smart cities: Assessment of Brazilian municipal e-government platforms. *Energies* 12, 2813.
11. Meijer, A., Bolívar, M.P.R. (2013). Governing the smart city: Scaling-up the search for socio-techno synergy. In: *Proceedings of the European Group for Public Administration (EGPA)*, Edinburgh, Scotland, 11–13 September 2013; pp. 100–113.
12. World Bank. (2021). *Good Governance and Its Benefits on Economic Development: An Overview of Current Trends*. Available online: https://pdf4pro.com/cdn/good-governance-and-its-benefits-on-economic-development-442998.pdf (accessed 20 April 2021).
13. Grindle, M.S. (2004). Good enough governance: Poverty reduction and reform in developing countries. *Government: An International Journal of Policy Administration and Institutions* 17, 525–548.

14. Grindle, M.S. (2007). Good enough governance revisited. *Development Policy Review* 25, 553–574.
15. Premat, C. (2016). Smart cities in a digital nation: Are Swedish cities enough innovative? In: *Smarter as the New Urban Agenda A Comprehensive View of the 21st Century City*; J.R. Gil-Garcia et al., (Eds.). Springer: Cham, Switzerland, pp. 207–224.
16. Cheng, K.H., Cheah, T.C. (2020). A study of Malaysia's smart cities initiative progress in comparison of neighbouring countries (Singapore & Indonesia). *Journal of Critical Reviews* 7, 47–54.
17. Yau, K.L.A., Lau, S.L., Chua, H.N., Ling, M.H., Iranmanesh, V., Kwan, S.C.C. (2016). Greater Kuala Lumpur as a smart city: A case study on technology opportunities. In: *8th International Conference on Knowledge and Smart Technology (KST)*, Chiangmai, Thailand, 3–6 February 2016; pp. 96–101.
18. Bokolo, A.J., Majid, M.A., Romli, A. (2018). A trivial approach for achieving smart city: A way forward towards a sustainable society. In: *The 21st Saudi Computer Society National Computer Conference (NCC)*, IEEE, Saudi Arabia, 25–26 April 2018. pp. 1–6.
19. Malek, J.A., Lim, S.B., Yigitcanlar, T. (2021). Social inclusion indicators for building citizen-centric smart cities: A systematic literature review. *Sustainability* 13, 376.
20. Lim, S.B., Malek, J.A., Hussain, M.Y., Tahir, Z. (2018). Citizen participation in building citizen-centric smart cities. *Geografia* 14, 42–53.
21. Lim, S.B., Malek, J.A., Hussain, M.Y., Tahir, Z. (2019). The behaviours and job positions of citizens in smart cities' development. *Planning Malaysia* 17, 133–145.
22. Lim, S.B., Malek, J.A., Hussain, M.Y., Tahir, Z. (2020). Participation in e-government services and smart city programs: A case study of Malaysian local authority. *Planning Malaysia* 18, 300–312.
23. Lim, S.B., Malek, J.A., Hussain, M.Y., Tahir, Z. (2020). Malaysia Smart City Framework: A trusted framework for shaping smart Malaysian citizenship? In: *Handbook of Smart Cities*; Augusto, J.C. (Ed.). Springer International Publishing: Cham, pp. 1–24.
24. Wok, S., Mohamed, S. (2017). Internet and social media in Malaysia: Development, challenges and potentials. In: *The Evolution of Media Communication*; Acuña, B.P., (Ed.). Intechopen: London, pp. 45–64.
25. Lim, S.B., Malek, J.A., Hussain, M.Y., Tahir, Z., Saman, N.H.M. (2021). SDGs, smart urbanisation, and politics: Stakeholder partnerships and environmental cases in Malaysia. *Journal of Sustainability Science and Management* 16, 190–219.
26. World Bank. (2021). *World Bank Country and Lending Groups*. Available online: https://datahelpdesk.worldbank.org/knowledgebase/articles/906519 (accessed 1 May 2021).
27. Serajuddin, U., Hamadeh, N. (2021). *New World Bank Country Classifications by Income Level: 2020–2021*. Available online: https://blogs.worldbank.org/opend ata/new-world-bank-country-classifications-income-level-2020-2021 (accessed 1 May 2021).
28. Noack, R. (2015). *World's Least Religious Countries*. Available online: www.washing tonpost.com/news/worldviews/wp/2015/04/14/map-these-are-the-worlds%02least-religious-countries/ (accessed 1 May 2021).
29. Worldometer. (2021). *Countries in the World by Population*. Available online: www. worldometers.info/world-population/population-by-country/ (accessed 1 May 2021).
30. Feng, B. (2013). *Chinese Respondents Top Materialism Poll*. Available online: https://sinosphere.blogs.nytimes.com/2013/12/20/chinese-respondents-top-materialism-poll/?mtrref=undefined&assetType=PAYWALL (accessed 1 May 2021).
31. Haerpfer, C., Inglehart, R., Moreno, A., Welzel, C., Kizilova, K., J., D.-M., Lagos, M., Norris, P., Ponarin, E., Puranen, B. (2020). *World Values Survey: Round*

Seven – Country-Pooled Datafile JD Systems Institute & WVSA Secretariat: Madrid, Spain & Vienna, Austria.

32. Cohen, J. (1988). *Statistical Power Analysis for the Behavioral Sciences*, 2nd ed; Lawrence Erlbaum Associates: Hillsdale, NJ.

33. Alemán, J., Woods, D. (2016). Value orientations from the World Values Survey: How comparable are they cross-nationally? *Comparative Political Studies* 49, 1039–1067.

34. Inglehart, R.F. (2016). After postmaterialism: An essay on China, Russia and the United States: A comment. *Canadian Journal of Sociology* 41, 213–222.

35. Uhlaner, L.M., Thurik, R., Hutjes, J. (2002). *Post-materialism as a Cultural Factor Influencing Entrepreneurial Activity across Nations*. Erasmus University Rotterdam: Zoetermeer, Netherland.

36. Economist Intelligence Unit (EIU). (2020). *Democracy Index 2020: In Sickness and in Health?* Economist Intelligence Unit: London, UK.

37. Inglehart, R.F. (2021). *Religion's Sudden Decline: What's Causing It, and What Comes Next?* Oxford University Press: Oxford, UK.

38. Banerjee, R. (2016). *On the Interpretation of World Values Survey Trust Question – Global Expectations vs. Local Beliefs*. Institute for the Study of Labor, University of Bonn: Bonn, Germany.

39. Curini, L., Jou, W., Memoli, V. (2013). How moderates and extremists find happiness: Ideological orientation, citizen-government proximity, and life satisfaction. *International Political Science Review* 2, 129–152.

40. Inglehart, R. (1971). The silent revolution in Europe: Intergenerational change in post-industrial societies. *American Political Science Review* 65, 991–1017.

41. Inglehart, R. (2016). Modernization, existential security and cultural change: Reshaping human motivations and society. In: *Advances in Culture and Psychology*; Gelfand, M., Chiu, C.Y., and Hong, Y.-Y., (Eds.). Oxford University Press: Oxford, UK.

42. Inglehart, R., Welzel, C. (2005). *Modernization, Cultural Change, and Democracy: The Human Development Sequence*. Cambridge University Press: Cambridge, UK.

43. Cardullo, P., Kitchin, R. (2019). Being a 'citizen' in the smart city: Up and down the scaffold of smart citizen participation in Dublin, Ireland. *GeoJournal* 84, 1–13.

44. Metaxiotis, K., Carrillo, F.J., Yigitcanlar, T. (2010). *Knowledge-Based Development for Cities and Societies: Integrated Multi-Level Approaches*. IGI Global: Hersey, PA, USA.

45. Green, B. (2019). *The Smart Enough City: Putting Technology in Its Place to Reclaim Our Urban Future*. MIT Press: Cambridge, MA.

46. Yigitcanlar, T., Kamruzzaman, M. (2019). Smart cities and mobility: Does the smartness of Australian cities lead to sustainable commuting patterns? *Journal of Urban Technology* 26, 21–46.

47. Giffinger, R., Fertner, C., Kramar, H., Kalasek, R., Pichler, N., Meijers, E. (2007). *Smart Cities: Ranking of European Medium-sized Cities*. TU Vienna: Wien.

48. Preston, S., Mazhar, M.U., Bull, R. (2020). Citizen engagement for co-creating low carbon smart cities: Practical lessons from Nottingham City Council in the UK. *Energies* 13, 6615.

49. United Cities and Local Governments (UCLG). (2016). *Executive Summary of Co-creating the Urban Future: The Agenda of Metropolises, Cities and Territories*. UCLG: Barcelona, Spain.

50. Yigitcanlar, T., Desouza, K., Butler, L., Roozkhosh, F. (2020). Contributions and risks of artificial intelligence (AI) in building smarter cities: Insights from a systematic review of the literature. *Energies* 3, 1473.
51. Yigitcanlar, T., Kankanamge, N., Vella, K. (2021). How are smart city concepts and technologies perceived and utilized? A systematic geo-Twitter analysis of smart cities in Australia. *Journal of Urban Technology* 28, 1–2, 135–154.
52. Lim, S., Malek, J., Yigitcanlar, T. (2021). Postmaterialist values of smart city societies: International comparison of public values for good enough governance. *Future Internet* 13(8), 201.

9 Augmenting Community Engagement

9.1 Introduction

The last decade has presented many challenges for cities around the world. First and foremost, urban migration continued to rise as projections estimated the world's urban population to be as high as 68%. As of 2020, North America's urban population was estimated at 83%, Australia at 80%, and Europe at 75% [1]. The past two years have also seen the COVID-19 pandemic challenge city resilience and slow forward-looking policy in response to handling the immediate emergency and uncertainty about a future "post-COVID-19" recovery [2]. Rapid population growth in cities often requires changes in the urban landscape to accommodate for new housing, mobility, and other shared services. These changes can often affect large amounts of the pre-existing population.

For these changes to be well-suited to both new and existing populations, city administrations will often look to community engagement strategies that hope to inform and consult with those most affected. In doing so, city administrations can attempt to ensure their decision is more defensible against critiques and the project is less likely to encounter roadblocks or pushback. The concept of City 4.0 introduces a new paradigm in which city administrations utilise digital technologies to connect all city stakeholders in a way that produces more sustainable urban outcomes. Furthermore, community engagement is a broad term used in an urban context to describe the different types of engagement from citizens in urban issues [3]. While research can often discuss this in terms of participatory planning [4,5,6], we utilise the term community engagement because it is a term shared by both researchers and city administrations alike.

Research on community engagement puts a strong focus on the politics of participation and how different approaches to community engagement can have vastly different results [7,8]. Participatory and collaborative approaches particularly look at broadening the base of stakeholders involved, and especially at "giving a voice" to traditionally marginalised groups [9,10]. The community engagement literature has seen a few interesting new developments in participatory design methodologies [11], interventions within public space [9,12], or applications of novel technologies [4] that address the challenge of inclusion. Furthermore, the COVID-19 pandemic has accelerated the adoption of QR codes and remote communication, whilst

DOI: 10.1201/9781003403647-11

Facebook's announcement of their "metaverse" plan brings concepts of mixed reality and blockchain to the mainstream, offering new opportunities for technologically mediated interactions in community engagement processes. Likewise, the new and popular city blueprints, such as smart cities or City 4.0, also underline the crucial importance of community engagement [13–16]. City 4.0 utilises technological developments and digitalisation to transform local public services and the local economy. It leverages these digital technologies and data to connect citizens, producing sustainable and desired urban, environmental, and societal outcomes for all.

In the context above, augmented reality (AR) is gaining attention as an enabler of situated engagement [17], improved urban conversation [18], and participation in cities [4]. AR allows digital information to be situated in physical space, so in an urban context, development details can be shared between stakeholders at the physical location or displayed and embodied at scale. The main affordance of AR—to overlay digital information over the physical world—is touted as a key driver in encouraging engagement with planning proposals, or in consulting with citizens about future developments [5,18,19]. Whilst there has been research into what this can mean for co-design in participatory planning, it is noted that the greater political systems in place still ultimately decide the face of participation in any given engagement process [4]. As such, a critique of AR or the implementation of any novel technology in cities is that, while the technology may offer new interactions, without a fundamental shift in the political relationship between councils and citizens, the technology will simply offer new opportunities for top-down "engagement theatre" and consensus-building activities.

Our research studied four different AR experiences intended to explore bottom-up and middle-out forms of engagement. The experiences ranged from the re-creation of existing community engagement methods in AR to entirely new interaction paradigms used to blend physical and digital.

- The city builder: This experience presents a list of options that allow the user to build their own city in augmented reality. Each option queues a separate musical loop, so that they end with a unique city and song. This experience was intended to test how AR could offer new interactions for gathering feedback from the community and visualise the results of citizen choices back to the participant in real time.
- The city spaces quiz: This experience acted like an augmented reality photo gallery, showing photos of space designed for cars or for people. It was designed to highlight the large amount of space required by cars, compared to people. Users would be quizzed on what level of scale they thought the photo represented. We intended this to be a form of interactive and educational tool that would help us gauge how receptive individuals are to education delivered through this medium.
- Bridges for Experience: This experience displayed 3D models of different bridges overlayed across a map of Brisbane River. Showcasing the potential to demonstrate future development plans to citizens in AR. Like the above

experience, we wanted to understand how users would react to an AR experience that mimicked more traditional community consultation strategies.

- The portals: This final experience displayed a portal in physical space that users could walk through to enter a virtual city. They could walk around this virtual city and experience a virtual world situated in the same space as the physical world.

These experiences were offered as "probes" to demonstrate different interaction paradigms in context and understand the opportunities and challenges of adopting AR technology in community engagement practices. We offered these experiences firstly to participants as part of a city-wide STEAM festival that lasted three weeks and secondly in a half-day workshop with four participants.

What emerged from our findings was that a key value of augmented reality for improving community engagement practices is not just about the unique interaction paradigms it affords, but more so about what opportunities it represents for the individual citizen within the community engagement political dynamic. Participants often discussed the feelings of agency that our city builder and portal experiences offered, and that while the interaction itself was novel, it was more that the participant felt that their voice was heard and that they were contributing. Participants were much less interested in our one-way informative experiences like the gallery, and much more interested in the experiences that allowed them to create for themselves.

Therefore, we contribute that, while AR affords us interesting opportunities to overlay digital information in physical locations, this is perhaps only relevant in community engagement when it empowers a sense of agency in the individual engaging with it. Simply put, a re-creation of existing engagement processes in AR is unlikely to be successful purely because of AR's affordances, however, AR's unique affordances do allow for an improved sense of agency for individuals in public space and a rethinking of the greater engagement experience. This was evident in the responses of our participants between the city builder and the Bridges for Experience. While the Bridges for Experience and city builder both use AR to overlay digital information on the physical world, the city builder was much more positively received due to the information being created and customised to hold significance to the end user.

Below, we explore the literature surrounding community engagement, participatory planning, and urban human–computer interaction (HCI). We do this to explain our use of the term community engagement and situate this focus within the participatory planning literature. Furthermore, it is important for us to draw on the urban HCI literature to contextualise our findings and show how urban HCI research has previously conceptualised the use of AR. Following this, we discuss our early conversations with stakeholders, our reasoning for and design of each study, and the results that we found. We then highlight the areas of interest that emerged from these studies before finally discussing some interesting directions for future urban AR research.

9.2 Literature Background

9.2.1 *Community Engagement and Participatory Planning*

We start this related works section by highlighting the literature surrounding community engagement and participatory planning. In most urban research, participatory planning is the term used to highlight the relationship between councils and citizens in relation to the development of urban areas [6]. However, the term participatory can carry slightly different meanings that shift the focus of research in the area. In the context of participatory design, participatory planning will often focus on the individual and design interventions, such as media façades, urban screens, and mixed reality, that encourage participation in design with individuals from the bottom up [9,20]. In other cases, the focus of participatory planning research is more political, analysing varying levels of civic participation in relation to greater democracy. In particular, Legacy's [8] paper highlights the way a large majority of the participatory planning literature tends to analyse top-down and bottom-up perspectives and how they can affect participation. While these topics certainly are not mutually exclusive, it is worth noting how the focus can shift from participation as an individual design activity to participation as a civic duty or participation within the political process.

Smith [6] presents an interesting summary of this, defining the rational and consensual aspects of participatory planning. The rational aspect considers that "individuals are more intimately involved with environmental changes; they can provide a planning process with information and judgements regarding local systems". The consensual aspects consider "societal units, being involved in the determination of planning processes related to the domain of that societal unit, which may lead to a further integration of power with authority, a move toward a democratic society". This theoretical basis for participatory planning [6] posits these two aspects in a way that has been accurately reflected in the analysis of research for years to come. We relate the rational aspects more closely to participatory design research, and the consensual aspect as the political focus of participation.

One constant in participatory planning research, however, is its focus on planning processes. That is, most of the participatory planning research understandably conceptualises participatory planning as something related to a specific project that will invite change in the urban area. A gap that arises in this literature is that its strong focus on planning processes and the politics of participation narrow its focus in such a way that it can miss the other motivations for engagement exhibited by citizens. To further this, community engagement literature has covered engagements between different stakeholders in medical research, such as the cultural barriers regarding the uptake of a vaccine [21], or in education research, to help embed cultural knowledge in an educational curriculum [22]. Aligning with the community engagement terminology, we are able to draw insights from city administration practice and the broader engagement literature perspectives, inclusive of participation, planning, and politics, but not restricted to these lenses. With this in mind, we utilise the term community engagement for two reasons: (a) community engagement is not specifically tied to the planning and development of an urban area, but more so to citizens' engagement with councils, and (b) community engagement is often utilised as a tool by city administrations within participatory planning processes. In the first instance, community engagement allows us to investigate the relationship between councils and citizens from a broader perspective, rather than in relation specifically to urban planning. Secondly, often in practice, community engagement is the terminology used for strategies that encourage broader participation. In this chapter, we often refer to traditional community engagement strategies and therefore feel it relevant to use this terminology as our basis for comparison.

9.2.2 Top Down, Bottom Up, and Middle Out

When analysing community engagement strategies and the relationship between city administrations and citizens, there are often three different relationships that are discussed: top down, bottom up, and more recently, middle out.

Top-down relationships position engagement as led by city administrations or governments, and often focuses on the way that city administrations consult with communities or deliver information to communities [8,23]. This form of engagement, when critiqued, is said to be more performative or sees the role of the citizen as tokenistic [24,25]. This is often because the decisions regarding the planning have been made, and community engagement is used as a strategy to inform citizens of the decisions. In other cases, it is found that the policy environments and power dynamics between varying levels of government can often sideline community objectives [26].

Bottom-up relationships position engagement as something that empowers individuals to create, design, and actively participate in interventions at a grassroots level [23,27]. While it could be said that some bottom-up interventions could still be empowered by city administrations, they are typically led by a community group, social movement, or individuals and look to collaborate on decision-making according to the chosen intervention. In this way, community engagement is a more collaborative process than the post-decision-making process of the top-down perspective. However, sometimes overlooked in these positions is the challenge of scale and the individual's perceived relevance of the project [26].

Bottom-up projects tend to be driven by individuals or community groups, and the shared purpose of that group adds perceived relevance of the intervention to all members of that group [3]. The projects of city administrations, however, can sometimes be so large that they affect a much wider group of the population and, as a result, it is increasingly difficult to ensure the engagement feels personal and relevant to everyone affected [3]. The final body of literature follows middle-out engagement.

Middle-out engagement looks to draw on the collective knowledge of all actors to provide opportunities for collaborative community engagement processes. The pop-up interventions of Fredericks and Caldwell [9] enlisted the help of both councils and local community stakeholders in their design, implementation, and deployment. These interventions utilised the strengths of both groups of stakeholders to ensure the interventions could be deployed at scale and for the benefit of broader councils, whilst still drawing on the knowledge and design of individuals at a local level to ensure their relevance and value to that local community. More local, state, and national urban policy is moving in a similar direction with a recent white paper from England's Ministry of Housing, Communities and Local Government proposing that better information be delivered to local communities, and technologically mediated solutions be developed that allow for a more democratic system between residents, communities, entrepreneurs, businesses, and councils [28]. Furthermore, research by Usavagovitwong et al. [29] highlights the concept of "community architects" across Asia, specifically demonstrating the value of architects in enabling a link between poor communities, local organisations, planning and development agencies, and broader government initiatives. In both of these works, the value that comes from enabling engagement between all city stakeholders and adopting a middle-out engagement approach is made clear.

Our research aimed to explore the value of a middle-out engagement approach, by partnering with local councils to host our digital experiences and offering interactions that specifically elicited feedback and knowledge from individuals and included their participation through creation within the experience (Table 9.1). We ultimately wished to explore how this approach can develop into more conversational platforms between citizens and councils, where the middle-out ethos can be coupled with urban HCI interventions that contribute to a broader city platform.

Table 9.1 Engagement approaches

Approach	Definition	Advantages	Disadvantages
Top-down	Led by city-administration. Tends to deliver information regarding planning decisions	Can deliver information at scale, and utilise existing IT infrastructure	Often feels "tokenistic" as citizens are not included in decision-making. Little engagement from citizens as perceived as irrelevant and impersonal
Bottom-up	Led by individuals or community groups, designs grass-roots solutions with citizens	Relevance to particular group, further engagement due to personal feel. Collaboration before decision-making	Difficult to scale, solutions specific to smaller urban groups. Often niche issues, and under-resourced
Middle-out	Aims to utilise knowledge of all actors, enlisting the help of councils to facilitate, and individuals to contribute	Utilises the value of all stakeholders, facilitates a relationship between stakeholders that is usually challenged	Limited previous work to draw on. Broader group of stakeholders makes project planning and execution much more difficult

9.2.3 Urban Human–Computer Interaction

Urban HCI is often discussed in research in both the context of community engagement and the context of social movements and digital activism. Like the way in which participation can be viewed through a political lens and a more design lens, the intersection of public space and technology often explores the way technology can shape the political landscape at a grassroots level, and the way individuals can use technology to create and design their own communities or experiences within that space [30]. Vadiati [31] highlighted the shift technology has on public space into an augmented urban space continuing beyond its physical boundaries. Furthermore, the way this matter affects urban governance was discussed, noting the narrative across research that ICTs are ultimately activating more citizens who would not engage in urban matters through traditional outlets [31].

While the influence of communicative technologies in urban space is increasingly evident, there are still many facets to explore around their implementation, the interactions they offer, and how they may or may not shift the current relationship between citizens and city administrations. Analysis of digital activism and citizen science [18,32–34] has highlighted the power for communicative technologies to empower individuals and social movements, such as the global effects of #MeToo and #BlackLivesMatter; however, the fact that these issues can transcend national boundaries can sometimes be to the detriment of their relevance or impact at the local level [18]. Alternatively, e-participation research will often investigate digitally mediated participation at a more local or state level, although this tends to revert to a focus on participation in planning or governance processes [35–37]. Ultimately, while there is a growing amount of research looking into the implementation of novel technologies at a local level, most of the focus lands on how these technologies can augment planning processes.

AR has been utilised many times in recent years as a tool to test new co-design methods for city planning. Its strengths as a visual communicator—allowing users to place objects and visualise proposals—is often touted as a key reason for its value in co-design methods, and its ability to run on modern mobile devices is seen as an incentive for younger audiences. In Bandung, Indonesia, augmented reality was used as a learning tool for future environmental planning. In this way, augmented reality allowed for more interactive storytelling that could combine local folklore with environmental challenges and was found to be adopted by the students in such a way that they could communicate with other community groups through augmented reality to collaborate on solutions to environmental challenges and educate those less aware of environmental issues [38].

Furthermore, in New Zealand, Allen et al. [39], developed an application that allowed members of the public to visualise 3D models of new building designs at their proposed physical location. The participants responded extremely positively to using AR as a visual tool in this way. Since 2011, many similar studies that use AR have taken place to co-design urban spaces, and in particular buildings and future developments [5,40]. Lastly, a paper by Saßmannshausen et al. [4] highlighted the value of these AR tools as extensions of community engagement practices that can entice a younger audience's participation. While this work was still grounded in planning activities, it also explored how AR can be used as an informative tool, a co-determination, and a co-design tool. In this context, it was not just about visualising existing plans, but about encouraging participation in the design of these tools that would then visualise information.

One aspect that we find particularly interesting is how using AR for participatory planning can open up new co-design possibilities outside the immediate realm of planning. That is, by enabling users to place and visualise digital objects in physical space, we can also enable new possibilities for collaboration between these individuals in public space. Furthermore, the development of algorithmic techniques allows for a procedural generation of building designs, so that architectural expertise can be generated without the need for expertise from the individual citizen [41]. In particular, Potts [42] analysed the way PokemonGo and augmented reality games (ARGs) could activate public spaces, increasing community interaction and facilitating the exploration of a city. Furthermore, numerous studies have explored the impact of AR to reappropriating public space [43,44]. These studies highlight the way these tools can be used for empowering individuals in urban space, not just in a planning context, but in the broader relationship between citizens, city administrations, and public space. Our research seems to sit at the intersection of these topics.

In sum, we use the term community engagement because we understand AR's affordances to extend beyond participation in planning activities and empower more broad community engagement. Having said that, we are not purely focused on the political empowerment of communities in opposition to city administrations in the city–citizen political paradigm. Lastly, while we recognise the value of AR as a visual tool in cities, in this work, we wish to explore what that means for improving the engagement of an individual within their community and public space, especially considering the smart city or City 4.0 context.

9.3 Methodology

This research took place over a period of about 12 months across several meetings with relevant stakeholders and two main studies. Our team consisted of two interaction design researchers and a post-doctoral game developer with expert knowledge of Unity3D and ARCore. This research is part of a broader exploration of augmented sociality [45] that seeks to find new opportunities for a community-oriented, user-generated mixed reality. Augmented reality itself is most easily understood as technology that overlays digital information over the physical world [18].

Preliminary research into smart cities [46] highlighted a shift in focus for city administrations from implementing technologies to address the assumed needs of urban challenges to instead using communicative technologies to talk to citizens and understand what challenges existed [18].

Given that our aim was to explore new opportunities for a socialised AR, we reached out to local stakeholders to understand their perspective on the state of current community engagement practices. For sake of clarity, we summarise the main insights gained from the stakeholder meetings in this section, because these informed the design of the four AR probes adopted in the subsequent studies. The findings from the two main studies are presented and discussed in the next sections.

The first study was conducted in the wild [47,48] during a public festival. As Rogers noted, research in the wild "is likely to reveal more the kinds of problems and behaviors people will have and adopt if they were to use a novel device at home, at work, or elsewhere" [47]. While studies in naturalistic settings often follow preliminary lab studies, we decided to conduct this preliminary exploration in a relatively uncontrolled setting with the aim to reach a wide public audience and gain an understanding of general expectations, technical challenges, and public interest.

The second study, conducted over six months after the public exhibition, consisted of a half-day workshop with four participants, during which specific thoughts on community engagement and the AR probes were shared and discussed. The workshop adopted an approach inspired by future technology workshops [49,50] and cross-cultural dialogical probes [51].

9.3.1 Stakeholder Consultations

Initial discussions involved employees of Brisbane city council in various offices with responsibilities spanning across community engagement and digital services. Since these consultations involved all participants in their professional roles, with a view of discussing possible collaborations and partnerships, these conversations were not conducted under the project's ethical framework and no "informed consent" declarations were collected at the meetings. We nevertheless omit reporting on their detailed roles or positions to maintain confidentiality. No audio or video recordings were made of these meetings and the summary below is based on the authors' detailed notes taken during the meetings. To ensure the participants' viewpoints are correctly represented, we shared a draft of this paper with them, seeking comments and inviting corrections.

The discussions focused on the technologies that were in use or that the stakeholders were potentially interested in and how these played a role in different community engagement strategies. We also discussed, in their view, how augmented reality may be utilised to address the challenge of community engagement at scale.

9.3.1.1 Opportunities

It emerged that collaboration and engagement were among the biggest use cases for introducing technological innovation in public projects, with a particular focus on connected community spaces and socialised or virtual platforms. The principle of fostering agency and sense of ownership was an important driver, in line with existing initiatives currently supported through more traditional means.

One important aspect was the drive to support existing community groups in implementing local engagement programmes and to remain financially viable, rather than exclusively focus on large-scale centralised support. Supporting these localised groups involves a deep understanding of how they operate, both internally and within the complex ecosystem of municipal offices and regulations.

Overall, a specific interest emerged for tools and applications to help deliver infrastructure projects. This involves supporting various goals and phases in a typical infrastructure project, from seeking feedback in the designs, informing the public on intended outcomes and benefits, and engaging with the community to help understand the project and create the best possible experience. This is within the understanding that councils ultimately own the assets and high-level planning decisions have typically already been made at the time consultation begins. It was noted that these processes are currently mostly supported by rather low-tech tools, often paper-based, or at best, online services.

9.3.1.2 Challenges

It also emerged that the downside of innovation rests in its inherent high level of risk. Decisions on adopting technological innovation are very sensitive to political cycles, and the availability of resources and funds can be ephemeral.

A particular emphasis was placed on the journey to deploy specific technologies within established council procedures. The need for infrastructure, the challenge of data management, and the community expectations and understanding of new technologies all pose problems.

A challenging goal also emerged from drawing in those who are hesitant and support the accessibility on a community scale with the aim of making the city more inclusive to vulnerable and homeless people. Symmetrically, an important but challenging goal was identified to explore new ways to gather, analyse, and use data from community engagement tools and initiatives.

9.3.2 Augmented Reality Probes

Following our preliminary stakeholder meetings, we distilled several design inspirations that we further developed through discussion in the research team and based on the relevant literature and previous works:

- Engage new audiences and members of the public who are otherwise hesitant to participate in community initiatives;
- Explore synergies with data mining, visualisation, and data-driven decision-making;
- Explore unique affordances of augmented reality, especially the appeal of visual interactive tools, localised contents and interactions, and similarities or resonance with virtual reality;
- Maintain a focus on deployment and accessibility by a broad audience.

While developing the AR probes, an opportunity arose to present them to a very large audience as part of the Curiocity festival. This STEAM festival has a strong

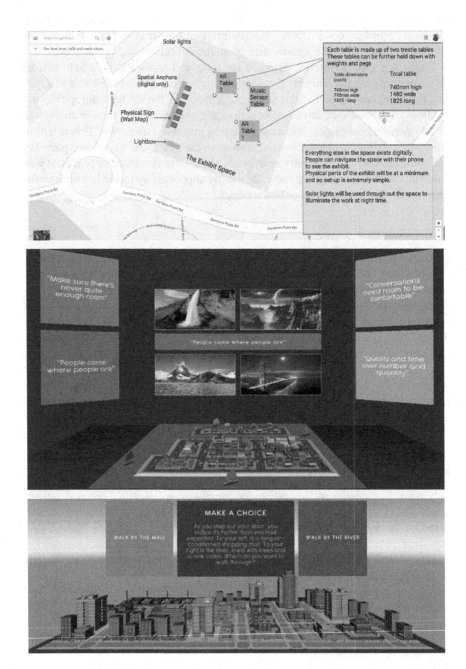

Figure 9.1 Initial designs brainstormed for the Curiocity festival.

focus on using science, technology, engineering, arts, and math to curate interesting public exhibits throughout Brisbane. Its goal is to encourage people to navigate around the city from experience to experience learning about both the city and the various applications of STEAM. The festival ran for three weeks throughout March and hosted over 60 installations, at least two-thirds of which were utilising augmented and virtual reality.

Curiocity aligned extremely well with our initial research agenda as it allowed us to showcase the experiences to the public and to gauge an interest in the public for augmented reality usage under the broader theme of the festival.

However, this opened our research to a whole new spectrum of challenges. Of course, being hosted by the Curiocity festival, the location of our installation was decided for us, which was outdoors. Secondly, being a part of a broader festival meant our participants would not be solely engaging with our exhibition and therefore would have little prior understanding of our installation and its purpose. Challenges like these shaped a few design decisions as it was important that we developed something intuitive, playful, and that could work outdoors.

A range of ideas were brainstormed and assessed based on likely environmental challenges, availability of material or software libraries, and COVID-19 constraints for sharing devices or manipulating surfaces. We considered offering a city builder experience, a gallery or quiz experience, a table with a Lego-city and sensors that trigger music, and a final AR wall that would overlay digital information on top of a Brisbane city map. These can be seen in Figure 9.1.

An important factor in refining the design ideas was to offer a selection of different AR interactions and replicate typical engagement methods. The quiz would be an interesting way to explore how councils could inform citizens in AR, whilst the map would show models in AR and highlight the potential for AR as a visualisation tool. However, the city builder, which had been chosen as the first experience, was instead intended to transform previous engagement processes and highlight the way interactive games could elicit the same information as a survey in a more playful way.

9.3.2.1 Printing Markers

For these AR experiences to work on location, we had to decide whether we would use image recognition or GPS. We could either use spatial anchors to place the experiences in a physical space so that they would be triggered when a user pointed their phone at that location, or we could use image recognition and image markers so that the experience would trigger when the user pointed a device at a particular image. We decided on image recognition for the three table experiences, the city builder, gallery, and model bridges, and spatial anchors for the portal. A spatial anchor was more useful for the portal as it required the user to walk through it, so we could not have a physical obstacle in the way of that interaction.

We wanted to design the markers in such a way that they were recognisable by the image recognition software, whilst still interesting for the participants and indicative of the experience on offer. We decided to double the markers as instructions

Figure 9.2 Image recognition designs brainstormed for the Curiocity festival.

and measured them out so that they would cover the entire tables we had hired. The markers can be seen in Figure 9.2.

These markers had to be printed on a specific type of plastic board so that they were water resistant and would not warp in the outdoor area under different weather conditions. The weather resistance of the board was useful, although this added a reflective layer to the marker that caused issues with the image recognition once placed outside. Again, not being able to test these on location, the challenges of image recognition did not become apparent until the markers were in place.

9.3.3 The Experiences

"Future Cities for Future People" is an Android smartphone application that can be downloaded from the Google Play Store to play. The name is an intended reference to Jan Gehl [52], who largely inspired the ideas presented throughout the AR experiences. The experiences within the application are as follows.

9.3.3.1 City Builder

The first game is a city builder. We present an empty city grid to the user and ask them to make choices about what should be in the city. Each choice presented is also linked to a musical loop. Once the participant makes all of their choices, they are presented with a unique city and an accompanying song. The choices that we presented to the user are as shown in Table 9.2.

The choices that we presented to the participant are, of course, not mutually exclusive in a real-world city planning context and, furthermore, we did not present them with any bias as to what may or may not be the correct answer. In some cases, we could visualise the results of choices, such as parking lots and public transport, wherein the parking lots choice would take up much more city space than if public transport was selected. However, it was not our intention to attempt to simplify what may be extremely complex issues. Instead, it was about presenting a questionnaire in an interesting and playful way to see if there was potential for this kind of conversation between city administrations and citizens moving forward. With the user's consent, their interaction could be recorded so that the choices could be processed and analysed. Again, this was intended to demonstrate how these interactions could spur real-time conversation between councils and citizens.

Once users had built their city, they could also activate a street view by clicking on a section of road. This would transport the user to that part of the road, and rather than look at the grid, they were free to move their phone around in space and view the city they had built as if they were standing in it (Figure 9.3).

Table 9.2 City builder choices

Lay Roads	
Standard housing	*Highrise buildings*
Public services	
Parking lots	Public transport
Supermarket	Market stalls
Stadium	Observation tower
Opera house	Tourist hotel
Stadium	Gardens

Figure 9.3 The city builder screenshots of third person and first person street view.

9.3.3.2 Bridges for Experience

The second experience displays a map of Brisbane and its river. Across the river are interactable buttons that the user can press to see different 3D model bridges. These bridges were designed by students from Bochum's University of Applied Sciences as part of an assessment exploring the education of students within media architecture and their approach to bridge design. The experience allows the bridges to be viewed in 3D space hovering above the map of Brisbane and displays a small description as to why the bridges were designed as they were. This experience is intended to showcase the possibilities for community consultation through AR. Using AR, we could quickly demonstrate future bridge designs to the community, hoping to engage them and demonstrate a way in which councils could engage with

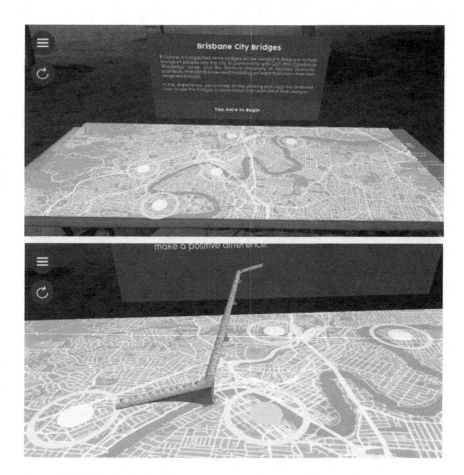

Figure 9.4 Bridges for Experience.

communities regarding future urban planning designs. Furthermore, it showcases the possibilities for university, industry, and council partnerships as 3D models can be exported from architecture programmes and displayed within AR applications (Figure 9.4).

9.3.3.3 City Spaces

The city spaces quiz is intended to be an interactive game that would help citizens think differently about a sense of scale in urban space. Taking much inspiration from Jan Gehl's book *Cities for People* [52], this game acts like a photo gallery in 3D space, displaying different photos of Brisbane's city environments to the participant. It showcases urban areas that are designed for cars, humans, and both, and

Figure 9.5 The city spaces quiz in augmented reality above the physical table markers.

aims to educate participants on the difference between human needs and needs for cars and the amount of space required for each (Figure 9.5).

9.3.3.4 City Portals

The final experience is a GPS-located AR portal. This portal exists at the physical location of the installation and can be interacted with by simply walking through it. Users can hold their camera up to the space to see the portal appear, and then walk through to experience an entirely virtual world. The above photos demonstrate how once inside the portal, the users' field of view becomes enveloped in the virtual environment. Here we hoped to demonstrate the affordances of AR as a situated and embodied interaction method (Figure 9.6).

Hold your phone over a table at the exhibit to begin an experience.

Hold your phone over a table at the exhibit to begin an experience.

Figure 9.6 The city portal.

9.3.4 The Participants

9.3.4.1 Study 1: Curiocity

Over the course of the 17-day festival, there were 90 downloads of the application. During the festival there was constant rain for roughly 5 days, and a COVID-19 lockdown for another three. As this installation was outside, this certainly played a part in the number of interactions we received. Of the 90 downloads, we received consent 125 times to receive data about the participants' choices. This number is greater because users were prompted every time they opened the application, so in some cases the participant may have used the application more than once, and therefore consented each time they used it. Of the 125 data logs retrieved, only 43 contained data regarding the users' specific interactions with the application. The remaining 82 displayed a "TEST" input, so that we know the application was opened but no further data were recorded. This tells us that no further experiences were triggered, which could be through user choice, or through a break in the application's functionality, such as the AR image recognition failing to work correctly.

9.3.4.2 Study 2: Workshop

This workshop took place indoors at our university campus with four participants, two men and two women, recruited via email. The participants were students, aged between 20 and 35, studying either computer science, architecture, or design. Each received a gift voucher as a token of our appreciation for their participation. Informed consent and image release forms were signed by all participants, and video and audio were recorded by the research team.

With all the challenges that the first study presented, it became clear that a second study was required to help gain further qualitative insights and allow for testing of the application in an indoor controlled setting. It was our aim to learn more about how participants interacted with the experiences at a qualitative level in a setting that would allow for a more focused discussion around their attitudes towards community engagement and augmented reality and allow them to test our application with support from our team in case there were any errors. The nature of Study 1 raised a few challenges and issues that Study 2 was able to compensate for. This workshop was inspired methodologically by Future Technology Workshops by Vavoula et al. [50]. In this particular methodology, the participants envisage future technologies and work backwards to co-design through current state activities. In our case, we wanted to break the pre-existing expectations surrounding augmented reality and community engagement to help them think about what community engagement could look like with this technology, rather than just what these technologies could replicate. The workshop ran in three sessions as outlined below:

- The first session ran for roughly 50 minutes and was strongly focused on how individuals perceived community engagement, and whether their perception of community engagement was always political. The discussion aimed to highlight the types of activities that the participants would engage with in their day-to-day life to understand what they might constitute as valid forms of participation just as much as political forms of participation.
- The second session ran for roughly 25 minutes and allowed each of the participants to use a tablet or phone to play with our AR experiences inside the workshop room. We had prepared each of the experiences on a separate table, and otherwise provided little instruction for the participants. We were particularly curious to see their entire interaction with the applications, from whether they would be able to understand and use them to their feedback and experience with them.
- After this, in the third session, we reconvened for a discussion surrounding the application to understand the participants' experiences with the AR experiences,

their attitudes towards them, and their thoughts on how or if they could be applied in a future community engagement context.

9.3.5 Analysis

Our research approach utilised both quantitative and qualitative methods. Our application can record all the choices that the user makes within. With the users' consent, we were able to record how they interact with each experience, the choices they make within that experience, and their total time spent in each experience. This provides us with an interesting quantitative picture, which was particularly useful in our first study when interviews were limited.

In the second study, we recorded the audio of each of the discussions as well as the video and photography of the participants' usage of our application. We attempted to use Dragon software to later transcribe the audio; however, the audio files failed to be recognised, so we transcribed the discussions ourselves. Of these discussions, we first read through the transcriptions separately, identifying some of our own perceptions of the data. We later had meetings to discuss our thoughts between authors as to the types of comments that had emerged from the transcriptions. Following this, we entered a more formal coding phase, reviewing the entire transcriptions multiple times to identify potential emerging themes.

9.4 Results

9.4.1 Curiocity Festival

Of the data collected, we recorded 206 total city builder choices and users entered a part of the city at the street view level 277 times. The average length of time users spent playing with the city builder was roughly three minutes. The remaining choices can be found below in Table 9.3.

Table 9.3 City builder choices

Choice	Options	Number of times chosen	Most popular
Choice 1	Standard housing	8	Highrise buildings
	Highrise buildings	15	
Choice 2	Parking lots	3	Public transport
	Public transport	19	
Choice 3	Supermarkets	5	Market stalls
	Market stalls	13	
Choice 4	Observation tower	15	Observation tower
	Stadium	3	
Choice 4	Opera house	9	Equal opera house
	Tourist hotel	9	and tourist hotel
Choice 5	Stadium	4	Gardens
	Gardens	13	

Table 9.4 City builder choices

Choice	Number of times selected
Bridge A	27
Bridge B	21
Bridge C	20
Bridge D	14
Bridge E	20

In this table, we have not included the button interactions that did not require the user to make a choice, such as the "Lay roads", "Public services", and "Explore" interactions. These interactions were mandatory and required the user to press them to move onto the next part of the game.

The bridge experience was triggered 27 times and the choices were as shown in Table 9.4.

The city spaces quiz was triggered 29 times and received 74 separate attempts to respond to its questions. The quiz would normally end after six different questions, but sometimes users would stop early or play the quiz multiple times. We displayed photos of Brisbane at different scales to the participants and asked them to guess whether this part of the city was at car scale (a highway), human scale (a quad or public space), or a combined scale (a market stall that had overtaken a street). We then recorded their answers for each. Of the 74 separate responses, we had 34 incorrect responses and 40 correct responses.

The final portal experience was triggered 40 times. This experience did not require any further interactions and therefore did not track any more information about the participant within the virtual environment. We simply recorded when they entered into and subsequently left the portal. The average time spent inside the virtual environment was roughly three minutes.

9.4.1.1 Observational Analysis

Firstly, many participants were not willing to download the application. Participants would walk past the installation or read about it, but upon realising they needed to download an application, they would stop their engagement. In other cases, the augmented reality aspect of the application would carry perceived complexity and act as a deterrent for individuals. Two comments heard were, "it is like the sims, except that was simple, now it's too technologically advanced", and "maybe we will download it when we get home". On average, roughly four to five people would walk past the exhibit each hour, but most would continue on to the next exhibit without downloading the application. Lastly, those who would interact with the installation and were happy to talk more about it were, interestingly, academics, architects, or retired couples.

Something that is perhaps not often discussed in the AR literature is the difficulty in delivering a consistent experience with the current technology, and even more so when it is set up outside and open to the public. In this scenario, the promise of using novel technology as part of a public festival to engage citizens completely blindsided us to the challenges of its successful implementation.

9.4.1.2 Technical Limitations

There were a few technical limitations that came with the development of this application.

Firstly, Android users had to have at least Android 8.0 or higher as the version of operating system on their device. A surprising number of devices were not compatible with this requirement, as this version of Android was only released in 2017.

Secondly, the quality of the camera on the device made a large difference as to whether it would recognise the markers in the physical space or not. Setting up this installation outdoors meant that the markers would catch a lot of sunlight. The markers were also printed on a PVC foam board so that in the case of rain or intense weather, they would not warp, fade, or have the image and colours run. This board was useful in durability, but surprisingly reflective and so, in full sun, it would often reflect light back at the device's cameras. On modern smartphones this presented little issue, as the cameras on these devices are quite high quality. However, we used tablets at the exhibit to lend to users who were not interested in downloading the application, and the cameras on these tablets struggled greatly to recognise the markers in full sunlight and, as a result, users were often unable to properly start the experience.

Thirdly, application size, processing power, and overall performance were all challenges that had to be prioritised in developing an easily accessible experience. We were acutely aware that asking participants to download an application to their device would add a layer of difficulty to the experience that would result in some users not taking interest and, as a result, we aimed to keep the application size as small as possible. This meant lowering the polygon count and resolutions of many of the objects within the experience. We managed to reduce the download size to 87 mb for the entire application and by reducing some resolution sizes and polygon count, we also hoped to increase performance across varying devices. Even so, performance was widely varied between modern phones and modern tablets. Smartphones would generally run the experiences with no framerate drops, although the phones would increase in temperature considerably within just a few minutes of playing. The tablets would often experience framerate drops instantly with the city builder experience and again would overheat considerably. Sometimes this overheating would result in even more framerate drops, which would result in the camera being unable to register the marker as well and the experience of jittering in and out of frame.

Lastly, whilst not an immediate issue, the low polygon counts of the application meant that the objects in the experience were reasonably simple and restricted our choices for the city builder or bridge to experience low-polygon assets. These low-polygon assets in some ways enhanced the playful nature of the experience but may have been less conducive to a believable or meaningful tool for community engagement. It was difficult to convey a level of weight to the users' choices and, as a result, may not have educated the user on urban planning as much as presented a simple fun experience.

9.4.1.3 Environmental Challenges

The festival began on 12 March 2021 and ran through till 28 March 2021. Brisbane is a sub-tropical city that tends to experience 25-degree weather for the majority of the year. March 2021 ended up being a surprisingly extreme weather period for Brisbane and, during the first two weeks of the festival, there was almost non-stop rain. This greatly limited the number of participants and really tested the durability of the installation. Daily checks were required to ensure the markers had not moved, bowed, or collected too much water. When the rain ceased, the temperatures would reach upwards of 30+ degrees and, during the middle of the day, the installation was so hot that it became almost completely unfeasible to expect participants to engage with our experiences. Furthermore, the reflectiveness of the markers would often confuse the image recognition software so that the augmented reality failed to trigger or the level of glare on the screen made it near impossible to see. While the installation was open to the public for three weeks, it only became usable for a few hours a day, a few days of the week. The final challenge was COVID-19, wherein during the final week of the festival, a spike in cases swept through Brisbane, eventuating in a snap lockdown.

9.4.2 Workshop Discussions

Below, we present the data from our workshops. While the data below cover a few different topics, there is an overarching discussion around agency both in an emotional sense—how the participant feels in the relationship between city and citizen—and a physical sense—how the interactions and controls provide the participant with agency in that moment.

The idea of agency was often discussed throughout the three sessions, where participants stressed the importance of feeling control, feeling heard, and feeling like their opinions were valued. Throughout the first session, there were many positive comments made about the way one council member had turned budgetary ideas for the suburb into a survey that residents could complete.

Participant A: "I remember a petition that he put out, which was very interesting for me, he sent it out to everybody who lives in that particular ward, and at that time I was living there, and it was a budget for improving different places within west end, and we as a resident could vote, and you didn't have to be a citizen, you just had to be a resident in west end, to vote where you wanted the money to go.

I thought that was very, very interesting because it was giving me agency in places that I use temporarily, but might not use in the future, and I still got a say right now".

Furthermore, in the second and third sessions, participants gave a lot of positive feedback towards the city builder experience purely because of the agency it offered.

Participant B: "that's why I would say the build your own city is interesting because I feel like I had a say. Right? So, I do respond by building, creating something, that means that I'm active in the sense of like having a real ownership of what the city is going to look like. So, you do have that agency over, at least you have this feeling, that you have agency, whereas, when you think about just responding or being informed, I'm not too sure to what extent you are actually engaged, or do you participate".

Participant C: "But I did like the opportunity to simulate my different choices, like, one city looks like this, and this is the music I get, and if I cancel, what happens if I do the opposite choices and it was very different and I found it rewarding to see my options matter in the game".

Alternatively, discussions around the design of the interface were focused on how the AR controls removed agency in a way that made the participants feel confused, or unable to see the value in AR specifically.

Participant D: "I just don't see why you need to make it AR for that experience, because I feel like you don't have much control, I mean from taking the perspective of a gamer, you have more control in the environment that you're in, but for that one, you can't even see to read the small text. Whereas, if it wasn't in AR, you could zoom, and you have more freedom".

Participant C: "Why do you need to walk around? When can you just sit down and move your mouse to navigate around the environment?"

Participant A: "When it goes to the interface, I think the written things shouldn't be with the visual, they should pop up before so that I know exactly what I'm seeing, and then I go into that interface and see it, and it should just be there as backup because it's pretty difficult to read, because it's so small".

The above comment was in relation to our design choice to include the interface in the augmented reality experience and that the instructions were floating positioned in physical space, rather than before or after the experience as a normal digital screen.

Participant C: "I was just thinking, I would see it as you can build your city on a desktop or normal mobile interface, and then when you want to see the city, you can portal yourself there and I think that's the only place where the AR makes sense".

A clear challenge in using novel technologies for community engagement is designing it in such a way that the user feels they have agency even though the technology is new and potentially complex. There are many factors in the design of the interface that can have unintended consequences, regarding the attitude of the user, that can shape their attitude towards the city administration overall. In our case, placing the interface within the AR resulted in some cases where participants felt that it was intentionally designed that way to give the illusion of agency without giving agency.

In this way, the interface and interactions of digital technologies are mediums through which to convey the attitudes or relationships from one stakeholder to another.

9.5 Findings and Discussion

The overarching aim of this research was to understand the potential for augmented reality to improve community engagement. The way augmented reality can allow users to visualise and interact with virtual environments in physical space creates a few interesting ways for councils to present information and modify consultation methods to feel more engaging. However, perhaps more important is the way that augmented reality can afford users agency over the space they occupy. Hence, the focus should not be on augmented reality solely as a technology, but instead as a new interaction paradigm that allows citizens an embodied interaction in the context of a specific place. As the related works show, there have been several studies based on visualising future plans through AR. Our findings suggest that the way AR can situate digital information in a physical space is not just interesting for its visualisation affordances, but more so for how it can empower citizens within a public space.

The popularity amongst participants for our portal and city builder experiences, supported by the discussions during our final workshop session, highlights a clear desire for agency in community engagement processes. This element of community engagement is perhaps one of the more discussed aspects of civic participation processes, where critiques of "engagement theatre" and "degrees of tokenism" often arise [8,25,53,54]. In the recent technology-enabled participatory planning literature, it is often explored how augmented reality can be used as a tool for more immersive visualisations and information sharing regarding planning projects [4,5]. It is hoped that a result of more immersive information and visualisation is improved participation, especially from younger demographics [4]. A shortcoming that is often realised in this research, however, is that ultimately the issues with engagement do not rest on the technology, but instead stem from the institutional processes. Whilst AR may offer more meaningful forms of visualisation, it does not necessarily offer any more meaningful engagement because in some cases the planning processes do not actually allow for citizen input.

There is a large amount of research demonstrating the success of AR visualisations for artists and improved culture within a city [43,44]. This was further highlighted by the success of several AR art visualisations offered during the festival that our first study participated in. However, we suggest that these successes are not purely due to the novelty of overlaying digital information on the real world, but instead due to what it represents in the relationship between individuals, councils, and public space. Digital urbanism and placemaking research highlight the use of AR in "guerilla" settings for individuals to protest within or regain ownership of a public space [55,56]. In these contexts, AR is often positively discussed due to the way it empowers individuals to place their own art or visualisations over the physical world, whereas, in top-down community engagement processes, technology is often discussed as potentially novel, but ultimately still limited by a few challenges presented by the political nature of the process or the perception of the public towards the city administration that implements it.

We find this to be especially true if AR is used to recreate existing forms of community consultation. During both our time at Curiocity festival and our workshop discussions, our least popular AR interactions were those that visualised existing digital information in physical space but did not offer any further customisation or creation. Those that delivered information in one way from the application to the users struggled to convey relevance to the participants or generate excitement from the users even with the novelties of AR. We see this as a natural extension to the sentiment in the paper by Saßmannshausen et al., where it seems that a lot of the successes found were regarding the co-design and collaboration involved with developing the AR prototypes [36]. While the AR technology helped enable interaction with a younger audience, the participatory design methodologies that were employed appear to be a key success factor in the audience responding positively to the applications [36].

9.5.1 Most Engaging Interaction Paradigms

We suggest that the value of AR regarding community engagement requires a reconceptualisation of its affordances. While the novelty of overlaying digital information in physical space may be useful for appealing to younger audiences [36], our findings appear to show that this holds most significance when it affords users the chance to create or have some control over the information they are experiencing. In this case, the visual and interaction affordances typical to AR seem to be most effective when they are used to afford a deeper level of agency in the user. When designing interactions for AR within community engagement, we suggest that a strong focus should first be on delivering a sense of agency or control. In the context of public space, AR can allow users to overlay digital information over a public space, allowing them agency over a public space in a way previously only possible through street-art or perhaps graffiti. This was reflected in our interviews with participants: "that's why I would say the build your own city is interesting because I feel like I had a say. Right? So, I do respond by building, creating something, that means that I'm active in the sense of like having a real ownership of what the city is going to look like".

A criticism often received in this context is "Why AR?". Most users do not feel that simply overlaying digital information on the physical world really adds extra value. Instead, these interactions become valuable when they allow the user to create or act in a way that makes the digital information relevant to them as users. Out of the four interactions that we explored in AR, we found that the experiences that recreated existing council–citizen interaction paradigms were overwhelmingly the least popular. The city spaces quiz and model bridge gallery—which both used AR to visualise information—struggled to engage participants in the same way that the city builder and portal did. Participants commented on the way that these experiences felt particularly "one-way". In these experiences, participants were able to use AR as a novel way to overlay digital information on the real world, but because they did not have any input into the creation of this information, they struggled to see its relevance. While other research suggests that AR can be used to extend existing community engagement processes [36], our findings suggest that perhaps an extension alone is not enough if these processes do not initially afford a sense of control to the end user.

The experiences that were the most popular were those that afforded the most agency. Participants thoroughly enjoyed the city builder and portal experiences and favoured less the city spaces quiz or model bridge experience. Interestingly, whilst these experiences were less relevant to the broader city in that they were not representative of future plans within Brisbane and were not visualising photos of Brisbane's public spaces, they were much more relevant to the individual who had created them. Whilst AR certainly enabled them to visualise their city in physical space, the key information is that it was "their" city. The level of agency over their creation continued to be a resounding positive comment.

9.5.2 Augmented Reality for Citizen-Centred Public Space

When conceptualising AR within processes of community engagement, it is key to consider AR not just as a technology for visualising council-defined information, but as a way for citizens to reclaim elements of public space and a sense of agency within the broader planning discussions. This is not to negate the clear affordances of AR in situating and overlaying digital information in physical spaces to create more engaging experiences, but instead to recognise that successful citizen engagement with these tools is also closely linked to the way they allow citizens to have control over a part of the discussion and appropriate the AR tools to promote their own projects and pursue their own agenda.

By placing more emphasis on the alternative ways that augmented reality can enable agency within urban planning, our design choices are not necessarily linked to visualisation or information sharing and can begin to open up to all sorts of unique, meaningful, and playful interactions. When our participants entered into the street view of the city they had created, they were more interested in sharing with each other the types of buildings that they had chosen. These low-polygon buildings were not necessarily exciting to look at, but the excitement came from the conversations that were enabled because of the choices made by the participant. In this experience, AR enabled a situated platform for conversation, more so than a space for visualising existing council plans.

Participant A: "we're using AR and then discussing about it, you have one medium it's a conversation starter, you sit and discuss".

Our initial research [18] aimed to explore the types of conversational platforms that AR could afford. Initially, we suggested that AR offers three affordances: (a) it could be used as a situated real-time enabler of conversation between councils and citizens; (b) it allows for visual, physical, embodied, and practical co-design; and (c) it enables a data-driven reflection of the above processes. Our city builder concept aimed to demonstrate these three affordances allowed participants to co-design their ideal city, not only through text-based interactions, but also as visual digital objects in a physical space. Using choices, we attempted to emulate the types of conversations that could be had between these two stakeholders and, lastly, by recording the data of consenting users, we were afforded a reflective quantitative picture of the conversations that had taken place. While an unintended finding was the deeper desire for agency that users discussed, we do believe that the city builder experience successfully explored what an AR platform for conversation could look like and the types of interactions that could maximise engagement from individuals. While its focus was on city building, its interaction methods demonstrated the ways that AR's visual affordances could be used to share information between stakeholders, not just about planning, but about broader city environmental or social concepts.

9.5.3 Challenges and Limitations

Once this deeper sense of agency is established, however, it is then difficult not to undermine it with underexplored interaction methods. Minor errors in interaction design can bleed into the users' feeling of agency in such a way that their attitudes towards the entire engagement process and the technology are then tarnished. Whilst in some cases, our participants thoroughly enjoyed the way they could move throughout physical space while inside a virtual environment, they were equally frustrated by the choices we made with interface and controls and struggled to see the value in AR as a standalone technology. It is a challenge for future research to explore how AR platforms can create a sense of agency in the citizen–council relationship and, at the same time, ensure that the methods of interaction do not undermine this feeling.

Interestingly, participants often suggested that a sole focus on AR was too strong, and that a more hybrid approach to AR should be utilised instead, using existing technologies for many aspects of the engagement process and only using AR for a particular use case where its strengths were obvious. Where we had kept our different interaction methods segmented, instead, the participants were more interested in a combination of the experiences that saw them building a city, using a portal to explore it, and using the gallery to explore the impacts of their choices.

9.5.4 Future Research Directions

In this way, we see AR as an extension of the number of smart-city conversational platforms that have been developing around the world. The smart city literature has noted the success of developing platforms for conversation first before large-scale implementations of technology [18,46,57]. Cities such as Amsterdam have demonstrated much greater success on a considerably smaller financial budget by developing platforms that allowed citizens, institutions, and councils to engage with each other and decide upon projects that were most important for the city [46,58]. For now, these platforms tend to exist mostly online, and once projects have been decided, then move towards physical labs and other consultation spaces.

We identified a gap in the literature for discussing AR's position in a broader set of city technology platform infrastructure. Common uses of AR focus so strongly on its ability to transform previous planning or educational activities that it is not often considered how AR can be integrated into the broad set of technologies that are already implemented in cities. As sensors, online websites, social media, and artificial intelligence are all widely researched in their implementation and inter-operability for improving city maintenance, resource efficiency, or civic participation, it should be further researched where augmented reality can sit in this greater tech-stack. AR on its own may sometimes struggle to convey usefulness to individuals outside of its novelty, but perhaps, in using city-wide sensor data and artificial intelligence, AR could be used to present real-time data to individuals to enable more informed conversations.

Participant B: "the city builder, the portal, the quiz, like the merging of these three is very useful in the sense that, and this is, I'm thinking from the perspective of, educating, making decisions, having some agency and then council getting something out of it".

Much research has been undertaken in the past five years that investigates the idea of City as a Platform. This research often investigates the way that open data, communicative technologies, and a multistakeholder participatory approach can be used to solve new environmental, social, and economic urban challenges [49–51]. However, at this stage, the platforms and research have a strong focus on artificial intelligence and the sharing of open data and little focus on the value of augmented reality to situate or visualise this information. When AR is discussed, it is more utilised in small-scale, standalone, local prototypes. An interesting avenue for future research is to understand how AR can be used as a part of the broader city platform. Where the concept of open data may only be useful to those with the knowledge to analyse and use it, perhaps AR could present these data in new, meaningful ways that encourage participation from non-technologists. Furthermore, the situated and embodied affordances of AR represented in our portal experience highlight the way that these platforms could shift from something digital and found only online, to something experienced in a physical space and interacted with by individuals in a more embodied way. For those perhaps too busy to interact with websites, surveys, and digital town halls, AR could augment the existing spaces that citizens inhabit in their day-to-day practices, shifting engagement from something required of individual citizens to something that is instead observed by city administrations or individuals within these spaces.

9.6 Conclusion

Augmented reality (AR) is often considered most valuable in an urban context when it can be used to visualise future plans for the area, especially in the context of a smart city or City 4.0. The successes of most research in this area, however, tend to highlight how much enjoyment and engagement the participants have in creating and placing their own models and buildings. Our findings suggest that while the visualisation novelties of AR are exciting for end users, what is most engaging is the sense of agency or control that can be found from the creation and ownership of digital content in a physical space. City 4.0 suggests that more sustainable outcomes can evolve from a digitalised connection of multiple city stakeholders. Furthermore, numerous case studies [4,20,28,29,32] demonstrate that by maximising citizen engagement in urban processes, more sustainable solutions are generated (such as improving the representation of poor communities so that they can plan their own urban futures relative to their unique social and cultural processes). When we consider AR's affordances in the relationship between citizens and city administrations, rather than just the affordances it can offer visually, we can start to understand the powerful role of AR in an urban context and the value it can bring to community engagement processes when designed correctly. Its ability to enable agency and contextualise information in an embodied and visual way can further empower citizens and improve council data and, as a result, create more equitable and sustainable outcomes for urban environments. Finally, we suggest further research is required to understand AR's role within the broader urban technological infrastructure, acting as a medium for conversation between citizens and city administrations, rather than just a visualisation tool for small-scale urban change [59].

Acknowledgements

This chapter, with permission from the copyright holder, is a reproduced version of the following journal article: Hunter, M., Soro, A., Brown, R., Harman, J., & Yigitcanlar, T. (2022). Augmenting community engagement in City 4.0: Considerations for digital agency in urban public space. *Sustainability* 14(16), 9803.

References

1. World Economic Forum. (2020). *How Has the World's Urban Population Changed?* World Economic Forum. Available online: www.weforum.org/agenda/2020/11/global-continent-urban-population-urbanisation-percent/ (accessed 1 February 2022).
2. Hunter, M. (2021). Resilience, fragility, and robustness: Cities and COVID-19. *Urban Government* in press.
3. Balestrini, M., Rogers, Y., Hassan, C., Creus, J., King, M., Marshall, P. (2017). A city in common: A framework to orchestrate large-scale citizen engagement around urban issues. In: *Proceedings of the Conference on Human Factors in Computing Systems*, Denver, CO, USA, 6–11 May 2017. Association for Computing Machinery: New York, NY, USA, Volume 2017-May, pp. 2282–2294.
4. Saßmannshausen, S.M., Radtke, J., Bohn, N., Hussein, H., Randall, D., Pipek, V. (2021). Citizen-centered design in urban planning: How augmented reality can be used in citizen participation processes. In: *Proceedings of the DIS 2021: ACM Designing Interactive Systems Conference: Nowhere and Everywhere*, Virtua, 28 June–2 July 2021; Association for Computing Machinery, Inc.: New York, NY, USA, pp. 250–265.
5. Bhardwaj, P., Joseph, C., Ikigailand, V. (2020). Gamified urban planning experiences for improved participatory planning. A gamified experience as a tool for town planning.

In: *Proceedings of the India HCI 2020: India HCI'20*. 11th Indian Conference on Human-Computer Interaction, 5–8 November 2020.

6. Smith, R.W. (1973). A theoretical basis for participatory planning. *Policy Science* 4, 275–295.

7. Shaw, M. (2011). Stuck in the middle? Community development, community engagement and the dangerous business of learning for democracy. *Community Development Journal* 46, ii128–ii146.

8. Legacy, C. (2017). Is there a crisis of participatory planning? *Planning Theory* 16, 425–442.

9. Fredericks, J., Caldwell, G., Tomitsch, M. (2016). Middle-out design: Collaborative community engagement in urban HCI. In: *Proceedings of the 28th Australian Conference on Computer-Human Interaction*—OzCHI'16, Canberra, Australia, 29 November–2 December 2016; ACM Press: New York, NY, USA.

10. Blanco, C., Kobayashi, H. (2009). Urban transformation in slum districts through public space generation and cable transportation at northeastern area: medellin, colombia. *Journal of International Social Research* 2, 75–90.

11. Klerks, G., Hansen, N.B., O'Neill, D., Schouten, B. (2020). Designing community technology initiatives: A literature review. In: *Proceedings of the OzCHI'20: 32nd Australian Conference on Human–Computer Interaction*, Sydney, Australia, 2–4 December, 2020; pp. 99–111.

12. Schroeter, R., Foth, M., Satchell, C. (2012). People, content, location: Sweet spotting urban screens for situated engagement. In: *Proceedings of the Designing Interactive Systems Conference, DIS'12*, Newcastle upon Tyne, UK, 11–15 June 2012; ACM Press: New York, NY, USA, pp. 146–155.

13. Yigitcanlar, T., Cugurullo, F. (2020). The sustainability of artificial intelligence: An urbanistic viewpoint from the lens of smart and sustainable cities. *Sustainability* 12, 8548.

14. Malek, J.A., Lim, S.B., Yigitcanlar, T. (2021). Social inclusion indicators for building citizen-centric smart cities: A systematic literature review. *Sustainability* 13, 376.

15. Rotta, M.J.R., Sell, D., dos Santos Pacheco, R.C., Yigitcanlar, T. (2019). Digital commons and citizen coproduction in smart cities: Assessment of Brazilian municipal e-government platforms. *Energies* 12, 2813.

16. D'Amico, G., L'Abbate, P., Liao, W., Yigitcanlar, T., Ioppolo, G. (2020). Understanding sensor cities: Insights from technology giant company driven smart urbanism practices. *Sensors* 20, 4391.

17. Fredericks, J., Fredericks, J. (2019). From smart city to smart engagement: Exploring digital and physical interactions for playful city-making. In: *Making Smart Cities More Playable*. Springer: Berlin/Heidelberg, Germany.

18. Hunter, M., Soro, A., Brown, R. (2021). Enhancing urban conversation for smarter cities—Augmented reality as an enabler of digital civic participation. *Interaction Design and Architecture(s)* 48, 75–99.

19. Shen, J., Wu, Y., Liu, H. (2001). Urban planning using augmented reality. *Journal of Urban Planning and Development* 127, 118–125.

20. Foth, M. (2018). Participatory urban informatics: Towards citizen-ability. *Smart and Sustainable Built Environment* 7, 4–19.

21. Carnegie, E., Whittaker, A., Brunton, C.G., Hogg, R., Kennedy, C., Hilton, S., Harding, S., Pollock, K.G., Pow, J. (2017). Development of a cross-cultural HPV community engagement model within Scotland. *Health Education Journal* 76, 398–410.

22. Riley, L., Howard-Wagner, D., Mooney, J., Kutay, C. (2013). Embedding Aboriginal cultural knowledge in curriculum at university level through Aboriginal community engagement. *Diversity in Higher Education* 14, 251–276.

23. Breuer, J., Walravens, N., Ballon, P. (2014). Beyond defining the smart city. Meeting top-down and bottom-up approaches in the middle. *TeMA – Journal of Land Use, Mobility and Environment*. 7, 153–164.

24. Arnstein, S.R. (1969). A ladder of citizen participation. *Journal of the American Planning Association* 35, 216–224.

25. Bowen, F., Newenham-Kahindi, A., Herremans, I. (2010). When suits meet roots: The antecedents and consequences of community engagement strategy. *Journal of Business Ethics* 95, 297–318.

26. Sanga, N., Gonzalez Benson, O., Josyula, L. (2021). Top-down processes derail bottom-up objectives: A study in community engagement and 'slum-free city planning'. *Community Development Journal* 57(4), 615–634.

27. Niederer, S., Priester, R. (2016). Smart citizens: Exploring the tools of the urban bottom-up movement. *Computer Supported Cooperative Work* 25, 137–152.

28. Ministry of Housing Community and Local Government. (2020). *Planning for the Future*. Ministry of Housing Community and Local Government.

29. Usavagovitwong, N., Luansang, C. (2010). *Housing by People: Performance of Asian Community Architects*, 81p. Available online: www.academia.edu/5103694/Housing_by_People_Performance_of_Asian_Community_Architects (accessed 14 August 2022).

30. Pancholi, S., Yigitcanlar, T., Guaralda, M. (2015). Public space design of knowledge and innovation spaces: Learnings from Kelvin Grove Urban Village, Brisbane. *Journal of Open Innovation: Technology, Market, and Complexity* 1, 13.

31. Vadiati, N. (2022). Alternatives to smart cities: A call for consideration of grassroots digital urbanism. *Digital Geography Society* 3, 100030.

32. Brown, A., Franken, P., Bonner, S., Dolezal, N., Moross, J. (2016). Safecast: Successful citizen-science for radiation measurement and communication after Fukushima. *Journal of Radiological Protection* 36, S82–S101.

33. Halupka, M. (2014). Clicktivism: A systematic heuristic. *Policy Internet* 6, 115–132.

34. George, J.J., Leidner, D.E. (2019). From clicktivism to hacktivism: Understanding digital activism. *Information and Organization* 29, 100249.

35. Lim, S.B., Yigitcanlar, T. (2022). Participatory governance of smart cities: Insights from e-participation of Putrajaya and Petaling Jaya, Malaysia. *Smart Cities* 5, 71–89.

36. Saßmannshausen, S.M., Radtke, J., Bohn, N., Hussein, H., Randall, D., Pipek, V. (2021). Citizen-centered design in urban planning: How augmented reality can be used in citizen participation processes. In: *Proceedings of the DIS 2021—ACM Designing Interactive Systems Conference: Nowhere and Everywhere*, Virtua, 28 June–2 July 2021; Association for Computing Machinery, Inc.: New York, NY, USA, pp. 250–265.

37. Purwandari, B., Hermawan Sutoyo, M.A., Mishbah, M., Dzulfikar, M.F. (2019). Gamification in e-government: A systematic literature review. In: *Proceedings of the 2019 4th International Conference on Informatics and Computing*, ICIC 2019, Semarang, Indonesia, 16–17 October 2019; Institute of Electrical and Electronics Engineers Inc.: New York, NY, USA.

38. Argo, T.A., Prabonno, S., Singgi, P. (2016). Youth participation in urban environmental planning through augmented reality learning: The case of Bandung City, Indonesia. *Procedia – Social and Behavioral Sciences* 227, 808–814.

39. Allen, M., Regenbrecht, H., Abbott, M. (2011). Smart-phone augmented reality for public participation in urban planning. In: *Proceedings of the OzCHI '11: 23rd Australian Computer-Human Interaction Conference*, Canberra, Australia, 28 November–2 December 2011; ISBN 9781450310901.

40. Imottesjo, H., Thuvander, L., Billger, M., Wallberg, P., Bodell, G., Kain, J.H., Nielsen, S.A. (2020). Iterative prototyping of urban cobuilder: Tracking methods and user interface of an outdoor mobile augmented reality tool for co-designing. *Multimodal Technologies and Interaction* 4, 1–21.

41. Postle, B. (2022). *Brunopostle/Urb/Wiki/Homemaker—Bitbucket*. Available online: https://bitbucket.org/brunopostle/urb/wiki/Homemaker (accessed 4 August 2022).

42. Potts, R., Jacka, L., Yee, L.H. (2017). Can we 'catch 'em all'? An exploration of the nexus between augmented reality games, urban planning and urban design. *Journal of Urban Design* 22, 866–880.

43. Biermann, B.C., Seiler, J., Nunes, C. (2011). *The AR|AD Takeover: Augmented Reality and the Reappropriation of Public Space*. Available online: publicadcampaign.com (accessed 14 August 2022).

44. Liao, T., Humphreys, L. (2015). Layar-ed places: Using mobile augmented reality to tactically reengage, reproduce, and reappropriate public space. *New Media Society* 17, 1418–1435.

45. Soro, A., Brown, R., Wyeth, P., Turkay, S. (2020). Towards a smart and socialised augmented reality. In: *Proceedings of the Conference on Human Factors in Computing Systems*, Honolulu, HI, USA, 25–30 April 2020; Association for Computing Machinery: New York, NY, USA, pp. 1–8.

46. Desouza, K.C., Hunter, M., Jacob, B., Yigitcanlar, T. (2020). Pathways to the making of prosperous smart cities: An exploratory study on the best practice. *Journal of Urban Technology* 27, 3–32.

47. Rogers, Y., Marshall, P. (2017). *Research in the Wild*. Springer: Berlin/Heidelberg, Germany.

48. Chamberlain, A., Crabtree, A., Rodden, T., Jones, M., Rogers, Y. (2012). Research in the wild: Understanding "in the wild" approaches to design and development. In: *Proceedings of the Designing Interactive Systems Conference, DIS'12*, Newcastle upon Tyne, UK, 11–15 June 2012, pp. 795–796.

49. Vavoula, G., Sharples, M. (2007). Future technology workshop: A collaborative method for the design of new learning technologies and activities. *International Journal of Computer-Supported Collaborative Learning* 2, 393–419.

50. Vavoula, G. (2021). *Developing the "Future Technology Workshop" Method Future Technology Workshop: A Method for the Design of New Technologies and Activities.*

51. Soro, A., Brereton, M., Taylor, J.L., Hong, A.L., Roe, P. (2016). Cross-cultural dialogical probes. In: *Proceedings of the First African Conference on Human Computer Interaction*, Nairobi, Kenya, 21–25 November 2016; ACM: New York, NY, USA, pp. 114–125.

52. Gehl, J. (2013). *Cities for People*. Island Press: Washington, DC, USA; ISBN 1597269840.

53. Fainstein, S.S., Lubinsky, A. (2020). The relationship between citizen participation and the just city: Can more participation produce more equitable outcomes? In: *Learning from Arnstein's Ladder*. Routledge: London, UK, pp. 129–147; ISBN 0429290098.

54. Monno, V., Khakee, A. (2012). Tokenism or political activism? Some reflections on participatory planning. *International Planning Studies* 17, 85–101.

55. Gonsalves, K., Foth, M., Caldwell, G., Jenek, W. (2021). Radical placemaking: An immersive, experiential and activist approach for marginalised communities. In: *Connections: Exploring Heritage, Architecture, Cities, Art, Media.* Vol. 20.1.; AMPS (Architecture, Media, Politics, Society): Canterbury, UK, pp. 237–252.

56. Di Bella, A. (2015). *Smart Urbanism and Digital Activism in Southern Italy. In Emerging Issues, Challenges, and Opportunities in Urban E-Planning.* IGI Global: Hershey, PA, USA, pp. 114–140.

57. Anttiroiko, A.-V. (2016). City-as-a-platform: The rise of participatory innovation platforms in Finnish cities. *Sustainability* 8, 922.

58. Desouza, K., Hunter, M., Yigitcanlar, T. (2019). Under the hood: A look at techno-centric smart city development. *Public Management* 101, 30–35.

59. Hunter, M., Soro, A., Brown, R., Harman, J., Yigitcanlar, T. (2022). Augmenting community engagement in City 4.0: Considerations for digital agency in urban public space. *Sustainability* 14(16), 9803.

10 Alleviating Community Disadvantage

10.1 Introduction

In recent decades, rural-to-urban migration influenced by factors such as increased employment opportunities, access to services, education, and communication networks has led to a period of rapid urbanisation [1]. Over 50% of the world's population live in cities, with this number expected to increase to 68% by 2050 [2]. While the environmental impact of providing transportation infrastructure in growing cities remains a primary concern in research [3], another important challenge relates to the provision of inclusive, accessible, and affordable transportation for all individuals [4]. This is important as having access to transportation is crucial to improve social inclusion and allow people to access essential services, employment, and recreational facilities. Access to transportation is a critical component in achieving quality of life—particularly among vulnerable groups such as the elderly and disabled [5].

Transportation disadvantage relates to an individual's ability to access transport and is particularly prevalent in areas without good access to public transportation. In these areas, individuals must rely on "private motor vehicles" (PMVs), which typically come with higher costs than public transport due to purchasing, fuel, maintenance, insurance, and storage costs [6]. This combined with increased population growth has had a significant impact on property values, with areas around public transport nodes experiencing higher property values [7]. Lower income earners are then forced into surrounding fringe areas, further increasing transportation costs and exacerbating issues surrounding transport disadvantage [8].

Smart mobility has been identified as a potential solution to alleviate many of the issues associated with transport disadvantage [9]. Smart mobility, a general term used to describe many of the transport-related technologies that have been implemented in urban areas, represents a new way of thinking about transportation, including the creation of a more sustainable system that is able to overcome some of the issues associated with PMVs [10,11]. While the number of research articles that focus on smart mobility is growing, little research to date has focused on how smart mobility can address transport disadvantage. Similarly, where specific smart mobility innovations, such as "autonomous vehicles" (AVs), "flexible transportation services" (FTSs), and "free-floating e-mobility" (FFM), or the integration of

DOI: 10.1201/9781003403647-12

intelligent technologies have been investigated as a potential solution to transport disadvantage, they are often treated as separate entities with only a few comprehensive attempts to conceptualise how their integration can contribute to or alleviate the issue [12]. This requires explicit consideration as these changes do not happen in a silo, but are rather concurrent, or even dependent, on each other.

This chapter attempts to contribute to existing research by analysing the way that smart mobility innovations can address transport disadvantage in cities. Using a systematic literature review as the research methodology, this chapter seeks to answer the research question: How can smart mobility contribute to alleviate transport disadvantage? To answer this question and ensure all technological advances are considered, we first reviewed the literature to determine the innovations relevant to the smart mobility field, how they relate to each other, and what the major benefits of these systems are to urban areas. Then, by looking through the lens of transport disadvantage, major contributions were identified and associated with our research aim and question. From the literature review, a conceptual framework representing the relationship between the benefits of smart mobility innovations and the various aspects of transport disadvantage was developed with the view that it could help researchers better understand the relationship between the two concepts. This chapter also highlights future areas of research that can help others look to smart mobility innovations to alleviate issues regarding transport disadvantage.

10.2 Literature Background

Smart mobility as a concept has its roots within the smart cities model: driven by policy, technology, and community, the primary goal of smart cities is to deliver productivity, innovation, liveability, wellbeing, sustainability, accessibility, and good governance and planning [13]. The conceptual framework shown in Figure 10.1 demonstrates this concept through a simple input–output–impact model. In the context of smart cities, the transportation system could be considered an asset of the city which is implemented through various drivers, including technology, policy, and community. When successfully implemented, these drivers should lead to more desirable outputs (or outcomes), the result (or impact) being a smarter city—or in this case a smarter mobility system [13].

Built into this concept of smart cities is the notion of smart mobility [10,14]. Similar to the broader smart city concept, smart mobility is partially driven by community and policy; however, much of the focus is on using technology as a way to transform the transportation system while addressing the societal, economic, and environmental impacts associated with PMVs, including issues regarding transport disadvantage [15,16]. Some of these innovations such as "demand-responsive transportation" (DRT) have been implemented by local governments as a way of offering services to those most in need or to replace underutilised public transport systems. They are often viewed more as an extension of the existing public transport network than a stand-alone system [17]. Similarly, ubiquitous infrastructure ("U-Infrastructure") harnesses technological advances in ICT, "intelligent

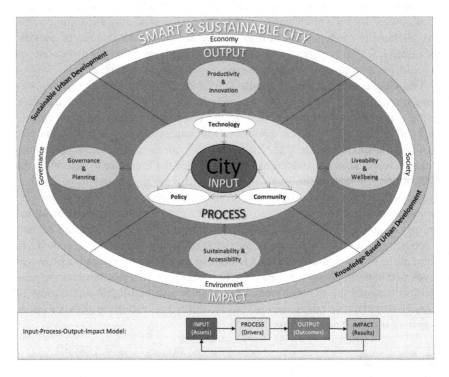

Figure 10.1 Smart city conceptual framework (derived from [13]).

transportation systems" (ITSs), and digital networks to improve the efficiency of urban infrastructure [18].

Other systems including car sharing, ride sharing, FFM, AVs, and alternative fuel vehicles are driven by private industry and with rapid advances in technology they are likely to disrupt the transport system, whether their benefits are harnessed by governments or they are left to evolve organically [19,20]. This was seen in 2015 in Australia following the introduction of Uber's ride-sharing platform. Regulators were effectively left playing catch-up to a disruptive technology that was implemented and already in widespread use prior to the appropriate legislation being developed. The impact of this lack of foresight not only led to issues regarding overnight loss of value to taxi licenses [21] but has also led to concerns about the underpayment of workers [22], and an eventual oversaturation of the market [23].

There is an important distinction to be made here about how smart mobility innovations are introduced into the market and the importance of managing disruptive technology. While modern visions of smart mobility are generally optimistic and show a transportation system where everybody has equal access and PMV travel is replaced with services that users can access on-demand, the reality could be very different. In fact, as with the introduction of the automobile in the early 1900s, there is a risk that this new technology will create even greater issues that we were unable to see or predict due to a persistent cloud of optimism that shades our judgement. Thus, critical in the realm of urban governance is to develop an understanding of the potential contributions of smart mobility so that its impacts can be managed effectively and the societal, economic, and environmental objectives of the smart city are achieved [24].

The conceptual background for smart mobility outlined above underlines the importance of further investigating the contribution smart mobility can make to urban areas. This is particularly true with regards to the issue of transport disadvantage which could potentially risk further decline if smart mobility innovations are implemented into urban areas without any actions taken by decision-makers. Similarly, misunderstanding the potential benefits of smart mobility could lead to missing opportunities to improve the equity of the transportation system.

10.3 Methodology

For this study, a systematic literature review was utilised as the methodology and based on the three-stage approach implemented by Yigitcanlar et al. [15]. The purpose of the review was to address the research question: How can smart mobility contribute to alleviate transport disadvantage?

The first stage in this process was planning. Our research objectives were defined as being to identify any relationship between smart mobility innovations and transport disadvantage. Based on this objective research aim and question, several keywords relevant to the subject area were developed. Primary inclusion criteria included articles that were peer-reviewed, published online, and in English. Secondary inclusion criteria were to only include articles that were relevant to the research aim. Exclusionary criteria were articles that did not meet the inclusion criteria. The keywords were then used to undertake an open-ended search to September 2020 using a university library search engine with access to 393 academic databases. Boolean search query was used with keywords, as shown in Figure 10.2. The initial search yielded 2136 articles.

The second stage of the process was performing the review. Abstracts of the proposed articles were scanned against the primary inclusion and exclusion criteria; duplicates and articles that did not comply with the criteria were removed. Following this, the full text of the remaining articles was read twice to ensure compliance with the secondary inclusion criteria. Articles irrelevant to the research aim were removed. In total, 99 articles were considered relevant to the research aim and included in the final qualitative review. Figure 10.2 provides a step-by-step outline of the literature selection and review.

The remaining articles ($n = 101$) were categorised using a directed content analysis method, whereby major themes were selected based on a theory or framework identified in the literature. An additional six publications relevant to the research topic but not otherwise meeting the search criteria were also added to the study. As the purpose of the review was to determine the contribution smart

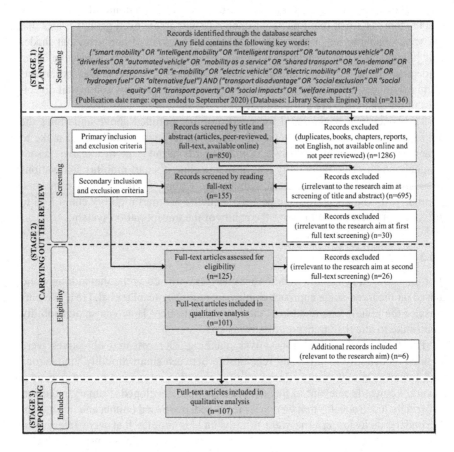

Figure 10.2 Literature selection procedure.

mobility innovations could make to alleviate transport disadvantage, a framework was selected to ensure all relevant dimensions were considered. Based on a previous review of transport disadvantage by Yigitcanlar et al. [4], it was decided that Suhl and Carreno's [25] six dimensions for transport disadvantage—i.e., physical, economic, spatial, temporal, psychological, and information—would be used as it was the most comprehensive. The articles were then reviewed using a descriptive rather statistical technique. Pattern matching and other qualitative techniques, such as scanning for common subjects, were also used to group the articles into the predefined categories. As a result, relationships were identified between the transport disadvantage dimensions and the number of final categories reduced to three: (a) physical and economic ($n = 39$); (b) spatial and temporal ($n = 33$); and (c) psychological and information ($n = 28$). Following a review of the literature a seventh category, "institutional disadvantage", was also discussed ($n = 7$). A description of the relevant dimensions is shown in Table 10.1.

Table 10.1 Dimensions of transportation disadvantage (derived from [4,25]).

Dimension	Description
Physical	Relates to the physical barriers that may limit a person from accessing transportation. Limitations may include inability to operate a motor vehicle and inability to physically access a vehicle or public transport due to a disability
Economic	Relates to the economic barriers that may limit a person from accessing transportation. Specifically concerns the personal cost of transportation and can include ticket price, fuel, insurance, storage, purchase, and travel time
Spatial	Relates to the spatial barriers that may limit a person from accessing transportation. Often associated with geographic-related transport disadvantage in areas where public transport coverage is inadequate, and individuals are forced to own PMVs to satisfy transportation needs
Temporal	Relates to the temporal barriers that may limit a person from accessing transportation. Often associated with geographic-related transport disadvantage in areas where public transport frequency is inadequate, and individuals are forced to own PMVs to satisfy transportation needs
Psychological	Relates to the psychological barriers that may limit a person from accessing different transportation modes. This barrier can include issues associated with perception and safety
Information	Relates to the information barriers that may limit a person from accessing different transportation modes. These barriers relate to an individual's ability to use and understand how to use transportation modes
Institutional	Relates to the institutional and governance barriers that may limit a person from accessing different transport modes. These barriers include policy, regulations, registration requirements, and other local laws that may limit an individual's ability to use transportation

The third and final stage of the process was reporting. In this stage, the analysis of the 107 articles completed during the screening stage was used to present the results by preparing and writing the final article. Finally, additional publications ($n = 31$) were used to support our findings, elaborate on our results, and provide a contextual background to this research.

10.4 Results

10.4.1 *General Observations*

Interest in the social issues surrounding smart mobility has grown over the past two decades. In fact, while only two of the selected articles were published before 2005, that number has continued to grow with four articles published during 2006–2008, five articles during 2009–2011, 13 articles during 2012–2014, 20 articles during 2015–2017, and 63 since 2018. The leading authors were affiliated with universities in Europe (*n* = 58), Oceania (*n* = 19), North America (*n* = 18), Asia (*n* = 9), South America (*n* = 1), and the Middle East (*n* = 2). The articles were published in a wide range of journals including *Research in Transportation Economics* (*n* = 9), *Sustainability* (*n* = 9), *Transport Policy* (*n* = 7), *Journal of Transport Geography* (*n* = 6), *Transport Research Part A* (*n* = 5), *Transportation* (*n* = 5), *Travel, Behaviour & Society* (*n* = 4), *Transport Planning and Technology* (*n* = 4), *Transport Reviews* (*n* = 4), *Journal of Transport & Health* (*n* = 3), *Energies* (*n* = 2), *Energy Research & Social Science* (*n* = 2), *Land Use Policy* (*n* = 2), *Local Economy* (*n* = 2), and *Transportation Research Part D* (*n* = 2). The remaining 41 articles were published in 36 different journals from a range of research areas including urban planning and policy, transportation, ethics, sociology, and health.

Articles were categorised into three groups based on the defined categories: physical and economic (*n* = 33), temporal and spatial (*n* = 31), and psychological and information (*n* = 26). With reference to the main smart mobility innovations, DRT was discussed in 40 articles, followed by AVs (*n* = 38), ITSs (*n* = 25), shared mobility (*n* = 17), "Mobility-as-a-Service" (MaaS) (*n* = 12), and "alternative fuel vehicles" (*n* = 12). Twelve articles discussed smart mobility generally but were not specific regarding technological innovations.

10.4.2 Smart Mobility Impacts

This section discusses the main innovations identified in the literature that are associated with smart mobility and what impacts these innovations will make to transportation. Understanding the broad impacts each of the innovations will have on the transportation system is important so that the flow-on effects can be analysed against each of the transport disadvantage dimensions.

The six major smart mobility innovations identified in the literature are: (a) DRT; (b) shared mobility; (c) ITSs; (d) alternative fuel vehicles; (e) AVs; and (f) MaaS. ITS, alternative fuel vehicles, and AVs represent direct technological advances that will affect vehicles and infrastructure. On the other hand, while technology is critical to the development of DRTs, shared mobility, and MaaS, they are more associated with innovations to the way transportation services are provided to the community rather than having a direct impact on the vehicles and infrastructure in the transport system. A description of each of these innovations and relevant literature is shown in Table 10.2.

The innovations often overlap to optimise the potential positive impacts. DRT systems and AVs enabled by ITS technology are often referred to as real-time or dynamic FTS [61] and connected AVs (CAVs), respectively [55,62]. Shared AVs (SAVs) incorporate elements of shared mobility and AVs [44], and FFM is essentially a combination of shared mobility, battery electric vehicles, and DRT [63]. MaaS forms an overarching platform in which each of these services can be bundled together [64]. A conceptual diagram is shown in Figure 10.3 to better understand the relationships between these innovations. This diagram is by no means exhaustive, for example, free-floating e-mobility incorporates elements of

Table 10.2 Smart mobility innovations

Innovation	Description	Reference
DRT	DRT provides a transportation options distinct from traditional fixed-route services in that they utilise dynamic, semi-fixed, or fixed routes with users able to pre-book based on travel needs and services operated on-demand. The main impacts on the transportation system relate to ability to provide greater coverage and flexibility. Although existing DRT services have been criticised for their inability to manage high demand and provide the required service coverage at an appropriate cost unless supported by other innovations including ITS, AV, and shared mobility	[26–33]
ST	Shared mobility refers to services where rides are shared with other users (e.g., ride-sharing) or vehicles are shared but used at different times (e.g., car sharing or bike sharing). Traditional types of shared mobility include car rentals, public transport, or taxis. Recent shared mobility innovations that make use of ITS, DRT, or battery-operated systems include FFM and peer-to-peer ride sharing apps such as Uber. The main advantage of shared mobility is that resources are shared among multiple users resulting in improved efficiencies in operation, storage, and cost. A move towards shared mobility is a critical component for smart mobility innovations including DRT, AV, and MaaS to achieve sustainable city goals	[34–42]
ITS	ITS refers to applications which utilise advances in ICT to effectively share data between vehicles, infrastructure, and users. ITS covers a broad range of applications including transport telematics, automatic information signs (ATIS), electronic ticketing, smart infrastructure, and in-car assistance, sensors, and other safety features. ITS is enhanced by advances in big data, Internet of Things (IoT), cloud computing, and artificial intelligence (AI), which contribute to more efficient data collection, processing, and analysis. The primary advantage of ITS within the transportation field relates to its ability to optimise the performance of other technological innovations	[43–46]
Alternative Fuel	Alternative-fuel vehicles refer to those vehicles which do not rely on petroleum-based fuel sources. These vehicles use batteries for their primary fuel source, which in turn are fuelled by non-petroleum sources such as the electrical grid, hydrogen, or solar power. Most literature focuses on the environmental benefits of this technology. However, with reference to transport disadvantage, the primary benefits of battery-operated vehicles relate to the convenience of FFM which provides users an assortment of conveniently placed powered transportation options which they can access on-demand	[47–50]

(*Continued*)

Table 10.2 (Continued)

Innovation	Description	Reference
AVs	AVs refer to vehicles that can be operated without input of a human driver. While there are various levels of autonomy for the purpose of this chapter any reference to AVs assumes the vehicles can operate without human input in all conditions—unless otherwise stated. The primary advantage of AVs relates to improved accessibility, operational efficiency, and safety	[51–57]
MaaS	MaaS is a concept whereby a range of transportation options, including ride-sharing, car-sharing, public transport, and FFM, is offered to customers via a single online platform, or app. Users subscribe to the service which gives them access to various transport options that were traditionally offered separately. The advantage of MaaS is that as an integrated system it can provide the platform from which mobility providers are able to shared resources, and could contribute to better transport outcomes as any issues can be better considered by looking at the transport system as a whole rather than only concentrating on individual parts. MaaS can also provide the operational structure from which new transport innovations are released into the market	[24,38, 58–60]

ITS, and, when offered as a bicycle service, it might not rely on electric-powered engines. In addition, DRTs are typically offered as shared mobility to improve efficiency and costs [65]. Nonetheless, the figure provides a conceptual outline to better understand the relationships between the various smart mobility innovations identified in the literature.

10.4.3 Physical and Economic Dimensions

This section discusses how smart mobility innovations can contribute to the alleviation of the physical and economic dimensions of transport disadvantage. Based on the reviewed literature, smart mobility could alleviate the physical and economic dimensions of transport disadvantage by: (a) improving accessibility to transportation for those unable to access or operate a vehicle; (b) creating a transportation system in which services are more responsive to user needs; (c) reducing the cost for users by improving the efficiency of the transportation system and promoting a move towards shared mobility; and (d) improving the "value of time" (VOT) spent in transit. A list of all reviewed literature is shown in Appendix 10.A.

Firstly, various smart mobility innovations have been shown to improve accessibility for those physically unable to access transportation or operate a vehicle. Access to a vehicle is an important factor in maintaining a good standard of living and providing security and freedom of movement to access social activities, employment, and other services, including healthcare [57,66], particularly in low-density areas [67]. DRT services that provide door-to-door transportation have

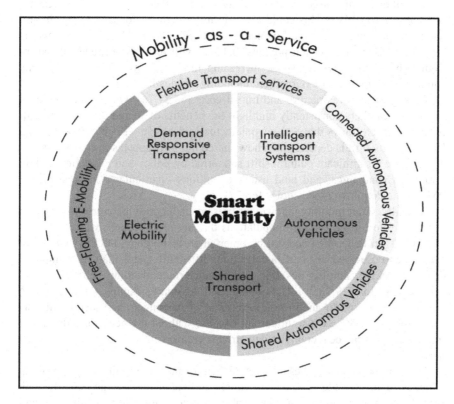

Figure 10.3 Relationship between smart mobility innovations.

been shown to improve user accessibility by reducing issues surrounding the first- and last-mile access of public transport [68]. In fact, when compared to traditional public transport services, one study showed high satisfaction with flexible DRT services resulting in a doubling of older users [69]. Furthermore, when operated as a shared service they have been shown to increase social interactions resulting in reduced feelings of isolation [68].

Despite the benefits of DRT, another commonly cited innovation to improve accessibility relates to AVs [57,70]. As AVs are able to drive without human input, the elderly, disabled, young, unlicensed, and those unfamiliar with local conditions may no longer be excluded from operating a PMV [51,71–73]. Even in a semi-AV setting, in-vehicle technologies such as crash avoidance; warnings for lane departure, collision, and blind spots; navigation systems; parking assistance; and adaptive cruise control may result in more elderly residents being able to hold onto their license for longer [52,74]. Some may also benefit from improved access to FFM including bike sharing, which would add additional accessibility options— particularly for short-distance trips [75]. Due to these advantages, it is important that these services are implemented with regulations to ensure equal access [40].

Nevertheless, increased accessibility means that there is a risk of increasing accessibility to PMVs. This could result in more demand for car ownership and increased per capita "vehicle kilometres travelled" (VKT) [10]. This premise is supported by research which predicts that AVs will result in a mode shift away from public and active transport, increasing total VKT by 15–59% [57]. This could lead to increased externalities including congestion and urban sprawl and result in greater infrastructure and transit costs [53,57,76]. Due to this potential impact, researchers consistently highlight the benefits of shared mobility [53,56]. If fact, research shows that SAVs would actually decrease VKT by 10–25% [57]. However, this shift is dependent on how shared mobility appeals to consumers and will require a significant cultural shift supported by policy and regulation, public awareness campaigns, and land use interventions—particularly in areas where PMV is the dominant mode choice [66,77].

Secondly, smart mobility innovations present an opportunity to provide services to the transport-disadvantaged populations that are more responsive to their specific needs. In fact, when enabled by other smart technology, DRT systems have been able to use advances in data collection, distribution, and analysis to improve decision-making, simplify ticketing, and enhance route planning, scheduling, and vehicle selection [29,78,79]. Data obtained from smart ticketing systems can be integrated and used to analyse the behaviour of passengers and identifying service gaps [80]. AVs are also important because without the need for a driver the internal layouts can be reconfigured to provide comfort and access based on special needs [72].

This is important as studies have found that, for shared mobility to be appealing, it needs to be flexible and able to satisfy individual needs—particularly with regards to having both on- and off-peak access to employment, healthcare, and recreational areas [81]. Integrated services such as MaaS can help by facilitating better multi-stakeholder collaboration and the sharing of information. The needs and trends of each individual user can then be used collaboratively to support the day-to-day operation of the entire system [82] and connect potential users with the most suitable providers [42].

Thirdly, there is potential for smart mobility to reduce transportation costs by improving the efficiency of the transportation system and promoting a move towards shared mobility. The integration of services through a MaaS-like system and the use of ITS has the potential to reduce administration and management costs. Cost savings related to the design of transportation systems could theoretically be passed on to the consumer or used to supply transportation services to the disadvantaged [24,79]. Using shared mobility as a replacement for PMVs would also remove many of the economic barriers associated with ownership—e.g., purchasing, maintenance, insurance, and storage costs [39]. Parking costs would also be reduced under a shared system as vehicles would spend less time idle [34,83]. However, the distribution of shared services is likely to favour areas with high demand and is unlikely to reduce issues associated with geographic-related transport disadvantage. Furthermore, disability-related disadvantage is unlikely to benefit from car and bike schemes alone [34]. AVs would be beneficial in this regard as removing the need for a driver would significantly reduce operational costs and help solve issues associated with accessibility. In fact, SAVs have the potential to reduce total transportation cost by over 80% when compared to traditional PMVs [39].

However, new technology also brings high upfront costs and low short-term return on investment. Thus, while research continues to show that there is a huge demand for more sustainable vehicles [84], residents are willing to pay extra for more environmentally friendly options [49], and shared mobility is cheaper than car ownership [85], it may be difficult to guarantee economic sustainability—particularly in the short term. For example, while the use of alternative environmentally friendly fuels often achieves better economic performance, the high cost of vehicles—particularly hydrogen fuel cell vehicles—can make the economic sustainability of such vehicles difficult [48]. Similarly, despite potential for lower maintenance costs, reduced accidents, and overall efficiency, the high upfront cost may limit the potential for market penetration [85].

Finally, cost alone might not be enough to sway users to a shared system. In fact, in many countries, the modes with the lowest cost of operation—e.g., public and active transportation—are often not the ones with the highest market share. Other factors, such as comfort and prestige, also play a part [39]. AVs could transform the interiors of private vehicles into mobile offices, dwellings, or entertainment and communication hubs improving the VOT by facilitating the ability to work, eat, socialise, and rest while in transit [56]. This could improve work–life balance and reduce stress—particularly among those who travel regularly. Conversely, increasing VOT may also lead to an increase in VKT, further exacerbating issues associated with infrastructure demand and urban sprawl [39,86].

From an economic perspective, the increase in demand for private AVs may also lead to disadvantaged populations being priced out of the market, leaving them unable to benefit from the advantages of the technology [40,56,87]. Similarly, with alternative fuel vehicles, users unable to afford the new technology may be charged with a Pigouvian tax to discourage the use of fossil fuels [47,50,88,89]. Increased use of private AVs and shared mobility may also lead to a reduction in public transport use, reducing revenue and resulting in higher costs and future degradation of services. This is likely to impact lower income and geographically disadvantaged residents the most [56,90].

There is also economic risk associated with an integrated transportation system such as MaaS. Where a single entity is responsible for the selection and distribution of mobility providers, the system itself may become a barrier to new transportation companies entering the market. This could result in monopolisation, increasing the risk of uncompetitive markets, price gouging, and other unfair business practices [76,91]. Conversely, government control could create tension with the private sector, which is critical in the development and funding of new transportation innovations [24,76]. If we are to rely on private companies to provide most of the services, it is unlikely that off-peak and low-demand services would be provided, and significant subsides, political engagement, and planning would be required to ensure that societal goals are being maintained [92].

10.4.4 Spatial and Temporal Dimensions

This section discusses how smart mobility innovations can contribute to the allevi-ation of the spatial and temporal dimensions of transport disadvantage. Due to the association with time and distance, this dimension is most closely related to issues surrounding geographic-related transport disadvantage. Based on the reviewed lit-erature, smart mobility could alleviate the spatial and temporal dimensions of trans-port disadvantage by: (a) filling gaps in the public transport network by improving the coverage and frequency of services; (b) strengthening the connection with public services by designing services to act as a feeder system which connects to major public transport nodes and employment centres; (c) improving the flexibility of public transport by offering services on-demand; and (d) creating more transpor-tation choices in areas where choice is traditionally limited. A list of all reviewed literature is shown in Appendix 10.A.

Firstly, literature on smart mobility consistently identifies smart mobility innovations as a way to fill gaps in the public transport network. In doing so, smart mobility can contribute to improved coverage and frequency of services [43,93]. DRT services, in particular, have been highlighted as a way to provide door-to-door transportation by using fleets of smaller shared vehicles as opposed to fixed-route services [94]. Other advantages of using smaller vehicles over traditional buses is that they have a lower operational cost per passenger and can access areas with smaller road widths [94]. However, these services often require significant govern-ment subsidies as they do not have the required number of users to support prof-itability over the required coverage [35,95]. While subsidising these services may be more economical than providing fixed-route public transport [96], ITS can also help better match supply and demand and develop locally specific strategies that also contribute to lower costs and better efficiency [95,97]. ITS has been shown to allow better real-time control over the networks and enhance the potential for DRT to provide increased flexibility and greater coverage while bringing costs closer to that of public transport [27,43]. SAVs have also been identified as a way to improve coverage particularly by reducing the instance of dead runs [33,98].

Notwithstanding, there will also be issues associated with providing the neces-sary infrastructure to facilitate suitable network coverage [99,100]. Furthermore, when promoting alternative-fuel vehicles that generate electricity from the grid, there may be issues associated with grid capacity. Infrastructure issues are intensi-fied in low-density and rural areas due to inadequate infrastructure and longer trans-mission distances [47,50,101]. As such, low-density areas would still attract higher transportation costs than high-density areas, and significant investment is required to ensure geographic equity [101]. One solution relates to cross-subsidisation, where profits made in areas with high demand are used to subsidise and fund the required infrastructure in areas with lower demand [47,95]. By sharing informa-tion and resources across the transportation system, MaaS can help facilitate this cross-subsidisation to ensure maximum profitability and promote social equity [83]. Furthermore, since subsidies may make low-density housing more attractive, planning interventions that promote walking, cycling, higher densities around employment and transit centres, and investment in high-speed public transport remain important [59,102].

Secondly, smart mobility can be used to support investment in high-speed public transport by using innovative services to act as a feeder system, which acts as a first- and last-mile connection to major public transport nodes and employment centres [96]. Theoretically, improved access to public transport would reduce car dependency and therefore reduce transportation costs [103]. DRT systems could be timed to public transport hubs to ensure reductions in transfer times. Public transport would therefore form the backbone of these "pulse networks", which could also allow for integrated ticketing and services [103]. The overall coverage of these networks could be supported by shared mobility such as FFM that would provide connections for shorter distances and provide more transportation options [37,104]. By limiting long trips directly into denser urban areas congestion will be reduced, which means individuals who are required to travel by PMVs will likely see a reduction in fuel cost and time spent in traffic [96].

Efficient trip chaining is also important as studies have shown that users are more sensitive to travel time than travel cost; thus, ensuring transfers are easy and free from unnecessary delays can contribute to improving the appeal of public transport [105]. ITS has a role in improving the efficiency of these transfer, by improving the ability to apply real-time alterations to routing [26,104,106]. In fact, studies have shown that DRT services that connect directly to major transportation hubs and are enabled by ITS contribute to increases in total public transport ridership [27,107]. Furthermore, a significant modal shift away from PMVs has been observed when "artificial intelligence" (AI) is used to configure routes to reduce travel time [108] or through the use of MaaS systems to create synergies between mobility providers [109].

Thirdly, by improving the flexibility of public transport and offering services on-demand, transportation systems can be designed to respond directly to the specific geographic and social characteristics of the local area [32,97]. For example, in some areas, such as those with large numbers of tourists, conventional public transport with fixed schedules and timetables may be more advantageous [28,110]. In addition, in areas with higher numbers of people unable to operate a vehicle, car-sharing schemes should be limited in favour of more flexible routes and timetables [111]. Similarly, in very low-density areas, semi-fixed, as opposed to door-to-door, services may be more efficient [33]. In designing transportation systems, planners should consider how changes respond to local characteristics and ensure the optimal allocation of available resources [32]. Furthermore, any local transportation plan should be able to be scaled up if demand increases to ensure equal and equitable coverage [96].

Finally, using smart mobility to create more options for users in areas where transportation choice is limited can be beneficial [59]. Having more mobility options available to users has been identified as an important step to overcome the culture of PMV ownership. Similarly, supportive policies with awareness of shared services would be useful [112]. MaaS provides an opportunity to bundle services and offer a range of options to consumers through a single online platform

[83,109]. Alternatively, transportation choice may also include the choice to not travel. Advances in the design of digital neighbourhoods, smart homes, ICT, and home delivery have the potential to remove the need for physical trips—particularly those related to employment [94,112]. Similarly, with the view to reduce PMVs, ICT and data obtained from ITS can be used to help residents make more informed decisions regarding residential or work location [113].

10.4.5 Psychological and Information Dimensions

This section discusses how smart mobility innovations can contribute to the alleviation of the psychological and information dimensions of transport disadvantage. Based on the reviewed literature, smart mobility could alleviate the spatial and temporal dimensions of transport disadvantage by: (a) improving the safety of travel; (b) improving the perception of existing transportation options; and (c) improving the ability to make informed decisions. A list of all reviewed literature is shown in Appendix 10.A (Table 10.A1).

Firstly, smart mobility innovations have been shown to contribute to improved safety in the transportation system. This is important as the perception of safety is critical to ensure individuals want to use smart mobility [54]. AVs have the potential to significantly reduce the number of vehicular accidents caused by human error [54,55,114]. CAVs can use advances in ITS, ICT, and AI data processing to communicate with other vehicles, infrastructure, and sensors, identifying dangers early and further improving safety for drivers and pedestrians [55]. In addition, given that no driver is required in the internal configuration, it can be reconfigured to add to the safety of the vehicle [55]. Similarly, DRTs that offers door-to-door transportation and shared mobility are perceived as a safer option than public transport—particularly at night [30,31,115].

Nonetheless, from the perspective of the user, safety not only comes from feeling safe while engaged in a journey, but also with regards to digital safety [36,116]. In fact, lack of trust in technology is consistently identified as a reason for not using new transport technologies, particularly among the elderly [54,117–119]. This is understandable as increased reliance on technology introduces additional risks including those related to data privacy, cyberterrorism, grounding of fleets due to grid failures, faulty data [55,120], unconscious bias [114], and questions of legal liability [121]. To build trust, significant investment is required in cyber and data safety. Information campaigns are also beneficial to garner support among late adopters [119].

Secondly, there is potential for smart mobility innovations to improve the perception of existing DRTs and public transport systems. Many DRTs have been implemented around the world; however, the perception of these services is often that they are for the old and disabled—even when they are offered to all in the community [122,123]. Furthermore, users who benefit the most from the services are often confused and unclear about how these new transportation services could serve them [123–125]. In fact, research has shown that attitudes towards smart mobility among those with disabilities were entirely dependent on having prior knowledge of the technology [125]. Those with more knowledge tended to be more positive [126].

More information about potential routes and scheduling could help users better navigate new transportation innovations [124]. MaaS can help with this by providing all services and relevant information through a single digital platform giving users an unbiased choice of various modes [38,60]. In addition, as all services are effectively bundled together, any offerings that are targeted towards those with special needs may no longer be viewed as an entitlement but would instead be part of a city, regional, or nationwide system that is synergised to benefit all of society [58].

Finally, smart mobility could improve the ability of commuters to make informed decisions. Technological advances in ITS can facilitate the collection and analysis of large amounts of data from cameras, sensors, vehicle locations, smart ticketing systems, social media, credit cards, mobile phones, and many other sources [13,45,127]. Automating the analysis of this "big data" could help individuals with route planning and vehicle selection [44,46,128]. The ability to make informed decisions based on real-time data can help commuters reduce uncertainty, fear, and discomfort, and enhance the user experience and improve confidence [44,45,115].

However, given the reliance on smart technology, there are issues associated with technical literacy and the digital divide [36,38,116,117]. The digital divide refers to the gap between those who can access ICT and those who cannot. This issue is not only associated with the spatial distribution of network coverage or equality of access to physical smart devices but also the ability for particular socio-economic groups to use and understand the technology [36,117,127]. Statistically, the elderly, lower income, female, and disabled are less familiar with new technology due to lower lifelong exposure to ICT. Therefore, they often struggle to quickly learn the required skills to access and pay for digital services [117,127,129]. This is where an integrated system such as MaaS can help. By integrating a range of mobility providers into a single platform, it could simplify the process for accessing transport by reducing complexity and the need to cycle through various mobility applications [127]. Stakeholder engagement and public participation are also important to understand the existing challenges within the community [130].

10.4.6 *Institutional Dimensions*

Upon reviewing the literature, a seventh and final transport disadvantage dimensions has emerged. The "institutional" dimension includes institutional and governance-related barriers including policy, regulation, and institutions that may limit an individual's ability to use a transport mode or service. Based on the reviewed literature, smart mobility innovations do not necessarily directly contribute to the alleviation of this barrier. However, given the fast-pace nature of technological change within the transport sector—including widespread trials of smart mobility services including DRT, AVs, and MaaS and the rapid emergence of new technologies associated with car-, bike-, and scooter-sharing—it is important that decision-makers understand the strengths and weakness associated with them so that opportunities and risks can be identified. This is important because the public sector does not necessarily function adequately in times of uncertainty [76] and a failure to address the short- and long-term issues associated with these transport services could exacerbate negative externalities associated with the transport system. It is therefore important that strategies remain flexible so that they can adapt to changing circumstances and community needs [30,131].

It is critical that institutional barriers do not inhibit the ability of users to access services which could have wider societal benefits including high cost and inconvenience of registering for new services [132], laws that explicitly ban the use or inhibit the ability to use a mode or services within a particular area [133], or lack of available infrastructure to support mode choice—e.g., lack of dedicated active and public transport infrastructure [134]. Of equal importance is the use of institutional measures to promote and support the development of smart mobility. These could include: (a) establishment of standards for data management and sharing, which should be established on a national or transnational level [135]; (b) institutional support structures to assist with community adaptation to new technology, particularly among disadvantaged groups including elderly, migrants, or disabled [136]; (c) development of parking restrictions to discourage private vehicle use [131], engaging the public in decision-making [130]; and (d) ensuring public value and societal goals are maintained [24,137].

10.5 Discussion and Conclusion

10.5.1 Key Findings

This review study investigated the impact of smart mobility innovations through the lens of transport disadvantage. Specifically, the review sought to answer the research question: How can smart mobility contribute to the alleviation of transport disadvantage? Firstly, some common smart mobility innovations were identified and the relationships between these innovations shown. These innovations include new vehicular and infrastructural innovations such AVs, ITS, and alternative-fuel vehicles, in addition to new and existing ways of offering services to the community including DRT, shared mobility, and MaaS. These innovations will likely benefit urban areas by improving accessibility, efficiency, coverage, flexibility, safety, and integration of the transportation system.

The study also showed how smart mobility innovations have the potential to contribute to the alleviation of all six dimensions of transport disadvantage: (a) physical; (b) economic; (c) spatial; (d) temporal; (e) psychological; and (f) information. We also discussed some implications associated with a seventh, "institutional", dimension. Potential risks have been identified, and there are a number of key actions that can be taken to alleviate these risks. Of these actions, the implementation of MaaS and shared mobility appears as a common thread to overcoming the risks associated with smart mobility.

Firstly, a move towards shared mobility is critical to ensure resources are shared efficiently and the services offered have the required accessibility, coverage, and flexibility to reach all users and do not result in excess consumer costs or reliance on government subsidies. This conclusion is reflected in studies on DRT [66], AVs [39,40,52], and MaaS [40].

Secondly, the review showed that it is often a combination of innovations that will best benefit the transport disadvantaged. For instance, DRT and AVs are shown to work more efficiently, and safely, when enabled by ITS and other smart technology including big data and cloud computing. Furthermore, the negative externalities associated with AV use, including increased VKT, suburbanisation, and infrastructure demand, are significantly reduced when operating within a shared economy. This highlights the specific advantages of MaaS, which as an integrated system can provide the operational structure from which new innovations are trialled and released into the market. It also can help connect users to shared mobility and provide a platform from which mobility providers share resources. Sharing data between mobility providers could help decision-makers achieve better outcomes as issues associated with transport disadvantage can be considered by looking at the transportation system as a whole rather than concentrating on individual parts. Similar conclusions regarding the importance of MaaS as an overarching operational structure are supported by a number of studies including Gonzalez-Feliu et al. [82], Mulley and Kronsell [58], Soares Machado et al. [38], and Beecroft et al. [116].

Lastly, a summary of smart mobility's potential contribution and risks and their association with transport disadvantage dimensions is shown in Table 10.3.

10.5.2 Conceptual Framework

Within the realm of smart mobility, a key challenge to overcome transport disadvantage is to understand how the specific benefits of new transportation innovations can be harnessed to respond to each of the dimensions of transport disadvantage. The results of the literature review highlight important relationships between the benefits of smart mobility innovations and the different dimensions of transport disadvantages. Specifically, this review has shown that the benefits of smart mobility can be specifically aligned with the corresponding transport disadvantage dimension. A conceptual framework showing the relationship between these factors is shown in Figure 10.4. For the purpose of providing a conceptual framework related to how smart mobility can alleviate transport disadvantage, the institutional barrier has been excluded from the framework as it is not a barrier that can be overcome by smart mobility innovations alone. Nevertheless, supportive policies, regulations, and other governance structures are critical to the implementation of smart mobility in a way that strengthens its benefits while responding to issues of transport disadvantage.

Firstly, when looking through the *physical* dimension of transport disadvantage, the primary contribution of smart mobility is its ability to improve transportation *accessibility* through implementation of AVs, flexible door-to-door transportation, strengthening connections with existing public transport networks, providing more

Table 10.3 Summary of literature review findings

Dimension	Contribution	Risk	Potential actions
Physical	Improved accessibility to vehicle Door-to-door transportation Connection to public transport Increased social interactions More transportation options More responsive to specific need	Unequal access to services Increased VKT per capita Increased suburbanisation Unappealing to user	Integration of services (MaaS) Marketing and education Policy and regulation Promote shared mobility
Economic	Improved efficiency of system Reduced consumer costs Increased VOT	Unequal access to services Increased VKT per capita Increased infrastructure demand Increased suburbanisation Monopolisation	Integration of services (MaaS) Promote shared mobility Land use planning interventions Subsidies Stakeholder engagement
Spatial	Improved coverage of services Fill gaps in public transport network Feeder system to public transport	Increased infrastructure demand Network coverage Grid capacity Unequal access to services	Active transportation infrastructure Cross-subsidisation Digital neighbourhoods Integration of services (MaaS) Marketing and education Promote shared mobility
Temporal	Improved flexibility of services Better real-time control of network Better match supply and demand Reduced transfer times Reduced congestion	Routing should be specific to needs	Analysis of local characteristics Digital neighbourhoods Invest in intelligent technology (ITS) Integration of services (MaaS) Marketing and education
Psychological	Improved safety of vehicle Safety of door to door transportation Improved perception	Data safety Cyber safety Unconscious bias Legal liability	Invest in intelligent technology (ITS) Marketing and education Promote shared mobility
Information	Improved integration Improve decision-making	Digital divide Technology literacy	Integration of services (MaaS) Invest in intelligent technology (ITS) Stakeholder engagement
Institutional	Opportunity for change	Rapid technological change Increase negative externalities Lost opportunity	Adaptive policy and regulations Supportive governance structures

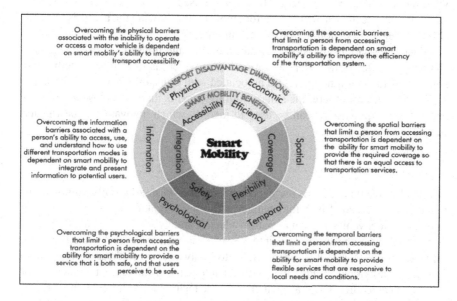

Figure 10.4 Conceptual framework of smart mobility and transportation disadvantage.

mode options, or specifically targeting user needs. Similarly, when looking through the *economic* dimension of transport disadvantage, the primary contribution of smart mobility is its ability to improve transportation *efficiency*, which could contribute to reduced consumer costs—whether by reducing the cost of actual travel or increasing the VOT spent in traffic.

Secondly, when looking through the *spatial* dimension of transport disadvantage, the primary contribution of smart mobility is its ability to improve transportation *coverage* by filling gaps in public transport or acting as a feeder system to major public transport nodes. Similarly, when looking through the *temporal* dimension of transport disadvantage, the primary contribution of smart mobility is its ability to improve *flexibility* by moving towards dynamic routing of transportation services, having more real-time control over the transportation network, better matching supply and demand, reducing transfer times, and reducing congestion for those who are required to travel by PMVs.

Finally, when looking through the *psychological* dimension of transport disadvantage, the primary contribution of smart mobility is its ability to improve transportation *safety*, whether through the use of AVs which remove the need for a human driver, ITS that communicates with vehicles and drivers regarding potential hazards, or door-to-door transportation that removes safety concerns associated with accessing fixed-route public transport stops—particularly in low-occupancy areas. Similarly, when looking through the *information* dimension of transport disadvantage, the primary contribution of smart mobility is its ability to integrate a wide range of data and services which can be used to improve decision-making, whether those decisions are made autonomously or following the analysis of available data regulators, mobility providers, and users.

Given the relationship between smart mobility and transport disadvantage, the challenge for decision-makers and mobility providers is to analyse specific case study areas to determine the issues associated with transport disadvantage that are most relevant. From there, the smart mobility benefits that most closely represent each of these dimensions can be used to identify which innovation is best suited for the local area.

10.5.3 Research Directions

Few studies identified in this review considered the six smart mobility innovations together as a broad driver for change in the transportation system. Given that alternative-fuel vehicles, such as battery electric and hybrid electric, and ITS have already started to be introduced into urban areas, and trials of AV are prevalent throughout the world, it is problematic to analyse each of these technological drivers as individual entities that will not interact and influence the success, or failure, of each other. The management of these technological innovations is therefore necessary to harness their benefits in response to transport disadvantage. That is why new operational structures and ways of looking at the transportation system including DRT, shared mobility, and MaaS remain important.

Nonetheless, while DRT systems are not new and have been implemented throughout the world—as an alternative to public transport and targeted toward those experiencing disadvantage—it has developed a stigma whereby it is often viewed as an option for only the aged and disabled. Similarly, shared mobility offered by private industry including ride-sharing, car-sharing, and FFM are typically targeted towards users in centralised, denser areas where the highest demand is available to ensure maximum profit. These services, therefore, rarely benefit those experiencing transport disadvantage, and often only exacerbate existing issues with unequal accessibility. As an integrated service, MaaS represents a new way of branding DRT, while enhancing public transport, shared mobility, and other elements of the transportation system. Furthermore, MaaS presents a unique opportunity to provide the platform from which new innovations are introduced into market, the data analysed, shared, and used to assess its suitability for alleviating transport disadvantage, and other related issues.

Prospective research should, hence, look at ways to use MaaS to harness the benefits of smart mobility innovations and attract users to shared mobility and public transport. MaaS is a relatively new topic so further research could focus on the barriers, and risks associated with implementing MaaS within urban areas. Analysis throughout a range of case study areas using transportation modelling, consumer surveys, expert opinion, and trials could also identify issues specific to the varying characteristics of different regions, including those associated with regulatory systems, policy frameworks, cultural differences, and geographic conditions.

Secondly, research could also focus on other innovative ways to integrate transportation modes, attract users to shared mobility, or develop alternative systems. Research could explore the role of other technological advances outside the field of transportation including 5G, AI, digital twins, virtual reality, blockchain, the IoT, big data, and cloud computing. For example, the use of virtual reality and augmented reality could be used to educate, market, and promote new transportation innovations towards individuals and business. Similarly, it could be used to let users experience new transportation technology prior to analysing their attitudes.

10.5.4 Concluding Remarks

Finally, given the recent events associated with the COVID-19 pandemic and its potential implications for consumer attitudes towards shared mobility, there is also a need to analyse whether the experience has changed user perspectives and willingness to ride-share and use public transport. This is important as attitudes may be changing due to increased awareness of vulnerabilities associated with virus transmission from passengers sharing close quarters in vehicles that often rely on centralised air-conditioning and little ventilation [138]. Furthermore, given these unprecedented events and the pressure on individuals and business to quickly adopt remote working and social environments, transportation researchers may be more inclined to ask whether no mobility is smarter than smart mobility. From a transport disadvantage perspective, research could be undertaken to compare individual transportation needs before, during, and after the lockdown experiences. Representatives from the commercial sector could be interviewed to discuss experiences with remote working, and how the experience will shape business models into the future, as one of the advantages of remote working is that for many jobs individuals may no longer be limited to employment opportunities due to location or issues with being able to afford or access transportation that is responsive to their needs [139].

Acknowledgements

This chapter, with permission from the copyright holder, is a reproduced version of the following journal article: Butler, L., Yigitcanlar, T., & Paz, A. (2020). How can smart mobility innovations alleviate transportation disadvantage? Assembling a conceptual framework through a systematic review. *Applied Sciences* 10(18), 6306.

Appendix 10.A

Table 10.A1 Reviewed literature pieces

Author	Year	Title	Journal
Mageean, J., and Nelson, J.D.	2003	The evaluation of demand responsive transport services in Europe.	Journal of Transport Geography
Brake, J., Nelson, J.D., and Wright, S.	2004	Demand responsive transport: towards the emergence of a new market segment.	Journal of Transport Geography
Brake, J., and Nelson, J.D.	2007	A case study of flexible solutions to transport demand in a deregulated environment.	Journal of Transport Geography
Ferreira, L., Charles, P., and Tether, C.	2007	Evaluating Flexible Transport Solutions.	Transportation Planning and Technology
Hensher, D.A.	2007	Some Insights into the Key Influences on Trip-Chaining Activity and Public Transport Use of Seniors and the Elderly.	International Journal of Sustainable Transportation
Zografos, K., Androutsopoulos, K., and Sihvola, T.	2008	A methodological approach for developing and assessing business models for flexible transport systems.	Transportation

Country	Category	Findings	Relevance
UK	Temporal and Spatial	Finding presents results from an evaluation of DRT in sites across Europe	Identifies transportation telematics as a way to improve the efficiency DRT systems.
UK	Temporal and Spatial	Findings highlight issues relating to the development of DRT.	Describes how DRT services can be enhanced by ITS to better deal with high demand, route planning, and integration.
UK	Temporal and Spatial	Findings demonstrate the evolution of public transport in the case study area and highlights the potential for better integration if deregulated	Provides insights into the use of the DRT to fill gaps in public transport networks particularly in dispersed areas.
Australia	Temporal and Spatial	Findings report on a recent study of the use of FTS in Brisbane, QLD.	Describes how FTS have the potential to increase public transport use by providing a more customer centric and adaptive solution to the first- last-mile problem.
Australia	Psychological and Information	Findings show that "the loss of a driver's license and a partner have the potential to be major contributors to social isolation in the absence of inadequate flexible public transport and or support mechanisms that enable access to the car as a passenger."	Identifies the potential for ATIS and ITS signs to provide dynamic information targeted directly to elderly drivers, such as avoiding challenging routes.
Greece	Physical and Economic	Develops a methodology for the development of flexible transport systems.	Describes how FTS allow flexibility in assigning routes, schedule, vehicles, and ticketing systems making them more responsive to local needs.

(*Continued*)

Table 10.A1 (Continued)

Author	Year	Title	Journal
Battellino, H.	2009	Transport for the transport disadvantaged.	Transport Policy
Mulley, C., and Nelson, J.D.	2009	Flexible transport services.	Research in Transportation Economics
Nelson, J.D., Wright, S., Masson, B., Ambrosino, G., and Naniopoulos, A.	2010	Recent developments in Flexible Transport Services.	Research in Transportation Economics
Santos, G., Behrendt, H., and Teytelboym, A.	2010	Part II: Policy instruments for sustainable road transport.	Research in Transportation Economics
O'Shaughnessy, M., Casey, E., and Enright, P.	2011	Rural transport in peripheral rural areas.	Social Enterprise Journal
Broome, K., Worrall, L., Fleming, J., and Boldy, D.	2012	Evaluation of flexible route bus transport for older people.	Transport Policy
Lucas, K., and Currie, G.	2012	Developing socially inclusive transportation policy.	Transportation

Country	Category	Findings	Relevance
Australia	Temporal and Spatial	Findings brings attention to the potential for scheduled transport services to fulfil transport needs in rural communities	Describes how DRT could be used to enhance the availability and scope of community transport to better service residents who need it most.
Australia	Temporal and Spatial	Findings that if implemented correctly flexible transport systems have the potential to improve bus services	Describes how the use of ITS to better match supply and demand can improve the efficiency of DRT and lead to lower costs more reflective of PT.
UK	Physical and Economic	Proposes the introduction of an organisational structure (FAMS) to help with the introduction of flexible transport services	Discusses the use of FTS to compliment conventional public transport by responding directly to user-demand.
UK	Temporal and Spatial	An analysis of policies related to sustainable road transport which fall into three categories: physical, soft, and knowledge policies.	Discusses how subsidised demand responsive taxis could replace conventional public transport in rural and low-density areas.
Republic of Ireland	Physical and Economic	Findings show that users of DRT are typically long-term residents, female, elderly, and those who live alone in isolated areas.	Describes how DRT services have helped increase independence, reduced feelings of social isolation and improve access to services for residents in rural areas without access to a PMV.
Australia	Physical and Economic	Findings show that when replacing fixed route with flexible service in Australia the use by older people almost doubled.	Provides insights into how DRT has improved accessibility and social inclusion for elderly.
UK	Temporal and Spatial	Findings identify that there are important differences between transport disadvantage in low income populations in UK and Australia.	Identifies that more flexible routes and timetabling is required to meet the needs of TDA.

(Continued)

Table 10.A1 (Continued)

Author	Year	Title	Journal
Nelson, J.D., and Phonphitakchai, T.	2012	An evaluation of the user characteristics of an open access DRT service.	Research in Transportation Economics
Shergold, I., and Parkhurst, G.	2012	Transport-related social exclusion amongst older people in rural Southwest England and Wales.	Journal of Rural Studies
Velaga, N.R., Beecroft, M., Nelson, J.D., Corsar, D., and Edwards, P.	2012	Transport poverty meets the digital divide: accessibility and connectivity in rural communities.	Journal of Transport Geography
Wells, P	2012	Converging transport policy, industrial policy and environmental policy.	Local Economy
Newman, D.	2013	Cars and consumption	Capital and Class
Ward, M.R.M., Somerville, P., and Bosworth, G.	2013	Now without my car I don't know what I'd do'	Local Economy

Country	Category	Findings	Relevance
UK	Psychological and Information	Results reveal that DRT system can improve accessibility, particularly for older residents.	Describes how users are more satisfied with DRT over conventional PT, particularly regarding safety of door-to-door services at night.
UK	Psychological and Information	Findings reveal that the availability of private vehicles "is not a strong indicator of overall location, although non-availability was important in limiting access to particular types of location."	Describes issues relating to DRT systems reliability and its perception as being for old people.
UK	Psychological and Information	Concludes that the provision of adequate transportation services to rural communities presents significant challenges because of issues relating to transport poverty and the digital divide.	Describes the use of GPS, ICT and other technology to enhance DRT.
UK	Temporal and Spatial	The "article identifies inter- and intra-regional dimensions of inequality that are emerging around the convergence of transport policy, industrial policy and environmental policy."	Provides insights into social equity issues surrounding future EM introduction.
UK	Physical and Economic	Concludes that electric vehicle will never be the ideal solution to promoting sustainable transport systems if they are used to promote increased consumption.	Discusses how electric vehicles are significantly more expensive than traditional vehicles.
UK	Psychological and Information	Findings show that, "while community transport services play a vital role in rural communities, many older people are confused or unclear about what these services do, how they can be used, and how to access them"	Describes how older people often confused and unclear about how DRT could serve them and that more information could help.

(Continued)

Table 10.A1 (Continued)

Author	Year	Title	Journal
Akgöl, K., and Günay, B.	2014	Prediction of Modal Shift Using Artificial Neural Networks.	TEM Journal
Harrison, G., and Shepherd, S	2014	An interdisciplinary study to explore impacts from policies for the introduction of low carbon vehicles.	Transportation Planning and Technology
Martinez, L.M., Viegas, J.M., and Eiro, T.	2014	Formulating a New Express Minibus Service Design Problem as a Clustering Problem.	Transportation Science
Stanley, J., and Lucas, K.	2014	Workshop 6 Report: Delivering sustainable public transport.	Research in Transportation Economics
Wang, C., Quddus, M., Enoch, M., Ryley, T., and Davison, L.	2014	Multilevel modelling of Demand Responsive Transport (DRT) trips in Greater Manchester based on area-wide socio-economic data.	Transportation
Beecroft, M., and Pangbourne, K.	2015	Future prospects for personal security in travel by public transport.	Transportation Planning and Technology

Country	Category	Findings	Relevance
Turkey	Temporal and Spatial	Findings reveal the potential of applying machine learning to calculate modal shift.	Provides insights into modal shift away from PMV when AI is used to optimise route planning.
UK	Physical and Economic	Establishes an ethical framework to "balance obligations to reduced greenhouse gases (GHG) emissions and rights to car ownership"	Provides insights into the importance of having access to a PMV.
Portugal	Temporal and Spatial	"Presents a novel and simple modelling approach to design innovative transportation services, such as the express minibus service."	Describes how future DRT models can be developed with real-time booking systems allow real-time routing changes to ensure the most direct routes for customers.
Australia	Physical and Economic	Develops "a set of general principles intended to further promote sustainable public transport."	Provides insights into how technology can improve DRT systems.
UK	Psychological and Information	Findings show that "the demand for DRT services was higher in areas with low car ownership, low population density, high proportion of white people, and high levels of social deprivation, measured in terms of income, employment, education, housing and services, health and disability, and living environment."	Describes how DRT appeals to areas of low population density, low car ownership and high levels of social deprivation. Explains that the perception of DRT is that it is safer than other forms of road transport.
UK	Psychological and Information	Develops "a set of policy recommendations, operator, and business opportunities, knowledge gaps and research priorities to support and enhance provision for personal security in travel by public transport."	Provides insights into the use of technology to improve safety and security on shared mobility services.

(Continued)

Table 10.A1 (Continued)

Author	Year	Title	Journal
Bigerna and Polinori	2015	Willingness to Pay and Public Acceptance for Hydrogen Buses.	Sustainability
Evans, G., Guo, A.W., Blythe, P., and Burden, M.	2015	Integrated smartcard solutions.	Transportation Planning and Technology
Gomes, R., Pinho de Sousa, J., and Galvão Dias, T.	2015	Sustainable Demand Responsive Transportation systems in a context of austerity.	Research in Transportation Economics
Grieco, M.	2015	Social sustainability and urban mobility.	Social Responsibility Journal
Haustein, S., and Siren, A.	2015	Older People's Mobility.	Transport Reviews

Country	Category	Findings	Relevance
Italy	Physical and Economic	"The results confirm that residents in Perugia are willing to pay extra to support the introduction of H2B."	Provides evidence that users are willing to pay more for sustainable public transport (Hydrogen Buses)
UK	Physical and Economic	"Findings suggest there is potential for an integrated TranCit card, facilitating easier access to services and travel options across boundaries, even at the international level."	Describes how data obtained from smart card ticketing systems can be used to better understand the behaviour of passenger and improve services.
Portugal	Temporal and Spatial	Finding show that "service design is critical" to ensure DRT services "answer sustainability and social inclusion challenges" while keeping costs low.	Discusses how DRT services can reduce costs and improve efficiency of transport network by using fewer, smaller vehicles, incorporating dynamic route planning and passenger allocation, and reducing instances of dead-runs.
UK	Temporal and Spatial	Findings show that "databases and methodologies around social sustainability have not been sufficiently developed to permit ready operationalisation" of advances in urban mobility.	Describes how intelligent data collection can help local authorities identify where transport services are required in order to reduce social inequalities resulting from physical or geographic conditions.
Denmark	Physical and Economic	Propose a hypothetical model based on the findings from a systematic comparison study. The modal "integrates the most relevant determinants of older people's mobility patterns and their interrelations.	Discusses how e-mobility, in-car assistance technology, and AVs will offer good opportunities for the elderly to remain mobile for longer.

(Continued)

Table 10.A1 (Continued)

Author	Year	Title	Journal
Kammerlander, M., Schanes, K., Hartwig, F., Jäger, J., Omann, I., and O'Keeffe, M.	2015	A resource-efficient and sufficient future mobility system for improved well-being in Europe.	Journal of Futures Research
Mackett, R.	2015	Improving accessibility for older people – Investing in a valuable asset.	Journal of Transport and Health
Thomopoulos, N., and Givoni, M.	2015	The autonomous car—a blessing or a curse for the future of low carbon mobility?	European Journal of Futures Research
Cheyne, C., and Imran, M.	2016	Shared transport.	Energy Research and Social Science
Clark, J., and Curl, A.	2016	Bicycle and Car Share Schemes as Inclusive Modes of Travel?	Social Inclusion

Country	Category	Findings	Relevance
Austria	Temporal and Spatial	Findings show that to achieve the vision of resource efficiency in the transport section a new way of thinking about mobility is required. "It is not about travelling fastest and frequently, but unhurried, infrequently, and sustainably."	Describes how DRT, and door-to-door transport, can reduce demand for PMV travel by providing a viable option in low populated regions.
UK	Physical and Economic	Findings show that the travel patterns of older people are consistent with the assumption that they contribute to society economically, by frequenting local shops and through volunteer work and childcare. The barriers older people face with regards to transportation may hinder an even greater contribution.	Describes how the potential ability for AVs to drive without human input means degenerative disabilities will no longer inhibit elderly and disabled individuals.
UK	Physical and Economic	Concludes that the introduction of AV is only likely to create a more desirable transport system if it is accompanied by social change.	Provides insights into how AV could eliminate transport related exclusion.
New Zealand	Physical and Economic	Findings from a survey, focus group, and analysis of census data in New Zealand highlight "a growing need for alternatives to private transport for residents of small towns."	Provides insights into the important of shared mobility being flexible in order to accommodate individual needs.
UK	Physical and Economic	"Argues that there is a need to consider the social inclusivity of sharing schemes and to develop appropriate evaluation frameworks accordingly."	Describes how shared bicycle and car schemes can remove economic barriers associated with owning your own car and how those with disabilities are unlikely to benefit from car and bike schemes alone.

(Continued)

Table 10.A1 (Continued)

Author	Year	Title	Journal
Davidsson, P., Hajinasab, B., Holmgren, J., Jevinger, Å., and Persson, J.	2016	The Fourth Wave of Digitalization and Public Transport.	Sustainability
Leibert, T., and Golinski, S.	2016	Peripheralisation.	Comparative Population Studies
Petersen, T.	2016	Watching the Swiss.	Transport Policy
Chen, Y., Ardila-Gomez, A., and Frame, G.	2017	Achieving energy savings by intelligent transportation systems investments in the context of smart cities.	Transportation Research Part D
McLeod, S., Scheurer, J., and Curtis, C.	2017	Urban Public Transport.	Journal of Planning Literature

Country	Category	Findings	Relevance
Sweden	Psychological and Information	Concludes that for transport operators, planners, and users to take advantage of the opportunities related to IoT and its impact on public transport a number of technical and non-technical challenges need to be addressed.	Discusses how smart mobility enabled by IoT could improve data collection and contribute to providing accurate, real-time information about vehicles, users, traffic, and air quality.
Germany	Temporal and Spatial	Findings argue "that the peripheralisation approach is a helpful tool to better understand how interaction of out-migration, dependence, disconnection, and stigmatisation shape the future of rural regions."	Describes there is a need for local specific strategies to address how DRT can be used more efficiently and equitably.
Australia	Temporal and Spatial	Analyses the characteristics of public timetable networks in the contest of rural transportation in Switzerland. Findings identify lessons for their potential application in other locations.	Discusses how first-mile, last-mile transport networks may provide better coverage and be more efficient they are timed to connect to public transport hubs to ensure reductions in transfer times.
USA	Psychological and Information	Findings from literature review, case studies and interviews has "found that the smart cities context has transformed traditional ITS into smart mobility with three major characteristics: people-centre, data-driven, and powered by bottom-up innovations."	Describes how technological improvements in ITS and ICT can facilitate the collection and analysis of data which can be used to improve the efficiency of the transportation system.
Australia	Temporal and Spatial	The "findings of this systematic review support the paradigm of PT oriented urban mobility and provide an optimistic insight into the future of sustainable travel in cities."	Discusses how DRT enabled by autonomous technology and shared mobility has the potential to increase the catchment of traditional public transport systems.

(Continued)

Table 10.A1 (Continued)

Author	Year	Title	Journal
Melo, S., Macedo, J., and Baptista, P.	2017	Guiding cities to pursue a smart mobility paradigm.	Research in Transportation Economics
Milakis, D., van Arem, B., and van Wee, B.	2017	Policy and society related implications of automated driving.	Journal of Intelligent Transportation Systems
Newman, D.	2017	Automobiles and socioeconomic sustainability	Transfers

Country	Category	Findings	Relevance
Portugal	Psychological and Information	Results show that traffic management systems that re-route can reduce travel times and enhance the efficiency of roads.	Describes how traffic management systems enabled by advances in ICT and data collection provide guidance information to drivers to assist route planning.
The Netherlands	Physical and Economic	Findings show that "first-order impacts (of autonomous vehicles) on road capacity, fuel efficiency, emissions, and accidents risk are expected to be beneficial. The magnitude of these benefits will likely increase with the level of automation and cooperation and with the penetration rate of these systems. "	Describes how AV provide another transportation option for those unable to drive a PMV.
UK	Physical and Economic	Proposes a mobility bill of rights that states: (1) everybody should have access to affordable mobility which meets basic needs; (2) transport should not harm us or the environment; (3) transport should not threaten health, safety or the environment; (4) transport pricing should not penalise those who use it less; (5) transport should be accessibly so we are not excluded from society; (6) we should not have to rely on private vehicles for our travel; (7) everyone should have access to a public transport system; and (8) transport should not contribute to depletion of natural resource	Discusses how electric vehicles offer very little to overcome transport related social exclusion.

(*Continued*)

Table 10.A1 (Continued)

Author	Year	Title	Journal
Sun, Y., Olaru, D., Smith, B., Greaves, S., and Collins, A.	2017	Road to autonomous vehicles in Australia.	Road and Transport Research
Adnan, N., Md Nordin, S., Bin Bahruddin, M.A., and Ali, M.	2018	How trust can drive forward the user acceptance to the technology?	Transportation Research Part A
Docherty, I., Marsden, G., and Anable, J.	2018	The governance of smart mobility.	Transportation Research Part A
Gonzalez-Feliu, J., Pronello, C., and Salanova Grau, J.	2018	Multi-stakeholder collaboration in urban transport.	Transport
Graham, H., de Bell, S., Flemming, K., Sowden, A., White, P., and Wright, K.	2018	The experiences of everyday travel for older people in rural areas.	Journal of Transport and Health

Country	Category	Findings	Relevance
Australia	Physical and Economic	Findings identify a number of key issues associated with the introduction of AV in Australia.	Discusses how increased VOT in AV could have a positive impact on those impacted by geographic-related TDA and there is potential for SAV to significantly reduce the costs of DRT.
Malaysia	Physical and Economic	Findings show "that the level of trust, which may vary on the sociodemographic profile of the users, has been studied as one of the factors for user acceptance."	Describes AV could improve accessibility for elderly and disabled including the potential for increased social interactions, greater connection to employment and health services, improved comfort, and increased VOT.
UK	Physical and Economic	Identifies public value as the key governance aim that should be implemented for the transition to smart mobility.	Describes how MaaS can facilitate the integration of a wide range of mobility providers and help strengthen the efficiency of public transport and DRT.
France	Physical and Economic	Provides an analysis and overview of a set of papers which focus on "the field of multi-stakeholder and collaboration in urban transport"	Discusses how an integrated system such as MaaS can facilitate multi-stakeholder collaboration, and the sharing of information and resources.
UK	Psychological and Information	Identifies three themes related to older people and their experiences of everyday travel: (a) experience with inadequate transport system; (b) importance of everyday travel to maintain lives; and (c) the symbolic importance of travel.	Describes how DRT and community transport is often stigmatised within the community and there is confusion about how to, and who can access it.

(Continued)

Table 10.A1 (Continued)

Author	Year	Title	Journal
Guo et al.	2018	Impacts of internal migration, household registration system, and family planning policy on travel mode choice in China.	Travel, Behavior and Society
Hopkins and Schwanen	2018	Automated Mobility Transitions.	Sustainability
Howard, A., and Borenstein, J.	2018	The ugly truth about ourselves and our robot creations.	Science and Engineering Ethics
Illgen, S., and Höck, M.	2018	Establishing car sharing services in rural areas.	Transportation
Jin, S.T., Kong, H., Wu, R., and Sui, D.Z.	2018	Ridesourcing, the sharing economy, and the future of cities.	Cities
Lam, D., and Givens, J.W.	2018	Small and smart.	New Global Studies

Country	Category	Findings	Relevance
USA	Institutional	Findings "suggest that – among other factors – continuing internal migration, relaxation of household registration system, and changes in family planning policy, are likely to affect travel mode choices."	Provides insights into the impact of policy and laws on travel mode choice.
UK	Institutional	Results "suggest that the UK has adopted a reasonably comprehensive approach to the governing of automated vehicle innovation but that this approach cannot be characterized as sufficiently inclusive, democratic, diverse and open."	Discusses importance of including general public in decision making
USA	Psychological and Information	Concludes that a range of measures should be taken to ensure bias is removed or mitigated from robotic technology – including self-driving vehicles.	Discusses how AVs will have to make decisions based on a range of alternative options and are therefore at risk of bias.
Germany	Temporal and Spatial	"Findings indicate a certain feasibility of rural car sharing development, while highlighting the positive effect it could have on car sharing demand in urban areas."	Provides insights into how ride sharing can contribute to further TDA.
USA	Psychological and Information	Findings describe how it is unlikely that ride sharing will reduce car ownership.	Describes how shared mobility and AVs can help smaller communities that do not have access to public transport by providing more options, more frequently.
USA	Temporal and Spatial	Using South Bend, Indiana as an example the study looks at the potential for smart cities in smaller communities.	Discusses the use of free-floating bike sharing for first- and last-mile connection to PT.

(Continued)

Table 10.A1 (Continued)

Author	Year	Title	Journal
Li, X., Zhang, Y., Sun, L., and Liu, Q.	2018	Free-floating bike sharing in Jiangsu.	Energies
Lim, H.S.M., and Taeihagh, A.	2018	Autonomous vehicles for smart and sustainable cities.	Energies
Milakis, D., Kroesen, M., and van Wee, B.	2018	Implications of automated vehicles for accessibility and location choices.	Journal of Transport Geography
Mulley, C., and Kronsell, A.	2018	The "uberisation" of public transport and mobility as a service (MaaS).	Research in Transportation Economics
Mulley, C., Nelson, J.D., and Wright, S.	2018	Community transport meets mobility as a service.	Research in Transportation Economics

Country	Category	Findings	Relevance
Singapore	Temporal and Spatial	Findings show that: (a) bike sharing was mainly used for travelling short distances; (b) lower costs, more education, and promotion of health benefits could be used to promote bike sharing; and (c) bike sharing is more attractive to higher income residents.	Describes how important the perception of safety is to ensure successful operation and use of AV.
Singapore	Psychological and Information	Findings describe how addressing privacy and cybersecurity related to AV is crucial to the development of smart and sustainable cities.	Describes how AV may lead to increased suburbanisation or density.
The Netherlands	Physical and Economic	Findings from Q-method study showed that experts expect AV to influence accessibility through all four level (land use, transport, temporal and individual)	Discusses advantage of a MaaS system would be that unlike existing DRT services the subsidised provision of transport may not be seen as an entitlement but instead be part of a larger system that benefits all.
Australia	Psychological and Information	Findings of workshop discussion show a difference between policy and mobility provider views, a need for flexibility, the importance of collaboration, and a need to address user safety.	Discusses how MaaS provides an opportunity to cross subsidise which could improve the transportation for disadvantaged groups (e.g., aged, disabled, and rural areas).
Australia	Temporal and Spatial	Findings show that CT operators in Australia are very enthusiastic about the potential for MaaS to offer mobility packages to services their users.	Discusses how AVs with the absence of strict policy measures could result in more demand for car ownership and miles travelled.

(Continued)

Table 10.A1 (Continued)

Author	Year	Title	Journal
Noy, K., and Givoni, M.	2018	Is "Smart Mobility" Sustainable?	Sustainability
Soares Machado, C., de Salles Hue, N.P.M., Berssaneti, F.T., and Quintanilha, J.A.	2018	An Overview of Shared Mobility.	Sustainability
Wong, S.	2018	Traveling with blindness.	Health and Place
Allen, J., and Farber, S.	2019	Sizing up transport poverty.	Transport Policy
Axsen, J., and Sovacool, B.K.	2019	The roles of users in electric, shared and automated mobility transitions.	Transportation Research Part D

Country	Category	Findings	Relevance
Israel	Physical and Economic	Findings from a survey of 117 entrepreneurs "shows that there is a mismatch between interpretation and understanding of what is 'smart' and what is 'sustainable'."	Discusses that for shared mobility to help achieve sustainable mobility objectives it is important to identify how existing public transport and shared mobility can be synergised to make them complementary and benefit the transport system as a whole.
Brazil	Psychological and Information	Findings determine that based on literature review the introduction of shared modes alone "will not solve transportation problems in large cities."	Discusses how people with visual impairment would greatly benefit if existing door-to-door transportation services were improved.
USA	Physical and Economic	Findings show "space-time constraints of people with visual impairments are closed linked to their access to transportation, assistive technologies, and mobile devices."	Describes how providing transportation for low density dispersed neighbourhoods is challenging due to dispersal of individuals and destinations.
Canada	Temporal and Spatial	Recommends that future investments in major transportation infrastructure should be focused in areas with high density of low-income households and low levels of accessibility. In areas of low density, subsidised ride sharing and DRT should be considered.	Describes how SAV could reduce total cost of ownership by over 80% per km travelled compared to a conventional car.
Canada	Physical and Economic	Findings summarise "characteristics of early users, as well as practical insights for strategies and policies seeking societally-beneficial outcomes from mass deployment of" transport innovations.	Describes how FTS can contribute to rural connectivity by providing door-to-door transport that does not rely on fixed routes and how MaaS is promising because it provides integrated customer experiencing linking users with a range of transport options on demand.

(Continued)

Table 10.A1 (Continued)

Author	Year	Title	Journal
Beecroft, M., Cottrill, C.D., Farrington, J.H., Nelson, J.D., and Niewiadomski, P.	2019	From infrastructure to digital networks.	Scottish Geographical Journal
Bennett, R., Vijaygopal, R., and Kottasz, R.	2019	Willingness of people with mental health disabilities to travel in driverless vehicles.	Journal of Transport and Health
Bennett, R., Vijaygopal, R., and Kottasz, R.	2019	Attitudes towards autonomous vehicles among people with physical disabilities.	Transportation Research Part A
Canitez, F.	2019	Pathways to sustainable urban mobility in developing megacities.	Technological Forecasting and Social Change
Creitzig et al.	2019	Leveraging digitalization for sustainability in urban transport.	Global Sustainability

Country	Category	Findings	Relevance
UK	Psychological and Information	Identifies connectivity as a central theme when looking at the development and evolution of transport geography research at the University of Aberdeen.	Provides insights into attitudes towards AV among those with intellectual disability.
UK	Psychological and Information	Findings show "three categories of attitude towards AVs arose from the STM; respectively involving freedom, fear and curiosity."	Discusses how public transport providers should look to integrated systems such as MaaS which can help with sharing of data, identification of demand, and connect potential users with the most suitable providers.
UK	Psychological and Information	Findings show that "attitudes towards AVs among people with disabilities were significantly influenced by their levels of interest in new technology, generalized anxiety, intensity of a person's disability, prior knowledge of AVs, locus of control and action orientation."	Provides insights into how AV could perpetuate or create new social inequalities.
Turkey	Physical and Economic	Findings "proposes a socio-technical transition perspective to examine and analyze the urban mobility systems in developing megacities. In addition, a multi-level perspective is offered to understand the dynamics of sustainable urban mobility transitions"	Provides insights into attitudes towards AV among those with intellectual disability and those without.
Germany	Institutional	Concludes that "only strong public policies can steer digitalization towards fostering sustainability in urban transport."	Provides insights into the importance of policy in smart technology development.

(Continued)

Table 10.A1 (Continued)

Author	Year	Title	Journal
Curtis, C., Stone, J., Legacy, C., and Ashmore, D.	2019	Governance of future urban mobility.	Urban Policy and Research
Dean, J., Wray, A., Braun, L., Casello, J., McCallum, L., and Gower, S.	2019	Holding the keys to health?	BMC Public Health
Freemark, Y., Hudson, A., and Zhao, J.	2019	Are cities prepared for autonomous vehicles?	Journal of the American Planning Association
Goggin et al.	2019	Disability at the centre of digital inclusion.	Communication Research and Practice,

Country	Category	Findings	Relevance
Australia	Physical and Economic	"Findings from industry engagement workshop highlight the complexity of issues and questions surrounding MaaS implementation."	Discusses how the change from a PMV to more sustainable system is reliant on the cost of transport, regulations, planning, land use, technology, public awareness and culture.
Canada	Psychological and Information	Findings show "there is general agreement that AVs will improve road safety overall, thus reducing injuries and fatalities from human errors in operating motorized vehicles. However, the relationships with air quality, physical activity, and stress, among other health factors may be more complex."	Discusses how when MaaS is implemented with AV there is a risk that those currently able to operate a PMV will have access to private AV.
USA	Physical and Economic	Findings show that: (1) planning for AV is not widespread; (2) bigger cities are more likely to have started planning for AV; (3) there is optimism among local officials regarding the potential increase in safety, and decrease in costs and pollution associated with AV; and (4) over one-third of local officials are concerned about the impact AV will have on VKT and public transport ridership.	Discuss how AVs can contribute to the improved safety but increased reliance on technology opens up additional risks.
Australia	Psychological and Information	Concludes "that 'disability and digital inclusion' should be specifically also placed at the heart of digital economy policy and plans"	Provides insights into digital divide and disability

(*Continued*)

Table 10.A1 (Continued)

Author	Year	Title	Journal
Groth, S.	2019	Multimodal divide: Reproduction of transport poverty in smart mobility trends.	Transportation Research Part A
Hawkins, J., and Habib, K.N.	2019	Heterogeneity in marginal value of urban mobility.	Transportation
Jokinen, J.-P., Sihvola, T., and Mladenovic, M.N.	2019	Policy lessons from the flexible transport service pilot Kutsuplus in the Helsinki Capital Region.	Transport Policy
Kandt, J., and Leak, A.	2019	Examining inclusive mobility through smartcard data.	Journal of Transport Geography

Country	Category	Findings	Relevance
Germany	Psychological and Information	Findings show that smart mobility can potentially contribute to transport poverty by: (a) providing an unequal distribution of mode options; (b) excluding those who are unable to use technology; and (c) excluding those who are unwilling to us technology due to privacy concerns.	Discusses how improved costs and accessibility associated with AV may reduce public transport use.
Canada	Temporal and Spatial	"Findings reveal the potential for social exclusion follow the adoption of MaaS."	Discuss how smart mobility may contribute to social exclusion.
Finland	Temporal and Spatial	Findings "provide a range of guidelines and lessons for future urban FMTS"	Discusses how MaaS would likely result in higher transport costs for those in low density areas and governments will likely need to provide subsidies and planning interventions in order to ensure equitable access to transport.
UK	Temporal and Spatial	Findings show "first, the decline in patronage occurs in three waves across the study period according to distinct activity patterns; second, formerly frequent (daily) passengers tend to abandon the bus and thus show the largest impact on the overall trend; third, the neighbourhood context of withdrawing passengers indicates social disadvantage, higher instance of ethnic minorities and lower car ownership rates, in other words higher risk of social exclusion."	Provides insights into the importance of DRT to direct users to major transport hubs, how users are more sensitive to travel time than cost, and how technology can improve efficiency of DRT.

(Continued)

Table 10.A1 (Continued)

Author	Year	Title	Journal
Kuzio, J.	2019	Planning for Social Equity and Emerging Technologies.	Transportation Research Record
Le Boennec, R., Nicolaï, I., and Da Costa, P.	2019	Assessing 50 innovative mobility offers in low-density areas.	Transport Policy
Legacy, C., Ashmore, D., Scheurer, J., Stone, J., and Curtis, C.,	2019	Planning the driverless city.	Transport Reviews
Liu, C., Yu, B., Zhu, Y., Liu, L., and Li, P.	2019	Measurement of rural residents' mobility in western China.	Sustainability
Martin, G.	2019	An Ecosocial Frame for Autonomous Vehicles.	Capitalism Nature Socialism

Country	Category	Findings	Relevance
USA	Physical and Economic	Findings show that 80% of metropolitan planning organisations have plans that included a response to social equity, however, only 20% of plans considered how new technologies would impact on social equity.	Describes how MaaS can contribute to improved public transport use in low density, less accessibility areas by providing a connection to major public transport hubs, and creating synergies between a range of transport options.
France	Temporal and Spatial	Develops a two-step decision-making tool to assist local governments with planning and implementing transportation policies .	Describes how the benefits of AV including the ability to work, eat, and rest while in transit could be highly desirable and result in increased cost, VKT, and demand on infrastructure.
Australia	Physical and Economic	Findings reveal "the conceptual gaps in the framing of AV technology – the prospects and limits – and how these are conceived"	Discusses how despite new technology encouraging walking is still key to reducing social exclusion as walking is costless, and contributes to improved health.
China	Temporal and Spatial	Findings "show that Qingyang's rural mobility is at a low level, but differences in the types of rural residents, districts and counties, and dimensions of mobility are observed."	Discusses how for AV to reduce some of the social equity issues associated with the PMV it should be introduced as part of a system integrated with existing transport providers.
USA	Physical and Economic	"As is usually the case with a new technological consumer product, discourse centers on its promises, not its perils. Largely ignored are potential impacts on social justice and environmental sustainability."	Provides insights into how information availability in lower density areas is critical for the success of many smart mobility applications.

(*Continued*)

Table 10.A1 (Continued)

Author	Year	Title	Journal
Martínez-Díaz, M., Soriguera, F., and Pérez, I.	2019	Autonomous driving: a bird's eye view.	IET Intelligent Transport Systems
Meelen, T., Frenken, K., and Hobrink, S.	2019	Weak spots for car-sharing in The Netherlands?	Energy Research and Social Science
Nordhoff, S., Kyriakidis, M., van Arem, B., and Happee, R.	2019	A multi-level model on automated vehicle acceptance (MAVA).	Theoretical Issues in Ergonomics Science
Ortar, N., and Ryghaug, M.	2019	Should all cars be electric by 2025?	Sustainability

Country	Category	Findings	Relevance
Spain	Psychological and Information	Provides an overall state-of-the-art of the development of AV and identifies the issues critical for its success.	Discusses risk that AV will be expensive and exclude low income residents and how subsidised SAV may provide a viable alternative.
The Netherlands	Physical and Economic	Findings "demonstrate how the relation between niche innovation and the socio-technical regime of private car ownership affects adoption patterns."	Discusses how while AV are expected to bring a much safer driving environment, acceptability among people over 50 is still quite low. .
Switzerland	Psychological and Information	Findings reveal "that 6% of the studies investigated the exposure of individuals to AVs (i.e., knowledge and experience). 22% of the studies investigated domain-specific factors (i.e., performance and effort expectancy, safety, facilitating conditions, and service and vehicle characteristics), 4% symbolic-affective factors (i.e., hedonic motivation and social influence), and 12% moral-normative factors (i.e., perceived benefits and risks). Factors related to a person's socio-demographic profile, travel behavior and personality were investigated by 28%, 15% and 14% of the studies, respectively. "	Discusses how car sharing contributes to improved accessibility for those without access to a vehicle—satisfying basic needs relating to transportation.
UK	Temporal and Spatial	Findings show that there is much uncertainty regarding how the transition between fuel-based and electric vehicles occurs including issues of efficiency, affordability and sustainability	Discusses how the general public perceives AV and identifies risks they associate with the technology.

(Continued)

Table 10.A1 (Continued)

Author	Year	Title	Journal
Ruan et al.	2019	Social adaptation and adaptation pressure among the "drifting elderly" in China.	International Journal of Health Planning and Management,
Sener, I.N., Zmud, J., and Williams, T.	2019	Measures of baseline intent to use automated vehicles	Transportation Research Part F
Sovacool, B., Martiskainen, M., Hook, A., and Baker, L.	2019	Decarbonization and its discontents.	Climatic Change
Tang, C.S., and Veelenturf, L.P.	2019	The strategic role of logistics in the industry 4.0 era	Transportation Research Part E
Viergutz, K., and Schmidt, C.	2019	Demand responsive – vs. conventional public transportation.	Procedia Computer Science
Waseem et al.	2019	Integration of solar energy in electrical, hybrid, autonomous vehicle	SN Applied Science

Country	Category	Findings	Relevance
China	Institutional	"The drifting elderly had poor adaptation regarding self-identity, daily activities, and social context."	Discusses issues of digital divide among elderly migrants
USA	Psychological and Information	Findings show "the strongest associations with intent to use (AVs) were observed for attitudes toward self-driving vehicles, performance expectation, perceived safety, and social influence."	Describes social equity issues surrounding the introduction of EM.
UK	Temporal and Spatial	Develops a framework for "energy justice" with four distinct dimensions: (a) distributive justice; (b) procedural justice; (c) cosmopolitan justice; and (d) recognition justice.	Discusses how AV bring a significant, and uncertain impact on the transport system.
USA	Psychological and Information	Concludes that companies must take measures to ensure underlying risks associated with technological advancements including: (a) cyber-attacks; (b) faulty data; (c) safety regulations; and (d) privacy.	Discusses how those in rural, or low density, sparsely populated areas may not be able to fully benefit from smart technology due to network coverage, and electricity prices.
Germany	Temporal and Spatial	Findings show that DRT services may not be the solution to public transport in rural areas and further research is need to balance access, financial, service, and pollution issues associated with DRT.	Discusses risks associated with AV and ITS.
India	Physical and Economic	"Overview of electric and hybrid vehicles suggests that in a developing country such as India, there is a huge demand for green-powered electric vehicles for the transportation sector."	Discusses demand for green-powered vehicles.

(Continued)

Table 10.A1 (Continued)

Author	Year	Title	Journal
Yigitcanlar, T., Han, H., Kamruzzaman, M., Ioppolo, G., and Sabatini-Marques, J.	2019	The making of smart cities.	Land Use Policy
Zhou, J.	2019	Ride-sharing service planning based on smartcard data	Transport Policy
Becker et al.	2020	Assessing the welfare impacts of Shared Mobility and Mobility as a Service (MaaS).	Transportation Research Part A
Bissell, D., Birtchnell, T., Elliott, A., and Hsu, E.L.	2020	Autonomous automobilities.	Current Sociology
Ferdman, A.	2020	Corporate ownership of automated vehicles.	Transport Reviews
Guo and Peeta	2020	Impacts of personalized accessibility information on residential location choice and travel behavior.	Travel, Behavior and Society

Country	Category	Findings	Relevance
Australia	Psychological and Information	Findings "disclose the need for a comprehensive smart city conceptualization to inform policymaking and consequently the practice."	Discusses how AV could assist the development of DRT in low demand areas, reducing costs, and making the system operate more efficiently.
China	Physical and Economic	Findings show "that some low-demand transit routes can probably be replaced by Uber at a lower level of overall costs."	Provides insights into cities that use technology enabled smart traffic systems.
Switzerland	Psychological and Information	"Results show that in Zurich, through less biased mode choice decisions alone, transport-related energy consumption can be reduced by 25%"	Discusses role of MaaS in providing users an unbiased choice of modes.
Australia	Physical and Economic	Shows "how a mobilities approach provides an ideal conceptual lens through which the broader social impacts of autonomous vehicles might be identified and evaluated."	Discusses social issues surrounding introduction of AV
Germany	Physical and Economic	"Proposes a new angle on the relationship between ownership models of automated vehicles and implications for travel."	Describe how for shared mobility to work in rural areas a broad base of users is required, large investments from the start, and strong connection with the broader region – particularly cities.
USA	Temporal and Spatial	Results "show that personalized accessibility information can potentially make relocators more informed about travel-related information, and assists them in selecting a residence that better addresses their travel needs based on higher accessibility to potential destinations."	Discusses the use of ICT to help residents make more informed choice.

(Continued)

Table 10.A1 (Continued)

Author	Year	Title	Journal
Guo et al.	2020	Personal and societal impacts of motorcycle ban policy on motorcyclists' home-to-work morning commute in China.	Travel, Behavior and Society
Hoque et al.	2020	Life Cycle Sustainability Assessment of Alternative Energy Sources for the Western Australian Transport Sector	Sustainability
Liu et al.	2020	A tale of two social groups in Xiamen, China: Trip frequency of migrants and locals and its determinants.	Travel, Behavior and Society
Meng et al.	2020	Policy implementation of multi-modal (shared) mobility.	Transport Reviews
Rojas-Rueda et al.	2020	Autonomous Vehicles and Public Health.	Annual Review of Public Health

Country	Category	Findings	Relevance
USA	Institutional	"These results suggest that policy and infrastructural support for using public transit, walk, and bike modes, household mobility, and plan to purchase a car were likely to affect the personal and societal impacts of the motorcycle ban policy on travel mode shifts"	Provides insights into the impact of policy and laws on travel mode choice.
Australia	Physical and Economic	"The results show that the environment-friendly and socially sustainable energy options, namely, ethanol-gasoline blend E55, electricity, electricity-E10 hybrid, and hydrogen, would need around 0.02, 0.14, 0.10, and 0.71 AUD/VKT of financial support, respectively, to be comparable to gasoline. "	Discusses economic sustainability of alternative fuel vehicles
Hong Kong	Institutional	"Highlights the importance of context and population differentiation and calls for more in-depth research on migrants' travel behaviors as well as their determinants."	Provides insights into barriers related to infrastructure provision.
Australia	Institutional	"Suggests that policy entrepreneurship in collaboration with other partners, policy innovation, and the notions of merit goods and second-best policymaking can enable policy initiatives towards multi-modal shared mobility and provide supporting arguments if policies encounter failures."	Discusses the importance of policy in development of shared mobility
USA	Physical and Economic	Provides recommendations for the use of AV to improve public health.	Provides insights into some benefits and issues with AV from a public health perspective.

(*Continued*)

Table 10.A1 (Continued)

Author	Year	Title	Journal
Soares Machado et al.	2020	Placement of Infrastructure for Urban Electromobility	Sustainability
Tao et al.	2020	Investigating the impacts of public transport on job accessibility in Shenzhen, China.	Land Use Policy
Tomej, K., and Liburd, J.J.	2020	Sustainable accessibility in rural destinations.	Journal of Sustainable Tourism
Turoń and Kubik	2020	Economic Aspects of Driving Various Types of Vehicles in Intelligent Urban Transport Systems, Including Car-Sharing Services and Autonomous Vehicles.	Applied Science

Country	Category	Findings	Relevance
Brazil	Temporal and Spatial	Results "shows that districts with the largest demand for charging stations are located in the central area, where the population also exhibits the highest purchasing power"	Discusses issues associated with electric mobility in low density and rural areas.
China	Physical and Economic	"Highlights land use and transport policy countermeasures to improve job accessibility by public transport."	Discusses how job accessibility is greatly improved if one has access to a PMV
Austria	Temporal and Spatial	Findings "demonstrates the use of sustainable transport accessibility as a measure for transport evaluation that considers both environmental aspects and social justice framed as sustainable tourism participation for all."	Provides insights into the use of DRT in rural areas with high levels of tourism.
Poland	Physical and Economic	"Results indicate the relation of travel parameters (including vehicle type) to the total cost of travel in urban transport systems."	Discusses the economic sustainability of AV and shared transport

References

1. Ingrao, C., Messineo, A., Beltramo, R., Yigitcanlar, T., Ioppolo, G. (2018). How can life cycle thinking support sustainability of buildings? *Journal of Cleaner Production* 201, 556–569.

2. Arbolino, R., De Simone, L., Carlucci, F., Yigitcanlar, T., Ioppolo, G. (2018). Towards a sustainable industrial ecology. *Journal of Cleaner Production* 178, 220–236.

3. Lee, S.H., Yigitcanlar, T., Han, J.H., Leem, Y.T. (2008). Ubiquitous urban infrastructure: Infrastructure planning and development in Korea. *Innovation* 10, 282–292.

4. Yigitcanlar, T., Mohamed, A., Kamruzzaman, M., Piracha, A. (2019). Understanding transport-related social exclusion. *Urban Policy and Research* 2019, 37, 97–110.

5. Currie, G., Delbosc, A. (2010). Modelling the social and psychological impacts of transport disadvantage. *Transportation* 37, 953–966.

6. Duvarci, Y., Yigitcanlar, T., Mizokami, S. (2015). Transportation disadvantage impedance indexing. *Journal of Transport Geography* 2015, 48, 61–75.

7. Yigitcanlar, T., Dodson, J., Gleeson, B., Sipe, N. (2007). Travel self-containment in master planned estates. *Urban Policy and Research* 25, 129–149.

8. Delbosc, A., Currie, G. (2011). The spatial context of transport disadvantage, social exclusion and well-being. *Journal of Transport Geography* 19, 1130–1137.

9. Yigitcanlar, T., Wilson, M., Kamruzzaman, M. (2019). Disruptive impacts of automated driving systems on the built environment and land use. *Journal of Open Innovation: Technology, Market, and Complexity* 2019, 5, 24.

10. Noy, K., Givoni, M. (2018) Is 'smart mobility' sustainable? *Sustainability* 10, 422.

11. Yigitcanlar, T., Kamruzzaman, M. (2019). Smart cities and mobility. *Journal of Urban Technology* 26, 21–46.

12. Golbabaei, F., Yigitcanlar, T., Bunker, J. (2021). The role of shared autonomous vehicle systems in delivering smart urban mobility: A systematic review of the literature. *International Journal of Sustainable Transportation* 15(10), 731–748.

13. Yigitcanlar, T., Han, H., Kamruzzaman, M., Ioppolo, G., Sabatini-Marques, J. (2019). The making of smart cities. *Land Use Policy* 88, 104187.

14. Yigitcanlar, T., Kamruzzaman, M., Foth, M., Sabatini-Marques, J., Da Costa, E., Ioppolo, G. (2019). Can cities become smart without being sustainable? *Sustainable Cities and Society* 45, 348–365.

15. Yigitcanlar, T., Desouza, K., Butler, L., Roozkhosh, F. (2020). Contributions and risks of artificial intelligence (AI) in building smarter cities. *Energies* 13, 1473.

16. Yigitcanlar, T., Butler, L., Windle, E., Desouza, K., Mehmood, R., Corchado, J. (2020). Can building 'artificially intelligent cities' protect humanity from natural disasters, pandemics and other catastrophes? *Sensors* 20, 2988.

17. Kaufman, B. (2020). *1 Million Rides and Counting. The Conversation 2020.* Available online: https://theconversation.com/1-million-rides-and-counting-on-demand-services-bring-public-transport-to-the-suburbs-132355 (accessed 1 May 2020).

18. Mahbub, P., Goonetilleke, A., Ayoko, G.A., Egodawatta, P., Yigitcanlar, T. (2011). Analysis of build-up of heavy metals and volatile organics on urban roads in Gold Coast, Australia. *Water Science & Technology* 63, 2077–2085.

19. Dowling, R. (2016). *Smart Cities: Does This Mean More Transport Disruption. The Conversation 2016.* Available online: https://theconversation.com/smart-cities-does-this-mean-more-transport-disruptions-63638 (accessed 1 May 2020).

20. Kane, M., Whitehead, J. (2017). How to ride transport disruption. *Australian Planner* 54, 177–185.

21. De Percy, M. (2016). *Taxi Driver Compensation for Uber is Unfair and Poorly Implemented. The Conversation 2016.* Available online: https://theconversation.com/taxi-driver-compensation-for-uber-is-unfair-and-poorly-implemented-64354 (accessed 1 May 2020).
22. Munton, J.R. (2017). *Explainer: What Rights Do Workers Have to Getting Paid in the Gig Economy? The Conversation 2017.* Available online: https://theconversation.com/explainer-what-rights-do-workers-have-to-getting-paid-in-the-gig-economy-70281 (accessed 1 May 2020).
23. Barratt, T., Veen, A., Goods, C., Josserand, E., Kaine, S. (2018). *As Yet Another Ridesharing Platform Launches in Australia, How Does This all End? The Conversation 2018.* Available online: https://theconversation.com/as-yet-another-ridesharing-platform-launches-in-australia-how-does-this-all-end-98389 (accessed 1 May 2020).
24. Docherty, I., Marsden, G., Anable, J. (2018). The governance of smart mobility. *Transportation Research Part A: Policy and Practice* 115, 114–125.
25. Suhl, K., Carreno, M. (2011). Can transport-related social exclusion be measured? In: *Proceedings of the 8th International Conference,* Vilnius, Lithuania, 19–20 May 2011; pp. 1001–1008.
26. Mageean, J., Nelson, J.D. (2003). The evaluation of demand responsive transport services in Europe. *Journal of Transport Geography* 11, 255–270.
27. Brake, J., Nelson, J.D., Wright, S. (2004). Demand responsive transport. *Journal of Transport Geography* 12, 323–337.
28. Battellino, H. (2009). Transport for the transport disadvantaged. *Transportation Policy* 16, 123–129.
29. Nelson, J.D., Wright, S., Masson, B., Ambrosino, G., Naniopoulos, A. (2010). Recent developments in flexible transport services. *Research in Transportation Economics* 29, 243–248.
30. Nelson, J.D., Phonphitakchai, T. (2012). An evaluation of the user characteristics of an open access DRT service. *Research in Transportation Economics* 34, 54–65.
31. Wang, C., Quddus, M., Enoch, M., Ryley, T., Davison, L. (2014). Multilevel modelling of demand responsive transport (DRT) trips in Greater Manchester based on area-wide socio-economic data. *Transportation* 41, 589–610.
32. Gomes, R., Pinho de Sousa, J., Galvão Dias, T. Sustainable Demand Responsive Transportation systems in a context of austerity. *Research in Transportation Economics* 2015, 51, 94–103.
33. Viergutz, K., Schmidt, C. (2019). Demand responsive – vs. conventional public transportation. *Procedia Computer Science* 151, 69–76.
34. Clark, J., Curl, A. (2016). Bicycle and car share schemes as inclusive modes of travel? *Social Inclusion* 4, 83–99.
35. Illgen, S., Höck, M. (2020). Establishing car sharing services in rural areas. *Transportation* 47, 811–826.
36. Jin, S.T., Kong, H., Wu, R., Sui, D.Z. (2018). Ridesourcing, the sharing economy, and the future of cities. *Cities* 76, 96–104.
37. Li, X., Zhang, Y., Sun, L., Liu, Q. (2018). Free-floating bike sharing in Jiangsu. *Energies* 11, 1664.
38. Soares Machado, C., de Salles Hue, N.P.M., Berssaneti, F.T., Quintanilha, J.A. (2018). An overview of shared mobility. *Sustainability* 10, 4342.
39. Axsen, J., Sovacool, B.K. (2019). The roles of users in electric, shared and automated mobility transitions. *Transportation Research Part D: Transport and Environment* 71, 1–21.

40. Martin, G. (2019). An ecosocial frame for autonomous vehicles. *Capitalism Nature Socialism* 30, 55–70.
41. Meelen, T., Frenken, K., Hobrink, S. (2019). Weak spots for car-sharing in The Netherlands? *Energy Research & Social Science* 52, 132–143.
42. Zhou, J. (2019). Ride-sharing service planning based on smartcard data. *Transportation Policy* 79, 1–10.
43. Brake, J., Nelson, J.D. (2007). A case study of flexible solutions to transport demand in a deregulated environment. *Journal of Transport Geography* 15, 262–273.
44. Davidsson, P., Hajinasab, B., Holmgren, J., Jevinger, Å., Persson, J. (2016). The fourth wave of digitalization and public transport. *Sustainability* 8, 1248.
45. Chen, Y., Ardila-Gomez, A., Frame, G. (2017). Achieving energy savings by intelligent transportation systems investments in the context of smart cities. *Transportation Research Part D: Transport and Environment* 54, 381–396.
46. Melo, S., Macedo, J., Baptista, P. (2017). Guiding cities to pursue a smart mobility paradigm. *Research in Transportation Economics* 65, 24–33.
47. Wells, P. (2012). Converging transport policy, industrial policy and environmental policy. *Local Economy* 27, 749–763.
48. Hoque, N., Biswas, W., Howard, I. (2020). Life cycle sustainability assessment of alternative energy sources for the western Australian transport sector. *Sustainability* 12, 5565.
49. Bigerna, S., Polinori, P. (2015). Willingness to pay and public acceptance for hydrogen buses. *Sustainability* 7, 13270–13289.
50. Ortar, N., Ryghaug, M. (2019). Should all cars be electric by 2025? *Sustainability* 11, 1868.
51. Thomopoulos, N., Givoni, M. (2015). The autonomous car—A blessing or a curse for the future of low carbon mobility? *European Journal of Futures Research* 3, 1–14.
52. Milakis, D., van Arem, B., van Wee, B. (2017). Policy and society related implications of automated driving. *Journal of Intelligent Transportation Systems* 21, 324–348.
53. Milakis, D., Kroesen, M., van Wee, B. (2018). Implications of automated vehicles for accessibility and location choices. *Journal of Transport Geography* 68, 142–148.
54. Lim, H.S., Taeihagh, A. (2018). Autonomous vehicles for smart and sustainable cities. *Energies* 11, 1062.
55. Dean, J., Wray, A., Braun, L., Casello, J., McCallum, L., Gower, S. (2019). Holding the keys to health? *BMC Public Health* 19, 1258.
56. Bissell, D., Birtchnell, T., Elliott, A., Hsu, E.L. (2020). Autonomous automobilities. *Current Sociology* 68, 116–134.
57. Rojas-Rueda, D., Nieuwenhuijsen, M.J., Khreis, H., Frumkin, H. (2020). Autonomous vehicles and public health. *Annual Review of Public Health* 41, 329–345.
58. Mulley, C., Kronsell, A. (2018). The "uberisation" of public transport and mobility as a service (MaaS). *Research in Transportation Economics* 69, 568–572.
59. Hawkins, J., Habib, K.N. (2020). Heterogeneity in marginal value of urban mobility: Evidence from a large-scale household travel survey in the Greater Toronto and Hamilton Area. *Transportation* 47(6), 3091–3108.
60. Becker, H., Balac, M., Ciari, F., Axhausen, K.W. (2020). Assessing the welfare impacts of shared mobility and mobility as a service (MaaS). *Transportation Research Part A: Policy and Practice* 131, 228–243.
61. Van Engelen, M., Cats, O., Post, H., Aardal, K. (2018). Enhancing flexible transport services with demand-anticipatory insertion heuristics. *Transportation Research Part E: Logistics and Transportation Review* 110, 110–121.

62. Yigitcanlar, T., Kankanamge, N., Vella, K. (2021). How are smart city concepts and technologies perceived and utilized? A systematic geo-Twitter analysis of smart cities in Australia. *Journal of Urban Technology* 28(1–2), 135–154.

63. Winter, K., Cats, O., Correia, G., van Arem, B. (2018). Performance analysis and fleet requirements of automated demand-responsive transport systems as an urban public transport service. *International Journal of Transportation Science and Technology* 7, 151–167.

64. Matyas, M., Kamargianni, M. (2019). The potential of mobility as a service bundles as a mobility management tool. *Transportation* 46, 1951–1968.

65. Czioska, P., Kutadinata, R., Trifunović, A., Winter, S., Sester, M., Friedrich, B. (2019). Real-world meeting points for shared demand-responsive transportation systems. *Public Transportation* 11, 341–377.

66. Harrison, G., Shepherd, S. (2014). An interdisciplinary study to explore impacts from policies for the introduction of low carbon vehicles. *Transportation Planning and Technology* 37, 98–117.

67. Tao, Z., Zhou, J., Lin, X., Chao, H., Li, G. (2020). Investigating the impacts of public transport on job accessibility in Shenzhen, China. *Land Use Policy* 99, 105025.

68. O'Shaughnessy, M., Casey, E., Enright, P. (2011). Rural transport in peripheral rural areas. *Social Enterprise Journal* 7, 183–190.

69. Broome, K., Worrall, L., Fleming, J., Boldy, D. (2012). Evaluation of flexible route bus transport for older people. *Transportation Policy* 21, 85–91.

70. Faisal, A., Yigitcanlar, T., Kamruzzaman, M., Currie, G. (2019). Understanding autonomous vehicles. *Journal of Transport and Land Use* 12, 45–72.

71. Mackett, R. (2015). Improving accessibility for older people. *Journal of Transport and Health* 2, 5–13.

72. Adnan, N., Md Nordin, S., Bin Bahruddin, M.A., Ali, M. How trust can drive forward the user acceptance to the technology? *Transportation Research Part A: Policy and Practice* 2018, 118, 819–836.

73. Wong, S. (2018). Traveling with blindness. *Health Place* 49, 85–92.

74. Faisal, A., Yigitcanlar, T., Kamruzzaman, M., Paz, A. (2021). Mapping two decades of autonomous vehicle research: A systematic scientometric analysis. *Journal of Urban Technology* 28(3–4), 45–74.

75. Haustein, S., Siren, A. (2015). Older people's mobility. *Transport Reviews* 35, 466–487.

76. Curtis, C., Stone, J., Legacy, C., Ashmore, D. (2019). Governance of future urban mobility. *Urban Policy and Research* 37, 393–404.

77. Canitez, F. (2019). Pathways to sustainable urban mobility in developing megacities. *Technological Forecasting and Social Change* 141, 319–329.

78. Zografos, K., Androutsopoulos, K., Sihvola, T. (2008). A methodological approach for developing and assessing business models for flexible transport systems. *Transportation* 35, 777–795.

79. Stanley, J., Lucas, K. (2014). Workshop 6 Report: Delivering sustainable public transport. *Research in Transportation Economics* 48, 315–322.

80. Evans, G., Guo, A.W., Blythe, P., Burden, M. (2015). Integrated smartcard solutions. *Transportation Planning and Technology* 38, 534–551.

81. Cheyne, C., Imran, M. (2016). Shared transport. *Energy Research & Social Science* 18, 139–150.

82. Gonzalez-Feliu, J., Pronello, C., Salanova Grau, J. (2018). Multi-stakeholder collaboration in urban transport. *Transport* 33, 1079–1094.

83. Mulley, C., Nelson, J.D., Wright, S. (2018). Community transport meets mobility as a service. *Research in Transportation Economics* 69, 583–591.
84. Waseem, M., Sherwani, A., Suhaib, M. (2019). Integration of solar energy in electrical, hybrid, autonomous vehicles. *SN Applied Sciences* 1, 1459.
85. Turoń, K., Kubik, A. (2020). Economic aspects of driving various types of vehicles in intelligent urban transport systems, including car-sharing services and autonomous vehicles. *Applied Science* 10, 5580.
86. Sun, Y., Olaru, D., Smith, B., Greaves, S., Collins, A. (2017). Road to autonomous vehicles in Australia. *Road and Transport Research* 26, 34–47.
87. Kuzio, J. Planning for social equity and emerging technologies. Transp. Res. Rec. 2019, 2673, 693–703.
88. Newman, D. Cars and consumption. Cap. Cl. 2013, 37, 457–476.
89. Newman, D. Automobiles and socioeconomic sustainability. Transfers 2017, 7, 100–106.
90. Freemark, Y., Hudson, A., Zhao, J. Are cities prepared for autonomous vehicles? JAPA 2019, 85, 133–151.
91. Ferdman, A. Corporate ownership of automated vehicles. *Transport Reviews* 2020, 40, 95–113.
92. Legacy, C., Ashmore, D., Scheurer, J., Stone, J., Curtis, C. Planning the driverless city. *Transport Reviews* 2019, 39, 84–102.
93. Santos, G., Behrendt, H., Teytelboym, A. Part II: Policy instruments for sustainable road transport. *Research in Transportation Economics* 2010, 28, 46–91.
94. Grieco, M. Social sustainability and urban mobility. *Social Responsibity Journal* 2015, 11, 82–97.
95. Mulley, C., Nelson, J.D. Flexible transport services. *Research in Transportation Economics* 2009, 25, 39–45.
96. Allen, J., Farber, S. (2019). Sizing up transport poverty. *Transport Policy* 74, 214–223.
97. Leibert, T., Golinski, S. (2016). Peripheralisation. *Comparative Population Studies* 41, 255–284.
98. Lam, D., Givens, J.W. (2018). Small and smart. *New Global Studies* 12, 21–36.
99. Liu, C., Yu, B., Zhu, Y., Liu, L., Li, P. (2019). Measurement of rural residents' mobility in western China. *Sustainability* 11, 2492.
100. Sovacool, B., Martiskainen, M., Hook, A., Baker, L. (2019). Decarbonization and its discontents. *Climate Change* 155, 581–619.
101. Soares Machado, C., Takiya, H., Quintanilha, J. (2020). Placement of infrastructure for urban electromobility. *Sustainability* 12, 6324.
102. Le Boennec, R., Nicolaï, I., Da Costa, P. (2019). Assessing 50 innovative mobility offers in low-density areas. *Transportation Policy* 83, 13–25.
103. Petersen, T. (2016). Watching the Swiss. *Transportation Policy* 52, 175–185.
104. McLeod, S., Scheurer, J., Curtis, C. (2017). Urban public transport. *Journal of Planning Literature* 32, 223–239.
105. Jokinen, J.P., Sihvola, T., Mladenovic, M.N. (2019). Policy lessons from the flexible transport service pilot Kutsuplus in the Helsinki Capital Region. *Transportation Policy* 76, 123–133.
106. Martinez, L.M., Viegas, J.M., Eiro, T. (2014). Formulating a new express minibus service design problem as a clustering problem. *Transportation Science* 49, 85–98.
107. Ferreira, L., Charles, P., Tether, C. (2017). Evaluating flexible transport solutions. *Transportation Planning and Technology* 30, 249–269.

108. Akgöl, K., Günay, B. (2014). Prediction of modal shift using artificial neural networks. *TEM Journal* 3, 223–229.
109. Kandt, J., Leak, A. (2019). Examining inclusive mobility through smartcard data. *Journal of Transport Geography* 79, 102474.
110. Tomej, K., Liburd, J.J. (2020). Sustainable accessibility in rural destinations. *Journal of Sustainable Tourism* 28, 222–239.
111. Lucas, K., Currie, G. (2012). Developing socially inclusive transportation policy. *Transportation* 39, 151–173.
112. Kammerlander, M., Schanes, K., Hartwig, F., Jäger, J., Omann, I., O'Keeffe, M. (2015). A resource-efficient and sufficient future mobility system for improved well-being in Europe. *European Journal of Futures Research* 3, 1–11.
113. Guo, Y., Peeta, S. (2020). Impacts of personalized accessibility information on residential location choice and travel behavior. *Travel Behaviour and Society* 19, 99–111.
114. Howard, A., Borenstein, J. (2018). The ugly truth about ourselves and our robot creations. *Science and Engineering Ethics* 24, 1521–1536.
115. Beecroft, M., Pangbourne, K. (2015). Future prospects for personal security in travel by public transport. *Transportation Planning and Technology* 38, 131–148.
116. Beecroft, M., Cottrill, C.D., Farrington, J.H., Nelson, J.D., Niewiadomski, P. (2015). From infrastructure to digital networks. *Scottish Geographical Journal* 135, 343–355.
117. Groth, S. (2019). Multimodal divide. *Transportation Research Part A: Policy and Practice* 125, 56–71.
118. Sener, I.N., Zmud, J., Williams, T. (2019). Measures of baseline intent to use automated vehicles. *Transportation Research Part F: Traffic Psychology and Behaviour* 62, 66–77.
119. Martínez-Díaz, M., Soriguera, F., Pérez, I. (2019). Autonomous driving: A bird's eye view. *IET Intelligent Transport Systems* 13, 563–579.
120. Tang, C.S., Veelenturf, L.P. (2019). The strategic role of logistics in the industry 4.0 era. *Transportation Research Part E: Logistics and Transportation Review* 129, 1–11.
121. Nordhoff, S., Kyriakidis, M., van Arem, B., Happee, R. (2019). A multi-level model on automated vehicle acceptance (MAVA). *Theoretical Issues in Ergonomics Science* 20, 682–710.
122. Shergold, I., Parkhurst, G. (2012). Transport-related social exclusion amongst older people in rural Southwest England and Wales. *Journal of Rural Studies* 28, 412–421.
123. Graham, H., de Bell, S., Flemming, K., Sowden, A., White, P., Wright, K. (2018). The experiences of everyday travel for older people in rural areas. *Journal of Transport and Health* 11, 141–152.
124. Ward, M.R., Somerville, P., Bosworth, G. (2013). Now without my car I don't know what I'd do. *Local Economy* 28, 553–566.
125. Bennett, R., Vijaygopal, R., Kottasz, R. (2019). Willingness of people with mental health disabilities to travel in driverless vehicles *Journal of Transport and Health* 12, 1–12.
126. Bennett, R., Vijaygopal, R., Kottasz, R. (2019). Attitudes towards autonomous vehicles among people with physical disabilities. *Transportation Research Part A: Policy and Practice* 127, 1–17.
127. Velaga, N.R., Beecroft, M., Nelson, J.D., Corsar, D., Edwards, P. (2012). Transport poverty meets the digital divide: Accessibility and connectivity in rural communities. *Journal of Transport Geography* 21, 102–112.

128. Hensher, D.A. (2007). Some insights into the key influences on trip-chaining activity and public transport use of seniors and the elderly. *International Journal of Sustainable Transportation* 1, 53–68.

129. Goggin, G., Ellis, K., Hawkins, W. (2019). Disability at the centre of digital inclusion. *Communication Research and Practice* 5, 290–303.

130. Yigitcanlar, T. (2006). Australian local governments' practice and prospects with online planning. *URISA Journal* 18, 7–17.

131. Meng, L., Somenahalli, S., Berry, S. (2020). Policy implementation of multi-modal (shared) mobility. *Transport Reviews* 40, 670–684.

132. Guo, Y., Wang, J., Peeta, S., Anastasopoulos, P.C. (2018). Impacts of internal migration, household registration system, and family planning policy on travel mode choice in China. *Travel Behaviour and Society* 13, 128–143.

133. Guo, Y., Wang, J., Peeta, S., Anastasopoulos, P.Ch. (2020). Personal and societal impacts of motorcycle ban policy on motorcyclists' home-to-work morning commute in China. *Travel Behaviour and Society* 19, 137–150.

134. Liu, J., Xiao, L., Yang, L., Zhou, J. (2020). A tale of two social groups in Xiamen, China: Trip frequency of migrants and locals and its determinants. *Travel Behaviour and Society* 20, 213–224.

135. Creutzig, F., Franzen, M., Moeckel, R., Heinrichs, D., Nagel, K., Nieland, S., Weisz, H. (2019). Leveraging digitalization for sustainability in urban transport. *Global Sustainability* 2, e14.

136. Ruan, Y., Zhu, D., Lu, J. (2019). Social adaptation and adaptation pressure among the "drifting elderly" in China. *International Journal of Health Planning and Management* 34, e1149–e1165.

137. Hopkins, D., Schwanen, T. (2018). Automated mobility transitions. *Sustainability* 10, 956.

138. Wong, Y.Z. (2020). *To Limit Coronavirus Risks on Public Transport, Here's What We Can Learn from Efforts Overseas. The Conversation 2020.* Available online: https://theconversation.com/to-limit-coronavirus-risks-on-public-transport-heres-what-we-can-learn-from-efforts-overseas-133764 (accessed 20 March 2020).

139. Butler, L., Yigitcanlar, T., Paz, A. (2020). How can smart mobility innovations alleviate transportation disadvantage? Assembling a conceptual framework through a systematic review. *Applied Sciences* 10(18), 6306.

Part 3

Smart City Futures

This part of the book concentrates on providing an understanding beyond the current smart city practice. It offers insights into having a smart city focus beyond service efficiency, and rethinking smart cities considering the big picture view of the humanitarian and planetarian challenges that are upon and ahead of us.

DOI: 10.1201/9781003403647-13

11 Beyond Service Efficiency

11.1 Introduction

Smart urbanisation has become a popular discourse in urban policy circles across the world. This is due to the increasing popularity of the smart city notion, where its main premise is achieving heightened economic development, quality of life, and sustainability through the use of digital data and technology for generating urban service efficiency (Ahvenniemi et al., 2017). The *smart city* movement has created numerous initiatives globally, however almost all of them have failed or lack adequate potential to generate sustainable urban futures (Cugurullo, 2018). The main reason behind this inadequacy is that current smart city practice portrays technologically determined and reductionist approaches to the city. These approaches overlook urban, human, and social complexities, and create conditions for new forms of social control, and increased social inequality and marginalisation (Bina et al., 2020). This chapter highlights the fundamental shortfalls around smart city conceptualisation and practice, and points to an approach—i.e., utilising technology, policy, and community as interconnected and balanced drivers—for securing sustainable urban futures for all.

11.2 The Problem

Humanity, today, is going through an extremely challenging period. This is due to—to name just a few—the global impacts of climate crisis, biodiversity collapse, natural disasters, pandemics, unsustainable development, ruthless neoliberal economy-driven inequalities, and economic downturn/recession (Yigitcanlar & Cugurullo, 2020).

On the one hand, while some groups and decision-makers have been denying or ignoring these catastrophic threats to our existence or dignity—e.g., far-right and neo-fascist groups and their supporters, fossil fuel lobbyists, corrupt or populist political actors—some activists have started to demand policymakers listen to the scientists and initiated large protests against the inaction—e.g., Extinction Rebellion, Fridays for Future (Axon, 2019).

On the other hand, while some organisations and governments have developed initiatives to mitigate these catastrophic threats—e.g., the UN's Sustainable

DOI: 10.1201/9781003403647-14

Development Goals, Paris Agreement, local government climate emergency declarations, Green New Deal—some companies saw these threats disguised as lucrative business opportunities—e.g., Cisco, IBM—particularly by taking advantage of technological advancements to create new avenues for business (Hollands, 2015).

In early 2000s, a techno-centric approach to urban development was established under the banner of the smart city movement. About two decades of smart city practice have revealed that rather than providing comprehensive and sustainable solutions to the problems of our cities and societies, the movement, so far, has mainly generated growth in the business portfolios of major technology, construction, and consultancy companies (Desouza et al., 2020). Moreover, the exploitation of technology, in the context of smart cities, has resulted in unintended negative externalities—e.g., security and privacy issues, increases in energy use, technology/digital divides. Furthermore, in his seminal work on the paradoxes of technology, Feenberg (2010) stressed the errors of common sense in technology having political consequences in domains including development, health, and environmental policy.

In recent years, an increasing number of scholars have started to point out various smart city shortcomings. Some of the notable ones include, but are not limited to, the following. Boeing et al. (2021) highlighted the systematic biases of smart city technology platforms and big data. Goodspeed (2021) raised the issue of not knowing or estimating the actual impacts of smart urban technologies in shaping our cities. Marantz (2021) portrayed the smart city as nothing more than just an expensive support tool for local governments to collect and disseminate data for informed decisions. Likewise, Bruno and Fontana (2020) emphasised the absence of comprehensive integration of smart city perspectives in the systems of governance—particularly in urban strategic plans. Lung-Amam et al. (2021) underlined the lack of community engagement initiatives for advancing an equitable, community-centred and place-based smart city agenda. They also criticised smart city interventions as solutions in search of problems, rather than solutions that seek to meet the needs of cities and their disadvantaged residents. As for Shamsuddin and Srinivasan (2021), the smart city is in conflict with the just city as the technology is used to make the city better for the privileged, instead of everyone. On that very point, Butler et al. (2020) and Zhang et al. (2020) evidenced how smartness-induced urban mobility could lead to the widening of transport inequality.

11.3 The Panacea

Aforementioned critiques and many more—on the shortcomings of smart cities mainly owing to their heavy technocentric nature—resulted in a search for a comprehensive conceptualisation of the smart city notion. Nam and Pardo (2011) came up with a multidimensional perspective to smart cities by identifying technology, policy, and community as the main building blocks or drivers of these cities. This multidimensional perspective expanded the traditional smart city approach—that bounds with data and technology to generate urban service efficiencies—to a contemporary one that utilises technology for dealing with complexity, policy for dealing with uncertainty, and community for dealing with ambiguity. In this multidimensional perspective, the establishment of a balanced and organic connection among the three smart city drivers is seen as of utmost importance. With the technology (frugal, sustainable, and ethical), policy (sound, strategic, and transparent) and community (engaged, aware, and learning) drivers at play, we are better suited for moving towards building desired smart urban futures for all (Yigitcanlar et al., 2020a).

Building on Nam and Pardo's (2011) smart city drivers (i.e., technology–policy–community) principle, a consolidated smart city conceptualisation that utilised the Input-Process-Output-Impact Model was developed (Figure 11.1). In this conceptual framework, the "input" is the city and its assets. By using this asset base, the "process"—involving technology, policy, and community—produces strategies, action plans, and initiatives. This generates the "output" for economy, society, environment, and governance domains of the city. When the output is aligned with knowledge-based and sustainable urban development goals, principles, and practices, this creates the desired "impact" and subsequently brings a smart city to

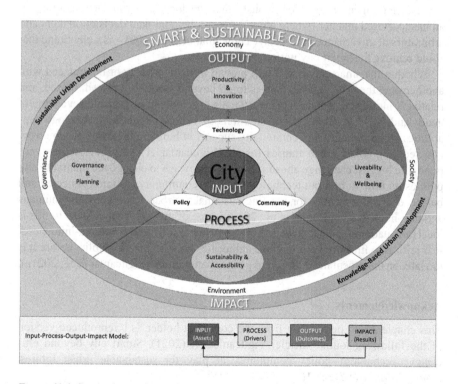

Figure 11.1 Smart city conceptual framework (Yigitcanlar et al., 2019b).

life (Yigitcanlar et al., 2019b). The conceptual framework also offered a renewed definition of the smart city as "an urban locality functioning as a robust system of systems with sustainable practices—supported by community, technology and policy—to generate desired outcomes and futures for all humans and non-humans" (Yigitcanlar et al., 2019b, p. 3).

11.4 Conclusion

Despite many cities around the globe jumping on the smart city bandwagon, the popular smart city movement has repeatedly failed to produce cities or urban development blueprints with offerings beyond limited service efficiency improvements (Kitchin, 2015). As presented above, the new conceptualisations advocate the need for a balanced and organic connection among the key smart city drivers of technology, policy, and community. Whilst there are promising conceptual developments being materialised in the smart city domain, today advancing smart technologies (with urban applications) are also creating new hypes. For instance, as a consequence of the advancements and increasing popularity of artificial intelligence (AI), some scholars envisage a new urban brand centred around this technology. For instance, an artificially intelligent city—a locality that utilises urban artificial intelligences to autonomously manage local government operations in an unsupervised manner (where algorithms are the dominant decision-makers and arbitrators of governance protocols) (Yigitcanlar et al., 2020b)—is a city brand that could remove the smart city notion from its throne.

Whether the smart city brand will prevail in its popularity or be replaced with another one, the critical issue here is to go beyond the highly priced, biased, and relatively ineffective technology investments in achieving sustainable development goals, and move towards holistic solutions by bringing together technology capabilities, good policies, and community support in building the cities of tomorrow and securing smart urban futures for all (Yigitcanlar et al., 2021). At this very point, the biggest challenge ahead is finding new ways to change the mentality and politics on how to best put technology–policy–community (as interconnected and balanced drivers) at play for creating sustainable urban futures for all—humans and non-humans (Yigitcanlar et al., 2019a). One of the major roadblocks to this is local (and national) politics that is short-termist, populist, and corporate-influenced. It is critical to find ways to convince authorities and the general public, before it is too late, on the urgent need for a change in urban politics (Yigitcanlar et al., 2021a).

Acknowledgements

This chapter, with permission from the copyright holder, is a reproduced version of the following journal article: Yigitcanlar, T. (2021). Smart city beyond efficiency: Technology–policy–community at play for sustainable urban futures. *Housing Policy Debate* 31(1), 88–92.

References

Ahvenniemi, H., Huovila, A., Pinto-Seppä, I., Airaksinen, M. (2017). What are the differences between sustainable and smart cities? *Cities, 60*, 234–245.

Axon, S. (2019). Warning: extinction ahead! Theorizing the spatial disruption and place contestation of climate justice activism. *Environment, Space, Place, 11*(2), 1–26.

Bina, O., Inch, A., Pereira, L. (2020). Beyond techno-utopia and its discontents: On the role of utopianism and speculative fiction in shaping alternatives to the smart city imaginary. *Futures, 115*, 102475.

Boeing, G., Besbris, M., Schachter, A., Kuk, J. (2021). Housing search in the age of big data: smarter cities or the same old blind spots? *Housing Policy Debate, 31*(1), 112–126.

Bruno, A., Fontana, F. (2020). Testing the smart city paradigm in Italian mid-sized cities: an empirical analysis. *Housing Policy Debate, 31*, 151–170.

Butler, L., Yigitcanlar, T., Paz, A. (2020). How can smart mobility innovations alleviate transportation disadvantage? Assembling a conceptual framework through a systematic review. *Applied Sciences, 10*(18), 6306.

Cugurullo, F. (2018). Exposing smart cities and eco-cities: Frankenstein urbanism and the sustainability challenges of the experimental city. *Environment and Planning A, 50*(1), 73–92.

Desouza, K.C., Hunter, M., Jacob, B., Yigitcanlar, T. (2020). Pathways to the making of prosperous smart cities: An exploratory study on the best practice. *Journal of Urban Technology, 27*(3), 3–32.

Feenberg, A. (2010). Ten paradoxes of technology. *Techné: Research in Philosophy and Technology, 14*(1), 3–15.

Goodspeed, R. (2021). Smart cities in community development: from participation in cybernetics to building knowledge infrastructures. *Housing Policy Debate, 31*(1), 171–173.

Hollands, R.G. (2015). Critical interventions into the corporate smart city. *Cambridge Journal of Regions, Economy and Society, 8*(1), 61–77.

Kitchin, R. (2015). Making sense of smart cities: Addressing present shortcomings. *Cambridge Journal of Regions, Economy and Society, 8*(1), 131–136.

Lung-Amam, W., Bierbaum, A.H., Parks, S., Knaap, G.J., Sunderman, G., Stamm, L. (2021). Toward engaged, equitable, and smart communities: Lessons from west Baltimore. *Housing Policy Debate, 31*(1), 93–111.

Marantz, N.J. (2021). Promoting housing affordability by making cities smarter about land-use regulation. *Housing Policy Debate, 31*(1), 174–177.

Nam, T., Pardo, T.A. (2011). Conceptualizing smart city with dimensions of technology, people, and institutions. In: *Proceedings of the 12th Annual International Digital Government Research Conference: Digital Government Innovation in Challenging Times* (pp. 282–291).

Shamsuddin, S., Srinivasan, S. (2021). Just smart or just and smart cities? Assessing the literature on housing and information and communication technology. *Housing Policy Debate, 31*(1), 127–150.

Yigitcanlar, T., Foth, M., Kamruzzaman, M. (2019a). Towards post-anthropocentric cities: reconceptualizing smart cities to evade urban ecocide. *Journal of Urban Technology, 26*(2), 147–152.

Yigitcanlar, T., Han, H., Kamruzzaman, M., Ioppolo, G., Sabatini-Marques, J. (2019b). The making of smart cities: are Songdo, Masdar, Amsterdam, San Francisco and Brisbane the best we could build? *Land Use Policy, 88*, 104187.

Yigitcanlar, T., Cugurullo, F. (2020). The sustainability of artificial intelligence: an urbanistic viewpoint from the lens of smart and sustainable cities. *Sustainability, 12*(20), 8548.

Yigitcanlar, T., Desouza, K.C., Butler, L., Roozkhosh, F. (2020a). Contributions and risks of artificial intelligence (AI) in building smarter cities: insights from a systematic review of the literature. *Energies, 13*(6), 1473.

Yigitcanlar, T., Butler, L., Windle, E., Desouza, K.C., Mehmood, R., Corchado, J.M. (2020b). Can building "artificially intelligent cities" safeguard humanity from natural disasters, pandemics, and other catastrophes? An urban scholar's perspective. *Sensors, 20*(10), 2988.

Yigitcanlar, T. (2021a). Smart city beyond efficiency: Technology–policy–community at play for sustainable urban futures. *Housing Policy Debate, 31*(1), 88–92.

Yigitcanlar, T., Kankanamge, N., Vella, K. (2021). How are smart city concepts and technologies perceived and utilized? A systematic geo-Twitter analysis of smart cities in Australia. *Journal of Urban Technology, 28*(1–2), 135–154.

Zhang, M., Zhao, P., Qiao, S. (2020). Smartness-induced transport inequality: privacy concern, lacking knowledge of smartphone use and unequal access to transport information. *Transport Policy, 99*, 175–185.

12 Rethinking Smart Cities

12.1 Introduction: Can Technology Save Us?

The current Anthropocene era is characterised by greenhouse gas emissions and human domination (Crutzen & Steffen, 2003). As a result, the world is being confronted with severe environmental, economic, and social crises (Moore, 2017). This is combined with rapid urbanisation, increased mobilisation, heightened globalisation, ruthless neoliberal capitalism, vigorous industrialisation, intensified agriculture, excessive consumption, and highly materialised lifestyles (Yigitcanlar & Dizdaroglu, 2015; Monbiot, 2016). At this dire strait, contemporary urban policy and practice tend to place all their bets on technology as a panacea to ensure our survival (Wiig, 2015). Yet, can technology alone really save us?

Rapid advancements on the technology front—particularly as a result of the second wave of the digital revolution and the Fourth Industrial Revolution, along with aggressive marketing by technology companies gave policymakers and urban administrators a false hope (Söderström et al., 2014). The hope is that the impacts of global-scale environmental and socioeconomic crises can be reversed through feasible technology solutions. Consequently, the amalgamation of technology and the city is widely seen as an effective instrument to manage the challenges that cities and societies are facing (Yigitcanlar, 2016). This fusion of technology and city, today, is referred to as "smart cities", which has evolved through different stages (Foth, 2018; Yigitcanlar et al., 2018).

12.2 Smart City in the Making

12.2.1 The First Generation: Intelligent Cities

Even though the smart city concept was popularised by the technology companies around the mid-2000s, its origin dates back to the intelligent city notion of the 1990s. The "intelligent cities" paradigm brought together the trajectories of the knowledge and innovation economy, and the spread of the Internet and World Wide Web as major technological innovations (Komninos, 2011). Intelligent cities (the first-generation smart city) were the realm of technology companies providing innovative technologies to local governments in order to improve and optimise

DOI: 10.1201/9781003403647-15

the efficiency of specific city functions. This conceptualisation was heavily expert-focused and almost no opportunity was given for citizens to participate in the decision-making process.

12.2.2 The Second Generation: Smart Cities

In the late 2000s, as an extension of the intelligent city movement, the "smart cities" concept emphasised a greater degree of involvement of local authorities in deploying smart technologies (Yigitcanlar, 2015). Targeting city infrastructure and services, these technologies established a new digital data layer to drive efficiencies through smart metres and shared mobility. This second-generation smart city employs sensors and other Internet of Things (IoT) devices with a growing emphasis on urban informatics, urban science, and data analytics aiming to solve urban problems (Lim & Taeihagh, 2018). Yet, the highly top-down approach in investment and governance remains—leaving only limited room for the community's voice in the policymaking process.

12.2.3 The Third Generation: Responsive Cities

As a reaction to the conceptualisation and practice limitations of smart cities, a new type of city model is envisaged: A city that provides citizens with active engagement in and usage of smart solutions to improve living standards and urban sustainability. This is referred to as "responsive cities" (Goldsmith & Crawford, 2014). These cities restore the citizen's right to the digital city by giving citizens power to use smart technology to contribute to the planning, design, and management of their cities (Foth et al., 2015). The responsive city (the third-generation smart city) relies on the IoT and mobile devices communicating autonomously with the aim of improving urban life.

12.3 The Challenge: Can Smart Cities Address the Causes of Our Urban Ills?

The progressions from intelligent to smart and from there to responsive cities are positive moves and contributed cumulatively to urban policymaking practice. However, city innovation remains largely technocentric with much needed governance, policy, and regulatory reform lagging behind in both speed and scope (Noy & Givoni, 2018). Technocratic approaches generate serious doubts about their capability of addressing the aforementioned root problems causing environmental, economic, and social crises (Kunzmann, 2014).

In recent years, various international, national, and regional city ranking exercises listed the best-performing smart cities, and various studies provided insights into smart city best practices (Giffinger & Gudrun, 2010). These exercises and studies celebrated the achievements of a number of global smart cities—including Amsterdam, Barcelona, Boston, London, New York, Paris, San Francisco, Seoul, Singapore, Stockholm, Tokyo, and Vienna. However, a closer look into the environmental performance of these cities reveals unsustainable levels of per capita greenhouse gas emissions despite some regulations (Hoornweg et al., 2011; Arbolino et al., 2017).

Moreover, recent empirical studies have reported that smart cities are not after all that smart as they fail to live up to sustainability expectations. For example, a recent study of 15 UK smart cities found no evidence that urban smartness contributes to sustainable outcomes (Yigitcanlar & Kamruzzaman, 2018). Another research on Australian cities revealed the smartness of cities does not lead to sustainable commuting patterns (Yigitcanlar & Kamruzzaman, 2019). Additionally, studies on smart cities in Africa and South Korea—including Songdo recognised as the world's "smartest" city—evidenced the environmental downfalls of these ambitious projects (Watson, 2014; Yigitcanlar & Lee, 2014). Furthermore, it is argued that cities cannot be truly smart unless they produce zero waste (Zaman & Lehmann, 2013) and make a net positive contribution to the ecosystem (Birkeland, 2012).

While useful to describe the changing attitude of local governments towards smart city investments, the trend from "intelligent", "smart" to "responsive" cities remains highly constrained by its focus on technology and technical systems (Anthopoulos, 2017). This, in turn, begs questions about the depletion of rare earth metals and the accumulation of e-waste. A technocratic approach is also not adequate in recognising our ecological entanglements with nature (Houston et al., 2018). It does not avoid the ecocide and existential crisis we face in light of forthcoming catastrophes of the Anthropocene era (MacDougall et al., 2013)—such as ecosystem collapse of the Great Barrier Reef (Pandolfi et al., 2003).

12.4 Towards the Fourth Generation: What Does a Truly Smart and Sustainable City Look Like?

The current smart city practice is generating a Frankenstein urbanism by forcing the union of different and incompatible elements in cities—in a disingenuous attempt at addressing quality of life and sustainability (Cugurullo, 2018). There is, hence, an urgency to reconceptualise urban planning, design, and development paradigms and to act upon these accordingly and immediately. In such reconceptualisations that question human exceptionalism (Houston et al., 2018), urban space cannot be seen as an entity separate from nature and thus it cannot be designed just or primarily for humans. Decentring the human in urban design (Forlano, 2016) will help to develop post-anthropocentric cities or more-than-human cities (the fourth-generation smart city?) that are truly smart, sustainable, and equitable (Foth, 2017; Franklin, 2017).

12.5 Conclusion: Towards a Post-Anthropocentric Urban Turnaround

The current smart city practice, at its best, is a zero-sum game for sustainability—environmental gains are cancelled out by the impacts of increased technology and energy use (Ahvenniemi et al., 2017). The biggest challenge, at this time, is finding a way to change our mentality and politics on how we shape our cities, societies, and the environment. We need to move forward instantaneously and quickly by focusing on an ecological human settlement theory (Liaros, 2018) that will create cohabitation spaces to house humans and non-humans in a sustainable and inclusive way in the post-anthropocentric cities of tomorrow.

The sixth extinction is already upon us (Celabllos et al., 2015). Building post-anthropocentric cities for more-than-human futures might be the last resort for humankind to evolve and not become extinct in the not-too-distant future. Nevertheless, currently, human civilisation is standing at a crossroads. A number of critical decisions must be taken and implemented immediately—for example, moving away from an aggressive population, urban, and economic growth dominant viewpoint. Furthermore, the right answers to the following questions will also be extremely critical for our future existence on the planet and its living conditions (Yigitcanlar et al., 2019a):

a) How can urban scholars, planners, designers, and activists convince urban policymakers and the general public of the urgent need for a post-anthropocentric urban turnaround?
b) How can we—jointly by public, private, and academic sectors along with communities—pave the way for post-anthropocentric cities and more-than-human futures?
c) How can we establish an ecological civilisation to sustain our existence on the planet in the long term?
d) How can a smart city blueprint be developed to support the emergence of an ecological civilisation?

Acknowledgements

This chapter, with permission from the copyright holder, is a reproduced version of the following journal article: Yigitcanlar, T., Foth, M., Kamruzzaman, M. (2019). Towards post-anthropocentric cities: Reconceptualizing smart cities to evade urban ecocide. *Journal of Urban Technology* 26(2), 147–152.

References

Ahvenniemi, H., Huovila, A., Pinto-Seppä, I., Airaksinen, M. (2017). What are the differences between sustainable and smart cities? *Cities* 60, 234–245.
Anthopoulos, L. (2017). Smart utopia vs smart reality: Learning by experience from 10 smart city cases. *Cities* 63, 128–148.
Arbolino, R., Carlucci, F., Cirà, A., Ioppolo, G., Yigitcanlar, T. (2017). Efficiency of the EU regulation on greenhouse gas emissions in Italy: The hierarchical cluster analysis approach. *Ecological Indicators* 81, 115–123.
Birkeland, J. (2012). *Design for Sustainability: A Sourcebook of Integrated Ecological Solutions.* Oxford: Routledge.
Ceballos, G., Ehrlich, P., Barnosky, A., García, A., Pringle, R., Palmer, T. (2015). Accelerated modern human-induced species losses: Entering the sixth mass extinction. *Science Advances* 1, e1400253.

Crutzen, P., Steffen, W. (2003). How long have we been in the Anthropocene era? *Climatic Change* 61, 251–257.

Cugurullo, F. (2018). Exposing smart cities and eco-cities: Frankenstein urbanism and the sustainability challenges of the experimental city. *Environment and Planning A* 50, 73–92.

Forlano, L. (2016). Decentering the human in the design of collaborative cities. *Design Issues* 32, 42–54.

Foth, M. (2017). The next urban paradigm: Cohabitation in the smart city. *IT-Information Technology* 59, 259–262.

Foth, M. (2018). Participatory urban informatics: Towards citizen-ability. *Smart and Sustainable Built Environment* 7, 4–19.

Foth, M., Brynskov, M., Ojala, T. (2015). *Citizen's Right to the Digital City: Urban Interfaces, Activism, and Placemaking.* Singapore: Springer.

Franklin, A. (2017). The more-than-human city. *The Sociological Review* 65, 202–217.

Giffinger, R., Gudrun, H. (2010). Smart cities ranking: An effective instrument for the positioning of the cities? *Architecture, City and Environment* 4, 7–26.

Goldsmith, S., Crawford, S. (2014). *The Responsive City: Engaging Communities Through Data-Smart Governance.* London: John Wiley & Sons.

Hoornweg, D., Sugar, L., Trejos-Gomez, C. (2011). Cities and greenhouse gas emissions: Moving forward. *Environment and Urbanization* 23, 207–227.

Houston, D., Hillier, J., MacCallum, D., Steele, W., Byrne, J. (2018). Make kin, not cities! Multispecies entanglements and 'becoming-world' in planning theory. *Planning Theory* 17, 190–212.

Komninos, N. (2011). Intelligent cities: Variable geometries of spatial intelligence. *Intelligent Buildings International* 3, 172–188.

Kunzmann, K. (2014). Smart cities: A new paradigm of urban development. *Crios* 1, 9–20.

Liaros, S. (2018). *An Ecological Human Settlement Theory* (2018, June 14), retrieved July 30 2018, from https://greenagenda.org.au/2018/06/ecological-human-settlement-theory

Lim, H., Taeihagh, A. (2018). Autonomous vehicles for smart and sustainable cities: An in-depth exploration of privacy and cybersecurity implications. *Energies* 11, 1062.

MacDougall, A., McCann, K., Gellner, G., Turkington, R. (2013). Diversity loss with persistent human disturbance increases vulnerability to ecosystem collapse. *Nature* 494, 86–89.

Monbiot, G. (2016). *How did We Get into this Mess? Politics, Equality, Nature.* London: Verso Books.

Moore, J. (2017). The Capitalocene, Part I: On the nature and origins of our ecological crisis. *The Journal of Peasant Studies* 44, 594–630.

Noy, K., Givoni, M. (2018). Is 'smart mobility' sustainable? Examining the views and beliefs of transport's technological entrepreneurs. *Sustainability* 10, 422.

Pandolfi, J., Bradbury, R., Sala, E., Hughes, T., Bjorndal, K., Cooke, R., Warner, R. (2003). Global trajectories of the long-term decline of coral reef ecosystems. *Science* 301, 955–958.

Söderström, O., Paasche, T., Klauser, F. (2014). Smart cities as corporate storytelling. *City* 18, 307–320.

Watson, V. (2014). African urban fantasies: Dreams or nightmares? *Environment and Urbanization* 26, 215–231.

Wiig, A. (2015). IBM's smart city as techno-utopian policy mobility. *City* 19, 258–273.

Yigitcanlar, T. (2015). Smart cities: An effective urban development and management model? *Australian Planner* 52, 27–34.

Yigitcanlar, T. (2016). *Technology and the City: Systems, Applications and Implications.* New York: Routledge.

Yigitcanlar, T., Dizdaroglu, D. (2015). Ecological approaches in planning for sustainable cities: A review of the literature. *Global Journal of Environmental Science and Management* 1, 159–188.

Yigitcanlar, T., Foth, M., Kamruzzaman, M. (2019a). Towards post-anthropocentric cities: Reconceptualizing smart cities to evade urban ecocide. *Journal of Urban Technology* 26(2), 147–152.

Yigitcanlar, T., Kamruzzaman, M. (2018) Does smart city policy lead to sustainability of cities? *Land Use Policy* 73, 49–58.

Yigitcanlar, T., Kamruzzaman, M. (2019). Smart cities and mobility: Does the smartness of Australian cities lead to sustainable commuting patterns?. *Journal of Urban Technology* 26(2), 21–46.

Yigitcanlar, T., Kamruzzaman, M., Buys, L., Ioppolo, G., Sabatini-Marques, J., da Costa, E.M., Yun, J.J. (2018). Understanding 'smart cities': Intertwining development drivers with desired outcomes in a multidimensional framework. *Cities* 81, 145–160.

Yigitcanlar, T., Lee, S. (2014). Korean ubiquitous-eco-city: A smart-sustainable urban form or a branding hoax? *Technological Forecasting and Social Change* 89, 100–114.

Zaman, A., Lehmann, S. (2013). The zero waste index: A performance measurement tool for waste management systems in a zero waste city. *Journal of Cleaner Production* 50, 123–132.

Index

Printed in the United States
by Baker & Taylor Publisher Services